Acknowledgements

I'd like to say thanks to Peter Yakoob for all his help, support and encouragement. Without your help my memoirs would still be hidden in the back of my cupboard.

A huge thank you to both Peter and Ben Seales for helping me edit my book.

I'd also like to thank Chris Sansom and Sam Ceccatty from Authoright, for putting up with my endless phone calls and changing my mind while my book was being made.

Gaby

Cover:
Clockwise; Ali Yafai (My father), Issy, Muna (Gabriella Gillespie) & Yas

Chapter One
Mum

"Ouch!" I screamed, as Yas smacked me in the face, "I'm telling Dad on you!"

"Go ahead, he was the one who told me to do it," she replied.

Yas and I had been sitting on the floor in our living room watching TV. I was around five years old and Yas, my older sister, around six and half. I'd picked up a bad habit of making funny movements with my face without realising I was doing it, stretching my nose and mouth in a downwards position. I ran out of the living room screeching as loud as possible to get Mum's attention, and towards the kitchen where Mum was, straight into her arms.

"Muna, baby, what's wrong with you?" she asked as she picked me up and cuddled me while wiping away my tears.

"Yas punched me in the face," I lied.

"No I did not!" Yas came storming in. "You're such a liar! I just gave you a little slap to stop you from making those stupid faces, and anyway Dad told me to do it!"

"Dad told you to do what?" Mum asked. She wasn't happy with Yas for hitting me, but hearing Dad told her to do it made her angry.

"He said if you catch your sister pulling those silly faces again give her a slap!" Yas replied.

"No, Yas, that's not the way to stop her from doing it, so I'm telling you to apologize to your sister and do not hit her again." Yas was always the stubborn one.

"No way that's not fair! Dad told me to do it so get him to apologize when he gets back; it's not my fault, why do I always get the blame?" Yas stormed out of the kitchen and upstairs, stomping her feet as she went along so we would get the message that she was upset; the next thing we heard was the bedroom door slam.

"Don't worry baby, I will talk to your Dad, but you really need to stop making those faces, they spoil your pretty face!" Mum kissed me and told me to go upstairs and make up with my sister.

I went upstairs into the bedroom that I shared with Yas. I sat next to her on her bed but she shoved me off with her feet. "Get off my bed!" she sulked.

"Sorry for telling Mum on you Yas, but you hurt me," I replied.

"Yea I know Moo, and I'm sorry, but if you keep pulling that stupid face you're going to end up staying like that forever, so if I see you doing it again I'm going to smack you! Anyway you know Mum and Dad are going to argue now, don't you?"

There were four of us sisters, Ablah was around nine and half years old and Issy, whose real name was Ismahan, was about eight, then there was Yasmin who we called Yas, and me, Muna, who they called Moo. Yas also called me Moo cow because she said I was a cow bag, and I had big eyes like a cow! She also said I talked a load of bull and had a wild imagination! That evening after dinner we all sat down to watch TV in the living room. As usual we girls would all sit on the floor in front of the TV. Yas sat to the side of me, her eyes glued to my face, and as soon as I pulled the face, *smack!* I let out a huge scream!

"I can't believe you did that again!" Mum shouted at Yas.

"Dad told me to do it, didn't you Dad?" was my sister's calm reply, as she looked at Dad.

Dad was sat comfortably in his chair. "She needs to learn," he mumbled. That set off an argument between Mum and Dad! Mum didn't believe in smacking whereas Dad apparently didn't have a problem with it. Mum sent us all to our rooms while they kept on arguing, the next morning everything seemed fine. Yas and I tiptoed downstairs as quietly as possible, we made it to the kitchen.

"Come on, bunk me up," I whispered. Yas was still trying to bunk me up onto the kitchen top when mum came through the door!

"Caught red handed once again, you two!" she teased as she started to chase us around the kitchen. "You need to wait for your sisters. Ablah, Issy, come on, hurry up!" Mum shouted out.

As they were coming downstairs Mum reached up into the kitchen cupboard and took out a bottle of malt. As she turned around to get a spoon from the drawer she laughed when she saw I was already stood there with a spoon in my hand! "It's a good job you love this stuff isn't it?" she smiled.

Since we were babies Mum had propped us on the kitchen top every morning come rain or shine and given us each a spoonful of malt. She would always tell us, "This will help you grow to be tall and beautiful!" We loved it so much we would always beg for more.

Mum was called Mary Yafai and she was from Birmingham. Every morning she would take us to school without fail, and she always watched us go in and waved us goodbye. Then she would go off and see her friends, mum had lots of friends in the area, even though she wasn't from the area that we were living in. We were living in Grafton Road, Newport, South Wales.

She was really beautiful and when she walked down the street heads would turn; she was tall and slim with long dark hair, and long legs that she liked to show off!

She had met Dad when she was really young. Dad was also a good looking guy with his Middle Eastern looks; he was Ali Abdulla Saleh Yafai, a Yemeni guy who had moved to England around 24 years earlier. I think they met when Mum was only around 15 because she married really young and she had Yas when she was only 16.

Ablah and Issy were not Mum's biological daughters, although Mum loved them just as much. Mum insisted she bring them up when she found out they were in a care home because their real mum had given them up after she left Dad. Mum insisted she wanted us all to grow up together, she believed sisters shouldn't be apart.

Yas and I never knew at first that our older sisters were not Mum's daughters. We found out when I was around five and Mum and Dad had a huge argument and Mum took us to her parents' house in Birmingham.

Dad refused to allow my older sisters to come with us, saying Mum wasn't their real mother so had no rights to take them. We returned after a couple of days because neither Mum nor us could stand being away from our sisters.

Mum's family hated Dad and were not supportive of her relationship with him. We visited them every once in a while, usually when our parents had an argument. Dad never came with us, he wasn't welcomed in our grandparents' home.

Dad worked away a lot; he had different part time jobs. He was a part time butcher and would deliver meat in a van he owned. He also worked in Llanwern steelworks in Newport Gwent and part time as a labourer up and down the country.

He had lots of friends from his home country; he would take us to their homes and would chat to them for hours in a language we couldn't understand. He and his friends would say to us, "You need to learn Arabic, you will need to speak it one day!" We would run off laughing blurting out, "Blah, blah, blah!"

Mum hated it when Dad took us to his friends' houses and they would constantly argue over it. If she found out we had gone alone to play with other children and gone inside their houses without permission she would be furious with us!

Even though Mum and Dad argued a lot we girls were happy. We would hardly ever leave Mum's side and she always loved to dress us up in the latest fashion. She and Dad had different ideas on what clothes we should wear, but Dad was never around so Mum got to dress us up just like she wanted, skirts instead of trousers like Dad wanted!

Mum loved having a house full of kids. At one time we had four other children living with us. There were two boys and two girls whose father was also Arabic. I think they lived with us because their Mum had left them and their Dad had a new girlfriend who didn't look after them properly. Whatever the reason, they stayed with us for many months.

It was the day before Mum's 26th birthday, on 2nd September 1971. Mum took us to school and told us she would see us that afternoon. My sisters and I were excited because we always did something special on someone's birthday. After she dropped us off we were secretly planning what we could do or give her for her birthday; we decided to make her a card that evening.

It was Dad who picked us up in his meat van, something he had never done before. When Yas asked where Mum was he told us she had gone to stay with her parents and wouldn't be back for a while.

4

At first we all thought Mum would come back the next day, it was her birthday and she would never celebrate without us, but she didn't. We held on to her birthday card and cried, asking questions about where she was and why we couldn't go and see her, but all Dad would say was she had left and he didn't know where she was.

Three days later when Mum failed to return home Dad reported her missing.

The police started a huge nationwide search, one of the largest of its kind back in those days. Over 30 police offices and two police dogs were involved in the search. Newspapers reported sightings of her in different cities, none of them turned out to be true.

Dad participated in the search with the police travelling up and down the country handing out leaflets with Mum's picture on them; he spent a fortune searching for her. Months went by with no sign from Mum. The newspapers even put an article from my sister Yas on her birthday in November begging Mum to come home, but again nothing.

It wasn't long before the newspapers started printing stories about Mum having an affair before she disappeared. It was alleged she was intending to leave Dad and take us girls with her. They said that she had intended to meet her lover the day she went missing but had never turned up. Of course this was talk that my sisters and I were not supposed to know about.

Sometime in early 1972 we were asked by the police to leave our home in Grafton Road; they needed to search it for evidence. We moved into another house in Corporation Road with Dad's friends.

The police started searching Grafton Road; they were searching for Mum's body or any evidence that she was killed in our house. They dug up the garden, ripped up floorboards and even smashed into walls. They reportedly found blood stains under a carpet in one of the rooms but couldn't identify who they belonged to.

Around August 1972, after questions were raised about our welfare, Dad voluntarily handed us over to social services care and we were put into a care home. Dad was interviewed more than 30 times before he was arrested more than a year after Mum disappeared.

The Regional Crime Squad and CID started gathering witness

statements. One witness was our next door neighbour who gave evidence that she heard Mum screaming, "No! No! Please don't... I'm sorry, don't," the day mum disappeared. She also said she heard a fight going on, sounds like furniture being thrown against the walls, then she said it went silent. A little while later she said she heard scrubbing sounds coming from our kitchen. She also told how she saw Dad and two men carry out a big rolled up carpet later that night and load it into Dad's meat van.

The two other men, who were Dad's Arabic friends and who were identified as those seen carrying out the carpet the night of Mum's disappearance, were also arrested and charged.

The jury found Dad guilty of manslaughter, even though Mum's body was never found; he was given six years in jail. The judge told the jury they needed to take into consideration the fact that Mum had provoked Dad into losing his temper and killing her by having an affair, therefore not to find him guilty of murder. The two Arabic men were cleared of all charges.

We were distraught. Even though Mum and Dad argued all the time, we were convinced our father was innocent.

We were rescued from the care home by Jim and Thelma. Jim was from Fiji and Thelma was a Welsh lady. Jim had been living in the UK most of his life; both of them had been friends with my parents and decided they couldn't see the four of us separated so took us in.

Jim and Thelma already had three daughters of their own. Carol, Linda and baby Keeran. Carol and Linda were from Thelma's first marriage, while Keeran was Jim's only child. Carol and Linda were the same age as Yas and I while Keeran was about three years old. Our foster parents were loving towards us; although strict with us, they truly cared for us.

We were abandoned by Mum's family after Mum's disappearance so Jim and Thelma had a lot to take on. Their family became our family, and Thelma had lots of family in Newport that we visited regularly. Our foster parents didn't get much assistance from social services. Every now and then they would get bits of food from them, but not much. Jim worked long hours on the railways to bring in extra money.

When we arrived at our foster home we were all displaying

problems in one way or the other from losing our parents. We were four little girls whose lives had been turned upside down, we had been left confused, angry and feeling lost; I'd already claimed to have seen Mum's ghost come out of a cupboard in our bedroom, which I was told was part of my wild imagination. We didn't receive any help or support from social services and were never asked how we were managing after Mum's disappearance, or Dad's imprisonment.

I was around eight by then and I'd also started pinching things and getting into trouble at school. Yas was a tomboy and wanted to fight everyone. Issy was around twelve and very into her image from an early age, but more the quieter one. Ablah was the oldest at around thirteen and a half and very independent. She was more mature and despised Dad and out of all of us she was the only one who always felt he was guilty. She also hated the fact that we were in foster care and couldn't wait to be of an age where she could leave.

I won't be mentioning Ablah much more in my book, other than to say I love her very much.

We called our foster parents Uncle and Aunty from the beginning. They did everything they could to make our time with them a happy one. My happiest memories of our foster home were our holidays.

Uncle Jim owned a caravan in Pembroke, South Wales; this was where we had our holidays every summer. When we were home we had constant homework or chores, it was a busy house and there was always something to do. Our holidays were the one time we were all allowed to run free and play! All seven of us girls would leave the caravan early morning and head to the beach to spend our days catching crabs, cockles and mussels. We built sand castles, did acrobats in the sand, squabbled over boys and would only return to the caravan to grab our food before we headed back out to play.

Uncle Jim would proudly follow us around with his camera to take the 'family shots' to show off to his family back home in Fiji, Aunty Thelma's family and friends back home in Newport, and of course our neighbours!

When we moved into our foster home we moved up a school

and things changed even more for us. Everyone knew us as the girls whose Dad murdered their Mum. Even though I don't remember being bullied or asked about it, I remember I didn't have many friends.

Issy was cool and beautiful and got on with everyone, but she was also quiet and kept her head down. Yas was known as the hard girl in school so nobody would mess with her, whereas I was also known as the trouble maker and the mouthy one.

I would always run to Yas for help; even though she was allowed to push me around and smack me whenever she felt like it, nobody else was! Yas has always been my protective big sister and has always protected me. If anyone wanted to fight me they had to fight my big sister first; and back then Yas always won.

I was always in trouble for one thing or the other when we first went into care. I remember one time in school when I was sent out of PE for misbehaving and told to wait in the locker room until the class had finished. At first I was upset for being sent out of class, but then I realised I was all alone in the locker room with the bags of both teachers and students. I quickly emptied out the purses of the teachers, not worried about leaving anyone any money, or the fact that I'd been the only one left in the locker room by myself, therefore the only suspect! It wasn't long before lunchtime where I generously shared out my good fortune to my sister and a few students, hoping to make new friends.

Soon afterwards I got called into the headmaster's office. I was caught with lots of money on me and made to tell what I'd done with the rest! Then I was escorted by a teacher and made to go around collecting the money back off the students I'd handed it out to! I was even less popular after that.

We visited Dad as often as Uncle Jim could take us. It wasn't a pleasant journey going to see him behind bars, but Dad would always collect his chocolate bars and give them to us on our visits. He would also make little things out of match sticks just for us as presents and we saw that as our treat from him!

Dad would always talk about him coming home and us going back to live with him, but he never talked about Mum or where she was.

As the years went by our love and respect for our foster parents grew. It took us a while to settle down but we soon found ourselves looking up to Uncle Jim as our own father, and our foster home as our home. We told social services we didn't want to go back to live with Dad when he was due for release and they knew we were settled where we were.

Shortly before Dad's release we got a visit from Ahmed and Kasim, the two men who had been implicated in the trail with dad. They claimed Dad had given them permission to come and take us away from our foster home and to go to stay with them.

Uncle Jim was furious and beside himself with worry, he realised then that Dad was up to something bad and was determined to find out what it was. He got into a big argument with them and refused to allow them near us.

Not long after, we got a visit from social services saying that the two men had got a solicitor to call their office and complain that when they visited us they saw bruises on our thighs and buttocks. Our foster parents had to allow us to be examined while they answered questions. Uncle Jim was furious. He couldn't understand why social services were not investigating how these men had claimed to have seen our thighs and buttocks in the first place, and why these men had come to our home to take us out of his care.

We were checked and no bruises were found on us, so social services left. There was no further investigation done by social services into Ahmed or Kasim. However, Uncle Jim didn't like what was going on so he started his own investigation.

He found out that Dad had got himself into a lot of debt and owed money to both these men and other men from his country, money he had borrowed while the trial for Mum's murder was going on, and money he had used in an appeal against his sentence. Knowing this, and many other things that had taken place over the previous years, Uncle Jim became really concerned for our safety.

Dad was released in February 1975; he had served fewer than four years out of his six year sentence. We didn't believe that Dad killed our Mum and although we didn't want to live with him at this time because we were settled in our foster home, we were happy to have him around again. We were still living with our foster parents because Dad didn't have a house at first; he was living in a one bedroom flat.

Dad would come and take us out all the time and he would spoil us rotten, buying us whatever we wanted and taking us to visit his Arabic friends and their children.

Uncle Jim would always be sat on egg shells waiting for us to return home. He was always worried that Dad would take us and never bring us back.

Dad had applied for a council house so that he could resume care of us, and social services told the housing department they supported Dad's application for a house big enough for us to move back in with him.

It wasn't long after Dad came out of prison that we first met our Uncle Nasser, Dad's brother. Dad was still living in his flat at the time and our uncle had come from the Yemen to visit Dad, but Uncle Jim didn't like him at all.

Uncle Jim was convinced that Uncle Nasser and Dad were up to no good. Uncle Jim was always checking around trying to find out what it was, but Uncle Nasser didn't stay long so we didn't really get to know him.

It was after Uncle Nasser went back to Yemen when we were at Dad's flat and we found some letters to Dad from his family in Yemen.

One of these letters said something about the importance of Yas and I going to the Yemen and being 'bound by a kinship' which distinguished us from our half-sisters. We gave Uncle Jim the letter and he took it to social services because he was convinced that Dad was up to no good, although he never told us what his real fears were. But once again he was met with disappointment, as social services failed to see any wrongdoing from Dad.

Uncle Jim tried so hard to keep us in his care, but in 1976 we were handed back into Dad's care after he got a council house big enough for us to live in.

We didn't know the details of the arguments going on between Uncle Jim and social services, only that he didn't want us living with Dad. We had started calling Uncle Jim Dad by then because he cared for us and loved us like a real father should.

Uncle Jim made it clear that his door would always be open for us, he also told us to be wary of the Arabic men Dad hung around with. We were too young to understand why Uncle Jim was so wary of them, but it wouldn't be long before we would find out.

We moved into Sycamore Avenue in Newport in November 1976. At first things with Dad were OK, he spoilt us and we could do whatever we wanted, but he quickly changed.

He started working away again as a builder, and would leave us alone for days at a time. He would leave us a budget for our food and just leave. We struggled to cope, I was barely 12 and my sisters not that much older, and we soon started missing school and hanging around doing nothing.

Uncle Jim would come and visit us all the time, if we were not in school he would come searching for us; he tried his best to keep us on the straight path. He would give us money so that we could go to school and time after time he went back to social services with information that we were being neglected, but they never came around to visit.

When Dad was home his temper was worse than I'd ever remembered. He even turned up one day with a redhead prostitute called Jill; he said he picked her up from the docks in Newport so she could take care of us when he was away. She lived with us for a while; we hated her because she would be out all night and sleeping or lazing around the house all day! She left in the end because we couldn't stand her, and her and Dad fought all the time.

There was one time at Sycamore Avenue when we all caught lice. Dad was fuming with us and he had us leant over the kitchen sink while he pulled and combed our hair, slapping us and banging our heads on the sink while screaming and shouting at us.

We went to Uncle Jim many times asking if we could go back and live with him but he told us he needed social services' permission to take us, which they refused to do. One of my worst memories of that house was being locked in a small cupboard for hours.

Dad had been away for days and was due back this day, but we were all worried because we had spent our food money on everything other than food!

We knew Dad would be furious with us so my sisters decided to run away and go to Uncle Jim's. They refused to take me with them because I was such a pain, telling me to wait at home until Uncle Jim came for me. They didn't think Dad would hurt me, but when he came home and found me alone he went crazy, asking me where my sisters had gone!

I'd promised my sisters I wouldn't tell Dad they had gone to Uncle Jim's for help so I refused to tell him anything, saying that I didn't know where they had gone. I can't remember much, only that Dad dragged me into a cupboard and locked me in.

While I was locked in the cupboard Uncle Jim came back with my sisters; he tried to get Dad to allow him into the house to see me but Dad refused, saying I was asleep. Yas later found me crying in the cupboard.

Uncle Jim tried time after time to get social services to listen to his concerns about what Dad had been up to, but they refused to take any notice of him.

Dad always took us to see his Yemeni friends and we would play with their children; these visits became more frequent after he was released from prison. Dad's friends would always have lots of food to eat and we would always get money from them and presents. We would listen to them babble on in Arabic while they would tell us that we needed to learn the language, but we didn't want to learn Arabic, as far as we were concerned we would never need it, we were English girls and only needed to speak and learn English!

Dad had Yemeni friends up and down the country. One of these men was called Nejmie, and we were told to call him Uncle. Uncle Nejmie was an Ambassador in London at the Yemen Embassy and one of the men who helped Dad during his trail; we would spend days at a time in London visiting Dad's friends, especially Uncle Nejmie.

Uncle Jim would always quietly question us when we came back about where we went and who we spoke to. Although we told him everything, we never knew why he asked us so many questions and why he didn't trust our Dad.

It was May 1977 when Dad promised us an exciting holiday abroad to the Yemen. We took no notice of Uncle Jim's concerns because we couldn't wait to go on holiday, we had never travelled before and the idea of going abroad thrilled us.

Dad took us shopping and allowed us to pick out all our own

holiday clothes. Dad and his friends had always told us how the Yemen was such a beautiful and hot country. They told us that exotic fruits would just fall from the trees and were available to everyone, that we would be able to just open our window and pick this fruit, that's how beautiful it was over there.

Uncle Jim tried one last attempt with social services, begging them to step in before it was too late, but they were not interested in helping us.

I remember very clearly the last time we saw my sister Ablah and Uncle Jim. We were at the train station on our way to London to catch our flight. Ablah sobbed as she held on to Issy.

"Please don't go, I have this feeling I'm never going to see you again!"

But we couldn't understand why they were so worried. We told them not to be silly, we would be back in a few weeks! We sat on the train and waved goodbye to Ablah and Uncle Jim as the train pulled off, out of the station, out of sight, and out of our lives.

On the way to the airport Dad gave us some devastating news.

"I'm sorry girls, something's come up and I can't travel with you today," he said unexpectedly.

We moaned and kicked up a fuss about travelling alone, but Dad reassured us that he would be following us in a few days; he told us that Uncle Nasser would be at the other end ready to pick us up.

He gave us a little spending money and told us to enjoy our holiday until he arrived. I myself wasn't bothered; I had my older sisters looking after me as always and anyhow, nothing was going to spoil my day.

Today was very special for me; it was May 28th 1977, my 13th birthday! This was going to be a holiday I would never forget!

Dad saw us through the airport and we were off, and although we weren't happy about travelling alone, we soon started to make plans to enjoy a few days alone without Dad.

We laughed and giggled on the flight and chatted about what we would do on holiday, all the beautiful beaches we would visit, places we would go, and of course, holiday romances!

Chapter Two
Given Away

When the plane flew over Aden, North Yemen, we were all excitingly trying to peer through the window to see what we could spot from high up, but it didn't look very exciting from what we could see. We had never been abroad before so didn't think anything of it, and couldn't wait to touch down and get out of the aeroplane.

Although we were a little apprehensive about Dad not being with us, we were young girls looking to get up to mischief and Dad not being there just meant we could do whatever we wanted!

In our tiny skirts and crop tops, together with our platform shoes Dad had allowed us to buy for our holiday, we headed to the aeroplane door, but when I stepped out into the open it was as if I'd put my head inside an oven!

It was so hot I had to take an extra breath! It was humid, and there was no breeze at all. I instantly started to sweat.

"Oh my god, I've never been this hot in my life," I moaned as we walked down the steps onto the runway.

There was no shuttle bus to take us off the runway so we followed the crowd inside the airport and through immigration to collect our bags. The airport was tiny and crowded and even hotter than outside. It had ceiling fans swinging around making lots of noise, but doing nothing to ease the heat.

As we looked around, we could see men with machine guns walking around the airport. They looked like soldiers because they had uniforms on and what looked like army hats, but whatever they were, they scared me.

We were being stared at by everyone as we made our way through the airport, and not realising it was because of the way we were dressed, it made us feel even more uncomfortable than we already were.

Issy held my hand as we went through immigration and kept telling me not to worry, while Yas just laughed at me and called me a sissy for worrying.

As we come out of immigration we could see Uncle Nasser stood behind a group of people who were waiting, and as soon as he saw us he ran over and greeted us, cheerfully hugging and kissing us on both cheeks.

"Come, come," he said, waving us behind him as he picked up some of our bags and walked towards the entrance. Once outside he turned to us.

"I need passports," he uttered, putting his hands out to us.

"Why do you need our passports?" Issy asked, looking worried.

We had passed immigration, so she wanted to know why he wanted them.

"Police need see them," he relayed in broken English, waving his hand impatiently. Issy had our passports with her in her hand-bag so she reluctantly handed them over.

We had seen loads of men with guns in the airport and we didn't know what the laws of this country were, so we thought it best to let Uncle Nasser take care of it.

Once he had our passports he whistled over to a little dirty white bus that was waiting on the other side of the road and the driver drove over to us. As Uncle Nasser loaded our bags we looked around, shocked at how the people were dressed!

We had never seen anything like it before, the men were wearing what looked like long dresses that went all the way down to their ankles with flip flops or sandals, and they had scarves wrapped around their heads made into some sort of a hat. As for the women, we looked around and couldn't see one female, but we could see figures dressed from head to toe in black, even their faces were covered in black veils! I wondered how they could see to walk with their faces covered like that. It was a frightening sight!

We climbed into the bus, wiping the dust from the seats so as not to ruin our brand new clothes, and as it started up to pull away it made a banging sound as if it was going to break down there and then! It looked as if it would too; the seats were ripped and it was dusty and dirty inside, the windows were stuck and wouldn't move up or down!

We looked at each other and pointed to the state of the bus, quietly making comments so that Uncle Nasser, who was sat up front, couldn't hear us.

On our way to our destination we looked around and became terrified with what we saw.

"Look at the state of this place, it looks like it's been hit by a bomb!" Issy whispered, pointing to what looked like houses as we drove along.

The buildings were old and crumbling, and the streets were dirty, with litter scattered everywhere.

Everywhere we looked we kept seeing those figures in black. "I wonder who they are... I really hope things get better once we get to Aden," I sulked, worried that I really wouldn't want to stay here, wherever here was.

Twenty minutes later we drove into Aden and pulled up outside a high block of flats and to our horror, Uncle Nasser turned to us and with a cheerful smile announced, "We home! Come, come!"

Our hearts sank! We were in the middle of Aden, and this was meant to be the best area. We got out the bus and looked up at the flats. They looked uninhabitable, and the smell was even worse!

We looked at each other and we could each see the fear in each other's eyes. As Uncle Nasser was taking our bags out of the bus, Issy turned to him. "Are we supposed to be staying here?" she asked.

"Yes! Come," he happily replied, ushering us towards the entrance.

The entrance to the flats was down a side alley, the short path to it filled with litter and dirt.

Once we managed to trample through the litter with our platform shoes, we got to the stairs and Uncle Nasser carried on walking up.

"Oh, please tell me there's a lift?" I begged, but he ignored me and carried on walking. Issy could see I was struggling with the heat because by that time the sweat was dripping off me.

"Come on, I'm sure it's just a few more steps," she said, trying to encourage me to keep going.

Yas offered to take my bag but she was already struggling with her own, so I said I was OK, as we continued up the stairs. As it was we were staying on the top floor, six floors up, but felt more like sixty, and by the time we got there the only thing on my mind was a shower and food.

Uncle Nasser knocked on the door and a lady opened it, covered from head to toe in a long dress and her hair was covered with a scarf. Although she looked shocked at what we were wearing, she had a smile on her face as she welcomed us in, kissing us on both cheeks before introducing us in Arabic to a group of other women who also continued to kiss us in the same way.

The other women were all wearing long black coats and scarves, some of them had their faces covered, and it was then that it registered that those figures we had seen before were the women.

My sisters told me to be quiet as I tugged at them, pointing out that the women in black were the people we saw in the street, telling me they had already figured that out for themselves!

By the time they had all finished fussing around us we were confused and tired, we had no clue as to what was happening. This was meant to be our holiday, but it wasn't feeling much like one now!

We didn't understand why the women were dressed the way they were, and didn't like the way people were staring at us because of the way we were dressed.

I looked over to Uncle Nasser who was stood talking to the lady who had opened the door.

"Can I go to our room for a bit please? I'm tired," I asked, putting my hand up and rubbing my forehead as the sweat dripped from me.

There were four rooms off the hallway to the entrance, Uncle Nasser came over and guided us to one of them which was a small room.

As we walked in all we could see in the way of furniture were three bundles of sheets and blankets laid out on the floor made up to look like beds.

"You're bloody kidding me!" Issy said in a sharp tone.

"Just leave it, we'll deal with it later, let's just put our stuff down and have a rest," Yas said, flinging her bag on one of the bundles of blankets. Then Yas turned to Uncle Nasser, who was stood outside the door watching us.

"Do you mind? We need some privacy," she said, shutting the door in his face. We all sat down on a bundle on the floor claiming our right to a bed each.

"This is crap! I can't believe Dad did this to us, I think we should call him and tell him we want to go home," Yas sighed, looking around the room.

The room was painted an off white; it looked like it had been painted many years earlier because it was flaking. There were a few little pictures hung on the walls of buildings that we later found out were mosques, and there was a little window that looked over onto a courtyard that was full of junk and litter. It stank!

"I need the toilet," I said, holding myself like I needed a pee. "Yas, you ask pleeeease!" I begged.

Yas got up and opened the door only to see Uncle Nasser still lurking in the hallway.

"Toilet?" she mumbled under her breath. None of us could be bothered to talk to any of them at that point but it was necessary!

I begged my sisters to come with me so Uncle Nasser walked us all over to a little door next to what looked like the kitchen and opened it.

Inside this tiny square room was a concrete floor with a hole in the corner, with a bucket full of water on the side that had a little jug in it.

"I really need to pee, but I don't know what that is." I turned to Uncle Nasser, a look of desperation on my face.

He sharply called out and the female who opened the door came running out of one of the rooms, he then said something to her and walked off. The female, who could speak good English and was called Sofia, went inside the toilet and started to demonstrate to us how to use the toilet, by squatting down and showing us that we needed to pee over the hole then use the jug of water to wash ourselves with it.

"Is she taking the piss?" Issy joked as Yas started to giggle, but I couldn't see the funny side, I was bursting to go to the toilet!

"Pleeeease tell me someone's got some tissue, I reeeally need to go!" I pleaded, but my sisters just looked at me with smirks on their faces as they shrugged their shoulders.

"I really don't know why you're smirking, you will need to go in a minute as well!" I yelled at them, reluctantly making my way into the toilet.

All three of us took it in turn to use the toilet, then went back to our room moaning about how horrible it was to have to use a toilet in that way.

As soon as we got to our room, uncle Nasser came and told us we needed to go and sit with the women in the other room, but Issy told him we were tired and wanted to rest; although he wasn't happy with us, he left us alone.

We stayed in the room for a bit fiddling about in our suitcases and talking when, all of a sudden, at the same time, we spotted a cockroach running across the room and up the wall! We started screaming and scarpered out into the hallway, bringing Uncle Nasser and the women running from the room wondering what on earth was going on!

"There's a flipping cockroach in our room!" Issy screamed at them.

Not understanding what she was saying, we stood at the edge of the door and pointed to the cockroach, which was by this time on the top wall by the ceiling.

"It's OK, it's OK, no hurt you," was all Uncle Nasser had to say, then he made his way inside the room to hit the cockroach down from the wall.

We all screamed when he then started flattening it with his shoe! By the end of this I was shaking and my sisters had had enough!

"Can we call our dad please? We want to speak to him now!" Yas demanded, but Uncle Nasser wasn't listening to any demands.

"No, tomorrow. No phone here, I take you tomorrow, now come sit with us, have food," he insisted, putting his arm out and escorting us into the room where the other women were sat. We had no choice but to do as we were told, it felt as though if we didn't do as we were told something bad would happen, we felt scared, almost intimidated.

There were only three women left by this time, and although they all wore long dresses and head scarfs none of these women had their faces covered.

We were happy Sofia could speak good English; the flat belonged to her and her husband, who was Uncle Nasser's friend. The other two females were her mother-in-law and her husband's grandmother.

We couldn't eat the food they cooked that day because we didn't know what much of it was; although we liked the rice it was too spicy for us, so we ate very little and ended up eating bread with a cup of tea. After we ate we decided we were going to bed and went to our room for the night.

It had been a long day for all of us and we were tired. We took as many clothes as we could and stuffed them under the door to try and stop any cockroaches from coming in to our room through the gap under the door.

As we lay down on our blankets and went over the day's events, we couldn't believe what had happened to us. We decided we would ring Dad first thing in the morning and let him know what was going on. Obviously things must have changed since Dad was last here. Dad couldn't know how bad things were now, otherwise he would never have brought us here. There were no fruit trees, no beautiful streets and the heat was unbearable!

We tried to fall asleep that night but it took forever because the floor was made of concrete and we only had blankets to sleep on. The ceiling fan was buzzing around but just like the airport, it was making lots of noise but bringing no relief to the heat.

I woke up the next morning and for a split second before I opened my eyes I prayed that everything that had happened had been a bad dream, but as soon as I tried to move I knew it wasn't. My back was in agony from sleeping on the floor.

I looked over at my sisters and saw they were lying there with their eyes open, just silently staring at the ceiling. I sat up to stretch but my back was as stiff as a plank of wood!

"Oh my God! Anyone's back hurting as much as mine?" I moaned in agony.

"Yep!" they both replied together.

"I really want a shower, but I'm scared they're gonna take me outside and hose me down," Issy said sarcastically.

"Oh c'mon, they must have a shower!" I said, looking over for reassurance.

"Did you see a shower hanging from anywhere in that toilet? Because all I saw was a bucket and a jug!" Issy continued. "Anyway, I'm going to ask because I stink!" she said, sniffing her armpits.

We got up and dressed, then we started to dig out our tooth-brushes and stuff from our bags. We headed towards the door to take the clothes away that we had stacked up against the door the night before, but as we picked the clothes up we nearly died with shock as cockroaches emerged from inside the clothes and started running around the room disappearing into our beds!

We squealed in fear, running around the room, grabbing each other in panic, then as quickly as we could we opened the door and ran outside into the hallway.

Sofia was stood in the kitchen doorway, a look of complete shock on her face as we ran out jumping around.

"What's wrong?" she asked, worriedly, as we continued to scream.

"Bloody cockroaches, they're everywhere!" I sobbed, tears running down my face, "I can't take this anymore, I want to go home. I want my dad!"

My sisters hugged me while I cried like a baby, I could feel them shaking and saw that they were trying hard to hold back their own tears.

"It'll be OK Moo, I promise, we'll go and clean the room, won't we Issy?"

I could see Issy had no intention of cleaning anything; she was just as scared as I was! Yas stroked my hair while she tried to calm me down.

"How are you going to clean them? They are everywhere, I hate them!" I sobbed.

Sofia came over to me. "It's OK really, they are harmless, I will spray your room so they won't come in any more, is that OK?" she asked.

She went into the kitchen and came back with some spray. "See, this will kill them all, you go in the other room and I will clean your room," she told us with a smile.

Sofia went and sprayed our room; she also picked up our shower stuff we dropped in our panic to get away from the cockroaches.

When Issy asked where our uncle was she told us he had gone out and would be back later. So then we asked her if we could have a shower and just like Issy had thought, there was no shower.

Sofia then showed us the routine of having a shower, which meant we would have to boil water in a huge saucepan on a tiny stove, and then transfer it to a huge bucket. Then we would have to pour it over ourselves from the bucket with a jug while washing ourselves. It took a while to get used to, but when you're hot and sweaty you will do anything to cool down!

After we had all showered we had some bread and cups of tea as there was very little much more we could find that we liked to eat.

Sofia then showed us around the flat. The kitchen was tiny, it had a tiny sink with a hosepipe that came from a hole in the wall and had a tap attached to it. The cooker had two cooker heads with a small oven; they also had a small fridge. There was no washing machine, and when we asked her about one she didn't have a clue what we were talking about!

Most of the flooring in the flat was very old tiles and they had a few little rugs here and there; there were no beds and no chairs or tables or cupboards, their clothes were all in big trunk-like suitcases in the side of their bedrooms. In the main room where everyone sat, there were mattresses with covers on them on the floor and that's where everyone sat. The room had a nice big rug in it. Sofia's mother-in-law and grandmother spent most of their time in their own room; it looked like they shared a room at the time because we had taken somebody's room.

That day while Uncle Nasser was out, we asked Sofia questions about why the women wore those black clothes. She told us that almost all the women in Yemen wore that black long coat to cover up. It was called an 'abaya', a one-piece long coat with a head covering called the 'niqab' which covered the whole face except the eyes, and then there was a veil to cover the whole face. The head scarf was called the 'hijab' and that was always worn inside the house. She told us it was worn for religious purposes because they are Muslim women, but not all women wore it even if they were Muslim.

She told us those who choose not to wear it get frowned upon by some people because they are looked upon as bad girls or not from a good family. Sofia said women can wear whatever they want underneath their abayas or when they were alone at home.

The long dresses that the men wore are called 'zennas' or 'thobe'; also clothing that was their tradition was a skirt called 'footah' which they wrapped around their waist and was held up with a belt. Mostly the men wore sandals or flip-flops with this clothing because of the heat.

After Sofia had cleaned our room we got ready and decided we were going out to try and phone Dad, after all our uncle did promise us we could call him today; we also wanted to go out and have a look around.

Just as we were about to leave Sofia stopped us; she warned us that our uncle told her we weren't allowed to leave until he came back. She assured us he was just worried we may get lost or get hassled by men because women didn't go out alone in Yemen, they only went out accompanied by men or in groups of women and that's only if they are covered.

We were furious, but not with Sofia - she was only doing what she had been told - we were angry with our uncle for not allowing us out of the house. This was supposed to be our holiday, but now we were told we couldn't leave the house unaccompanied.

We hung out with Sofia while she cooked dinner and around lunch time Uncle Nasser and Sofia's husband came back. It was the first time we met him and he seemed friendly enough, he was called Jalal and looked older than Sofia, maybe in his 40s.

Once again we struggled with the food and ate very little but tried not to show that we were struggling, we just said that we weren't that hungry. After dinner Uncle Nasser got up to leave again with Jalal, but we followed him to the hallway.

"When can we call Dad?" Issy asked.

"I speak him today, he say you wait him, no call father," he replied as he turned to leave, but Issy grabbed his arm.

"That's not fair! You said we could call him today, we don't want to stay here anymore, we want to go home!"

Uncle Nasser aggressively pushed her away from him. "You do as told, stay here!" he warned.

We all began yelling at him, telling him to leave her alone, telling him we wanted to go home. The arguing got so loud that Jalal, Sofia and his mother were trying to calm us down, but all we wanted to do was leave.

"Come on let get our bags, we are not staying here!" Issy's voice was trembling with rage as she spoke to us, then she turned to our uncle.

"Give us our passports, you can't make us stay if we don't want to, we aren't prisoners!" But he just glared at us, evil in his eyes.

"No passport no goes home, this home, you stay here!"

Issy tried to push past him heading for the door, but Jalal and Uncle Nasser blocked her way while Jalal's mother locked the door with the key, then she put the key in her pocket.

"You can't make us stay if we don't want to, we will just run away!" Issy shouted as we ran into our room sobbing, slamming the door behind us.

Our Uncle followed. "These clothes no more! Trousers only, these long," he said pointing at our short sleeved tops and skirts. And with that he left the room.

We realised then what a mess we were in. We didn't know anybody there who could help us and we didn't even know how to contact Dad because we didn't have his phone number. We had no passports and very little pocket money. All we could hope for was that Dad would hurry up and get here.

We heard Uncle Nasser and Jalal leave, and peeping through the keyhole of our room we saw Jalal's mother lock the front door and take the key. We decided to act nice and see if she would trust us, so we wiped away our tears and went out to the other room to sit with them.

All three women were sat in the room by then. Sofia tried her best to convince us that everything Uncle Nasser was doing was for our own good, which Dad had told him to do, but how dumb did they think we were? We knew our Dad better than anyone and he would never tell him to keep us locked up like this.

A while later and the flat started to fill up with women, each time Jalal's mother would unlock the door to let them in, then lock it again.

Sofia told us it was tradition for female family members, neighbours, and friends to gather in the afternoons for special occasions, and us coming from England was a big occasion. All the women wanted to see the new English girls!

One family that came over were two sisters that lived in the same flats just a few doors down; one of them was a young girl called Nahla, she was around 17. She stood out to us because she was wearing jeans and a long sleeved top and her hair wasn't covered.

We instantly liked Nahla and started chatting to her because she spoke really good English, she told us she was a student and that her family didn't make her wear the abaya or hijab because they were more westernised and trusted her to do the right thing.

She was staying with her sister while studying in Aden but her family were from another town. She told us she got hassled a lot and stared at by both men and women when she went out for not covering up, but she didn't care, because she still stuck by her religious beliefs and was doing nothing wrong.

The afternoon came and went, and after everyone had gone Uncle Nasser returned with some Arabic cakes and sweets for us. Maybe he did it as a peace offering, but whatever the reason, we took them and ate them because we had eaten very little food since arriving.

Once again that night we slept knowing that whatever we did it wouldn't keep the cockroaches away, and nothing could take away the dreadful heat.

One day started to blend into another. After about a week our Uncle started to allow Sofia and Jalal's mothers take us to the shop with them. The thought of running away entered our minds on many occasions, but we had nowhere to go, and no one to run to. We had no choice but to follow orders.

We were also allowed to go and hang out with Nahla and her sister in their flat. We would listen to our English cassettes that we had brought over and teach Nahla the words to the songs and how to dance.

Nahla taught us a little Arabic; she also taught us how to dance the Arabic style and how to put eyeliner on the Arabic way. They used a black gritty dust that was in a tiny thin glass vial, it had a long thin smooth metal pin that you would dip in the dust then gently put it on the corner of your eye, pushing the metal pin back and forward so the black dust would become as eyeliner. It would make our eyes water and the dust would go everywhere, you had to know how to use it and we didn't! Nahla became our best friend and we saw her every day.

Two weeks passed with still no sign of Dad and we still hadn't been allowed to phone him. Every time we asked Uncle Nasser he would just say, "He comes soon," and that's all we got.

One day when visiting Nahla, her sister was out visiting other relatives and we were alone in the flat. Nahla had often told us about a shop she knew that sold English foods; that day, although reluctant, she agreed to take us out shopping alone without adult supervision.

By that time we had all become accustomed to wearing only trousers and long sleeved tops so off we went, all four of us in our jeans, with our hair uncovered. We knew if we got caught we would get told off, but we didn't care because we just wanted to go out alone. Walking along the road the car horns were beeping and we were getting shouted at by men, but Nahla just told us to ignore them.

"This is what they do if you're uncovered, don't look up, take no notice and keep walking," she advised us.

We got to the shop which was only about ten minutes' walk away from the flat, and once inside we looked around to see what we wanted to buy. There wasn't really much food that we recognised because the packages were different from back home and everything was written in Arabic, but what we did see was cornflakes, so we got a few packs of those, we also got some chocolate Mars bars. Once we had what we wanted we made our way home, happy with the fact that we had enjoyed half an hour out by ourselves without any grown-ups!

We got to the top of the steps and were greeted by a furious Uncle Nasser who was waiting for us outside Nahla's flat. He was shouting and cursing at Nahla in Arabic, so we couldn't understand what was being said, but we knew she was in trouble. Nahla waved at us saying she would see us later, she looked concerned as Uncle Nasser shoved us into our flat telling us we shouldn't have gone out alone because it could have been dangerous for us.

Once inside the flat he snatched the bag out of Yas's hand to see what we had bought, then once he was satisfied it was only food he gave it back.

Even though we were upset and scared by his behaviour, we were getting used to his outbursts by now, so we just let him rant on and tried not to get upset. We gave him a few snide comments in quick English, that way we knew no one but us three could understand, and then we took our goodies and disappeared into our room.

The next day we went to see Nahla, but her sister said she wasn't in. When we asked her to pass on a message that we had called, she told us that Uncle Nasser had told Nahla she was no longer allowed to hang out with us or talk to us.

We confronted our uncle when he came back and tried to ask him what his problem was. He said he didn't like Nahla and thought she was a bad influence on us; he forbade any more contact between us. We told him he couldn't stop us from having friends especially female friends, and that we would carry on seeing her no matter what he said.

That night we wrote a letter to Nahla and asked her to meet us while Uncle Nasser was out. We told her we missed her friendship and we promised to keep our friendship a secret. We passed the letter to her sister who reluctantly passed it on to Nahla. She wrote us a letter back.

She told us our uncle had threatened to have her sent back to her family, and her education taken away from her, if she continued any contact with us. She told us that our uncle could make up any lie he wanted about her, she said she would not be able to defend herself or be listened to; this was just how girls got treated in Yemen.

This letter broke our hearts; we couldn't understand how our uncle could be so heartless as to do this to our friend just because she was trying to be nice to us. For Nahla's sake we decided to leave her alone. I hated our uncle from that moment onwards, no matter what he did I would never trust him, or have any love or respect for him ever again.

It had been fifteen or so days since we arrived in Aden and out of the blue Dad's other brother Uncle Mohammed arrived from Sanaa, South Yemen. We had never met him before but he was fluent in English because he had lived most of his life in America.

The first two days with him were great; he took us to a beach in Aden that we didn't even know existed. We weren't allowed to swim of course because that was forbidden for females, but we sat on the beach and ate ice-cream. He also took us to a cinema, we sat and watched a whole film in a language we couldn't understand, but we loved it because we were out of the flat!

He spoilt us so much more than Uncle Nasser had, but that was just to soften the blow!

One afternoon after lunch we were sat in our room lazing about. Both our uncles and Jalal were in the main room while the other women were in another room. We were all excited when Uncle Mohammed came to our room and told us he needed to tell us some important news. Thinking he was going to tell us Dad was coming we were eager to listen to what he had to say, but devastated when he started talking.

He told us the next day Issy and I were going to be travelling with him to Sanaa in South Yemen, but Yas was not coming with us. He said she was going to live in Uncle Nejmie's house in another part of Aden, as she had been promised to him in marriage, she was now his wife.

We all started to panic. "What do you mean promised in marriage?" Yas gasped, trying to catch her breath. "I'm just a kid, are you joking? This is a joke, right? You're winding us up, aren't you?" she mumbled.

"This is no joke, your father promised you to Nejmie before you left England, the arrangements have been made, you will go and wait for your husband to arrive from England. His family are good people and you will stay with them until he arrives."

Uncle Mohammed stood up to leave the room. "You all need to pack your clothes because we leave first thing in the morning."

We all stood up and blocked the door to stop him from leaving, holding hands. I just cried, I couldn't speak because I didn't understand what was going on.

"No, no, we won't go, we called Nejmie 'uncle', Dad wouldn't do this to us, he wouldn't do this to Yas, his own daughter! This is all you and Uncle Nasser, you can't order us around and tell us what to do and you are not giving my little sister to a pervert, she's just a kid!" Issy yelled in Uncle Mohammed's face.

Our uncle stood calmly in front of us as we stood blocking the door. "Believe me when I tell you this, your father is the one who arranged all of this and you will all do as you are told. I am only doing what my brother has asked of me and your sister is no child; she is a woman, you are all women, and you must all start behaving like women!"

He pushed past us and left the room, leaving us all holding on to each other, stunned, afraid and shocked!

I didn't really understand much of what was going on around me. I listened to Issy and Yas as they discussed events that had happened back in England, how Uncle Jim must have known this was going to happen to us because he had tried so hard to stop us from coming, and how we should have listened more to his advice. How Dad had always been so friendly with Nejmie, and must have had this planned all along.

Although I didn't know much, I knew we needed to be worried, I knew my big sister was about to be taken away from me and I was petrified! I also knew Dad had lots of Arabic friends back in England and here. How could he do this to Yas, and what did he have in store for Issy and me?

That night we made plans to run away, we didn't know anyone or where to go, we had no passports or money, but we couldn't stay to get given away to men like this.

We decided we would wait till late that night and sneak out. We refused to speak to anyone or eat anything for the rest of the day, shutting ourselves away in our room.

When everyone finally went to sleep we opened our bedroom door and went to sneak into the hallway. Uncle Mohammed made us jump as he spoke; he was sat outside our room hiding in the corner.

"We are not stupid so don't treat us as such," he warned in a low stern voice.

"Why shouldn't we? You treat us like we are stupid!" Issy shouted back at him. I was so scared I instantly burst out crying and hid behind her; within seconds Uncle Nasser appeared in the hallway.

"We won't do as you want!" Yas cried, grabbing my hand and pulling me back into the room.

We could hear Issy arguing in the hallway with our uncles. They were making it clear they would stay outside our door all night so that we couldn't go anywhere, she was making it equally clear to them that they were not taking our sister away from us.

She finally gave up arguing with them and came back into the room, slamming the door as hard as she could. "I hate them sooo much!" she shouted as loud as she could so that they could hear.

We cuddled up together on one bed, talking and crying at the same time, terrified of what the morning would bring.

Every now and then Issy would open the door and check to see if the hallway was clear for us to escape, when she was met with disappointment she would slam the door as hard as she could, just to piss them off.

I nodded off at some point but I don't think my sisters did because when I woke up in the morning, they were still talking.

The next morning, when that horrible moment came, our uncles came into the room.

"Time to go," Uncle Mohammed calmly said, looking directly at Yas. We were all cuddled up together on the same bed, holding on tightly to each other.

"No way, I'm not going anywhere with you!" Yass voice was shaking.

Both our uncles came over to separate us and we all started screaming as they grabbed her to take her away.

The look of total fear and desperation in my sister's eyes, knowing what was about to happen to her, and the fear I had of losing our sister was unbearable and indescribable.

I could feel my heart breaking as we begged and pleaded with our uncles not to take her away from us, but when that failed, we kicked at them, punching and scratching as much as we could to keep them away from her. But that only ended up with us tugging her back and forth.

Jalal, Sofia and his mother and grandmother heard the screaming and came rushing in to help our uncles take her away. In the end all we could do was try and hug her and kiss her and tell her how much we loved her, that we would sort things out to get her back.

We were pushed back into the room while the door was blocked by Jalal and his family, whilst our uncles dragged Yas away kicking and screaming out of the flat, down the stairs and out of our lives.

It seemed like things were happening in slow motion, but at the same time things happened so fast.

Issy and I were left sobbing on the floor, helpless. We lay there and just held each other and cried, then all of a sudden Uncle Mohammed came back upstairs.

Issy jumped up wiping the tears off her face, a look of hope in her eyes. "Where's my sister?" she pleaded, looking behind him.

"I told you, she has gone to her husband's home, your Uncle Nasser has taken her and we are going to Sanaa now, so come on bring your things, let's hurry, the car is waiting," he said as he picked up our bags.

"Why are you doing this to us? I want to be with my sister," I sobbed. But there was no sympathy in his voice.

"Please let's not have a repeat of what just happened, we need to go, now hurry!" Uncle Mohammed made a gesture with his hand that he wanted us out the door.

"Come on Issy, we better go," I sobbed as I grabbed her hand and made my way to the door.

Issy followed quietly, we both knew we were going to be made to do as we were told, by choice, or by force.

We were escorted to a big open-back jeep. Uncle Mohammed sat up front next to the driver and we sat in the back seat; the open back was full of men who were also going to Sanaa. They stank and whatever teeth they had left were stained, and they did nothing but stare at us for the whole journey.

We cried throughout that journey. Mostly silent tears, as we ignored Uncle Mohammed's failed attempts to engage us in conversation; it was as though he had no idea of what he had just done to us. Taking away our sister was like ripping away a piece of our heart, and for us to know she had been given to a man she had once called uncle was something we couldn't bear to think about!

As we drove out of the tarmac roads of Aden and on to the dirt roads that lead to wherever we were going, the views started to change. The hills and mountains stretched for miles and miles. I could see in the distance on top of the many hills what looked like villages and houses that were so high up. I wondered how people could even get to them with these roads!

We passed small villages with farms and I could see both men and women working in them. The women had different coloured clothes on the further we drove, but they were all covered; some had their faces covered by black veils and some didn't.

The houses looked ancient and it looked like the small ones were made from mud but the bigger ones were made from stone as well as mud.

The little houses had little round holes for windows, while the big houses had huge big square windows that had wooden shutters painted in all different colours.

Some of the bigger windows had metal bars on them; I wondered why they had them. Were they there to stop people from falling out, or to stop people from escaping?

There were hardly any cars or trucks on the road but there were lots of people riding along the side of the roads on donkeys. The donkeys were weighed down on each side by huge saddle bags that looked packed with stuff.

There were women casually walking along with huge buckets and other things on their heads, as if it was the most normal thing to do!

One minute we were driving through green fields and villages for miles and miles, the next we were driving through rough rocky mountains that looked as if it had been burnt by a huge fire because it looked so black and ashy.

We stopped every now and then by a road side shop. All the shops along the road just looked like a little huts but Uncle Mohammed stopped every now and then to buy us refreshments. We accepted drinks from him purely because it was so hot and we were thirsty.

If this had just been a holiday, and we hadn't been in such a bad situation, there could have been many questions I would have asked on that journey, but everything looked horrifying to me and

I knew we were going to be taken to a place that we didn't know, or want to be in.

We had been tricked into thinking this was going to be a fantastic holiday, but now it was anything but a holiday.

I couldn't get the image of my sister being ripped away from us out of my head. Issy held my hand real tight all through the journey. As I lay my head on her shoulder and we quietly wept together, I began to realise what had happened to us: we had been kidnapped!

Chapter Three
Dad's Secret Family

When we arrived in Sanaa it was early evening and it was dark. We had been travelling all day and we were tired and in no mood to talk to anyone. So when we got to our destination and were greeted by a screaming lady who was running towards the jeep we really didn't know what to do, or how to deal with her.

She was wrapped in what looked like a huge red, black and white tablecloth that covered her from head to toe, except her face. Her face was separately covered by what looked like a scarf that was shaped like a balaclava, with only her eyes showing.

We got out of the jeep and she just came at us, hugging and kissing us, she just wouldn't let us go!

"That's your sister Nebat," Uncle Mohammed said as he pulled our bags out the jeep. Issy and I looked at each other in utter disbelief.

"We don't have another sister!" we both said, as this woman continued touching us as if she was trying to make sure we were real.

"She is your father's first born, your father married Nebat's mother and had Nebat before he left for England," Uncle Mohammed continued.

"This just can't get any worse! I'm getting really freaked out by things we don't know about Dad!" Issy hissed through her teeth as she held tightly onto my hand.

"Come on, it's OK, I got you," she told me, trying to reassure me, but I was shaking with fear and she could see it.

Next to Nebat was a tall thin man who was her husband

Ahmed. He and Nebat chatted away as they took us inside and sat us down, but we couldn't understand a word they said to us; they didn't speak English.

Nebat could see from our faces that we were upset so she turned to Uncle Mohammed for an explanation. He must have told her we were upset about Yas because she came to try and comfort us and started to ramble on in Arabic.

"What is she saying?" I asked him. I really didn't want to speak to him but I wanted to know what she was saying.

"She's saying she's your sister now, that you can come to her if you need anything," he replied, looking at us both. Issy stared at Uncle Mohammed, her eyes full of hate and welling up with tears.

"Are you really crazy or just plain bloody stupid?" she snapped. "You don't just take away one sister then try and replace her with someone we didn't even know existed until a few minutes ago, we don't want another sister! We want Yas back!"

Issy burst out crying, then so did I. Straight away Nebat came over to try and hug us but Issy pushed her hands away, screaming out.

"Just get off me! Leave me alone!"

At this point so much had happened in the day, things had gotten too much and Issy and I were both crying out loud, we couldn't stop ourselves; then Nebat started to cry.

Uncle Mohammed didn't know what to do or say to shut us up, so he came and knelt in front of us to try and calm us down. For the first time since meeting him I looked at his face and thought how much he looked like Dad. He was a little taller than Dad but they had the same hair, eyes, nose, mouth, they looked so alike.

"I know you all want to blame me for this, but like I have told you, I am only doing what has been asked of me by your father, when your father comes you can shout and scream at him, but please, I don't want you to shout at me anymore," he said, trying to defend his actions.

"But you don't seem to understand how we are feeling, you just expect us to shut up and do as we are told," Issy sobbed, not wanting to give in to him.

"Until your father arrives yes, you need to do as he has asked. Once he is here you can talk to him and try and change his mind;

A Father's Betrayal

your father will be here next week. Until then let's try and not shout at each other." Uncle Mohammed stood up and went away, leaving us to wipe our tears.

I looked at Nebat; she had taken off her covers by that point and was only wearing her hijab so we could see her face. She too looked sad; I couldn't help but feel for her. I couldn't help but wonder what she must have gone though in her life.

When she looked at me I tried to give her a little smile and felt a slight bond towards her as she gave me a little smile back.

That night we slept in a room that Nebat had prepared for us. The sleeping arrangements were slightly better than in Aden. We had mattresses to sleep on instead of bundles of blankets and thankfully there was not a cockroach in sight.

We lay awake most of the night wondering what Yas was doing, how she was being treated and how she must have been feeling being all alone.

It was still hot but not as hot as Aden, however they didn't have ceiling fans in Nebat's house.

The toilet and washing arrangements were the same, the only difference was Nebat had boiled loads of water ready for us so that when we woke up in the morning we didn't have to do it ourselves, we could go straight in and wash.

Nebat had also cooked us fresh bread in her clay oven the next morning. It was the best thing we had eaten since we arrived in Yemen.

Issy and I had spoken the night before and decided we would try our best with Nebat. She had done no wrong to us and after all, she was a sister of ours even though we didn't know her. We also decided that although we hated his guts and didn't want to talk to him, Uncle Mohammed was our translator and we needed him, but we would talk to him as little as possible.

Uncle Mohammed told us we would only be spending the one day with Nebat. The next day our journey would continue to our final destination. This was Dad's parents' house; up until this day we didn't even know that Dad had parents. I silently wondered if they would treat us good and kind like grandparents are supposed to.

We spent the day with Nebat while she ran around the house

36

trying to do everything she could to make us feel welcome. That afternoon as usual the house filled up with women from all around wanting to get a glimpse of Nebat's English sisters. She was in her element showing us off to everyone! Although we really didn't want to sit with them, we had no other choice. Nebat only had two rooms and the room we had slept in the night before was the other room. Uncle Mohammed and Ahmed were now in that room.

The next morning we were up early and ready to go. We said goodbye to Nebat as she cried and hugged us, and then we got into another jeep, again there were other men in the jeep who wanted to be dropped off on the way.

We had no clue to where we were going, or what was in store for us once we got there. The drive took about five hours and once again the scenery on the way was of mountains, hills, villages and fields and all that came in between.

If we passed a village that was close to the road, children would run up to the jeep and the men on the back would usher the children away from the jeep as they ran alongside it. Most of the children didn't even have shoes on their feet and they were covered in dirt and dust!

As we got closer to our destination, I noticed we came off the dirt road and started to drive towards the mountains.

"Oh God! It looks like we are going to one of those villages!" I whispered to Issy, panicking as I pointed to some houses in the distance. Issy squeezed my hand as we drove past the houses and behind the mountains further and further into nowhere.

Behind the mountains the roads were winding, bending and so bumpy, then all of a sudden we could see more fields, hills and land all around us, and we were wondering where the hell we were!

Then we saw the village, Dad's village. It was called Al Mugraba and as we drove up to it my heart sank. The roads that led to it let off so much dust they had to shut the car windows.

The houses looked as though they were the aftermath of an earthquake, they looked as though they were falling down and crumbling! I looked around as we entered the village and all I saw was what looked like a ghost town; I couldn't see anybody. Some of the houses were huge, some were small but they all looked as though they were made out of mud.

The roof tops were flat and I could see washing draped over the sides of the roofs like they were about to fall off. As we drove through the houses I started to see one or two people walking around. The men looked grubby and had worn out zennas on, and the females wore dresses down past their knees with trousers underneath, baggy and dragging in the dust. They wore scarves around their heads but their faces were uncovered.

We pulled up outside a huge house and Uncle Mohammed got out and opened the door for us. "This is your Granddad's house!" he said cheerfully as if he thought we would be happy to be there.

Straight away a big lady came out of the house and started to welcome us and usher us towards the front door of the house.

After Uncle Mohammed took our bags out of the jeep it drove off, leaving us alone, with nowhere else to go!

"This is your grandmother, Fatima," he said as she continued to usher us towards the door; then, with the loudest voice, she leant her head forward and shouted up the stairs, "Farouse!" We looked inside the doorway to see who she was shouting for.

There were loads of steps leading upstairs when all of a sudden, this young girl around my age came running down them, only to tumble midway and land flat at the bottom of the steps!

Gran started yelling at the girl but she took no notice. She just jumped up as though nothing had happened and started hugging and kissing both of us as if we had been best friends all our lives!

"That's your cousin Farouse!" Uncle Mohammed laughed as Farouse grabbed Issy and me by our hands and dragged us upstairs.

The stairs were made from cows' dung and straw. We walked up about ten steps before the steps bent to the right, but just before the bend there was a little door that was about waist high. We didn't take any notice of it at first and followed Farouse up about another five stairs. On the middle floor were four doors, Farouse took us into the one door on the right that was open.

Farouse was scruffy and talkative but never stopped smiling; she had so much energy! She was about the same age as me. We found out they didn't exactly know her real date of birth, but she was about twelve years old. She was skinny but the same height as me; she was Uncle Nasser's daughter but had been taken off her mother when she was younger because her father divorced her mother and her mother remarried. Farouse lived with our grandparents.

Gran had very dark skin compared to other Yemenis I'd seen. She was a big lady with a big back and thick arms and legs, she had very masculine features that were a bit scary! The dresses they wore had high waistlines that sat just under their breasts and hers looked really tight from the top because her breasts looked enormous! I couldn't really tell her age but she looked late 40s. She wasn't our real grandmother. Dad's mum died shortly after giving birth to her youngest son many years early. Fatima was Dad's stepmum.

It was dinner time by the time we arrived and Granddad was just arriving from working in the fields. As he walked in I couldn't help notice the difference in size between him and Gran. He was small and skinny and looked much older that she did. He had a little bit of straw-like white hair that was covered by some sort of cloth he had wrapped on his head to make it look like a hat. I caught myself looking at his hat wondering how it just sat on his head and didn't fall off! He greeted us with a kiss on both cheeks and a hint of a smile, and that was that from him.

We were sat in a room on the middle floor and it was a long room that went from one end of the house to the other. There were mattresses on the floor that we sat on and the floor itself was made from cows' dung and straw. Along the whole length of the room were square windows about 25 inches both in length and height. They were at elbow's reach as you sat down so that you could look out if you were sat at the window; like the ones I'd seen on our journey, these all had wooden shutters and metal bars on them.

Farouse ran in and out of the room bringing in the food and placing it all in the middle of the floor, and then she came around with a little dish of water. Starting with Granddad, then Uncle Mohammed, she let everyone dip their hands in the dish to wash their fingers.

When she came to me I looked at her and smiled. "No thanks," I said politely, waving my hands in a gesture of 'no' so she could understand.

Farouse looked puzzled and said something to Granddad who in turn said something to Uncle Mohammed. "Are you not eating dinner with us?" he asked me.

"Yeah but I'll use a folk or spoon thanks," I answered.

"We don't have them here, we all eat with our fingers, together, out of the same bowl or plate."

I looked at the food in the middle of the room; there was a round bowl with a lump of what looked like cement made into a pyramid shape in the middle of the bowl. Surrounding it was something that looked like soup. On another plate was rice with what looked like potatoes curry on top, then in a big round basket on the side was bread, the same that Nebat had cooked us at her house.

"I don't know about you sis, but I'll just have some bread. I'm not that hungry," Issy said to me. I agreed with her, there was no way I wanted to eat with my fingers, especially the food that was in front of us.

Uncle Mohammed said something to Granddad and after he grunted and mumbled something back, Farouse brought over the basket of bread and placed it in front of us. Then they all sat in the middle of the room and started to eat.

As I watched them eat the food I was so happy I'd refused to eat with them. They would break off a bit of cement (as we nicknamed it, it was really called aceed) then they would mix it in the soup turning it over and over and then scooping it into their mouths while licking their fingers before repeating it all again. Every now and then they would throw a blob of this yellowish frothy mixture (hilba) into the soup. Then mix it in with their fingers, again licking their fingers as they went along, topping up the soup from a bowl nearby when it got low, or too thick from all the mixing.

After the cement was finished they started on the rice and potatoes, mashing the potatoes with their fingers and mixing it in with the rice. Only this time it was worse because when they scooped the rice into their mouths, any remaining food in their hand they would flick back onto the plate, mixing it in with the rest of the food.

After all that was finished, Granddad got the bowl that had the soup in it and started picking out pieces of chicken from inside it. He started breaking the chicken into tiny little pieces, passing firstly to Uncle Mohammed, then Gran then he passed to me but I kindly refused; so did Issy. He hadn't washed his hands before he had started to break the chicken and the image of him scooping his food into his mouth was still in my head. He shook his head in disappointment as we refused and said something in a harsh voice to Uncle Mohammed. We were sure he was cursing us but we really didn't care!

After dinner Farouse took us up to what was to be our room. Uncle Mohammed had made it known to us that we were staying in the guest room which was the best room of the house. We came out of the middle floor and went up about six more steps that bore right and in front of us there was a kitchen. We looked in and saw that again the floor was made from cows' dung and straw, but in the corner on the floor was a small cemented area with a hole and a bit of pipe that leads outside: that was the sink area.

At the other end of the kitchen were two built-in clay ovens, there were also two little holes in the wall, one either side of the kitchen just big enough to stick your head out of and another big hole right above the clay oven for the smoke to exit. We carried on past the kitchen and up yet another five more stairs to the top floor and a square landing. Straight ahead in front was one door, and to the right the door of the room we were staying, and to the left was a little wooden door that led on to the lower roof.

As we went to go into our room I looked to my right only to see a few more steps leading up to another floor. I tugged on Farouse's arm and made a gesture to ask what was up there. "Da, ally," she said grabbing my hand for us to follow her up there.

At the top of the steps was another small cemented area with a hole in the corner and a piece of broken pipe that lead outside. She knelt down to demonstrate that this was the shower area, there was no door or curtain to protect us from anyone coming up or down the stairs, so I didn't know how anyone was supposed to wash there without being seen? Up a step off the shower area was another wooden door that led to the upper roof.

"Let's have a look later when we are alone," Issy said as she made her way back down the steps and into the room.

The size of this room was the same as the one we had ate dinner in; the only difference was this room had been split in two. There was another door just to the left just as you came through the main door. This room had only taken a small size off the main room; it was full of mattresses, pillows and blankets. It had a small window in there.

The main room was a bit better than the middle room as it had a very long rug that covered the dung floor and the mattresses were thick and covered in pretty-looking covers. They had thick colourful pillows that boarded the room, and on top of the mattresses were armrests scattered all around the room.

I could smell the smoke from the bakhoor that still lingered in the air. I'd smelt bakhoor many times since arriving in Yemen because all the women used it to make their houses and cloths smell nice. Bakhoor is a scent that comes from burning fragrant woods; it's made by soaking the wood in natural oils, perfumes and sometimes spices.

The windows in this room were much bigger and didn't have metal poles on them. I dumped my stuff on the floor and headed straight for the window; I found the latch, flung the window open and stuck my head out.

Farouse came charging over. "La, La," she said in a terrified voice trying to close the window.

"Hey... what the hell's wrong with you?" I snapped at her, re-opening the window.

There was no point us trying to communicate because we couldn't understand each other. Although we knew basic words by now and I knew she did not want me to open the window, I just didn't know why.

I could hear Gran with her loud voice calling Farouse again so Farouse ran off, leaving me with my head out the window.

"Hey! Look!" I said to Issy, "there's a shop out there." Issy came over and joined me by the window and we both hung our heads out.

The window looked over the front door and to our left we could see another house; next to the huge front door to that house was a shutter like window that looked like a shop. As we looked out of the window we could see some goats, sheep and chickens in a stable just a few feet right opposite our front door.

"I wonder who they belong to," I said.

"Most probably Granddad, see that little chicken running around over there? Well its brother or sister was on our dinner table today!" Issy joked.

I pretended to gag at the thought of what she had just said and we continued to look around at what we could see of the village from the window.

We both had our heads hanging out of the window, so we didn't notice Gran walk into the room, but she gave us a huge fright when she started yelling at us.

"Ayp al ek ya Bennet!" (Shame on you girls!) Although we didn't understand what she was saying at that time, her voice was such that we nearly fell out the window!

"What the hell is wrong with you people"! Issy screeched. "What's wrong with us looking out the stupid window?"

Gran marched over and pulled the window shut but Issy wasn't having any of it.

"No! It stays open," she yelled as she flung it back open.

Cursing us as she left the room Gran marched off, the next thing we knew Uncle Mohammed walked into the room. "Now what!?" Issy snapped as we both came in from the window.

"Your Gran said you shouted at her," he said, but Issy was in no mood to listen to him and cut him off before he could finish speaking.

"She yelled at us for nothing! What is wrong with looking out the window? What's the harm in that?" she asked sitting down with her arms crossed.

"It's shameful here for girls to be seen with their heads stuck out the window," Uncle Mohammed continued as he sat down next to us. "Especially if you're not covered up, she was only looking out for you so that you don't get a bad reputation, you've only just arrived, you should listen to her guidance."

"Yeah well, that's easier said than done!" I sulked. "How we are supposed to listen to anything or anyone? You're the only one we can understand!" I said.

"Well if you need to ask me questions I only live a few houses away," he replied.

"What? You don't live here? Who's going to let us know what they are saying?" I asked.

I was terrified of Uncle Mohammed leaving us alone with these people. Although I didn't like him at least we could understand what he was saying!

He told us not to worry; he said that Farouse would look after us because she was so excited to finally have us here. He said he lived with his wife and children who we would meet that afternoon as they were coming over with many other women to meet us.

Uncle Mohammed left Issy and me to prepare for another day of being put on display for the women to look at! By this time we were so fed up with having to sit amongst people we didn't know or understand, and having to allow them to stare at us as if we had come from another planet!

As we were getting ready we chatted about Yas, wondering what she was doing, hoping she was alright. It was the first time in my life I'd ever been away from my sister and I was finding it difficult and Issy could see that. She was being extra nice to me; at least we had each other. Yas had no one.

After we got ready I went downstairs to look for Farouse who was in the kitchen to ask her where the toilet was. I asked her in Arabic as I'd learnt it by then. "Hamam," I asked.

Her face lit up with a big smile as I said the word and she came rushing out and took me by the hand, babbling on most probably thinking I could understand more of what she was saying when I couldn't. She took me down the stairs and to the little waist high door I'd noticed when I first came in and she opened it.

It was a long tunnel-like room with a small round window at the other end, and under the window was a hole in the floor and a bucket of water in the corner. It was dark and the only light came from the tiny window; there was no light fitting in sight.

To get over to the hole at the other end you had to bend down and, as you were hunched over, make your way into the toilet and stay that way until you left. The ceiling was made from tree branches and little thin bits of wood that were covered in cobwebs. The hole for the toilet dropped to the bottom of the house and the draught came up as you squatted over it. It stank, and it was so uncomfortable I wished that I never had to use the toilet ever again in my life, ever!

When I finished I ran upstairs and told Issy about the toilet. She didn't believe it was as bad as I said, so I took her downstairs to see for herself. She was horrified! It was even worse for her because she was taller than I was, so she had more bending down to do.

I mentioned the fact that there were no light fixtures in the toilet and that I hadn't seen any anywhere around the house, so off we went to explore. As I thought, there were none to be seen anywhere. However, we thought, there must be electricity, otherwise how do they have light? Use the appliances? Or watch TV? I went in search for Farouse once again and tried to demonstrate a light switch to her. She looked puzzled so I tried a light bulb, and again she was puzzled. I told Issy we might as well give up and wait for Uncle Mohammed to come back and ask him, because there was no way there were no lights!

The gathering took place in the middle room of the house. The women came from all over the village bringing with them huge pots of teas. The teapots were so big I never knew they made them that size! They kept them warm by covering them in the side of the room with big huge blankets. By the time all the women had arrived the room was full and the pots of tea were stacked high.

We were puzzled that the women kept forcing money into our hands; not realising it was one of their customs, we tried to refuse, but Gran kept telling us off, forcing the money back into our hands, so we took the money and put it in our pockets.

Uncle Mohammed's wife came and she was quite pretty, she had a young boy and two young girls. Issy and I were made to sit at the head of the room while the women sat all around us.

Farouse went around with about ten tiny tea cups, handing out one each as far as they went, and then she went and took a pot of tea from under the blanket. She then went around and filled the cup of whoever had one. The women drank the tea down as quickly as they could and then Farouse collected the cups and handed them out again without even washing them! Starting from the female she had ended with when the cups ran out, she started handing them out again and pouring tea.

The tea they drank was not like tea we knew, these afternoon teas were different. Some were brown with big bits in them called gishr, made with sugar; another was called buon which was a coffee with ginger, made without sugar and not the most popular drink.

We refused to drink, and I think Farouse understood it was because the cups hadn't been washed. So after the cups had gone around the room a few times, Farouse brought down a bowl of clean water to wash them; she then offered us a clean cup before anyone else which we took. I enjoyed the taste of the gishr; it became one of my favourite drinks!

The women here were so different to the women in Aden and the dress style so different. Some females here were dressed in colourful high-waisted and puffed out at the bottom dresses. They had average high necks and came below the knees. But they also wore tight fitting trousers underneath.

The headscarves they wore were again colourful. They wrapped the hanging bit of the scarf under their chin and back up to the top of their head tying it in a little knot at the top of their heads. They were such big heavy scarves that extra material would leave a 'v' shape part hanging down from the neck to cover any showing cleavage. However, their faces were uncovered even when walking through the village.

The colourfully dressed females, we found out, were the married women. The other little girls or younger females wore baggy, shabby dresses with high neck lines, mostly black or grey, and had baggy trousers underneath that dragged in the dusty floor. Although a few of them wore black scarves, they mostly wore these silly looking pointy things on their heads that were neither scarves nor hats, but something in between, they also didn't have to cover up outside.

The afternoon went by and the women left after a few hours. Gran didn't say a word as Issy and I sat at the downstairs windows and watched as she herded the goats, sheep and chickens from the outside stables into the inside stables which, we found out, were inside the house on the bottom floor. The reason Gran was OK with us sitting at the downstairs windows was because they were protected by metal poles so you couldn't stick our head out, so we couldn't really see much, and nobody could really see us.

As it got darker we got anxious to see what was going to happen about the electricity because we hadn't seen Uncle Mohammed so we still didn't know. When Farouse walked into the room with a hand held lamp and started lighting candles and putting them around the room, my heart sank. She walked over to us and handed us a candle and a torch.

"I really, really just want to cry right now!" I sulked with the saddest look on my face. Issy looked up at Farouse.

"Uncle Mohammed, can you take us to Uncle Mohammed?" she asked in very slow English to try and get Farouse to understand. It worked! Farouse ran off and we could hear her and Gran arguing downstairs, and then it went silent.

About ten minutes later Uncle Mohammed turned up, his mouth the size of a small ball on one side; he was chewing ghat, a green leaf that almost all the men, and sometimes women, chew in the afternoons when they get together. The juice from the ghat gives them a mild sedative affect that makes them relaxed. They chew on the leaf until they have a ball in the side of their mouths. They suck the juice out of the leaf and swallow it as they chew, sometimes spitting out the juice if it's too much in their mouths.

We asked him about the electricity and he told us there was none in the village or any of the villages nearby. Only the big cities and towns had electricity at that time. Our village was hoping to receive it in a few years, together with water pipes.

Once again our hearts sank. We had no idea that the house had no water connection! He told us that they used hand held lamps, candles and torches for light; however he tried to reassure us that Granddad had a tape recorder that he would allow us to borrow - if we used it sensibly, because batteries were expensive.

He told us the water was brought in from the wells on a daily basis and the wells are in the fields not far away. After we moaned at Uncle Mohammed for an hour or so he said he needed to go home to his family, but would be back in the morning to check on us. Then he left us, leaving Issy and me to deal with our first night in our new home.

That night we stayed upstairs with our candles and refused to go downstairs. Farouse came up and tried to get us to go down and sit with them but we didn't see any point in it. We did not know these people, and had no wish to get to know them. We liked Farouse, but at that moment in time we had so much to come to terms with.

We sat together and talked about Yas and Ablah and how much we missed them. Ablah must have been so worried about us by not hearing from us at all since we left England. Yas was all alone in Aden; we wondered how she was coping and whether or not she had any friends to talk to.

We cried a lot that night, and silently I prayed that Dad would come quickly and bring Yas back to us. We put our mattresses together and cuddled up to go to sleep.

"Goodnight Issy, goodnight Yas, goodnight Ablah, love you all!" I whispered as I closed my eyes.

Next morning we were woken at the crack of dawn by Gran's voice shouting at Farouse; it was as if she never stopped. We tossed and turned as much as we could to get back to sleep, but in the end we couldn't so we got up.

It was barely light outside but everyone must have been up for hours because we could smell the smoke from the clay oven burning. We went down to the kitchen and found Gran and Farouse cooking breakfast.

Gran was busy making 'foul' on the smaller clay oven. Foul is a brown bean which looks similar to a kidney bean and made into a curry so that you can dip the bread into it. Farouse was making the 'maloowja' which is a bread cooked in the larger clay oven.

There are two different types of breads made, one called maloowja and one called 'khobs' but the daily and most commonly made is maloowja. As we watched Farouse make the bread, we were amazed she didn't set herself on fire!

Once all the wood and anything else that was in the clay oven had finished burning, there was a round pile of burning flames coming from inside. These flames were being kept alight by a big piece of wood that was stuck through a hole at the bottom of the clay oven.

From a big bowl of dough made the night before, Farouse would break off a big handful of dough. Then she kept transferring it from one hand to the other, smoothing it out and stretching it. While doing this she added a yellow slimy substance on one side which was called 'hilba', this was the un-whipped version of what was added to the soup the day before. The hilba helped the dough from sticking to her hand when she needed to transfer the dough onto the inside of the clay oven wall.

Once the dough was stretched and hanging from her hands Farouse leant over the oven, putting one leg up onto the side of the clay oven for balance. Then she put her hands into the oven and transferred the dough onto the oven wall as quickly as she could, spreading it thinly across an area of the wall. While spreading it across the oven she would quickly take her hands out and dip them into a bucket of water placed on the floor next to the oven. This was supposed to help her with any pain she felt from the flames rising from the oven.

She did this three times until the oven wall was completely covered in bread. Then she covered the oven with a very large round metal lid that had a little handle, and a little small hole to look through to check when the bread was cooked. Once the bread was cooked, she gently tugged on the sides of the bread, easing them off the wall of the oven with her fingers and then pulling them out. If any of them broke and fell into the fire Gran would shout at her and Farouse would have to put her hands into the fire and rescue the bread quickly before it burnt. We watched in awe as Farouse made at least ten breads that morning, enough for the day ahead.

After breakfast was made Gran transferred some foul into a little bowl. Then she wrapped some bread in a piece of cloth and poured some tea from an old black kettle that had been brewing on the smaller clay oven, into a smaller black kettle. After she had done all this she put everything in a little basket, covered them with a little thick blanket, put them on her head and set off to the fields to take breakfast to Granddad, who had been working in the fields for hours!

We had our first taste of hot maloowja smothered with homemade butter dipped in foul and washed down with sweet black Arabic tea that morning. Farouse let us have our own dishes since Gran was in the fields with Granddad, it tasted good and we ate loads!

Uncle Mohammed did not visit us that morning so after breakfast we helped Farouse with the chores. She took us down to the stables that were under the stairs on the bottom floor of the house, they were to the left as you came through the front door. She had to light the lamp to go in because it was so dark and I could hear the animals inside before we entered.

There were three different stables, one for the goats, one for the sheep and one had loads of chickens in it! The stables were big and dark and the smell was so strong and overpowering I could barely breathe! She opened the stables one by one and the animals ran out and made their own way into the stables outside, except the chickens, they ran wild for a while outside the front door before she managed to gather them up and put them in their rightful place.

Farouse then took us to the other rooms that were on the middle floor. The room straight in front as we came up the stairs was Gran and Granddad's; it was always locked.

The other two to the left were store rooms. One of them was a store room where they kept their clothes and belongings and any food that didn't need to be stored in a cool place. The other room was a really cold room and had lots of small round windows like holes in it. That's where all the food that needed to be kept cold would be stored and it was as cold as a fridge. There were pieces of dried meat hanging from wires in the ceiling, the meat was dry and shrivelled up and looked like they had been hanging there for years!

She was eager to show us how she did her chores, starting with the cleaning and brushing the stairs. She used a brush made from tree branches that were tied together with a piece of string. First of all she would sprinkle water onto to stairs with her hand from a small bucket, and then she would dip the brush in water and shake it. This would stop the brush from breaking and make it last longer, and also stop dust from coming up from the floor as she swept, because the floors were made from cows' dung and straw. Every couple of months they would go over these stairs with a new layer of cows' dung to keep them looking new.

As we were helping I noticed three big barrels of fresh water down by the stables, covered up with plastic lids. There was one just like them upstairs in the kitchen that Farouse and Gran were scooping water out of in the morning when making breakfast. I wondered what they were for. I didn't ask Farouse at the time because she was busy.

We helped clean the kitchen, washing the breakfast dishes in the sink on the floor with just hot water that had been boiled on the oven that morning. We watched as she prepared meat and rice in big black pots and added water and spices to them. Then she buried them between the coal that was still burning hot inside the clay ovens from the morning, before putting the lid on the oven, and covering the oven with a huge old blanket! She soaked the hilba ready for lunchtime. It was a powder that was sprinkled over a bowl of water and left to soak for a few hours.

Farouse was cheerful, happy and eager to teach us everything she knew; she was also eager to learn. She pointed out everything, telling us in Arabic what things were called then asking us what they were called in English.

She would repeat everything we said to each other. She even started calling me 'Moo' and Issy 'Issy' instead of Ismahan, because that's what she heard us call each other. She was clumsy and forever falling over and dropping things and banging her head. She just made us laugh.

After we finished in the kitchen she took us outside and pointed over to the fields. "Wardy," she said, telling us we were going to the fields.

Then she picked up a few little buckets and handed one each to Issy and me and took one large bucket for herself. Off we went to the wardy to get water.

We thought the fields were just around the corner, as Uncle Mohammed did say they were not far away, but we were so wrong!

We walked for about two miles, passing fields full of both men and women working on their hands and knees. We were stared at by everyone and were joined on our way by about ten other girls, all with their huge buckets chatting happily away as if they were going shopping. They waved hello to other women on their way back from the well carrying huge buckets of water perfectly balanced on their heads, not a drop being splashed about, and they weren't even holding onto their buckets!

"I really hope no one's expecting us to do that? Can you imagine us trying to balance anything on our heads like that and walk without holding on? We will be here forever!" I moaned to Issy.

"Holding on or not, there's no way I'm carrying anything on my head! Oh my God! Look at that donkey! I wonder what it's got on its back, it can hardly move!" Issy said, pointing to a donkey with a saddle on both sides of its back.

The saddle was hanging so full and low the donkey was swaying from the weight and behind the donkey there was a little girl about eight years old with a stick whipping it to keep it going. I nudged Farouse.

"What's that?" I asked pointing at the donkey. Farouse showed us it was a water saddle on the back of the donkey. Only the well-off people in the village had a donkey. We had one, but Granddad had our donkey in the fields that day, and most days, that's why we were fetching the water on our heads.

On our way to the well I spotted a funny looking mountain with a flat top in the distance. "Wow! Look at that volcano!" I pointed out to Issy, but she just laughed at me.

"Don't be stupid! That's not a volcano, it's just a little mountain, one day we should sneak out the house and go up to the top," she suggested.

"Yeah, I'm up for that!" I said as we carried on walking.

We got to the well and could see Granddad and Gran working in the fields nearby. There were loads of women at the well, all eager to come and say hello to us English girls and get the gossip from Farouse on her new English cousins.

The well belonged to our family so as soon as we got there we jumped the queue and filled our buckets from a large pipe that was pumping water onto the fields nearby. Farouse filled her bucket then took a scarf she had wrapped around her waist, rolled it into a round circle, and used it as a padded cushion for underneath the bucket on her head. Then one of the other females helped her as they lifted the bucket onto her head. Within seconds she let go of the bucket, looking around and walking as if she had nothing on her head.

"She'd be in the flipping circus if she was in England! Just think how much money she would get paid for doing something like that! She hasn't dropped a single drop of water!" I gasped in amazement.

Issy and I looked like idiots as we filled up our pathetic little beach size buckets and carried them in our hands while following her home. By the time we got back to the village we were knackered! Farouse carried her bucket upstairs to the kitchen, and then poured it into a funny shaped water barrel on a window sill. The barrel was on a sill carved deep in the kitchen corner to keep it cool for drinking only.

Farouse told us that day we were lucky we didn't need to go

back to the fields to get more water, because sometimes she would have to go up to six or seven times a day!

Our buckets were poured into the big barrel on the side that was used for cooking, washing and showering. The barrels that were by the stables were for when the barrel in the kitchen ran out and needed topping up.

It was lunchtime and we had dinner to prepare. Gran was still working in the fields with Granddad since breakfast, so we helped Farouse with dinner. She enjoyed our company as she showed us how to make the hilba and all the other things.

Issy had her hand in a deep bowl whipping the hilba in a circular motion; Farouse and I were in stitches watching her as it was going everywhere. She couldn't grasp how to hold the bowl!

Farouse showed her there was an art to it; she sat her on the floor and put the bowl between her legs and told her to grip the bowl with her legs, that way her hands were free to grip the bowl at one top with one hand while whipping the hilba with the other hand.

She showed us how the rice and meat she had buried between the burning coals in the morning was now cooked because the clay oven and its heat had worked like a slow cooker; the juice from the meat was now the soup we had seen the day before. Once she had taken everything out of the clay oven she put more tree branches and a little wood in it.

She put a huge, heavy metal cross bar over the top of the oven and set the oven alight from the little hole at the bottom. The kitchen immediately filled with smoke leaving me and my sister coughing our guts up and heading towards the door, our eyes watering as we gasped for air!

Farouse just sat on the kitchen floor and waited for the smoke to lift through the hole above the oven into the open air and clear the kitchen. It took a matter of minutes! Once the smoke cleared Farouse filled a load of black kettles, pots and pans full of water from the barrels and mounted them on the cross bar to boil. Once one of the pans had started to boil she got ready to make the main meal of the day: the 'cement'!

She took a load of flour out of a huge sack that was in the corner of the kitchen and placed it in a bowl on the floor by the oven.

Then she got a really long wooden spoon with a big square head to it and placed it next to it.

With all her stuff ready she took one of the big boiling pots off the oven, placed it on the floor in the corner between the oven and the wall and sat down next to it. Quickly placing a piece of cloth next to the pot and pressing against it with her feet, she scooped flour into the water, and with the big wooden spoon she mixed it all together as fast as possible to stop it from lumping while keeping the pot in place with her feet.

When she had enough flour in it she had both her hands on the spoon and began mixing it and beating it until it was a doughy, smooth mixture. She placed it back in the oven and added a little more boiling water to it for a few minutes before returning it to the floor and repeating to mix again. With the cement cooked, Farouse flipped the pot over into a round clay bowl that had been heating on the side of the oven. She rubbed a little butter into her hands and patted it down and covered it with a clay top that had been made to fit the bowl. She put it to the side and covered it with a blanket to keep warm until everyone got home.

We watched as Farouse ran around and took charge of everything while Gran was working in the fields, and wondered how a young girl of her age could do so much. She was the same age as me, maybe younger, but she did everything, and to her this was normal. She had been awake since the crack of dawn, cooking, cleaning, fetching water, looking after animals, and it was only lunch time!

Gran's voice was louder than a trumpet! As soon as she arrived home we heard her shouting out Farouse's name from the front door. It seemed like she was always shouting at her for anything and everything.

We went through the same routine at dinner time because once again, we didn't want to share plates and were not allowed to have our own, so we just had bread.

We didn't see Uncle Mohammed until after dinner; he said he had needed to go into town so he apologised for not coming that morning. We asked if he had heard from Dad but he said he hadn't, and as far as he knew he would still be arriving the following week.

Another day went and another came. Every night I would pray that Dad would come and bring Yas back to us, come take us back home to England, but there was no sign of them.

We had the same routine every morning with the chores. Every afternoon more women came to see us, again they gave us money; it was as though they were paying us for allowing them to stare at us!

One day after they left, we went to our room moaning about how hungry we were and what we could do to get some food, so we decided to use the money the women had given us and sneak downstairs and go to the shop to get some stuff to eat, so off we went to the shop.

The shop was tiny; it looked more like a small shed than a shop. We peered through the window, which was a wooden flap held up by a hook, to see what we could find.

The shop keeper was sat on the floor amongst his boxes smoking his 'madaa'. This was a long water pipe they smoked tobacco through; as soon as he saw us he stood up and came outside from the front door of his house. He ushered us through the front door and a side door into his shop where he babbled on, pointing to everything in his shop. He was most probably telling us to look through the boxes that were stacked one on top of the other, leaving hardly any room to manoeuvre!

We didn't have a clue what he was saying because he was talking in Arabic, but by then we had got used to letting people just babble on. It was when he realised we couldn't understand a word he was saying that he started tapping his chest and said to us in English, "Uncle Abdurupa!" That was all he could say in English.

We knew he wasn't our real uncle; everyone was introduced to us as an uncle! However, Uncle Abdurupa was kind and friendly. He was a small man around Granddad's age and he wore these huge black spectacles that were way too big for his face. We were allowed to take our time and look through all the boxes.

It was difficult; we hardly knew what anything was because the only writing on them was in Arabic and the boxes only had little holes in them, barely big enough to look inside. After ages looking we finally had our shopping.

A few cans of tuna, some honey, some chewing gum and most importantly, some cigarettes! Uncle Abdurupa looked at me as we picked up the cigarettes. I could see the look of disapproval in his eyes. Yemeni girls didn't smoke cigarettes.

"Oh no, they're not for me! Uncle Mohammed, he told me to buy them for him, Uncle Mohammed!" I lied as I held up the cigarettes and pointed towards the house.

His smile told me he bought my lie as we took out our money and handed it to him. We didn't have a clue how much we had or how much things cost, but lucky for us we had enough money - we even got change!

We rushed towards the house eager to hide our valuables from everyone, but one person hot on our trail was Farouse. She was stood by the door eager to see what we had bought from the shop, so we allowed her to rush upstairs with us so we could show her our stash.

Farouse was horrified to see the cigarettes, but when I put my finger to my lips telling her to "shush", begging her to keep quiet, she understood what I meant and stuck her thumb up as if to say she would. We had been able to communicate with Farouse quite quickly, maybe it was an age thing, but whatever it was it worked. She saw us struggling to find a place to hide our ciggies, so she took us downstairs and into the normal store room, where she pulled out a broken piece of stone revealing a little hole in the wall. This was also her hiding place; in this hole Farouse hid her own money in a tiny piece of cloth to hide it from our Gran. This also became our place to hide things.

Night time came and we had begged Gran to allow Farouse to sleep in our room that night. Granddad was against it but Gran had the last say and she said it was OK. We were planning a feast; we also had the cassette player, which had only been loaned to us under strict terms and conditions relayed through Uncle Mohammed. So once bedtime came, which was usually around 7.30 pm, we were sneaking into the kitchen to steal bread to go with our tuna and honey; we also took some extra candles.

Once back upstairs we locked the door from the inside with the flimsy latch that opened as soon as the door was shaken, but we still locked it and put on some of our English music, tucking into our tuna wraps dipped in honey.

After we finished our food we decided to light a cigarette, and with the music on we were soon giggling away, turning up the music, not realising how loud it was.

It wasn't long before Issy decided she needed a pee, and, not wanting to go downstairs in the horrible toilet, she ran upstairs to the cemented area just above our room to pee in that, thinking it would just drain out of the pipe, but in her hurry to go upstairs her candle blew out, and in her rush to pee she missed her target. Her pee dripped down the stairs making a puddle on the landing just above the top steps.

No sooner had she come back in the room could we hear Granddad's voice on the bottom of the stairs. He was heading upstairs, cursing us about the noise! As soon as we heard him we turned off the radio, blew out the candles, and dived under our covers pretending to be asleep.

It only took him a few shakes before he managed to open the flimsy door lock! Then he stormed in the room cursing, thumping and even kicking us through our blankets, but we carried on pretending to be asleep. Once the thumping stopped I peered from under my blanket while he was searching the room for the cassette player, which he found and took before he stormed out of the room.

He was wearing only his boxer shorts and a tiny little half rounded hat that just rested on the top of his head. As soon as he left the room we all threw our blankets off and sat up giggling, but as we did we heard a noise coming from the hallway. Granddad had slipped on Issy's pee and fallen down the stair!

We all held our breath, not knowing if he was OK or not, but after a few seconds he started cursing us again and we heard him storm downstairs and slam his bedroom door!

The next morning Gran woke Farouse up at the crack of dawn and we could hear her shouting at Farouse in the kitchen; we were sure it was about the night before. We could smell the bread and really wanted to get up but felt best to wait till Gran left for the fields.

We knew Granddad would have told her everything about the night before and we didn't want to deal with her. Once we could no longer hear her voice, we snuck down and peered into the kitchen.

"Is she here?" I whispered.

"No! She's gone wardy," Farouse giggled, pointing in the direction of the fields.

We spent the morning helping Farouse again. Uncle Mohammed and his kids came around for a while and he seemed happy to see us getting on with Farouse. Once they left we went to the fields to get water; this time we made more than one trip and the heat was getting to us by the time we finished.

It was while we were sat at yet another gathering that we decided to sneak off and go to the mountain we had spotted a few days earlier on our way to the fields. Issy got up first and left the room, then after a few seconds I followed. We snuck out the house and out of the village. We didn't tell Farouse because we wanted to go alone.

The village was quiet in the afternoons because most of the females were at gatherings, and the men were chewing ghat or working in the fields. We walked as fast as we could out of the village and then ran to the mountain, which was in a different direction to the fields. We could see Granddad in the fields but he didn't see us; as soon as we were out of his view we took a deep breath and walked up the mountain knowing we couldn't be seen.

It took us about ten minutes to get there and by the time we got to the top we collapsed in a heap of sweat! The top of the mountain was flat, but it had huge black rocks on it.

We lay down flat on our backs for a while and just enjoyed the peace and quiet, and the cool breeze that blew by because we were so high up.

"This is so nice, I wish Yas was here with us, she would love it up here, I wonder what everyone's doing back in England?" While I chatted away, Issy just lay there with her eyes closed not answering me. After a while I stood up and looked around.

"Hey look, there's our village, and there's another village over there!" I said, excitedly pointing to another small village in the distance the other side of the mountain. Issy stood up and looked over to where I was pointing.

"Oh yeah, looks about same size as this one. You know we should be getting back soon because they are going to find out we are missing, and all hell's going to break loose!" Issy said, looking fed up.

I stood up and picked up a sharp-edged stone that was on the floor beside me.

"Before we go, let's make this our secret place. Shall we scratch our names into that big rock over there?" I said, pointing to a huge black rock on the other edge of the mountain.

"OK! Race you over there, last one there is a sissy!" Issy shouted back at me as she took off and started running over to the rock.

"Hey, that's not fair, you've got longer legs than I have!" I laughed as I chased after her.

"What shall we write?" she asked when we got to the rock. "I know, Issy, Yas and Muna forever!" I suggested. Issy agreed and we both took it in turns to scratch the names into the rock.

We made our way back to the village and just as we had anticipated, Gran was furious with us. Most of the women had gone home by that point and the only ones left were Uncle Mohammed's wife and close neighbours. Gran started shouting at us, insisting we tell her where we had been, but we just ignored her and went upstairs to our room.

It was late afternoon so we figured we would just stay there the rest of the night and ignore everyone. Not long after Uncle Mohammed turned up, Gran had sent Farouse to get him to find out where we had been. He sat next to us on the mattresses; he was chewing ghat so he was calm and relaxed.

When he asked us where we had been, we told him we had just had enough of everyone staring at us in the gatherings and needed to get out, so we went to the fields for a walk. He didn't seem angry with us; instead he said he had some very exciting news for us!

"I've just received news from your father today," he said, as our eyes lit up with excitement, "He is in Sanaa and will be here tomorrow." Before he even finished his sentence I jumped up with joy.

"Dad's coming tomorrow! Dad's coming tomorrow!" I sang, dancing around and jumped up and down. "We are going home!" I jumped on Issy and as we both hugged and laughed I looked over at Uncle Mohammed, thinking that he too would be happy for us, but his face said otherwise as he got up and left the room.

That night we packed our bags; Dad was coming to rescue us. Issy thought that even though Dad had made a few mistakes along the way, he would take us home once he saw how unhappy we were.

I on the other hand was more naive and didn't believe Dad was involved in any of this that had happened to us; I believed it was all the work of our uncles!

Chapter Four
Girls, Let's Go Home!

The next day we woke as usual. Gran had asked Uncle Moham-med's wife to come and help prepare the food that day because they had invited a few guests around for dinner. Dad was arriving back home after being away in England for a very long time, so this was classed as a big occasion.

We tried to help with the chores but we were so excited and distracted, every time we heard a noise we would run downstairs to see if it was Dad! Gran would shout at us to stay put but we no longer cared what she said; Dad was on his way, and we were going home!

Once lunch was ready and the guests had arrived, we were anx-iously waiting for Dad, when all of a sudden we heard a com-motion from the street. I stuck my head carefully out of the tiny kitchen window and saw a jeep.

"Dad! It's Dad!" I screamed as I pulled my head in from the window and darted down the stairs with Issy straight behind me.

The jeep had pulled up before I got to the door and Dad was already being greeted by Granddad and some of the men that had been invited for dinner, mainly the elders of the village.

I stood by the door waving at him. "Dad! Dad!" I shouted, jumping up and down, frustrated that he didn't come straight to me and Issy, who was stood by my side. When he finally came over I grabbed him and kissed him.

"Dad I missed you soooo much!" I said, hugging him as tight as I could!

"I missed you both too," he laughed, kissing us both. "Now, I have a really big present for you both in the car but I want you to be very, very careful with it, OK?"

"OK!" You could hear the excitement in my voice as we both ran over to the jeep, expecting to find presents from England. The looks on our faces were of pure delight as we opened the jeep door and we heard the sound of a female voice!

"Surprise!" It was Yas.

We wept with joy, squeezing her and kissing her. I couldn't believe she was back. "See, I told you!" I insisted, turning to Issy. "I told you Dad would never take Yas away from us! I told you he would bring her back!"

Even though I'd prayed day and night to have my sister back, we hadn't expected to see her; then all of a sudden to have her back with us, we were over the moon! I still trusted Dad and believed in him, no matter what he was our father, he would always protect us.

Dad went upstairs with all the men into the middle room ready for dinner, so we took Yas by the hand and walked her into the house. Then we started showing her around.

"Now, don't be alarmed by what you see," Izzy whispered. "We will explain everything to you later, but for now here goes! That's Gran, we don't like her just yet, this is Farouse, Uncle Nasser's daughter, she's alright, we've been teaching her English!" Farouse came up to Yas and gave her a big hug.

"Hi Yas!" she said in English. Yas looked at her and gave a little smile. "Hi Farouse," she said very quietly. I couldn't help but notice how thin and pale she looked, but we carried on showing her the rest of the house.

After introducing Yas to everyone, we didn't have much time with her because it was hectic with dinner being rushed down and people back and forward.

We didn't eat dinner with the men that day because they were not family members, and females are not allowed to interact with men unless they are very close family members, so we had to sit and eat in the kitchen.

We took some rice on a separate plate and ate with Yas. Gran cursed us for not eating with them, but this time we ignored her and just carried on eating and chatting with Yas, telling her about the village; she was very quiet and just listened to us.

After dinner, when Dad came up to the kitchen, I begged him to allow us to take Yas out for some fresh air.

"Pleeeease, please Dad can we take Yas for a little walk to the fields?" He looked at us all one by one, a cigarette hanging from his mouth.

"Oh I don't know, I will have to ask your Gran." He was just about to ask her but I stopped him.

"Please Dad, we will only be gone for a bit, you're our Dad, it's your choice."

"OK, but don't be long!" he said, giving us a smile.

We grabbed Yas and ran out the kitchen and down the stairs.

"Come on," Issy said, "we've got a secret place to show you." With that, we headed for our mountain.

We were out of breath by the time we got to the top but we took Yas straight over to the rock.

"Look what we wrote," I said, jumping up and down, happy to have my sister with us again. "We came up here and did this, we missed you sooo much, do you like it?" I asked, hugging her.

"I love it, I really do, Moo," Yas said, sitting down.

We knew she was happy to be back with us, but something was wrong. All of a sudden she started to cry, putting her hands over her face. Issy and I sat each side of her and held her.

"Please don't cry, you're back with us now," I begged as my eyes welled up.

"Please tell us what happened?" Issy asked, trying to stay brave for Yas by holding back her own tears.

Wiping her face, Yas told us how she had been kept prisoner in Nejmie's parents' house with his mum, dad and three sisters who were all very strict and religious.

He still hadn't arrived from England. She was referred to only as 'Nejmie's wife' and had to wear a ring that he had bought for her to prove she now belonged to him.

She was shown a bedroom that had been prepared for them but was told that it was being kept until their wedding night. Until then she wasn't allowed any privacy and was made to sleep in the same room with his sisters. She was made to act a certain way now that she was 'Nejmie's wife', because he had paid a good price for her!

His family told her that Nejmie had paid Dad a lot of money to marry her; when she asked how much, they refused to say.

We all cried together as Yas told us the only reason she was returned to Dad was because she took an overdose of painkillers and tried to end her life; she couldn't deal with the thought of being alone and never seeing us again.

After doing this, Nejmie's family said she was 'damaged goods' and sent word to Dad in England to come and collect her straight away. They demanded Dad take her away and return Nejmie his money.

We sat there for a while, trying to comfort our sister the best we could, but it wasn't easy. Yas had been sold and more or less held prisoner; she had suffered terribly, being separated from everyone she loved.

On our way back to the village we decided we were going to sit with Dad that afternoon and confront him. We all wanted to go home. But by the time we got back, Dad had gone off to eat ghat with Uncle Mohammed, and once again we were forced to sit with all the females at yet another gathering, only this time, all eyes were on Yas!

That night we waited for Dad and when he finally came up we were in our bedroom. He was still chewing ghat and he came in and sat down beside us on the mattress.

"When are we going home?" Issy asked, starting the conversation. Dad didn't even bother looking at us as he carried on shoving ghat into his mouth.

"You are home," he coldly answered.

Issy looked at him, unimpressed. "You know what I mean Dad, home to Newport."

Dad took a deep breath. "This is our home now, we are never going back to Newport so you girls have to forget about Newport, forever, we don't have anything back there anymore, I've sold everything I own to get us here..."

Yas had heard enough by this time, and she sharply interrupted him.

"Yeah... that included me, didn't it, Dad?"

We all started shifting from side to side uncomfortably in our seats, speaking at the same time, protesting about wanting to go home.

"Shush! Be quiet all of you!" Dad hissed impatiently, but Issy was fuming with him.

"No! I won't be quiet, what about Ablah? When are we going to see her again?" she screamed.

"That's her fault, she should have come with us, I'm just doing what's best for you girls!" Dad shouted as we all began to weep.

"Dad please, we just want to go home," I begged as he stood up. But nothing any of us said would make any difference.

"From tomorrow you will all help your grandmother and cousin with the chores, you will learn to speak Arabic and you will wear Arabic clothes. You will become good Muslim girls and you will all marry good Muslim boys! You will obey me, and your grandparents! Do you understand me? Do you!?"

I'd never heard Dad speak as meanly to us as he did that day; he looked at us with ice-cold eyes. None of us answered as he left the room and left us in a state of uncertainty.

We had once hoped that Dad would come and rescue us, now all our hopes and dreams had been shattered.

I saw a spark leave Issy's eyes that day. Ablah was her everything.

That night we lay awake but we didn't cry any more, there was no use in crying. We lay there wondering about our future, not knowing if we would ever see Ablah again, or ever leave the Yemen. Nobody was coming to rescue us anymore!

The next day we were given dresses, trousers and scarves by Gran and told to wear them. We had no choice but to do as we were told; our English clothes were taken away from us and we never saw them again.

Because Issy was so tall, the trousers they gave her were too short and only reached her ankles, she begged Gran to allow her to keep some of her jeans to wear under her dresses, but her pleas fell on deaf ears.

Issy was distraught. Her image meant a lot to her, now everything she needed or wanted was being taken away from her.

Gran was mean and loud and forever shouting at all of us. I learnt to do just as I was told and get on with things, in my own mind thinking that things would change one day and we would go back to England. Issy became more and more depressed, while Yas became rebellious!

We were put to work properly this time, no more just helping out! In the kitchen we were shown how to make the bread in the ovens and how to cook everything from the soup to the cement.

We burnt ourselves on a daily basis from the flames whist making the bread and scalded ourselves from the boiling water whilst making the cement, but we were shown no mercy by Gran.

Farouse always tried to help us out and cover for us when things went wrong, even taking the blame herself so that Gran would shout at her and not us; we grew fonder of Farouse every day!

We were made to sit with everyone and eat from the same bowl as them. It was difficult; we used to pick from the edges of the bowl and sometimes pretend to chew for ages just until the food was all eaten up.

We were taught how to make 'domage'. This was something that was added to the fire to help the clay oven burn longer, it was disgusting to make!

We would have to gather as much cows' dung and donkey droppings as possible by walking around the fields where they had been grazing, picking it up and carrying it home in a tin bucket on our heads. At times we would find quite a lot and if the animal had just dropped it, it was smelly and heavy and because we hand to pick it up with our hands we also stunk!

We would gather all of this into an old oil barrel that was buried deep in the ground. Over weeks we would collect this together with goats' and sheep's droppings taken from the stables. This was one of the chores I hated the most.

We had to take a brush, usually one that was no good for the stairs any more, take a lamp and go into the dark stables under the house. We had to hang the lamp on a nail hanging from the stone walls that were full of cobwebs. Then we would have to gently sweep the floor of the stables so that we could sweep up the droppings of the sheep or goats, but not disturb the dust underneath the droppings.

Once we had got all the good droppings safely scooped up in a basket we had to go back in and sweep up again, removing the under dust which also had droppings in it, but had been trampled by the animals. The under dust was added to what was in the oil barrel but the good droppings would be spread out in a corner in a separate stable out the back in the sun, and left to dry. Once dry this was also used in the fire to help it burn.

The most awful thing about cleaning the stables was the animal flies! These were tiny black things that bit you and jumped from one part of your body to another; it was impossible to find them in your clothes because they would hide in the seams and we would be left with bite marks everywhere and we were constantly itching.

I seemed to suffer the worst with these bites and would resort to spraying my whole body with fly spray in the hope of keeping them away from me; it never worked!

Once we had everything in the oil barrel we would add straw and water to the mix, then we would have to roll up our trousers to our knees and jump in the barrel, then trample it until it was all mixed together. Next we had to scoop it out of the barrel a handful at a time, pat it down on the floor into around one inch thick, 12 inch round circles, and leave them out on the floor in the stable behind the house to dry in the sun. We would have to make dozens of these at one time and by the time we finished we would be up to our neck in shit… literally!

The domage, sheep's and goats' droppings together with wood allowed the clay oven to burn slowly for hours, and to our surprise although it made the oven smoke a bit when it was first lit, it didn't make the bread taste strange!

We had to take our clothes to the fields to wash at the well. This was a task that took hours, we would usually do this in the afternoon and Granddad would have to start up the well just for us to wash the clothes.

We would gather everyone's clothes that had been dirty for about a week; they were filthy! Then we would pile them into a big round washing tin and mount it on our heads, set off to the fields and wash everything by hand, spreading them out over rocks and branches to dry as we went along.

We tried our best to fit in and do the chores, but our best was never good enough.

Gran always had something negative to say about us but mostly about Issy, no matter how hard she worked. Gran was always shouting and going on at Granddad and Dad about how old Issy was, that she should had been married by then.

Issy was barely 17 at this time but she was being talked about by everyone because she was so tall, and, to them, so old! It was very unusual for girls Issy's age to still be unmarried in Yemen. Girls would get married as young as ten, or even younger.

Dad and Granddad would argue a lot and although we didn't speak that much Arabic at that time, we knew it was because our grandparents wanted Issy married as soon as possible and Dad was trying to put them off.

One big argument between them happened after we had dinner one day; it was about a week after Dad had arrived. We were in the kitchen cleaning and Dad and our grandparents had been in the middle room arguing about Issy. Dad was shouting as he came up the stairs.

"They are my daughters, it's my decision! If you don't want us here we will leave!" He stormed into the kitchen. "Girls, pack your things, we are going home!" We all jumped up, not believing what he had just said.

"Going where?" Issy asked, looking at us; she could see we were also in a state of disbelief.

"Where do you think I mean? We are going back to England, now get your things together and wait till I get back!"

He turned around and stormed down the stairs to fetch a car, so we all ran to our room and started gathering our things. We didn't have the clothes we came with but we didn't care! We jumped around, excited about the fact that Dad had finally come to his senses, we were going home to see our sister! We chatted about how good it would feel to finally get back to normal, back to school; back to the people we grew up with. We talked about stopping over in Sanaa and saying goodbye to Nebat, picking up a present for Ablah; we were so excited!

We waited and waited for Dad that afternoon to come and take us home. When he finally came back early evening chewing his ghat, he was angry at us for even thinking we were ever leaving Yemen. He said he was just angry at Granddad but had no intention of ever going back to England.

He took his things and headed to sleep in the fields that night, leaving us once again crying ourselves to sleep.

Dad did this to us a few times within the first few weeks of him arriving and for the first couple of times I believed him, even though my sisters gave up believing him after the first time.

Yas started refusing to do much around the house, which caused huge arguments between her and Gran! Dad shouted at her and tried to talk to her but she said she didn't like the work and wasn't going to do it, and that was that! If Granddad shouted at Yas she would shout back at him too.

With all the problems between Yas and our grandparents, Dad would end up taking Yas to the fields with him most days just to keep the peace! Our grandparents hated the fact that Yas spent all her time with Dad instead of doing chores, but Dad insisted on it, and in the end they gave up.

Dad stayed away from the house a lot, he would work in the fields on the ghat and Yas worked with him; she didn't mind field work, it was only house work she hated.

Granddad owned a lot of land and grew a lot of ghat; when the ghat leaves grew to a certain height, someone would have to sleep in the fields at night to make sure it didn't get stolen. Usually Granddad would pay someone to do this but now that Dad was there, this was his job.

They also had about six guard dogs that stayed in the fields tied up day and night, and if anyone other than members of our family went near the ghat, they would bark until Dad or Granddad told them to shut up. They were the scariest dogs I'd ever seen and I dreaded to think the damage they would have done to someone had they bitten them.

Dad would sleep in the fields most nights and one of us would take him his breakfast in the morning. Because he had the dogs, he could sleep most nights if he wanted to because they had huts; if anyone came near the ghat he would get woken by the dogs barking.

Once Dad had eaten his breakfast he would carry on working until dinner time; after that he would come home, eat dinner, then either go back to the fields or go chew ghat with other males somewhere in the village. Early evening he would come home, collect his food for the night and some scraps of food for the dogs and be gone!

Dad also carried a huge rifle; all men in the village carried them and many young boys! Males would just walk around with these huge guns hanging off their shoulders, they terrified me!

The nights were the worst; we had by now been taken out of our privileged guest room upstairs and made to sleep in the middle room. This meant we could no longer use the upstairs room to escape when we needed to be alone; it was now locked and off limits, kept for guests only.

The middle room was used for all purposes day and night, and although the chores never stopped there were sometimes a couple of hours each night that we had free before bedtime. Those few hours dragged on. There was just the candle light and silence.

Although I'd learnt to put my head down and get on with things, I was also the wind up merchant of all three of us and the trouble maker! Farouse was my accomplice more often than not!

One night, as we all sat in complete silence yet again, I got bored. Granddad had a habit of nodding off while slumped in his spot and if anyone made a noise, instead of getting up and going to bed, he would wake up and shout at us to be quiet. It was not as if we could watch TV or read a book; we weren't even allowed to talk!

That night I had with me a tiny piece of tree branch, so once we were all sat down I gently stuck the branch up my nose, tickling my nose just enough to make myself sneeze. Gran shot a stare in my direction as Granddad stirred and mumbled something under his breath, I hid the piece of branch in my hand and rested my hand under my chin, then I apologised for sneezing.

A few moments later I did it again and let out another sneeze; this time my sisters and Farouse all started giggling because they knew what I was doing! Gran cursed me as Granddad woke up, also cursing the day his son ever brought his daughters to his home, then he closed his eyes to go back to sleep.

Farouse looked at me and gestured for me to break her a bit and pass it to her, which I did. We both tickled our noses trying to make ourselves sneeze when all of a sudden Farouse let out a little tiny sneeze, but I had a sneezing fit and couldn't stop!

Granddad jumped up and came at me, grabbing me without warning. He grabbed me by the scruff of my dress, and then he sank his teeth into my shoulder, biting me as if he were a dog! I screamed in pain as Yas jumped up.

"You idiot, get off my sister before I kill you! You sick old man!" she screamed, pulling him off me and pushing him aside.

Issy was also screaming abuse at Granddad. At this time I was bawling my eyes out because my neck was hurting from the bite, while Farouse just sat there shaking with fear, not knowing what to do.

Gran joined in, shouting at Yas for grabbing Granddad and telling Issy to shut up; it turned into one huge screaming match! It was dark outside but Yas ended up storming out of the house, saying she was going to the fields to get Dad because Granddad had bit me.

We tried stopping her but she had developed such a temper by then, once she got something in her head there was no stopping her! She stormed off and didn't come back that night. We waited and waited for her until we finally fell asleep.

It turned out Dad decided he couldn't take any more arguing and kept Yas in the fields with him that night. This became a regular thing for Yas, she would argue with our Grandparents because she would refuse to do housework, then she would storm off and stay in the fields with Dad, sometimes staying all day and night.

Dad even allowed Yas to walk back and forth from the house to the fields carrying his rifle ! Our grandparents and other villagers were furious with Dad for allowing Yas to behave this way, saying Dad treated her more like a boy than a girl. But I suppose Dad thought it was easier for him to let her stay with him for a while if it meant he got some peace and quiet!

It was only a few weeks after Dad arrived that Nebat came to visit. It was in the evening and we were all sat in the room when we heard a car pull up outside. When Gran opened the window to check who it was, we heard a whisper.

"It's Nebat!" Gran said excitedly, rushing downstairs to open the door. Nebat came up and greeted us all. She was with her husband Ahmed and after they said hello to us, our grandparents and Ahmed rushed upstairs to discuss something.

We could tell by the commotion and the atmosphere of the house that something else was going on other than just Nebat visiting but Nebat wouldn't say anything. Gran called Farouse upstairs and after a while Farouse came back down all happy and excited.

"My dad's here!" she whispered. "He's hiding in the village but he will be here shortly."

Uncle Nasser had come from Aden to Sanaa and had been hiding in Nebat's house. Now he got a lift with them to Granddad's house, but had got out of the car way before entering the village so as not to be recognised; he wasn't coming to the house until he knew the villagers would be asleep.

Uncle Nasser was a 'guerrilla', an enemy of the South and not allowed in the South of Yemen; if caught he would be killed. Just being in Granddad's house was a risk to everyone, so we all needed to keep his visit top secret.

When staying in Granddad's house, Uncle Nasser stayed hidden in the little room that was cut off from the guest room on the top floor. He only left the house in the middle of the night to meet up with other members of his guerrilla group. Gran's brother was one of the main leaders of this group and she did everything she could to assist when one of them came to the village.

This was the first time that Uncle Nasser had visited since we arrived in the village, so Granddad wanted to make sure we knew to keep our mouths shut. He came to the room to make it clear to us the trouble we would all be in if anyone found out he was staying. He told us all our family could end up in prison or dead, putting his fingers to his head and pretending to pull a trigger to scare us! I already hated Uncle Nasser from our time in Aden, this information only made me hate him even more!

We chatted to Nebat while lying in our beds trying to sleep, although none of us could even close our eyes because we were anxiously awaiting Uncle Nasser's arrival. Hours passed, then we heard Gran go downstairs and open the front door. We didn't hear a knock because he didn't knock on the door. He didn't want to make a noise because the door knobs were huge and made of heavy metal, so he threw a stone at Granddad's window.

We could hear their voices as they disappeared upstairs. Farouse wasn't allowed to see her dad that night; she said she never did see him the night he arrived because he spent time with our grandparents, but she would see him the next morning. The next morning we were told not to disturb him and to get on with the chores as if he was not there; if he needed anything he would ask and Farouse would see to him.

We spent the morning doing chores with Nebat; she was a guest but she got stuck in as if she had been with us all along. She was Gran's favourite because Gran had brought her up since she was a baby after Dad had gone off and left her behind and her mother remarried. Gran always compared everyone to her, even Farouse. She would constantly be going on at us all, "Watch your sister Nebat, look how well she cooks, look at the way she does this or that!" Gran drove us mad but we all loved Nebat and she would always apologise for Gran's behaviour, telling us:

"She only does it because she cares for us all so much and wants us to be the best!"

We felt sorry for Nebat, she had been married since she was around 11 years old but she had been unable to have children. She told us how she had tried everything she could to have children but it wasn't to be. She also did not know her real age because birth certificates are not issued in Yemen, but she thought she was in her late 20s.

Usually when females cannot get pregnant after a few years of marriage their husbands remarry, but her husband refused to do this to her because he loved her. We liked Ahmed after we found this out about him; he was funny and goofy and was always joking about!

Uncle Nasser woke up about midday and made his presence known; he was demanding and arrogant ordering us about. "Get me this and get me that."

I watched as Farouse ran around tending to her father's every need. I could see she adored her father and looked for his approval, but to him she didn't really exist other than to be a slave and do as she was told. I hated the way he treated her, and my face couldn't hide my contempt for him.

Dad came home from the fields and was happy to see his brother. He stayed home that afternoon and chewed ghat with him until early evening, then he went back to the fields. After Dad left, Farouse and I were told to go upstairs and clean up the ghat stalks off the floor while Uncle Nasser sat downstairs.

While we were cleaning I noticed a bottle of whiskey tucked in between the mattresses on the side of the room. I was shocked because I knew that alcohol was banned in the Yemen, and Muslims were forbidden to drink it.

"Look at this!" I whispered holding it up for Farouse to see. Farouse had a look of fear in her face as she rushed over and snatched the bottle out of my hand, returning it to its place while looking behind her to make sure her father wasn't coming back upstairs!

"Leave it alone and pretend you didn't see it, please, you can't say anything to our grandparents, promise me!" she begged, but I was so angry.

"No, why should I? He shouldn't be drinking, it's not fair that he gets away with breaking the rules but we have to do as we are told!" As we were talking, Uncle Nasser walked back in the room all smiley and happy because he had been chewing ghat.

"All clean up here?" he asked in a cheerful voice while swinging his bad arm back and forward as he did when he walked. Many years earlier he had been shot in the shoulder while fighting in the mountains; because he hadn't been able to get medical help, he had more or less lost all the use of his left arm. His hand had formed into a claw like shape, and he was unable to grip anything. But because he could bend it from the elbow he had one hell of a swing to it!

"Yeah all clean, should I throw this away?" I asked as I took the bottle of whiskey from between the mattresses and held it up in front of him. I saw the colour drain from Farouse's face as Uncle Nasser snatched the bottle from my hand and chucked it on top of the mattresses.

"What do you think you are doing, you stupid girl!" he growled.

"Me? You're the one drinking alcohol! Maybe I should see what Granddad thinks about this?" I threatened as I turned to leave the room. But before I could exit the door Uncle Nasser grabbed me and pushed me up against the wall, holding me by my neck.

I could hear Farouse begging her dad to stop but he told her to shut up and sit down, which she did without question.

"Maybe you would like to find out what happens to stupid little girls who don't know when to keep their mouths shut?" he threatened, squeezing my throat.

My eyes welled up with tears. I had a horrible feeling in my stomach as all sort of thoughts flashed through my mind imagining what he was about to do to me! My mind was telling me to fight back, but my body felt paralysed. Then all of a sudden he let me go and shoved me towards Farouse, who was cowering in the corner. "Take your stupid cousin downstairs and teach her how to behave," he demanded.

Farouse grabbed my hand and dragged me out of the room, down to the kitchen; we were both shaking as she begged me not to say anything to anyone. She warned me that her father had a very nasty temper sometimes and even if I told Granddad, nothing would change. She said Granddad would always take his son's side, always! She warned me not to go up against her father because I would be the one who got hurt because I was a girl, and that's just how it was.

I went downstairs and told my sisters what had happened. They were fuming with me for confronting Uncle Nasser like I'd done and even more upset with him for what he had done to me. It took a lot of persuading to make them let the matter go, because like Farouse said, her father had a temper and we had no idea what would happen if we approached him about his behaviour, or told on him.

The next few days we all tried to stay out of Uncle Nasser's way. Every night he would sneak out of the house and not return until early morning, then sleep until lunch time. When he was awake, Farouse attended to his every need; if anyone needed to go upstairs to help her, one of my sisters would go with her, that way I wouldn't have to be alone with him.

We spent a lot of time with Nebat. She told us about her other family. Nebat's mother had remarried and had another family that lived in a village close by. Nebat was allowed to visit her mother now that she was married and settled. However, when she was growing up as a child she wasn't allowed to see her mother after her mother remarried. This is a custom in Yemen. If a woman is separated from the husband for whatever reason, divorce or his death, if she remarries, she must leave behind any children she had with that man and never contact them unless the father agrees. If the father died then the next of kin (male) from the father's family makes the decisions on behalf of that child. Because Dad left, going to England with no intention of returning, his marriage to Nebat's mum got dissolved in his absence, which allowed Nebat's mum to remarry. Nebat lived with our grandparents but wasn't allowed to see her mum, even though she lived less than half hour walk away from her. After Nebat married she became the 'property' of her husband; Ahmed then allowed her to see her mother whenever she wanted to.

It must have been difficult for Nebat after Dad's return because Dad showed no affection towards her, not that he showed us any affection anymore either, but to him it was as though she never existed. She told us she was close with her mother now and had a really good relationship with her; she also had a half-sister from her mother's side.

On the day Nebat was going to visit her family we asked if we could go with her; although Dad was OK with this, Gran put her foot down and said no. We were so angry with Gran because it seemed like Dad did whatever she told him to do, it was as if he no longer had a mind of his own.

Nebat's visit to the village was short but sweet, and we missed her terribly when she went home. One thing we were happy about when she left was that she took our nasty Uncle Nasser with her.

We picked up the Arabic language very quickly; maybe it was because other than us sisters, nobody spoke English. Even Dad and Uncle Mohammed had started refusing to speak to us in English, unless they were shouting at us and really needed to get their point across. We would get told off if we were caught talking to each other in our mother language, but we would always ignore them.

We made many friends in the village, mostly young girls we met on our way to the fields or girls we met at afternoon gatherings. We would all meet up and walk together to fetch water, or go to do our washing together.

It was on a visit to the fields one day that I noticed one of the young girls called Ilham was missing from the group; she would always meet up with us but for the past few days I hadn't seen her so I asked Farouse where she was. Farouse told us Ilham was being 'prepared' for marriage; we wouldn't be seeing her until her wedding day, which was in a few days.

I was in shock Ilham looked younger than us but Farouse told us it was normal for girls her age to be married. Girls that are being prepared for marriage are not allowed to leave the house from the time of their engagement until their wedding, they are kept at home to be pampered and 'fattened' up to look good for their wedding day.

To make their skin look good they took a yellow powder (turmeric) added with a greener power, and then added a sprinkle of water or oil to make a thick paste out of it. Then they put this on to their faces, like a face mask. They did the same to their hands, arms and feet. This paste is left on day and night and if it came off it was retouched. This is supposed to make the skin look 'whiter'. They are also not allowed to work or put their hands in water, or go out in the sun. They are only allowed to do light work around the house.

The day of the wedding celebrations arrived and we were woken by gun shots. I nearly had a heart attack! I thought there was some sort of war happening, because it wasn't just one or two bullets but lots of bullets going off at once! Farouse reassured us that it was just the wedding party playing with their guns and celebrating. She told us this would be happening a lot over the next few days and not to worry.

Gran went off after breakfast to help the bride's family prepare food for their guests. On that day the groom's father and all the elders of the village, amongst other male family members, got together over dinner. The elders' wives and female family members all got together to help prepare and cook the food at the bride's house. Sometime during this dinner the groom and bride's fathers, together with the elders of the village, would 'seal the deal' and the wedding would officially begin.

After dinner all the males went to a neighbour's house to chew ghat and celebrate, while the females started to gather at the bride's house for their own celebrations. We finished our own dinner that day and got ready to go, Farouse excitedly chatted away letting us know what to expect.

She told us all the women dressed up in their best clothes to go to weddings, but I couldn't really imagine what 'nice' or 'best clothes' she could be referring to. As we made our way to the wedding I was shocked to see some of the women walking about the village covered up wearing their 'sharsharfs'. In Aden the long black coat is called abaya but here in the South it's called a sharsharf.

This was the first time we had seen women cover up since being in the village. The only time they covered up was when they needed to go into the city. Farouse told us it was because they were wearing makeup, and lots of jewellery, so were not allowed to be seen in public like that.

When we got to the house we were surprised at how different the women looked! The sharsharfs came off and we saw that every female was trying to outdo the next! The young girls and little girls that were still unmarried were dressed a little cleaner with their best dresses on, but no makeup or jewellery. However, the married women had on very colourful dresses, which most had sewn especially for that occasion.

The more colourful and thicker, or heavier the material, the more expensive it was! Some of these dresses were long and dragging on the floor called 'maxies', whilst others were short, much shorter than the ones we wore daily. The trousers they wore with the short dresses were flared and baggier.

Their faces were layered in makeup, way too much makeup! The face foundation was a pure white powder that would have made them look as white as ghosts, if it wasn't for the rest of the makeup. The eye shadow was colourful, way up to their eyebrows, the blusher a big pink circle in the middle of their cheeks and the lipstick was red and layered thick! Many of them had a black line that started at their forehead and went straight down over the nose, lips and chin and finished at their necks!

They had these cardboard crowns that were covered in a thin piece of cloth that allowed it to be tied to the back of the head; the cloth also had stones stuck to them that looked like shiny little diamonds, although they were obviously not diamonds! These 'crowns' allowed their hair to flow both under and over the crown to give their already beautiful thick long hair even more volume.

At the top of the room was a throne-like seat made up for the bride. Once all the women were seated and the music was playing, the bride was brought into the room amidst whistles from the women. These were not normal whistles, these were noises made from the women shaking their hands against their mouths and making a high pitched scream that sounded like a long on-going whistle! We couldn't see an inch of Ilham's body or face as she walked to her throne and sat on it, she was covered in a sharsharf and black veil. She wasn't allowed to show herself until her formal wedding, the next day.

The women danced and drank their teas all afternoon. The dance was a step dance made of five or six steps repeated over and over again. They danced until someone else got up and took over from whoever was on the floor at the time, usually in groups of two, three or four at a time. Ilham didn't move from her spot or drink anything and when we left a few hours later she was still sat on her throne!

The next day the celebrations got bigger. Every male in the village got invited for food at the bride's house. Her husband was from another village and he too would have been having big celebrations that day. For the bride, this was the day she got shown to the females of the village in her white gown.

She would go to her husband's house the following morning, that's where the biggest celebrations took place and where she would be put on display to him and his village. When we went that afternoon for the gathering, there were even more women than the day before. The room and landing were full and everyone wanted to see Ilham in her wedding dress.

The bride came in escorted by a woman known as 'Al Mouzayna', a professional women who is called in to 'help and guide' the bride. Ilham was covered from head to toe in a huge white wedding gown and white veil. Once she was sat on the throne, Al Mouzayna uncovered her veil and adjusted her gown to show off the entire bride's gold. She also exposed her hands and feet to show off the henna and negsha (black ink) art work that she herself had done on the bride.

Ilham looked like a little china doll, her face was covered in white powder makeup, the rest of her makeup layered on thick as a clown! The women made those whistles again all through the afternoon. They danced and were all happy and having fun, while Ilham looked lost and terrified as she sat on her throne with Al Mouzayna sat in front of her by her feet.

Al Mouzayna was a middle-aged lady with a stern face that scared you with just one look! Farouse told us that she would travel tomorrow with Ilham to her husband's house to tell her what to do when the time came for her to be with her husband, to lose her virginity! Ilham would arrive tomorrow morning and have to go straight to her husband's room where he would have to prove to his family and friends that she is a virgin. She would already have a throne-like seat waiting for her in her husband's bedroom; it would be covered in a brand new pure white cloth. She would need to sit on this throne and her husband would take her virginity, while she prayed that she bleeds like all virgins should! She won't be permitted to lie down for her first time because they believe that if you lie down there is a chance you may not bleed.

When he is finished with her, the white, bloodied cloth would be carefully folded then taken by the husband and handed to his father or mother. They would then show it to all the elders and other family members to prove that the bride was pure. Then the celebrations would really begin at the groom's house, and the bride would once again be paraded in her white gown for all the females of her husband's family, and friends. However, if the bride for any reason did not bleed she would be returned to her father's house in shame! Then her father, or brother if she did not have a father, would take her life in an honor killing by murdering her for shaming the family!

We listened to Farouse when she told us these stories but we didn't really believe her. We had played lots of tricks on her since arriving in the village and just thought she was trying to get her own back on us!

The next morning while I did my chores, I heard the fireworks and guns go off in the village as the convoy of cars arrived to escort Ilham to her husband's house and I couldn't help but feel sad for her. She was so young and she looked so scared yesterday sat on that throne in her wedding dress. She must have felt terrified of what was about to happen to her.

As I carried on sweeping the stables I could hear the cars beeping their horns as they left the village, and I knew it was only a matter of time until that same fate happened to me and my sisters.

Dad had become someone I hardly recognised, his mood swings and behaviour were unpredictable. I knew by now that he didn't bring us here for a holiday, he had other reasons for bringing us here; marriage was one of them. It had nearly happened to Yas once before, and I knew it would happen to us soon, but now I was wondering which one of us would be first?

Chapter Five
Goodbye Sweet Sister

We had been in Yemen for less than two months when Dad came to us to tell us of his plans for Issy. He was calm and cold; it was as though he was coming to tell us of a chore that needed to be done. He called us all into the middle room one day after dinner; our grandparents were already waiting for us. Farouse was told to stay in the kitchen.

"Ismahan, I have found you a husband, he is a good man and he can look after you well, you are not young anymore and you must marry. The wedding will take place in 7 days." Dad was calm as he looked at Issy.

Issy's response was weak; she struggled to get her words out.

"Wwwhat? Wwwhat do you mean?" I could see the colour slowly draining from her face; at the same time I could feel my own heart beating a million times a minute, but I couldn't think of a single word to say. I glanced at Yas; I could see the anger building up in her face.

"Oh! So it's her turn now, is it? You had to pay back the money for me so now you need to sell another one of us?" Standing up, she stood in the middle of the room pointing her finger around at them all one by one. "I hate you! I hate you all!" she screamed.

Granddad stood up and started yelling at Dad to control his daughter as Yas continued to scream abuse at them all. Then Gran stood up and started yelling at Yas to shut up; all of a sudden Issy screamed louder than everyone!

"I won't marry, I promise you Dad if you make me do this, I will kill myself! I swear it now!" I could hear the desperation in Issy's voice, hoping that Dad would reconsider, but Dad just stared at her, then he stood up.

"Well then go ahead and kill yourself, because the wedding happens in seven days," he sighed as he left the room, promptly followed by our grandparents as they both carried on cursing us for our disobedience, and Dad for not disciplining his daughters.

Farouse came running into the room wanting to know what the news was; she didn't realise what had happened until she saw the look on our faces.

"What's happened?" she asked, concerned.

"Dad thinks I'm going to marry some stinking pervert! Someone I've never even met. I don't think so!" Issy broke down as she spoke, sobbing, shaking with fear.

We tried our best to reassure her that this wasn't going to happen, but deep in our hearts we knew it would. We had fought with Dad and his family over many things since coming from England, however by now we knew if we were told to do something, no matter how much we argued, in the end we had no choice but to do it.

For the next couple of days we argued with Dad and his family, we refused to eat and do chores, but Dad just screamed and yelled at us all and refused to back down. Our grandparents told him to stand his ground with us, not to believe Issy when she said she would kill herself; he in turn listened to them.

Then one afternoon Farouse came to us with more disturbing news! "I've heard a rumour that the man you're going to marry is 60 and already married with children." Issy demanded to know who told her but Farouse refused to say. "All I can tell you is she doesn't lie," Farouse replied.

Issy stormed out of the room and upstairs to where dad was sat eating ghat with Uncle Mohammed; we were quickly behind her. She barged into the room, stood right in front of Dad and looked him square in the eyes.

"You seriously think you're going to give me to some old man who has kids and a wife!" she screamed, her voice full of hatred.

Both Dad and Uncle Mohammed looked shocked that Issy had

the nerve to approach him about this issue once again.

"He's a good man and he can provide for you!" Dad yelled back at her.

"I don't care who or what he is! I didn't choose this man and I'm not going to marry him!" The tears were streaming down Issy's face but Dad didn't seem to care how much he was hurting her.

"Yes you are, he's coming here tomorrow to meet you and you will see for yourself that he is a good man, now, I'm not discussing this with you any more!" he said as he carried on chewing his ghat.

Issy straightened her body and raised her chin up high; wiping the tears from her face, she firmly looked at Dad.

"If you force me to go ahead with this I promise you I will kill myself, and then I will come back and haunt you!" With that, she turned and left the room.

The next day the man my sister was to marry arrived in the village. He brought with him three big trunk suitcases full of dresses, trousers, shoes, scarves, makeup, toiletries, perfumes and underwear, jewellery and anything else a woman would need to start a new life. This is because the bride is not permitted to take anything with her from her old home to her new home.

His name was Atiq, and as I snuck a quick look out the window to see what he looked like, I was horrified! He was old, fat, short and bald. Issy was tall, young and beautiful and just starting her life. I couldn't understand why our father would do this to her?

Dad came into the room where we were sat. "You two need to leave the room, her husband is now coming in to speak to her," he ordered us, waving his hand at us to get up and leave.

"He's not my husband," Issy told him quietly; it was as though she couldn't be bothered to speak any more.

"Yes he is because we have finalised the deal, now you two move! I'm not going to tell you again, I'm losing my patience with you girls!" Dad snapped at us with a real sternness in his voice.

We looked at our sister, not wanting to leave her alone, "It's OK, I'm fine, let him do what he wants," she said in a defeated tone, not wanting us to get into trouble. Yas and I left the room not wanting to leave our sister to the horrible fate that awaited her, yet knowing that whatever we said or did would make no difference; we knew we would only be dragged out if we refused to leave.

We saw Atiq waiting in the hallway as we left, a smile on his face with the knowledge that he had something special waiting for him inside. I looked at him, wondering if he knew what damage he was doing to my sister, or more to the point, if he cared.

Issy didn't talk much after her meeting with Atiq; she had become withdrawn even from us. Something had also been worrying me; I couldn't stop thinking about what Farouse had told us about the girls here being killed if they were found not to be virgins. I'd spoken to Yas about it the day before because although we didn't think she had had any boyfriends back home, we knew Issy had been using tampons for years, and we were worried that meant she wouldn't bleed like a virgin. Yas told me not to worry, she said Issy would never allow Atiq to lay a finger on her even if the marriage did go ahead, but I couldn't help but worry.

I decided to tell Farouse about my fears for my sister and to my surprise she wasn't shocked when I told her I didn't think Issy would bleed. She told me many girls worried about the same thing on their wedding night and took precautions with them just in case things didn't go as planned. She told me that many girls took a tiny vial and filled it with animal blood the day of the wedding; there was no shortage of animal blood during the celebrations, as many animals are slaughtered. They hid it in their wedding dress and took it in the room with them; if they didn't bleed they could discreetly spill it on to the sheet without their husbands seeing. Farouse told me she would get me the blood; now all we had to do was convince Issy to take it with her, just in case.

The day of the wedding arrived and our grandparents agreed against calling in Al Mouzayna. They said she was old enough to guide herself, and knew Issy would refuse any art work done on her so it would be a waste of money.

Issy had refused to go to the gathering the day before and although Gran shouted and tried to intimidate her, she refused to back down, so we all stayed upstairs together. She was given the small room on the top floor to use during the wedding celebration to get ready in.

The next day the guests arrived for dinner, but Issy had been refusing to eat properly since she was told of the wedding and she was looking pale and ill. Yas and I tried everything to get her to have a proper meal but it was as if she had already given up on life.

Issy's wedding was different from the other weddings we had attended; she wasn't going to be paraded in front of everyone in her wedding dress, maybe because they knew she would refuse. That afternoon, after Dad had eaten with the guests, he came to the room. "Issy, please do this for me. I cannot change anything now because a deal has been made but if you give me time, after the wedding, if you are still not happy with your husband I will come and bring you back with me and you won't have to go back to him again," he promised. But Issy didn't even look at him when she answered.

"I don't want to marry him now, so if you really loved me you wouldn't do this to me. I don't trust you any more Dad, so no, I will not be doing you any favours, just like you have never done me any favours!"

Dad's tone changed from pleading to threatening. "That's enough! I'm not going to keep explaining myself to you, and just so you know you are leaving for your husband's house today!"

Yas and I gasped as reality hit us, Issy was going today!

"Oh no! No! She's not going today," Yas cried. "Why today? She's not supposed to go until tomorrow."

I looked at Issy and saw how helpless and defeated she looked; she had lost all hope of ever getting out of this situation. She didn't even argue with what Dad had just told her, she had lost her fighting spirit.

"Your sisters are allowed to go with you, they can stay for the three days of celebrations then they can come back with me, you have around 20 minutes to get ready before the car gets here, so hurry up and get ready," Dad told us as he left the room.

We quickly gathered our belongings, thinking that any moment Dad would come back and tell us we wouldn't be allowed to go with her. Issy wasn't allowed to take any of her old things but Yas quickly hid her favourite little round mirror in her suitcase for her; it was something she had kept of hers when we all had our belongings taken away from us after coming from England. At least that way she would have something of her old life with her.

We were all made to put our sharsharfs on because we were going to the city, by that time we were expected to cover and behave like proper Muslim girls. As we walked with our sister down those stairs I felt a mixed feeling of guilt and relief. The guilt that we could not save our sister from these monsters that were doing this to her, then the relief that we had been given permission to go with her to her husband's house for three more days to help her through this dreadful time. Usually only the father and Al Mouzayna travelled with the bride to her husband's house.

Gran was at the door; she tried to give Issy advice then a kiss, but Issy pushed her away telling her she didn't want her kisses or advice. Farouse grabbed her as she sobbed, telling her she loved her, then Farouse came to me and slipped me the tiny vial of blood into my hand as she hugged me goodbye.

There were two jeeps that took us to Sanaa; we were allowed to travel in one alone with our sister while Dad and Granddad travelled in the other. On the way I showed them the blood that Farouse had given me; although Issy said she appreciated what we were doing, she told us that she meant every word of what she had said to Dad, she would kill herself before the marriage was final, and Atiq would never lay a finger on her.

That was the first time Yas and I really believed our sister was serious about committing suicide.

It was a long drive to Sanaa and there were many tears cried along the way as we pleaded with our sister to wait and see what the outcome would be. We told her we needed her with us and that we couldn't live without her, but Issy had given up on life and saw no other way out.

When we came close to Atiq's house we were joined by ten more jeeps from his wedding convoy that led us and started shooting guns and letting off fireworks.

We pulled up outside a block of flats six storeys high. All of these belonged to Atiq, and one of them was to be Issy's new home. Once we were outside about 20 women came out to greet us, all making the high whistle wedding noises as they ushered us inside and upstairs to a first floor flat.

Once inside Issy was escorted by one of the females to a room which she was told was her bedroom, while some of the other women carried in the suitcases that Atiq had brought for his bride and left them on the floor inside the bedroom. As I looked around,

I let out a silent sigh of relief to see there was no 'throne' set up for my sister. The bedroom had a real bed and carpet; it had a cupboard, a chair and resembled an English bedroom more than we had seen since arriving in Yemen. Issy sat on the chair, Yas and I sat on the edge of the bed.

"What are we supposed to do now?" I asked as we looked around the room.

"Does anyone know if I have a brush or comb in those cases?" Issy asked, ripping off her sharsharf.

Yas said she would check the suitcases. As she got up and opened one of the cases she found the mirror she had hidden for Issy before we left, and was gutted to see it had been broken from the journey.

"Oh crap! It's broken!" Yas sulked.

Issy looked over to see her favourite mirror in Yas's hand. "Oh well, there you go, seven more years of bad luck," she said in a quiet, sad voice.

"Don't say that!" I pleaded with her.

"Why not? It's true! Our bad luck started seven years ago and it's going to continue," Issy told me as she got up and started to go through the suitcases looking for a comb to comb her hair.

"Can you two give me an hour or so? I really want to get some sleep because I'm tired, please," she asked.

We reluctantly gave her a hug and left her alone; we didn't want to leave her because we were worried about what she would do. She was really down and she had talked about suicide, but we thought as long as we kept an eye on her, then she would be OK.

Once we left her we went and looked around the flat. It was a big flat which had most things English flats would, it even had a real toilet and shower. If only Issy's husband was someone kind whom she loved, then she could have had a chance of being happy; why was life so cruel?

The women were celebrating in the big room; it was evening by then and most of them were going home at this time. We didn't know what the celebrations were like in Sanaa or if they were expecting Issy to come and join them, but they could wait all they wanted because she wasn't coming! We didn't even know if Atiq's first wife and children lived in this same block of flats or if she was even at the wedding! There was a lot we didn't know.

We sat with the women for a bit then decided to check on our sister. We quietly snuck into her room and opened the door, only to see her curled up on the floor clenching her stomach. We ran to her and picked her up, trying to find out what was wrong with her. Issy was heaving and trying to be sick and Yas knew she had done something awful, because it was something she had tried herself when she was sold to Nejmie!

"Pleeeease, please tell me what you've done? What have you taken, how many have you taken?" Yas kept asking over and over again. I wasn't sure what Yas was talking about because although I could see my sister in pain, I'd thought maybe she was having bad period cramps because she always suffered from them.

"Yas what are you talking about, taken what?" I asked, confused.

"She's taken a bloody overdose, go find Dad... move!" she screamed at me.

I ran out of the room and saw one of the women who had escorted us into the house earlier. "I need my dad, my dad, I need my dad please! Where's my dad?" I begged, with tears pouring down my face. The women pointed to a room down the corridor which had the door shut; I ran straight at it and flung the door wide open, searching the room with my eyes looking for Dad as I yelled out loudly.

"Dad! Dad! Issy's taken an overdose!" I struggled to get the words out of my mouth.

I spotted Dad and Granddad amongst the room full of men, including Issy's husband, sat in the room chewing ghat. They all glared at me in total disgust as I stood there in front of them, my face uncovered, daring to interrupt their gathering.

Dad immediately jumped up and rushed out behind me, following me as I ran back to where my sisters were, but by then Yas has picked Issy up and taken her to the toilet that joined her bedroom and was sticking her finger down her throat trying to make her sick. Issy had been sick by the time we got there and was slightly more coherent.

"What is this, are you all trying your best to put me and my family to shame?" Dad sneered. "Issy, what have you done?" Issy was still heaving as she spoke.

"I told you, I'm not going ahead with this marriage and I won't!"

Dad looked at us all, pure contempt in his eyes.

"You don't leave this room tonight. If anyone asks anything you tell them she ate something bad, you will not put my family to shame, do you hear me? This marriage will go ahead!" Dad stormed out of the room, leaving us alone to try and comfort our sister as she sobbed with her head halfway down the toilet.

Yas and I knew we needed to keep an extra eye on her from then on, so we decided to take it in turns and never leave her alone for a minute - but we only had three days left with her. We knew our sister didn't want this marriage and we didn't want it for her either, but we couldn't lose her, not like this. We had to convince Issy to hang in there and try to find a different way out.

We spent most of the night trying to persuade her not to do something stupid again. We told her how much we needed her and we tried to convince her that one day, in the future, we would all return home to England and things would be OK again. We tried to lighten the mood by remembering the things we used to do and places we use to go, all the while telling her to hold on to the hope that one day we would go back home.

Issy finally fell asleep so Yas and I decided to stay up and take it in turns to look after her. When morning came we were relieved that the night had gone well, but worried about the day ahead. This was the day that Issy was expected to be paraded in front of all the women in the afternoon. It was also the day that she was expected to lose her virginity to Atiq.

The flat quickly filled up with people coming to help with the cooking and to celebrate. Breakfast was brought in to the bedroom by Atiq's sister but Issy refused to eat; Yas and I ate very little.

While we were busy unpacking some things from Issy's cases, she went into the toilet. After a while when she didn't come back out Yas went to check on her, and found her lying on her floor with blood dripping from her wrists. She had taken some broken glass from the mirror into the bathroom with her and cut her wrists. I heard Yas scream and I ran in and found her trying to cover Issy's wrists with her hands to stop the blood; I instantly started to scream as loud as I could. That brought Atiq's sister running into the bedroom to see what was happening.

I froze with pure fear at what was going on around me and the next thing I remember Dad was there, and Atiq's other sisters were there; soon the bathroom was full with people shouting at Issy for doing what she had done.

I couldn't understand why nobody was helping her, my sister was lying on the floor with her wrists cut and blood pouring out of them, but there was no sympathy or concern for her welfare, just shouting.

Issy was taken into the bedroom where the door was closed and her arms were bandaged up to stop the bleeding. She hadn't managed to cut very deep because Yas had interrupted her, but she had done a considerable amount of damage to both wrists, and she was bleeding heavily.

Atiq's family were furious and arguing with Dad, but in the end they decided they still wanted the wedding to go ahead. They told everyone to patch her up and get her ready for the wedding; she wasn't allowed to go to hospital because they said she didn't need it.

We could hear Granddad in the hallway telling Dad to stick to the plan and take no notice of his daughter. He told him she would come to her senses soon enough, she would finally do as she was told, once the wedding was over.

We were beside ourselves with worry for our sister. She kept telling us how sorry she was about what she was doing, but told us she couldn't go ahead with the wedding. She told us she would never allow Atiq to lay a finger on her but knew that if the wedding happened she would be forced to have sex with him, and she couldn't bear the thought of that happening. We knew she was right. If the wedding happened she would be forced to have sex with Atiq and nothing she could say or do would change that, but we also knew we couldn't lose our sister!

We had nobody to turn to and nowhere to run. The one person who was supposed to protect us from this happening was the same person who was doing this to us. Dad was selling his own daughter and putting her life in danger.

Issy made it very clear to us that although she loved us and was sorry for the pain she was causing us, she would not fail the next time she tried to take her own life. We knew from the look in her eyes that we needed to be worried.

Nebat arrived at the flat and we were happy to see her. We told her what had been going on and she agreed to help us watch our sister. She had been asked by our family to bring all her gold for Issy to wear that afternoon because Issy didn't have much of her own. Atiq had bought her gold for the wedding but Nebat had a lot of gold that she had bought over the years. Necklaces, bracelets and rings worth a fortune that she had been saving to sell one day so that she could build her own house, and now she wanted Issy to wear them all.

Atiq's family had hired a woman to come and do Issy's makeup for her that afternoon and Issy didn't kick up a fight, she just went along with whatever people told her to do. She put on her wedding dress that Atiq had brought with the suitcases and the gold and had her makeup and hair done.

We didn't understand the way the wedding arrangements worked in Sanaa because after she had been made up, Atiq was called into the room to 'inspect' his bride. We didn't have to leave the room although all the women covered their faces; he just looked at her, a big smile on his face when he saw how beautiful Issy looked in her wedding gown. Issy didn't look at him or say anything as he spoke of his approval to his sisters, and then left the room to carry on with his own celebrations that were happening in the flat next door.

Issy looked weak from the events of the past week or so; she hadn't eaten and she had lost quite a bit of blood from her wounds, which were still bleeding even though they were bandaged up. If only she had been happy on that day then she would have looked beautiful, but the blank, lifeless look in her eyes, took away the beauty that was in the rest of her body.

Nebat tried to reassure her that everything would be alright and that in time she would learn to love Atiq. She told her that she herself was forced to marry her husband Ahmed when she was very young and on her wedding night she had contemplated jumping from the roof and taking her own life, but she didn't, and now she loved Ahmed.

As Issy was taken into the room, the women filled the air with their whistles as she was escorted to her throne. Issy had shut off all her emotion that day, she had stopped crying and fighting and was just doing as she was told, but that didn't stop us from worrying; in fact it made us worry even more.

Yas and I sat either side of her as she sat on her throne and all the women stared at her. They spoke of her beauty and commented on how well Atiq had done for himself finding such a young, beautiful, English bride. The women danced and drank their teas as they celebrated yet another forced wedding.

Issy left the room many times that afternoon to use the bathroom; she said she was feeling sick from the heat. The dress she had on was heavy, so was the gold, and it was difficult to keep up with her once she was up because there were so many women dancing and chatting in the hallway, but we did our best to stick to her.

On one occasion she told us she needed air and asked Yas if she would go with her so Yas went with her up to the roof top. Issy begged Yas to let her jump, she told her she no longer wanted to live in this life and just wanted to end everything. She begged Yas over and over again to let her jump while I was not there to see her go, but Yas refused to even think about such a thing and brought her back down.

Yas spotted Dad as they were coming back down the stairs; he was going into the flats next door so she told him what had happened. He asked if he could speak to Issy alone for a few minutes in her room. They went into Issy's room and Yas came to the room where I was sat with all the women to tell me what had happened. I saw her wave to me from the doorway and I instantly got up.

A tight knot pulling in my stomach told me something bad was about to happen, and just as I got to the room door I saw Dad come out of Issy's room. Dad walked over to Yas who was stood in the middle of the huge hallway that was packed with women.

"She's OK now, she's just brushing her hair, she will be out soon," he said with a smile. But just as he was speaking Yas spotted Issy leaving her room and running for the stairs! I could hear the fear in Yas's voice.

"She's gone for the roof, she's going to jump!"

Dad was closest to the door and first behind Issy. He ran as fast as his legs would take him with Yas right behind him, trying her best to catch up and get to Issy before she got to the rooftop. I pushed my way past the women in the hallway and made my way to the roof as fast as I could.

The next thing I remember, we were on the roof and Yas was screaming while hanging over the top looking down onto the street. Dad was on his knees, not far from the entrance to the roof; he had run into some metal bars as he got to the roof and that had stopped him from getting to Issy on time. He was slapping his head with his hands and crying like a child. I ran to Yas and grabbed her.

"I tried, I tried to stop her!" She kept saying as we both collapsed to our knees and started screaming with all the air in our lungs, as we clung on to each other as if our lives depended on it. Once our minds came back to us we staggered to our feet to look over the edge.

A huge crowd had gathered down below and we couldn't see our sister, but we knew we needed to get to her and take her to hospital. Dad had disappeared by then so we ran downstairs and pushed our way past the people on the stairs, who tried to stop us from leaving .We ran out onto the street but when we got there we couldn't manage to push our way through the crowd. So many people had gathered to see what had happened, there were hundreds of men on the street and we couldn't get past them!

We saw a car nearby so we just crouched behind it and curled up in each other's arms and cried, not knowing what else to do.

When the crowd eventually started to leave we pushed our way through them, but we couldn't find Issy.

We started screaming at everyone, demanding to know where our sister was, pushing people around and getting cursed at by them for our behaviour, when suddenly a man came over who we recognised from the wedding. He told us he was a relative and said Issy had been taken to hospital, and then he offered to take us to where she was. We went with him to the hospital and found Dad already there; his face was red and swollen from his tears.

"I'm sorry, I'm so so sorry. I should have listened to her, she's gone," he wept.

We both collapsed on the floor. Dad knelt beside us as we screamed and cursed and shouted abuse at him while everyone in the hospital stared at us in disgust, but Dad just let us be. In the end, all three of us huddled together on the hospital floor and cried.

It was late when we were taken to Nebat's house, where she was already waiting for us; she came to the door as soon as we arrived. She stood right in front of us, ripped off her head scarf, and then she stuck her fingers deep into her hair. She tangled her hair up in between her fingers, twisted it in her hands and started pulling her hair out as hard as she could while screaming at the top of her voice. People were trying to get her fingers out of her hair by bending her fingers back one by one but they couldn't because she had such a tight grip on her hair.

Yas and I wanted to hug her and comfort her but we couldn't, we could barely comfort each other. Eventually Nebat stopped and let her hair go. She had pulled out chunks of her own hair and everyone was cursing her for being so stupid and ruining her beautiful long thick hair.

Nebat's house was full of women who had heard of Issy's death and who had come to mourn her. They were making this horrible wailing noise that was a custom for them to make when someone died, but it sent shivers down my spine. It made things worse for us because we didn't want these people mourning for our sister, they didn't know her, and they certainly didn't care about her, or us! However now they expected us to join them in this awful gathering and come together to mourn our sister. We refused to join them so Nebat took us into her room where we sat alone and wept uncontrollably.

We tried to understand what had happened, but how could we? Dad had taken away the most important people in our lives. Mum was gone and we still didn't know the truth about her disappearance, now Issy; we had also lost all hope of ever see Ablah again.

We were in a situation where we couldn't stick up for ourselves or each other because anything we said or did made no difference. Only time would tell whether or not our sister's death would change the way Dad saw us, or treated us.

We didn't see Dad again until mid-morning the next day. As soon as we got back from the hospital Dad had left us alone with

Nebat and all the other women who were staying at her house, her friends and neighbours. Dad came to tell us to gather our things because we were going back to the village.

"Please Dad, we can't go without seeing Issy, we need to say goodbye," we pleaded with him, but it was too late.

"I'm sorry girls but that's not how it's done here, she was buried this morning," Dad said, fighting back his own tears.

"Why Dad, why did you do this to us? We didn't even go to her funeral," Yas wept.

"Why couldn't we go to her funeral, where's her grave?" I cried.

Dad was struggling to hold back his tears. "Women are not allowed to funerals and her grave is just another grave, your sister killed herself and that's frowned upon here so just leave it please!" he snapped.

"She killed herself because of what you and your family did to her so I hope you all rot in hell! I really hope she comes back to haunt you like she promised she would!" Yas screamed, full of rage.

"Yes, Yas, I know what I did and trust me, I'm in hell already, just make sure you are both ready to go this afternoon," he said, wiping the tears from his face as he walked away.

Granddad had already left the night before to tell everyone about Issy's death so by the time we got to the village everyone already knew. We arrived at the house early evening, Farouse ran down to the car and we could tell from her face that she had been crying a lot. She hugged us and started crying again, telling us how sorry she was, and as we hugged her we knew we could believe someone when they told us they were sorry for Issy's death.

Gran came down and went to kiss us but we refused to kiss her and she started to argue with Dad who for once told her to leave us alone, telling her we had just lost our sister and we were upset. She started to go on about how upset she was so Yas turned on her. "You're not upset! You hated her and so did your husband, you wanted her gone, well now she is!" she screamed in her face before running upstairs. I ran after her, past a house full of women who were sat in the middle room and straight up to the top landing where we sat on the stairs and started to cry again.

We refused to go downstairs where everyone was and stayed upstairs. Dad came up and tried to reason with us, saying that people just wanted to pay their respects to Issy, but we still refused. We wanted to be alone; we needed to come to terms with our sister's death in our own way. Only we knew how the other one was feeling.

Once again we stayed upstairs alone that night and out of the way. Farouse spent some time with us and we all cried together. Farouse told us the women would be coming to the house for days, maybe weeks, to mourn Issy's death. It wasn't something Yas and I wanted to hear, we really didn't want to have to sit and grieve our sister with these people, but we knew sooner or later we would be forced to.

The next day the house filled up with women, and because there were men upstairs chewing ghat and mourning with Dad we were forced to sit downstairs with everyone. They all dressed in black, sat around and cried, making the most awful wailing noises that sometimes broke into a song of mourning. Farouse told us this was what they sung when someone died, but it was horrible, and it got too much for us.

We both stood up to leave the room but were stopped halfway by an old woman who was sat next to Gran.

"Where are you going? Sit down!" she ordered us in a demanding tone.

"We are going out to get some air," I replied as we continued to walk off. Then the old women said in a loud voice so that we could hear. "She was young and had a good life ahead of her, now she's going straight to hell!"

I saw Yas's face change; she was full of rage, and for a moment I thought she was going to hit this woman, but she turned around to look her in the face.

"What did you say? You all pretend to come here to mourn my sister and you didn't even know her! She was our sister! Ours!" she screamed.

I grabbed her hand and pulled her towards the door, worried about what she would do if I didn't get her out of there.

"Where are you going?" Gran yelled at us as I tugged at Yas to leave with me.

"To hell!" I shouted back as we left the room.

We ran out of the house and straight to our special place on the mountain. We got to the top and sat beside the rock that had our names carved on it.

"What are we going to do now?" I asked Yas as we huddled together.

"Stick together and always make sure we are there for each other, no matter what happens," she told me.

"Do you think Dad will ever change?" I asked, starting to cry again.

"I don't know Moo, never rely on him, and never trust him, but you and me, we will always have each other," she said with a sigh.

"Promise me you will never do anything like Issy did, no matter what happens?" I begged.

"I won't, don't worry," she said, hugging me.

"Is that a promise?" I asked.

"I promise Moo, I will always be here for you, I swear on Issy's grave."

Chapter Six
Yas Pulls the Trigger!

After the mourning period finished everyone in the house went back to being their normal selves, but for us things would never be the same. It had only been around two months since we came from England and the cultural change alone was a lot to handle, but losing our sister had left us with an empty space in our hearts that could never be filled, or healed.

Everywhere we went and everything we did reminded us of our sister. We had come as three sisters, but now there were only the two of us left and we didn't feel whole. We talked about her and remembered the good times and would laugh about things we'd done together, but in the end we would always end up crying so much it hurt.

As the months went by, we would avoid talking about her because the pain was becoming so unbearable we couldn't carry on with our lives.

Yas and I became closer than ever. She stopped spending time with Dad in the fields and stayed at home with me so that she could help me with the chores; it wasn't that she couldn't do them, she just never wanted to.

We were not shown any mercy or special treatment just because our sister died. Within weeks of her dying we were put to work in the fields harvesting the crop, sugar cane, rice, wheat, grain and many more things that Granddad grew in his field; that's where Yas was best at work. She buried her head in work to try and block out the heartache, whereas I buried my pain somewhere deep in my head, a place I never revisited.

It was hard, back breaking work and the sun and heat made it even harder. Some days we would be put to work from as early as 4am and not stop until lunch time, and then we would have to go home and help Gran make dinner. Gran would stay home and make breakfast to bring it to us at the fields; she would then go back home and prepare dinner, but she would always leave the hard work for us until we got back from the fields at lunchtime.

Once we finished dinner we would have to do all the chores that we would have done had we been home, fetching water from the fields, cleaning stables, collecting fire wood that we would have to chop ourselves from old trees. We even had to take the animals to graze in the fields most afternoons. Most nights when the sun went down we were still working and as soon as our heads hit the pillow we would be out like a candle.

We rarely saw Dad; he became really withdrawn after Issy's death and started staying at the fields day and night. His food would be taken to him and most of the time he wouldn't even eat it himself, he would just give it to the dogs. We could hear our grandparents talking about him saying how they believed he was going crazy because he kept telling them that Issy was haunting him at night, but they just believed he was having nightmares.

When we did see him he was quiet and wouldn't talk to us much, only to tell us to do as we were told and listen to our grandparents. Our grandparents were getting stricter with us by the day. If I had time to myself in the nights before bed I would like to draw pictures with my pencils or read a book, but by now they had started shouting at me, telling me that, "Girls don't draw pictures or read books!" They took away our English books we had brought with us from England so we couldn't read any more.

We always swore we would never stop speaking to each other in English, no matter what they did to us, because that was our thing, something that was ours that could never be taken away from us! We even came up with our own English slang so that Dad couldn't understand us if we wanted to talk to each other when he was around. We would cut the beginning or end of words or speak with a funny accent to confuse him. Dad use to get so angry with us and shout at us all the time and tell us to speak Arabic but we wouldn't, not to each other. With everything else they had taken away from us our Mother's language wouldn't be one of them!

One night after we had gone to bed we could hear Dad and our grandparents arguing downstairs by the front door so we snuck out of our room and stood on the landing to listen to what they were saying. We could hear Dad trying to take one of the goats from the stables but Gran was shouting at him, calling him a madman and saying he was losing his mind because of what Issy had done!

Dad was disagreeing with her, telling them he needed to sacrifice a black goat because Issy was coming to him at night and haunting him, just like she promised she would before she killed herself. He said he had a dream and in this dream she told him to sacrifice a black goat. He wanted to do this because he believed if he did she would stop haunting him. We could hear Granddad calling on Allah for help and guidance for his son and Gran just shouting at Dad for being weak and foolish. In the end Granddad told Gran to let Dad take a goat. He said if it meant that Dad would get some peace of mind then so be it. Dad took the goat and sacrificed it in the fields that night.

When we went to the fields the next day we saw the goat's blood besides the hut in the dirt but there was no sign of the goat and it looked like dad had tried to cover up the blood with dirt. The goat sacrifice was never mentioned by anyone.

I was so relieved by the time the harvesting was over; it meant we could rest from working in the fields for a few months. Even though we were exhausted and had got everything from the fields to the house we now had to sort everything out. We had to grind the flour by hand on a big round stone flour grinder with a wooden handle, where you'd pour the grain in the top through a hole then pull the handle round and round until the flour came out into a bucket at the bottom. This would take weeks doing it a handful at a time; again it was hard work!

We had to break down the rice stalks until all the rice was off them and on a sheet that had been laid out. Then we had to separate the good rice from the bad rice. There was always work to be done and never enough time in the day!

We were never allowed to sit down, and after being in Yemen

for a few months and starting out hating the women's gatherings in the afternoons, we came to realise why women enjoyed them so much! That was the only time when they could get out of work and the house, just sit down and gossip to other females about things other than work!

Many of the young girls we had made friends with were pregnant, but they still had to work in the fields, some of them younger than me! One day I'd see a girl on her hands and knees working the fields or carrying a huge bucket of water for miles, the next morning I'd be told she had her baby. Some of them even gave birth in the fields! None of the girls would get to see a doctor from the time she got pregnant or when giving birth.

Some young girls were married off outside the village and we wouldn't see them again, many more were married within the village to their close relatives, first cousins.

Sometimes they would have gatherings in the evenings, especially at the times of harvesting because people would be busy in the afternoons. Just because we had finished our harvesting didn't mean other people had finished theirs. One evening we had been to see a young girl who had had a baby; this was a usual reason why women would gather together. We got back around 8pm and were looking forward to going to bed, but when we got back we had a visitor.

Uncle Nasser was at the house; he had come at an earlier time that evening, which was unlike him because he usually came in the middle of the night, but all I could think of was the fact that he was there. I hated him with such passion and he knew this!

He was already upstairs so we didn't have to see him that night, but I couldn't sleep knowing he was in the house. I just felt uncomfortable. Yas told me not to worry, she said she would look after me and make sure I was OK but I still couldn't sleep, I had a horrible feeling about him being there, a feeling I couldn't get rid of.

The next morning we carried on with the chores as usual. Uncle Nasser had been out most of the night so he was still asleep, and when he woke up Farouse ran around after him as usual. After dinner, while Uncle Nasser was downstairs in Granddad's room chatting with him, we went upstairs to clean and Yas found Uncle Nasser's hand gun.

I absolutely hated guns and was terrified of them! But Yas loved playing with guns so she picked it up and started playing with it, pointing it at me and pretending to pull the trigger. Farouse was begging her to put it down and as usual, I started to cry! Yas started making fun of me calling me a sissy and pointing the gun at me saying "Bang! Bang!" Then all of a sudden, Uncle Nasser walked in the room.

His face went red with fury when he saw Yas with the gun but he tried to stay calm.

"Yasmin, give me the gun, it's loaded and dangerous!" he told her.

He had his right hand down by his side but slightly risen, gesturing at her to hand him the gun. But as she went to hand him the gun it went off! The bullet took off two of his fingertips, then it went through his thigh and out through his buttock!

Of course I started to scream, but it wasn't for my uncle's sake. In my fear of seeing Uncle Nasser enter the room I hadn't seen Yas turn the gun away from me and I thought the gun had gone off in my direction! Stupidly I'd thought I'd been hit! Although I wasn't in pain I was frantically searching for a gun wound in my body!

Uncle Nasser didn't say a single word for a moment until Farouse saw the blood and started screaming that her dad had been hit.

Yas was in shock; she just stood there like a statue until Uncle Nasser calmly approached her and took the gun out of her hand.

"It's OK! I'm OK!" he calmly told her, but within seconds our grandparents were upstairs and when Granddad saw blood dripping from Uncle Nasser he went crazy!

"Who did that?" he demanded to know.

"It was an accident, she didn't mean to do it," Uncle Nasser said, looking at Yas, who was still stood there in shock.

With that, Granddad launched himself at Yas and sunk his teeth into her shoulder just beneath her neck, biting her so hard he instantly drew blood! Yas screamed and pushed Granddad off her throwing him against the wall, and then she ran out of the house and towards the fields.

Our grandparents were worried about Uncle Nasser, the bullet had gone clean through but he was bleeding badly. They couldn't take him to the hospital because he was a wanted man and it was too risky driving him out of the village at that time of day. Gran ran out of the house to get a medicine woman who lived in the village and I went to look for my sister.

I knew she wouldn't have gone to the fields because she would have been too scared of Dad, his mood was unpredictable. He was like a ticking time bomb and we knew sooner or later he was going to explode so we were trying our best to stay away from him. I went to the only other place I knew she would be. I found her at our mountain, she was shaking like a leaf and crying so I sat down beside her and put my arms around her.

"Is he OK?" she asked, wiping away her tears.

"Yeah unfortunately he is, he's lost a few fingers but he will manage!" I replied sarcastically.

"That's not funny Moo, really? Has he lost his fingers?" she asked, her voice trembling.

"Just the tip off one I think, or maybe two. The bullet just went through his leg, he's fine, he was laughing and joking when I left!" I lied, trying to make her feel better. I had a look at the bite marks on her shoulder and told her not to worry because they would soon heal; mine did when Granddad bit me. We chatted for a while and I tried to make her laugh. I could always make her laugh when she was feeling low.

We both knew that when we went back she was going to be in trouble so we stayed there until it got really dark. Dad was home by the time we got back and Granddad was fuming, pacing up and down the room and cursing Dad for bringing us from England and into his life. Dad was in a really bad mood and his voice was like a raging bull!

"Where have you two been?" he demanded to know.

"We just went for a walk, Yas was upset because..." before I could finish my sentence Dad slapped me as hard as he could across my face! It felt as if my face had caught fire and I burst into tears. My whole body started shaking and my legs felt like jelly, Dad use to terrify me when he was angry.

Yas was about to scream at Dad, but before her words came out he slapped her just as hard across her face; but instead of crying or even flinching she stood there in front of him, defiant, glaring in his eyes.

"Go on then, hit me some more, I'm not going to cry, I'm not scared of you!" she dared him.

"You will listen to me if it is the last thing you do, I promise!" he threatened with his fists clenched, then he stormed out of the room back to the fields.

That night Uncle Nasser was taken to a friend's house nearby, he had lost a lot of blood but he was OK. He had been shot many times in his life and had many battle scars to prove it so Yas's bullet wound was just another scar to him. The bullet went straight through and didn't hit any major arteries or bones so no permanent damage was done. He had lost the tips of two fingers but he managed without them.

Our grandparents didn't stop cursing us for days, and even though I didn't do anything wrong I still got cursed, because according to our grandparents we were Devil children. That's what our Grandparents called us on a daily basis: 'Devil Children'!

Chapter Seven
The Secret Matchbox

It had been around five months since we came from England and we tried our best to fit in and keep our heads down. We knew it would only be a matter of time before we got sold off and we thought if we kept quiet and tried our best to do as we were told we would somehow be spared. We had heard rumours about men asking for our hands in marriage but until then Dad had refused, however we knew this wouldn't last forever. Yas and I used to be terrified every time Granddad had a guest, thinking it was someone who wanted us.

Our village was a small village, it had one tiny shop and that was that. It never even had a school, but all of that was about to change because a small school had just been built in the village. The male teachers were being brought in from far away to teach the young boys. Girls were not permitted to go to school or have an education in our village.

Because the new teachers didn't live in any of the villages nearby, they were given a house in our village; that house just happened to be opposite our Granddad's house.

There were two teachers; one of them had dark curly hair, olive skin, broad shoulders and was just really good looking! The other one, he was taller, his hair was lighter and so was his skin, he was good looking too but not as good looking as the dark haired one!

Our Granddad was one of the elders of the village so it was his job to welcome the teachers to the village and to invite them for food in his home. That day the teachers were coming to dinner.

When they arrived, we were in the kitchen cooking dinner. They were not the only ones invited that day to our house. Granddad had invited the other elders of the village to come to dinner to talk to the teachers about what would be expected of them whilst they were living in our village. Because we never got many visits from people outside our village we were all hyped up not knowing what to expect!

In the kitchen we had two tiny round windows, just big enough to stick your head out of and look out onto the street. The windows were like the rest of the house, made out of cows dung and straw. The windows were quite small and deep so you would have to lean in and really stick your neck out before your head looked onto the street. If you tried to pull your head back in too quickly without twisting your head sideways, you would get a scrape on your chin from the roughness of the straw and dung!

Anyone coming into our house for dinner would have to come past one of the windows, because they were on either side of the house. We all wanted to get the first look at the teachers, so every time one of us heard a male voice coming from outside the window we would race to one of the windows! Our Gran was shouting and cursing us. "Shame on you girls!" she yelled as she tugged us down from the windows, and threatened to call Granddad if we didn't stop.

Gran went down to get something and swore that if she caught us in the windows when she got back we would be in trouble, but as soon as she left the kitchen we all jumped up to fight for who would get to the window first.

When they finally arrived I was the one with my head stuck out the window! The moment I saw the dark haired teacher I had a crush on him! I was banging my leg on the inside of the window to let the girls know they had arrived because I knew if I'd pulled my head back in I would miss them walk by, and there was no way in hell I was taking my eyes off him!

I could hear Farouse screaming at me to let her have a look and I could feel her tugging at my clothes. "Get off!" I said under my breath, not wanting to scream at her because I had my head jammed in the window, but as I did the dark haired teacher looked up at me. Anyone else would have tried to pull their head back in from the window but I couldn't take my eyes off him! He smiled at me and I smiled back, and with that he was gone.

I tried to pull my head in as quickly as possible to run over to the other window to see him again because that window overlooked the other side street from the front door, but in my haste I forgot to slightly twist my head to avoid scraping my chin and ended up with a big red scrape right on the tip of my chin!

"Crrrrap," I cursed under my breath, rushing over to the other window so that I could catch another look, but Yas had her head stuck in it. I was tugging at her dress to try and pull her out but she just kicked me. When she finally got her head out she just nodded slightly and said, "Not bad!" Then she walked over to the oven to carry on what she was doing before!

I followed her, confused. "What do you mean not bad? Did you see what I saw?"

Farouse had stuck her head out both windows in a last attempt to get a look at the teachers with no luck, and she was not happy. She starting going off on us. "What did you see? Why didn't you let me see? You both saw them and I didn't, that's not fair! What did they look like?"

"He's soooo gorgeous," I started telling her, but Gran came running up the stairs.

"They are all here, hurry up, let's get dinner dished up!" she said, but then she noticed the scrape on my chin.

"You've had your head out that window, haven't you?" she demanded to know.

My hand immediately went up to my chin to try and cover the mark while I thought of a good excuse to give her, but I couldn't think of any. "Uh, no, no, I..." Gran stopped me talking with a slap across the head, she couldn't be bothered to hear my lies, then she shoved me towards the oven. "You are the devil in disguise! Get over there and do some work," she ordered.

We quickly dished up dinner, but all I could think about was how cute the teacher was. Farouse was upset that she didn't get to see them and kept asking me to describe them. Yas just kept saying they were OK looking but not great!

I really wanted to get a closer look at him but knew that we were not allowed anywhere near the first floor where they were eating dinner. I knew if I got caught again Granddad would flog the living daylights out of me!

Dinner was over and the dishes had all been brought back up to the kitchen. The kitchen was on the middle floor and on the top floor was Granddad's guest room, so this was the room where he would take his guests when they came over to eat ghat.

When everyone had finished dinner they were ready to go upstairs; we were told to go inside the kitchen and close the door. Gran left us girls in the kitchen to wash the dishes and clean up but we decided to go on to the roof, this way we could get a better look at the teachers as they walked into the top room because the roof door had little holes in it. It was a risk, if Dad or Granddad caught us we were in big trouble, so we decided to take some washed clothes up with us to pretend we were bringing them in off the roof after they had been out there to dry.

We grabbed the basket and ran up on the roof just in time as the men came up the stairs. The teachers were the first to go into the room. We only caught a glimpse of them but it was worth it! "See, I told you he's good looking," I told Yas.

"Nah, the other one is better!" she argued.

"I think they are both nice!" said Farouse.

As we debated which one was better looking we heard Granddad calling Farouse from downstairs and she started to panic. "What should I do?" she asked, looking over the edge of the roof top.

"No good looking over there, unless you intend to climb down, think of something else!" Yas joked.

"He's going to kill me," Farouse screeched, crawling around the roof in a state of panic!

"Just take the basket and go in," I said. We could hear Granddad's voice calling out but we couldn't leave the roof because not all the men had gone inside the room, there were still men hanging around in the hallway! Now we all started to panic because she couldn't go in, even with the washing!

To make matters worse the rooftop wall was connected to the kitchen and by now we could hear both our grandparents talking in the kitchen. We couldn't make out the conversation in full, but it didn't sound good! Then all of a sudden it went quiet in the kitchen. We looked out of the door holes and saw Granddad go into the top room and close the door behind him; the hallway was clear.

"Quick let's go," Yas whispered as she quietly opened the door and we all tiptoed into the hallway to head downstairs!

Gran was stood at the entrance to the kitchen, looking up the stairs straight at us as we came down the stairs! We had nowhere to go. The look in her eyes was of pure disgust and disbelief!

"Oh God! Oh God! You devil girls! Get down those stairs right this minute!" Her voice was like thunder!

Farouse was first down the stairs and Gran grabbed her by the back of her scarf dragging her into the kitchen. "What were you doing up there?" she demanded to know, slapping Farouse across the head time after time.

At this time Farouse started sobbing, "I didn't want to but…"

Yas butted in. "Oh shut up Farouse! We went up to get the clothes from the roof and got stuck up there because the men started to come upstairs, that's all!"

Gran shot a sharp look Yas's way but Yas wasn't scared of her and Gran knew it. She looked at me; I was shaking with fear just like Farouse. "So, where's the clothes?" she asked. In our hurry to leave the roof we left the basket up there!

"We forgot it up there," Yas replied in a stubborn tone.

"And it took all three of you to go up and get one basket?" Gran continued. We all just looked at each other but no one answered. "Your grandfather will hear of this," she threatened walking out the kitchen door, "now get on and finish your chores!"

After she left the kitchen, Yas turned to Farouse. "You were going to tell her why we were up there weren't you?"

"It wasn't you she was hitting," Farouse sulked.

"Yeah, well if you and Moo didn't show her how scared you are of her she wouldn't pick on you all the time, you need to stop crying every time she touches you, I'm never going to let you in on a secret again!" Yas told her as she carried on with the cleaning.

"That's not fair, I tell you all my secrets, I promise I wasn't going to tell her," Farouse pleaded.

"We will have to think about it, won't we Moo?" Yas turned to me but I was daydreaming. "Hello, earth to Mooooo?" she laughed.

"Huh, what?" I turned around to see Yas and Farouse staring at me.

"Sorry Yas, I was thinking about the teacher, wasn't he just gorgeous? I wonder what his name is or how old he is, do you think I will ever get the chance to speak to him?" I wasn't speaking to anyone in particular at this point, I was just thinking out loud.

"Well if you do, keep it a secret from Farouse because she will only go telling her precious grandmother," Yas said with a little grin.

"No I wouldn't, you know I wouldn't, don't you Moo?" Farouse sulked. The conversation quickly stopped as Gran came back upstairs, but the teacher wasn't far from my mind!

Gran didn't tell Granddad on us that night, but when everyone left she made sure we didn't get to see the teachers again because we were all locked inside the downstairs room with her.

The next morning, as we were getting ready to go to the fields to collect water, I was outside the front door collecting the buckets when I glanced up to the house where the teachers were staying. I noticed that one of the big windows facing our direction was open.

My heart started beating really fast as I rushed upstairs to tell Yas. She just told me that maybe they had been cleaning the house and left it open for air, because school had started and they would be teaching at that time.

We carried on with our chores and by lunchtime time I knew that the teachers would be back because I could hear the kids in the street, but didn't know what their routine would be with it only being their first day.

Every time I heard a noise I stuck my head out the window knowing that for them to go back and forth from the school to their house they would need to pass our window. We were usually OK at lunchtimes because Gran would be busy at the fields or doing other things, so my head was more or less stuck out that window all through lunch break. Yas and Farouse were not impressed because they were left doing all the work!

I was almost going to give up when he walked by; he was alone. He looked up and smiled and in return I smiled back, my heart was beating with excitement and I had butterflies in my tummy! He had his hand by his side but I could see he was trying to tell me something without being noticed.

It took less than a few seconds for him to walk by so I pulled my head in and tried to make sense of what he was trying to tell me. I showed Yas what he had done with his hand; he had made a round motion with his hand, then put up his five fingers. Yas seemed to think it meant he would be back in five minutes.

That was all I needed to know; once again I had my head out the window. He came back within minutes but this time he had something in his hand.

It was a matchbox. He glanced up at me from the corner of his eyes and nodded discreetly, then raised his hand very slightly to show me the matchbox. He was doing all this whilst walking very slowly past the window. I couldn't nod or move to let him know that I could see what he was saying because the window was so small I could barely fit my head in it in the first place, but he saw that; with this he threw the matchbox on the floor to the side as if it were trash and carried on walking.

I pulled my head out the window. "He dropped something for me!" I squealed as I darted downstairs as fast as my feet could take me! My heart was pounding and I felt as though I was going to be sick, as I got to our front door I did my best to try and stay calm.

"How am I going to do this?" I thought to myself. The streets were clear but if anyone had seen him throw it away then see me just walk by and pick it up I'm in trouble!

I ran back upstairs and got a piece of cloth, then ran onto the roof. I then crawled across the roof on my knees so not to be seen; I crept up to the side, then threw the cloth off the roof so it looked like it blew off! It wasn't unusual for cloths to blow off the roof, it happened all the time!

I ran back down onto the street pretending to look for the cloth that just happened to be close to the matchbox... brilliant! I picked up the matchbox and wrapped it in the cloth then ran back inside and up the stairs.

My heart was beating so fast when I got back to the kitchen, Yas and Farouse were waiting anxiously to see what all the fuss was about, they thought I was just being silly.

"He threw me a matchbox," I huffed, out of breath. We all huddled around the matchbox and as I opened it there was a little piece of rolled up paper inside. "Oh my God, it's a letter!" I squealed in delight.

Hello my name is Mana and I like you,
What is your name? Please write to me.

It was written in English so he knew we were English. "He likes me, he likes me, I knew he liked me, and I've got his name! How did he know we are English?" I was dancing around the kitchen like a little school kid.

"Everyone in the bloody country knows about us new English girls Moo, anyway what are you gonna do?" Yas asked me.

"I'm going to write back, tell him my name and let him know I like him too! What do you think I should ask him?"

"Ask him how old he is and if he's married?" Yas replied sarcastically! I looked at her and frowned.

"Don't be horrible, of course he's not married, he's too young to be married, anyway he wouldn't be doing this if he was married, would he?"

"No one's ever too young to be married in this place Moo, you should know that by now! But I don't think he is, otherwise he wouldn't be looking at you," Yas replied, reassuring me after hearing the concern in my voice. "Anyway how are you going to get a letter to him?" she asked.

"The same way he got one to me, I will throw one out the window when he goes past!" I said cheerfully.

I hid the letter down the inside of my top, that way I knew nobody would ever find it; then I carried on with the chores. We all carried on chatting about the teachers, it was a nice change to have something happy to talk and smile about and we were still joking around when Gran came home. She knew we were up to something but she could never have guessed what! She always knew we were up to mischief but there wasn't much she could do unless she caught us red handed and that didn't happen very often.

It was late afternoon when I went outside again and noticed the window of the teacher's house still open, only this time they were both sat either side of the window looking out. The window was low down so when they sat at it they didn't need to lean or sit up to look out, they could just sit there and have a perfect view of the street. Once again my heart started beating fast as I ran upstairs to tell the girls. Gran was out and Farouse was busy elsewhere, so it was just Yas and I who ran downstairs and went outside to pretend we were working in the stables, which were directly in view of the teachers' windows.

They saw us in the stables and although we couldn't see their faces very well because they were too far away from us, we could tell they were happy to see us! Mana started holding up something to the other teacher and shaking it then pretending to throw it out the window. We started giggling, but he kept doing it over and over again until it clicked: he was trying to ask me for a letter. I nodded my head as if to say yes, then we ran inside so I could write him a letter. I found a piece of paper and started writing.

Dear Mana my name is Muna. I like you too. I am 13, how old are you? My sister's name is Yasmin. What is your friend's name? X.

That was enough for the first letter, Yas and I debated for a while whether or not I should have put a kiss on the end of the letter, but we both decided it was OK to put just one, so I did.

I wrapped the letter up really tight and looked everywhere for the matchbox Mana had threw his letter to me in. I couldn't find it! We had a matchbox in the kitchen that we used to light our fire with but it was still full of matches; I didn't care, I had to get this note out to Mana, so I emptied the matches on to the side and tucked the letter neatly inside the box.

We went back down to the stables and looked up to the window; they were still there. I raised my hand slightly to show him that I had a matchbox while still being aware that someone else could be watching. The teachers stood up and closed the window.

We stayed in the stables because we could still see the front door of their house from the stables and decided once they left I could run up to kitchen and throw the letter out the window. We carried on pretending to do stuff in the stables for a few minutes until we saw them leave the house and then we quickly ran upstairs where I stuck my head out the window.

The other teacher appeared first, then Mana, walking really slowly behind him. It was really awkward because once I saw him I didn't want to pull my head back in from the window, but I had to so I could stick my hand out to throw the matchbox out. Once I'd thrown the matchbox out I had no clue where it landed, so I quickly shoved my head back in the hole just in time to see him turn around and walk back to pick up the matchbox.

He looked up at me and gave me a lovely smile as he quickly caught up with his friend and walked off in the direction of the fields. The secret matchbox routine became a regular thing for us for a few weeks.

His friend's name was Mohammed. They were both 18 and first time teachers but they didn't come from the same village, even though they were friends and knew each other before coming to our village. Mana wrote good English and we would exchange letters every day; he was eager to try and meet up with me, however we were worried about getting caught so hadn't made any plans.

Yas and Farouse were happy that I was happy, Yas and Mohammed had a little flirt going on between them with glances and smiles but nothing like Mana and I. It was difficult sometimes to retrieve the matchboxes that he would drop for me, especially if Gran was around, and sometimes it would take ages before I could go and get them.

I'd become really concerned about being caught out because there was another young girl who had come to stay with her auntie for a while in the house opposite us that we didn't get on with and was always watching us! Their house was right in front of me every time I stuck my head out the kitchen window! Her name was Laila and she was also looking at Mana; I knew she liked him because every time he walked by she was watching him. She had started to make things really difficult for us!

One time when he dropped a matchbox she was on the roof of her house putting out washing and she saw him do it. Gran was in the kitchen and I couldn't get out of there to go and get it. I knew she had seen him do it and my gut told me she was going to pick it up because I saw her look over her roof and immediately leave the roof top!

Gran was busy at the oven making bread so I went over to Farouse and quietly told her about my concerns. Farouse quickly took off her shoe and threw it out the window.

"Gran look what Muna just did, she threw my shoe out the window!" she screamed! Gran turned around and gave me the most evil look!

"Why did you do that? Farouse, go and get your shoe quick before a dog gets it! Muna, get over here and make some bread! What did I ever do wrong in life for God to bring me you girls?" she yelled, pulling me over to the oven by the scruff of my neck. But I didn't mind at all because Farouse had gone to get my note!

Gran went downstairs to get some wood, leaving me in the kitchen to cook the bread. As soon as she left the room I stuck my head out the window just in time to see Farouse and Laila both run for the matchbox! Laila picked it up but Farouse snatched it out of her hand.

"That's mine!" Laila snarled at Farouse. Farouse pushed her back.

"I don't think so, I dropped it out my kitchen window, and it's a bit far from your house to be yours, isn't it?"

"I will tell," Laila threatened, but Farouse wasn't to be messed with.

"And I will rip your skinny little tongue out so you will never be able to speak again, do you know who my father is? He taught me everything he knows so go ahead!" With that Laila ran off and Farouse came back with her shoe and my letter! I really loved Farouse more for what she did for me that day.

I knew I had to be more careful, so the next letter I threw for him I made different plans; he could hide the letters behind a huge rock that was behind our house and that he passed daily. I would hide mine beside the house next to a different stone that he also walked by daily, only I would no longer drop them in a matchbox, but in a chewing gum wrapping paper! The plan worked well and we carried on with that for about a week but then we decided we were going to try and meet up.

Dad and Granddad had gone into town for the afternoon and were not due back until late that night. Earlier on that morning Dad had started up our water well in his field and we had filled up lots of barrels of water so that we could take all our clothes to the fields to wash that afternoon. Mana and I had arranged to meet at the fields that afternoon. He would keep a look out for us; once we had gone to the fields he would wait a few hours then follow. We could usually be at the fields all afternoon doing our washing and the well was about two miles away so nobody would see us.

At first we were worried about telling Farouse, we trusted her to a certain extent but sometimes when she got scared she would blurt out things without thinking! The only problem we had with not telling her was that we wouldn't have been able to go without her; we all had to go and wash the clothes that day, which was how it was always done.

We decided to tell her and she swore on her brothers' lives she wouldn't tell no matter what, and that was enough for us to trust her. Farouse would never swear on her brothers' lives then go back on her word! We gathered all our washing, put them in our washing tins and mounted them on our heads. They were heavy, but we were used to them by now so off we went. I made sure I paraded myself in front of the stable door so Mana could see we were off and then we began our journey to the fields.

We were excited but nervous at the same time because we knew if we were seen talking to the teachers we would be in big trouble. We got to the fields and began washing the clothes; I was washing my clothes as quickly as possible whilst checking the path from the village to see if I could see anyone coming. I was anxious; I was finally going to talk to Mana!

We were all chatting to each other about what I was going to say to him. How did I think I would feel? Would he be as nice as I imagined close up and face to face? I looked up to check the path leading from the village and could see two figures walking towards us in the distance.

"Oh my good God, it's them!" I screamed as the others both jumped up to check, then I started to panic! "How do I look? Do I look OK? Oh my God, I'm soaking wet from washing these flipping clothes! Look at the state of me, please somebody find me a dry dress in these clothes!" I begged as we all started to frantically search through the washing to find a dress that we hadn't washed. But everything was filthy and stunk. I was left with what I had on.

"What is he going to think of me? What if he doesn't like me?" I was panicking so much I was in a state and close to tears! Yas stood in front of me and grabbed my hand.

"Oh for crying out loud, Moo, pull yourself together, it's only a bit of water! Of course he's going to like you, why wouldn't he? Look at you, you're beautiful!" she said, giving me a hug to calm me down.

"I'm really nervous! I don't have a clue what to talk about. Please, Farouse, don't say anything stupid because you always say stupid stuff!" I begged, giving her a shifty look.

"No I don't! I don't Yas, do I?" she asked Yas, sulking.

"Yes you do, Farouse; you always say the stupidest things so you just stay quiet!" Yas told her.

Farouse started to sulk even more but we took no notice of her, we were too excited! The teachers were getting closer so we looked around to make sure no one else was in the fields before they got to us.

There were a few huts around so Yas ran over and looked inside; they were Dad's huts he used when he slept in the fields, but we wanted to make sure they were all empty and they were. So many things could go wrong with this plan.

Even though the fields we were in were miles away from the village and at that time of day more or less deserted, someone could easily walk by. The village was visible to us in the distance and so was the path, apart from a few bends here and there, but all around our fields were other people's fields with their crops in them and surrounding those fields were rocky hills and pathways leading to other villages. Anyone could appear from behind these hills or crops and see us talking. There wasn't much we could do to stop that other than be extra cautious.

When the teachers walked up to the well, my heart was beating a hundred times a minute and my legs and hands were shaking. Mana was looking straight at me; I glanced quickly at Mohammed and saw him smiling at my sister.

"Hello, how are you?" Mana put his hand out to shake my hand and Mohammed did the same for Yas.

"This is my cousin Farouse," I said as I turned around to introduce her, but she was nowhere to be seen.

"Farouse what you doing, where are you?" Yas shouted out.

"I am over here!" came a voice from behind one of the huts, which was a few feet away from us. Yas went over to the hut leaving me with the teachers and as we waited for her to come back Mana and I just kept looking at each other from the corner of our eyes, each time catching each other doing it then smiling while looking away. Yas came back.

"She won't come out, she reckons she's shy but she's not, is she Moo?" I shook my head but said nothing; my heart was beating so fast I thought it was going to jump out of my chest. "She said she will keep a look out for us to make sure no one comes, if she sees anyone she will shout for us. Shall we go sit over there?" Yas said, pointing at a huge rock the size of a small car. We walked over and sat down next to it.

Yas and I sat next to each other and then Mana sat next to me while Mohammed sat next to Yas, on either side of us. We were covered by the rock a bit more because we were facing away from the village, but Farouse could see us. It was a bit awkward to begin with getting the conversation started but once we did it was great.

They told us they had heard about the pretty English girls that lived in the village even before they arrived! Mana said he was surprised that I liked him because his family were not a wealthy family; although not poor, he said they didn't have a lot of money. Both Yas and I told the teachers that we didn't care about money and didn't look at people for what they have; we just wanted to be happy.

We told them that we were not supposed to be in the Yemen and one day we would find a way home. Mana told me he wished me all the happiness and if that meant going back to England and never seeing him again then that would be God's wish, however, his heart would be breaking because he would miss me and my smile.

Yas and Mohammed were laughing and joking and time was going by fast. They told us how they sat in that window all their spare time hoping to get a glimpse of us, they said it wasn't the best room in that house but it had the best view and that's why they chose it! They said many times they walked back and forth at night hoping that we would open a window to see them so we could talk or just see each other. That day we made a code, if I put a washing tin on my head and walked back and forth three times from the stables to our front door that meant we were coming to the fields and we would meet up again!

We could see Farouse trying to finish the washing alone whilst at the same time keeping a look out and we knew it was selfish leaving her to do all the work herself, but we didn't want the meeting to end; however, we had to go. We still had clothes to wash and the sun would be down soon and Gran would be fuming if we didn't get home to start cooking tea. We said our goodbyes with another handshake and lots of silly giggles, and off they went.

I had my eyes firmly on him until he vanished out of my sight. We told Farouse everything that was said and we giggled and chatted while we finished washing the clothes. We were washing and putting them out over the rocks and the tree branches to allow them to dry in the heat before we had to carry them home, the dryer they became the lighter they would be to carry. By the time we gathered up all the clothes and folded them in the washing tins, the sun was going down and we were much later than usual. We helped each other lift the tins onto our heads and walked towards the village as quickly as possible. We would just tell Gran that it took longer than usual to wash the clothes, this time we wouldn't give her an excuse, that way Farouse wouldn't get her story wrong like she usually did!

As we got closer to the village we could see Gran on the roof of our house looking out for us, we knew she was going to be angry! We made sure Farouse knew what to say and reminded her she had sworn on her brothers' lives. Gran was angry as usual and gave us a stern telling off for being late and again for the clothes still being damp. Farouse decided to throw a tantrum and storm off upstairs leaving Yas and I to deal with Gran. Gran called after her, but Farouse just shouted down how she was always getting shouted at and hadn't done anything wrong then carried on ignoring her.

Yas and I took the clothes upstairs while Gran brought the animals in from the outside stable. When we got to the roof we could see the teachers sat at their window so we continued to scatter the washing around the roof top for them to dry whilst glancing over at them. Farouse came rushing on to the roof. "Did you see what I did there with Gran? That stopped her from a million questions didn't it? I'm getting really good at hiding secrets now aren't I?" she boasted. We smiled and told her how well she had done. We finished up on the roof, had one more glance and went downstairs to cook tea; it had been a good day.

We met a few more times after that over the fields; it wasn't that often because Dad was at the fields most of the time. I was falling for Mana more and more. Yas and Mohammed didn't have the relationship that we did, they were just friends and had a laugh when we met up but were only tagging along for our sakes.

Although Farouse kept a lookout for us, she was getting more and more concerned that we were taking too many risks and that if we ever got caught there would be dire consequences. Yas and I didn't really understand why Farouse was always so scared. We knew that we would get into trouble, but we weren't sure what would really happen to us. We had been brought up in a country were girls and boys were allowed to see each other and speak to each other. The punishment for disobeying your parents on this matter may be a slap or being grounded, but nothing to stop you from ever talking to boys again! Farouse tried her best to explain to us what happened to girls in the Yemen that disobeyed their fathers, especially when it came to boys. She told us if you were even caught talking alone with a boy you could be put to death!

Farouse was loyal and nice to us because she felt sorry for us for what we had been through; we knew she would do anything for us but we could see she was getting more and more scared of the risks we were taking. We didn't really understand the risks, so we decided we would try and keep Farouse out of what we were doing with the teachers as much as possible, but I for one was not going to stop seeing Mana!

By this time, our grandparents had been talking about Dad taking us and moving into an empty house next door to theirs. If it was up to them we would have been married by now, but Dad was still refusing so the next best thing for them was us to move out. It was a stone's throw away and I could see the teacher's house from it so I wasn't bothered.

There was also talk about Dad remarrying, and the girl they had in mind for him was only in her 20s; she was from a village close by. Dad didn't really put up a fight; he knew Granddad wanted this wedding to go ahead so that Dad could take us girls out of his house and off his hands.

The preparations for the wedding began. Us girls spent days cleaning out the house next door. It was a big house with a huge wooden door that was opened by a huge metal key bigger than my hand, just like all the other houses. When you entered the house there was a landing of around four foot long. As you came through the front door to your right there was a really long hall-way, which was long and dark with a really high ceiling. Then again as you come through the front door to the right and to the back of the stairs were the three underground stables. Every house had these; it's where people kept their animals at night. They were also dark, creepy and full of cobwebs; I hated cobwebs!

The stairs went around a bend and up to the first floor, about ten steps, and on the first landing were three rooms. The middle size room straight ahead became Dad's room, the smaller size to the left was ours and the longer bigger room to the right was the guest room or lounge. Then, as you continued past the big room to the right, the stairs went up to a small square landing and then bent around into the kitchen. The kitchen was like all the other kitchens, around 20 feet by 20 feet. It had a floor sink which was a cemented floor with a hole in it that let the water run out onto the street below. It also had a large built-in clay oven in the corner that was used to cook all the food, and that was it! Then about five more stairs continued up to the roof, again a flat top roof with high edges that came to about waist high. This house only had one small room on the top floor.

Dad's wife arrived from her village and was welcomed with a cheer of celebration whistles. She was petite and slim and quite pretty and her name was Amina. She already had a daughter called Samira who was 11 but who was not allowed to be with her anymore because she had remarried our Dad. We thought that was really sad but that was just how it was in Yemen and there was nothing she could do about it. In Amina's case she had been married to an old man at a very young age and her first husband had died; her daughter was now living with her mother as the father's family didn't want her!

We got on OK with Amina, we didn't like or dislike her at first, she seemed nice but was always sad at first because she missed her daughter. Dad promised her he would find a way to get her to come and stay with us and that made her feel better. Although Dad had been a bit less bad tempered since Issy's death, we were never sure what to expect from him; one minute he would be all smiles and loving then the next minute we were not allowed to speak in case we said the wrong thing. For example if he was in a good mood and I slipped up and called him 'Dad' in English, he would not notice and be fine. However if he was in a bad mood and I did it he would snap at me and sometimes slap me and say, "Stop speaking English, call me Abba!" (Dad). We were hoping getting married would keep him off our backs and calm his temper.

It was only a few weeks after the wedding that Dad started sleeping by the fields again. It wasn't by choice; the ghat was growing and if nobody looked after the crops at night thieves could steal it and Dad would lose a fortune. He would go out in the fields late afternoon and come back early morning and sleep all day, only to repeat it again the next day. Sometimes he would wake around lunch time to eat dinner with us but other times we would wrap his dinner and he would take it to the fields with him.

Amina would be in bed by 7 pm, leaving Yas and me alone all night to do as we pleased. We didn't have much to do, all we had was a little cassette player, torches, hand held lamps and candles for lights, but by that time we had devised a plan with the teachers! If we went up to the roof and flicked a lighter three times that meant they could come and talk to us from under our bedroom window. We did that for a few nights then one night we felt brave! Amina was such a heavy sleeper so we decided to sneak the teachers inside the house!

We tiptoed downstairs and quietly unlocked the door to let them in; with only our torch and a hand lamp it was dark downstairs, so we went over by the stables to find somewhere to sit. It was disgusting with cobwebs everywhere and I was terrified of spiders! We sat and chatted for about an hour then decided they had to leave just in case Amina woke up, so we arranged to meet the next night in the same way.

The next night we went through the same routine, but when they came in we told them we were going upstairs to our room because we didn't want to sit in the stables with all the cobwebs! They were terrified about this because Amina was upstairs, but we assured them she was snoring away and no worry to us.

We snuck upstairs and into our bedroom. It was scary but funny; Yas and I couldn't stop giggling because we could see the fear of being caught on their faces. We chatted for a while in low whispering voices but then Yas and I got bored and decided we wanted to listen to music.

We put the tape recorder on, not too loud to wake Amina but we always listened to music at night so that wouldn't bring her into our room anyway, and once the teachers had relaxed we decided we wanted them to do a little dance for us to keep us amused! First of all they said they couldn't dance to our English music, but we sulked and finally got our own way! They got up and stated to dance Arabic style to the music. We were sat in front of them telling them to move their hips and wave their hands a bit more! Yas and I were in stitches laughing at them while they tried to impress us with their dance moves!

After their dance Mana came and sat next to me and put his arms around me. I cuddled up to him and that was the first time I'd felt the comfort of his arms, it was nice! The four of us got on well and chatted till early hours of the morning, then when we snuck downstairs to let them out Mana turned around and very gently kissed me on the cheek! That night I had my first cuddle and first kiss from Mana, it had been the best night I'd had since arriving in Yemen. We continued our meetings a few more times until one night he asked me a question.

"Are you promised to anyone in marriage?"

"No, why, do you want to marry me?" I asked, hoping he would say yes.

"I've loved you from the moment I set eyes on you and would do anything to marry you," he replied.

I knew I was only 13 years old and marriage was a stupid thing to be talking about at my age, but I also knew I wouldn't have a choice soon who I married so if I could choose, Mana would be the one.

I saw what happened to my sister; it was something I will never forget. I also saw what kind of man she was given to and I was terrified this would happen to me. I'd watched young girls over the last few months and seen how their behaviour changed after their wedding nights. I'd seen the abuse they suffered. Although many of them didn't tell us in full detail what their husbands did to them, I could see how they would lose their young lively spark they had before they were married. These were very young girls, some younger than my sister and I.

Even with our very childish ways and rebellious antics that we still carried with us from back home, we knew these would be beaten out of us sooner or later if we got given to the wrong man. I would do anything I could to hang on to my love for life.

I questioned Mana on how he would treat me if I agreed to marry him. I could feel he was a kind and gentle person and I felt as though I could trust him not to hurt me, but I needed to hear him say it. He told me it would be an honour to marry me and that he would always treat me as his queen. He was worried because his family were not from a wealthy background and he didn't think my father would accept him as my husband, but I told him if he truly loved me then he would at least try. Mana promised he would ask my father if he could meet him the next day, and ask for my hand in marriage.

The next day I was beside myself with worry; if Dad said no then my life would seem worthless because Mana was my only hope of happiness. I watched Mana as he set off for the fields to speak with Dad and paced around the house until I saw him come back.

"I'm meeting him this afternoon," he whispered as he walked past the window.

Dad came home for dinner and was in a good mood as he told us to clean the guest room because he was expecting guests! He watched me run around helping the others get things ready for our guests and I could see him giving me the odd glance here and there; I was sure he had a feeling that I knew something.

If this was any other man coming to ask for my hand in marriage I would have been terrified, but I wasn't. Although anxious things wouldn't go well if Dad found out Mana's family were not rich, I was more excited than scared!

Amina had no clue why Mana was coming because Dad hadn't told us anything, so my sister and I played along as though we were also clueless, and when they turned up we pretended to be shocked to discover it was them! Dad sent us all to the kitchen while he escorted them into the room, but we were all peeping from behind the stairs, which included Amina! She was just as childish and stupid as we were sometimes, she would have Yas and me in stitches with some of the stuff she came out with!

After he escorted them into the room Dad closed the door behind him but not before he glanced upstairs and caught us in the act! Surprisingly he had a grin on his face as he continued to shut the door behind him! Not one to miss out on gossip, Amina suggested we go and listen to what they were talking about, and with that we all snuck downstairs and quietly stuck our ears up against the room door.

We were there for a while trying our hardest to hear what was being said but all we could hear was mumbling voices, then all of a sudden we heard footsteps right next to the door! Yas and I darted for the stairs while Amina just stayed at her position until the door opened, then once she got caught in the act she pretended to be searching on the ground for something! We were only half way up the stairs when Dad opened the door

"Get back here young lady!" Dad called out to me, stopping me in my tracks. "And you can stop pretending, get up and get out of here!" he told Amina, who immediately ran off. I grabbed Yas's hand as we both walked back down towards Dad; he had a smile on his face.

"What are you two up to?" he asked, tilting his head as if to suss me out. I hadn't seen Dad like this in a very long time.

"Nothing, are we Yas?" I said, nudging her, but she just stood there shaking her head.

"Anyway, I have a young man in there who has asked for your hand in marriage, it's one of the teachers, his name is Mana, do you know him?" he asked looking curious.

"No, well, I mean I've seen him around, but I don't know him!"

My voice was shaky and I'm sure Dad knew I was lying from my face.

"Well he's waiting for an answer, should I say yes?" I quickly nodded my head up and down; Dad's face broke out into a huge smile as he gave me a big hug and disappeared back into the room. Yas and I ran back upstairs giggling away while we told Amina the news and then we ran over to Farouse and told her!

A few days later Mana went back to his home town to bring his father to our village to officially ask my father and grandfather for my hand in marriage. Waiting for Mana to return was an anxious time for me. I was praying that he would come back with his father's blessing, but my heart was breaking at the thought of parting with my sister.

If I was to marry him then I would have a slight chance of happiness for myself, but my sister would still be awaiting her fate of being sold to the highest bidder. I was torn between staying with my sister and taking my chance with Mana.

Yas and I had talked about this many times and she was adamant that I needed to take my chance of happiness. She knew that one day we might both be sold to separate villages and torn apart, so if one of us could go willingly and be happy then we should go. I knew that my sister was stronger now, that even though she had once attempted to take her own life, she would never try it again. When Issy committed suicide it left us both with a pain in our hearts from losing her that only another sister could feel; it was because of this pain, and because we loved each other so much, that we could never inflict that pain on each other again.

Chapter Eight
It's Yas, She's Dead!

Uncle Nasser came back while Mana was away; it felt like he had just left. His wounds had healed well and he was his normal drunken self, only this time he had brought his two sons with him. Farouse's younger brothers had been living with their mother, but now he wanted them to live at Granddad's house. By the tone of the conversation that went on between him and our grandparents, it didn't sound like Uncle Nasser had talked it through with them beforehand, or that they were happy about it! But in the end they gave in and accepted them into the family home.

They were called Anwar and Ehab. Anwar was small for his nine years of age; he was cute and childish with curly hair, while Ehab was taller at eleven years old and more grown up. Uncle Nasser spoilt his sons and expected everyone to treat them just as the grown men were treated, and that was to be waited on hand and foot.

I hated having to tend to Uncle Nasser and he would always wind me up to get a reaction from me. Sometimes the reaction, for everyone else watching, would be funny, even if I wasn't laughing myself, and I'd walk away to keep the peace. But most times I'd snap back and it would end up in disaster!

It was when Amina was away at her family home, and Yas and I were sent to stay at our grandparents for the night that all hell broke loose! Amina had gone to her family home for her after-wedding celebrations; this was something that the bride did a few weeks or months after the wedding. There was no time limit on when she would go back; it would just depend on how busy both households would be around fitting in the feast. When she went back home, there would be a big feast at the family home to celebrate the fact that her wedding had gone well. Amina would be gone a few days and in the meantime our grandparents had also gone away for the night to visit Gran's brother, who had snuck into a village nearby.

That day Yas and Farouse were upstairs with Uncle Nasser and his boys while I was in the kitchen doing something. I could hear them calling me but I tried to ignore them because I could hear them laughing and I knew they were making fun of me. In the end I went upstairs and saw all of them sat looking shifty, with Anwar lying down covered in a blanket. Anwar hadn't been well that day and hadn't eaten much and they all knew I had a soft spot for him.

"Anwar wants you to make him something to eat, don't you son?" Uncle Nasser said to me whilst looking at Anwar. Uncle Nasser had been drinking, and because our grandparents were away he didn't even bother to hide the bottle; it was on the floor right in front of him. Anwar nodded his head at me.

"Is it for you or him?" I asked my uncle.

"No, it's for him, I promise," my uncle said with a smug look on his face. Anwar told me he wanted boiled potatoes and chillies, and although I didn't want to make it I couldn't say no to Anwar. I went down to the kitchen and started the small fire.

We always had boiling water because we buried lots of pots between the burning coal in the oven after cooking dinner and it kept the water boiling most of the day, so it took me about 20 minutes. Once I finished I took the plate of boiled potatoes and chillies upstairs and handed it to Anwar, who was by this time sat up in bed. Uncle Nasser had a big smile on his face as his son took the plate out of my hand and handed it straight to him!

Everyone started laughing, because they could see my face turning red with anger as my Uncle dipped a potato in chili and shoved it in his mouth! I reached out and tried to grab the plate from him.

"If you want some food get your own bloody daughter to cook for you! This is for Anwar!"

I couldn't hide the hatred I had for him as I spoke. It had

become impossible for me to control the way I hated him, or the way I reacted when I was around him, but sometimes I'd wish I had! I grabbed the plate and we started tugging at it as he held it up away from me.

"Ah come on Muna, I'm hungry, let it go," he smirked, pulling the plate away from me.

I tried to pull it back off him but he was stronger than I was and I ended up losing. He looked at me with the plate in his hand, his eyes telling me he could do as he pleased, and then he laughed as he looked at his sons, then back at me!

The atmosphere in the room had begun to change and I could feel that everyone was feeling tense. He then dropped the plate on the floor and started stomping up and down on it, twirling around mashing the potatoes with his feet, pretending to dance with his arm in the air and trying to make everyone laugh, while singing some stupid song, but no one was laughing.

They could see my eyes filling up with tears. "I hate you!" I screamed in his face. "You're nothing but a lowlife bully and when Granddad comes back I'm going to tell him you're a drunk and you've been sat here drinking all day!"

Uncle Nasser had heard enough. Who was I to talk to him and threaten him in this manner? He turned around, turning his back to me, and then he swung his bad arm as he came back around to face me, but he swung with such force it caught me on the side of my head and flung me across the room!

They were all sat in the small room, but I had been flung out into the adjoining room. I felt dazed and the fear of what was happening finally hit me!

I heard Yas scream and I looked up to see her launch herself at our uncle. "You bastard," she screamed, "Leave my sister alone," but she didn't get very far.

He punched her in her face and she too ended up on the floor next to me. I looked over at Yas as she fell, and when I saw blood on her face any fear I had of being hurt by this man left my body. I got up and went to attack him, my hands waving out in front of me as I ran towards him, but I was still dazed from his last hit and he was much bigger and stronger than me. He swung at me again and punched me with such force I felt blinded as I hit the floor, blood pouring from my nose.

I could hear our cousins in the background crying and cowering in fear. I didn't for one moment blame them for not coming to our rescue, they knew only too well the repercussions for anyone that tried to help another when they were being punished, and we were about to find this out!

Once again Yas got up, blood dripping from her mouth as she ran at Uncle Nasser; cursing him for laying a finger on me and thinking he could get away with it! Telling him how he would live to regret it.

Uncle Nasser picked up his rifle that had been resting against the wall besides him where he had earlier been sitting. As I lay injured on the floor, I looked up and saw him pick up the gun, my body froze in fear but I could hear myself scream. All I could do was watch as he lifted the gun and pulled it back over his shoulder, and then he brought it back with all his force and hit Yas in the face with the butt of the gun, sending her crashing to the floor!

I crawled over to where she was lying as our uncle went back into the room and closed the door on him and his children. Yas was lifeless; I tried in vain to get a reaction from her as I shook her, screaming and begging for help from anyone who could hear me. I could hear him in the room ordering Farouse to stay where she was as I continued to cradle Yas in my arms. Her face was covered in blood and I didn't know what to do!

The next thing I remember I was running out of the house towards the fields. I could hear myself breathing heavier and faster, my heart was telling me to go back and be with my sister but my legs were taking me to Dad. A voice inside my head kept telling me over and over again, "Dad will know what to do; Dad will know what to do."

I didn't stop running until I got to the fields. It was dark but it was a full moon so I could see around and my glance quickly darted from one field to the other looking for Dad. I knew Dad would be walking around at this time making sure everything was secure. I could taste blood in my throat as I screamed for him.

"Daaaad, Daaad!" I shouted repeatedly until he appeared. He

saw me and hurried over, a look of utter worry and shock on his face when he saw my face covered in blood.

He was shaking me asking me what was wrong but I was in shock, I was crying and couldn't get my words out.

"Yas, Uncle Nasser, she's dead!"

Dad started running towards the house, yelling at me to keep up with him and tell him what had happened, but when I tried he didn't want to know about his brother drinking, only what Yas and I had done wrong. He then tried to reassure me that Yas was fine and was most probable just 'knocked out'.

When we got closer to the village I started to get more and more hysterical, telling Dad that Yas was covered in blood and that she was just lying there not responding to me. Dad stopped and looked at me.

"If she's not dead, I'm going to kill you for putting me through this!" He said, huffing and puffing out of breath.

He looked fed up, as if he had had enough of us! Dad banged on the front door when he got to it and I noticed someone had been down and locked it after I'd left. I'd stopped crying at this point and what Dad had said to me earlier had started to play on my mind.

I was stood at the door praying silently. "Please God let my sister be OK! Please God." But a nagging voice in the back of my head would say, "What if Yas was OK and she had only been knocked out? Dad was going to kill me if Yas was fine!"

I started to shake my head, frustrated with myself for thinking so stupidly! Of course I wanted my sister to be OK, but couldn't she at least be injured so that Dad wouldn't beat the crap out of me?

All these stupid thoughts were going through my head when the door started to open slowly. Dad started yelling at whoever was stood behind the door holding the candle, asking them why it took so long to open the door. When all of a sudden my eyes adjusted to the candle light, and at the same time so did Dad's. We both saw Yas holding the candle! I instantly jumped out of Dad's way, ducking and diving, waiting for him to lash out at me.

"I swear to God, Dad, she was dead! I swear it! Yas please tell him, weren't you dead?"

I begged my sister to back me up, but she just stood there and quietly let out a little giggle at how stupid I sounded, asking her to tell Dad she had come back from the dead.

"I'm OK Moo, a few bruises but nothing serious," she reassured me.

"But Dad, honest, I swear to you she was dead! I tried to wake her up and she wasn't breathing!"

My legs started to shake like they always did when I thought I was in for a beating, but luckily Dad was in no mood to deal with me that night. He walked over to Yas and looked at her face under the candle light but said nothing, and then he turned around, wagging his finger rigorously in my direction and shaking his head in disappointment as he let out a big sigh.

"Huhhh, I will deal with you tomorrow." He sounded more fed up than angry as he walked off back to the fields.

Dad didn't go upstairs or ask if we were OK, he never spoke to his brother about his behaviour, but then why would he? His family were permitted to treat us and do with us as they pleased, why else would our uncle behave this way towards us?

Our Uncle left the village the next night, but before that our grandparents had come back and heard all about the night before, minus the fact that Uncle Nasser had been drinking. Of course Yas and I got blamed for everything and got cursed, but spared any physical punishment.

That day our Grandparents came to a decision that from now on Uncle Nasser would not stay in their house when he came into the village. It was decided that Granddad's other house, that was about seven doors up from the one he lived in and empty, would be cleaned out and kept for him when he came into the village. Granddad thought that Uncle Nasser's visits were bringing too much attention to his house and he was worried something would happen. Another reason was they had just come back from a visit with Gran's brother who was a leader in the guerrilla group, he had told her they were going to be attending meetings in the village and needed a house to meet up in.

The day after Uncle Nasser left, Gran told us to go and clean the new house. She would be at the fields all morning so we had lots to do in both houses. As we were getting things together Farouse ran downstairs to get her father's alcohol from his hiding place in the stables. She had been given instructions by her father to take the drink and hide it in the new house.

We were all in the middle landing debating what to do with the alcohol because we were fed up with his drinking. Farouse said we should just replace it with water. Yas and I laughed at her; she never was very smart! I was up for replacing it with pee, which would teach him for messing with us! Then Yas said she wanted to get drunk and see what our grandparents did when they came home and found her drunk! She said it wasn't fair that men were allowed to do whatever they wanted but girls were kept on a tight leash.

The atmosphere soon changed from funny to fear when I realised Yas wasn't kidding and we both started tugging on the bottle of whiskey. Yas won the struggle and took the bottle, running towards the stairs as I ran after her calling her back.

"Yas, stop being a bitch; you're going to get us all in trouble!" I pleaded, grabbing her dress and pulling her back, but she lashed out with the bottle.

"You're such a spoil sport!" she yelled as she swung the bottle and hit me across the head. The bottle just clipped the side of my head, but I fell on the step and passed out.

I woke up on the step and Yas and Farouse were gone. I was most probably only out a few seconds but they were nowhere to be seen; they had gone to the other house. I went upstairs to the kitchen rubbing my head checking for blood. I had a little lump but no cuts. "What a bitch!" I thought out loud. "Leaving me alone like that on the stairs, I'd never do that to her!"

They came back a few minutes later; I could hear them on the stairs laughing as they walked up and my heart sank thinking they were drunk. As they walked in the kitchen I was rubbing water on my head, I didn't even look at them.

"You OK, Moo?" I could hear the concern in Yas's voice.

"What do you care? You left me passed out on the stairs and you ran off!" She could tell I was pissed off with her by the tone of my voice.

"No I didn't, I didn't even look back, I promise I didn't see you, I just thought you were sulking!" I could hear her desperation and I believed her, but I wasn't going to let her know she was off the hook just yet.

"So, how much did you drink?" I asked, worried.

They both assured me they didn't touch the alcohol. Yas had decided she couldn't be bothered with the hassle, so they did what they were told to do with the bottle and hid it in its new hiding place.

That night Yas snuck into my bed and cuddled up to me. "I'm sorry Moo for being a bitch, I'm just struggling a bit because you're going away, but that doesn't mean I don't want you to go because I do, it just means I'm going to miss you. I shouldn't be taking this out on you because it's not your fault, it's Dad's. Love you, Moo," she said, nudging me in the side with her elbow.

"Love you too, Yas," I said, nudging her back. We cuddled up under a blanket and chatted for a bit before she finally fell asleep.

"I know you didn't mean to hurt me earlier," I whispered as I drifted off to sleep.

Chapter Nine
Mana, Never Talk of Dying

We were back in our house with Amina when Mana came back to the village; he was accompanied by his father. We made dinner for everyone and that afternoon a price was agreed between both families and the deal was sealed, I was sold!

That afternoon I was allowed to sit with Mana for what everyone thought was the first time. We laughed and giggled and held hands and he told me that his family were over the moon that he had found someone he wanted to marry. Just like me, he hadn't told his family that we had been meeting in secret because they wouldn't have taken it well. They would most probably have thought I wasn't pure enough to marry their son, but we knew that our meetings were innocent and we had done nothing wrong.

Mana saw the bruises on my face from Uncle Nasser; I could see the sadness in his eyes as he promised me that once I was his wife no one would ever lay a finger on me again. We only had about 20 minutes together before Dad knocked at the door and then came and stood in the doorway to say that Mana had to leave. Mana shook my hand as he was leaving trying to pretend to be the stranger that was meeting me for the very first time, and as Dad stood at the door he whispered for me not to worry, he would be back soon and we would be together forever.

The next day Mana went back to his village with his father to prepare for the wedding and our preparations began. The wedding was happening in a week so I was to stay inside and do only minor housework. Yas and I spent every moment we could together and Dad agreed she could come to Mana's family home with me on my wedding day and stay until the celebrations ended. Our grandparents were fuming with Dad for agreeing with this but he insisted she was allowed to come and that was that.

On the day of the henna Al Mouzayna was brought in to do the henna and negsha to my hands and feet, but I'd asked Dad to send her home after she was done because I didn't want her with me when I travelled to Mana's house. I had Yas and she was all I needed. Dad was happy that I was happy with the wedding, and he was doing everything he could to make sure this wedding stayed a happy one, so he agreed.

A few days before the wedding Mana sent three suitcases full of things I would need to start my new life with him, including my wedding dress. He had told me he would choose everything himself and would buy me modern day clothes, not clothes that I would have seen other Yemeni girls wear in our village. He had tried the best he could to buy clothes resembling English dresses and trousers. Ready-made dresses and trousers that, although we would never wear them in England because they were not for young girls, over here people thought were beautiful.

Yas and I laughed and joked at the clothes, but gave him credit for trying to please me so much! It was then I remembered I still had an outfit I'd hidden away which I'd brought from England. We had all been made to hand over our clothes but we had hidden little things we loved so much, I'd hidden a pair of jeans and a little crop top. I didn't even know why I'd hidden these clothes, I never expected to wear them again, but now I wanted to take them with me to Mana's house. They were hidden in our grandparent's house so Farouse went and got them for me and I folded them at the bottom of my suitcase underneath my new clothes.

Nebat came the day before the wedding, it was the first time we had seen her since Issy's death and she looked thin and tired. She told us she hadn't been well; we hadn't really thought about how much Issy's death must have affected her. Although she hadn't grown up with us she was still our blood sister and she loved Issy. It must have been difficult for her, just when she found her sisters to have one of them tragically taken away from her. We also found out that all of her gold, worth thousands, that she had given Issy to

wear on her wedding day, and which had taken her a lifetime to collect, was stolen from Issy's body in the hospital whilst she lay dead!

Nebat insisted she didn't care about the gold and we believed
her, however, that gold had been what she was going to sell to
build her own home, now it was gone, along with her sister. Nebat
would need to start all over again and this was not something she
thought she was able to do; this laid heavily on her heart. We
would most probably never have heard about this from Nebat
because she wasn't the type of person to think materialistically. It
was Gran who told us as soon as she found out the gold had been
stolen and that wasn't long after Issy died. Gran didn't hesitate in
telling us that Issy's 'selfish actions' cost Nebat a fortune.

My wedding day arrived and I was a bag of nerves! Yas did
her best to be happy for me and I knew that in her heart she was.
She was happy that I was escaping this life of abuse by our family
and going somewhere where, hopefully, someone would treat me
better. I was also happy in that same way. I knew Mana was kind
because I could feel it when I was close to him and the look in his
eyes told me he would treat me right.

Yas and I could feel each other's hearts breaking. It was
only a matter of days before we would be saying goodbye and
we wouldn't know when we would be seeing each other again.
Although Mana promised me he would never stop me from seeing
my sister, Yas could be sold to a family who forbade her from
seeing me, we might never know what family she would be married into, or where? We could be kept apart, forever!

The emotions that went through my mind as I put on my wedding dress were confusing. My mind wandered back to Issy's wedding day and how she must have felt when they made her put on
her dress. I knew I was going to be spending my life with a man I
was crazy about and I was as happy as I could be given the situation I was in. However at the same time I was hurting; I felt lost
and trapped and if I could have found another way out I would
have taken it!

The women gasped as I walked into the room in my wedding
dress. It was pure white, huge and heavy. The tiara and white long
veil Mana had bought me was up to date with the latest fashion,

so the women had lots to gossip about. I didn't have fancy gold but I didn't care; although I could see and hear a few comments about the lack of gold I was wearing I took no notice. The afternoon went well and as my last night with Farouse came to an end, I couldn't help but wonder what her fate would be, or if I would ever see her again.

The next morning my convoy left the village in a blaze of gun shots and fireworks. Yas and I were sat side by side in the jeep wearing our sharsharfs; as the bride I had to have my face covered with my black veil, whereas Yas didn't.

We went far into the mountains and past many villages and eventually came to Mana's town, Al Naderah. As we drove up to the town we were joined by the groom's convoy that were waiting for us. They greeted us with gun shots and fireworks as they escorted us to Mana's family home. As soon as we arrived, dozens of women filled the street to welcome us and the whole street filled with the sound of the women's whistles as they escorted me into the house with Yas by my side.

Once inside the door a lady came up to me, a huge smile on her face as she gently took a sneaky peak under my veil so that only she could see.

"Marsh Allah! Marsh Allah!" she said as she put the veil down and kissed my head over my sharsharf.

It was Mana's mother, called Saada, and she was pleased with her son's choice for his wife. Mana's mother guided me into what was to be my bedroom. My heart started to beat when she opened the door and I saw the throne already set up! She was acting as though it wasn't even in the room, chatting away to us, but Yas and I looked at it and each other, and although we didn't say anything straight away we both knew what the other one was thinking! It was the speculation of what was about to happen to me.

Mana's mum left once she finished asking me if I needed anything and said she would be back in a bit, as soon as she left I turned to Yas. We had both sat on a bed that was next to the throne.

"Looks bloody scary, it's giving me the creeps just looking at it!" I said as a shudder went down my spine. Yas came closer and hugged me.

"You sure you're OK?"

"Yeah, honest I'm fine, it will all be over in a few hours!" I tried to reassure her, but I was nervous and she could tell.

It wasn't just that I was about to lose my virginity, but the way I was going to lose it and the consequences if things went wrong that terrified me! There was a constant nagging in the back of my mind. "What if I don't bleed?"

Mana's mother came back into the room; we had arrived just before dinner and she had come to tell us what the plan of the day would be. She was a nice lady, around five foot four and a little plump, but she had a nice smile and kept saying how beautiful I was and how happy she was to have me there. She told us we would have dinner brought in to the bedroom for both of us and then after dinner I would spend time with Mana before the women arrived for the gathering.

Yas had hold of my hand when she entered the room and as she carried on with the conversation, she kept squeezing it at points. By conversation I mean it was totally one sided with Mana's mother stood in front of us chatting away and us sat on the bed with a look of pure horror on both our faces while she spoke.

When she came to the bit where I would need to gently fold the white blood stained cloth and knock on the door to hand it over to her, because she would be stood outside, Yas squeezed my hand so hard I nearly passed out! Mana's mother kissed my forehead one more time and left us alone.

"Oh my God! She's going to be stood outside standing guard!" Yas whispered. "There's no bloody escaping now!"

I looked at Yas searching her face, I couldn't tell whether she was joking or not. "Why would I want to escape?" I asked. "And go back to what?"

She nudged me. "Yeah I know, Moo, but what if things go wrong? You can never find a gun when you need one!" she joked.

"Ha, ha, don't even joke about it Yas, and promise me no more stupid stuff when you go back to Dad's house!" Yas looked at me but then looked away. "No Yas, I mean it, promise me!" I nagged, giving her a stern look.

"I can't Moo, I'm sorry but I can't swear to you if I can't be sure. If they piss me off then I'll snap, you've done it too so you know what it's like, but I promise to try my best!"

I couldn't really push her for any more than that. I was leaving her all alone with those people and only the two of us knew what the other one was feeling. It would be easier for me from now on because I would have Mana to keep me safe; she would have nobody.

We were brought our dinner by a few family members; only the closest relatives are allowed to see the bride before her revealing and they were Mana's female cousins. They commented on my beauty each time they entered and left the room but I couldn't tell if this was something that was said to every bride or if they truly meant it.

After dinner the same females came back and helped me redo my hair and makeup, it looked stupid! Layered on thick and way too much, but that's how it was done so that's how I let them do it. I had a dress picked out for me by Mana's mother to wear because my wedding dress was being kept for the afternoon, after I had spent time with Mana; he would see me in it tonight after everyone had gone home.

We could hear all the commotion outside, guns going off, the drums beating and people singing. It had started far away in the distance but now it was getting closer. Mana and the men had eaten dinner down the street because this house was too full of women that had come to the wedding. He was now being escorted over on foot by hundreds of men all singing and dancing in the street, and he was nearly here!

I could feel my heart beating faster as the music got closer and I realised it wasn't just nerves, now I was becoming terrified and I was struggling to hold back my tears. I knew Mana wouldn't hurt me but the fear of what was about to happen and not knowing what could become of me over the next 24 hours brought a pain deep down into the pit of my stomach! I knew I couldn't fall apart because if I did then Yas would, and all hell would break loose! I pulled myself together and smiled, knowing Mana would protect me.

Mana's mother told everyone they needed to leave because her son was coming to the room so everyone rushed out, all except Yas who hung on to me like glue. "Go on, go, I'm OK, stop being silly," I told her, pushing her away, untangling her arms from behind my neck. She left with me telling her to go and her telling me how much she loved me; eventually the door was shut and I was all alone.

For those few minutes before Mana entered the room I quickly glanced around, biting my fingernails. I had never felt so alone or lost. I hadn't taken much notice of what furniture was or wasn't in the room, but now I was looking for a chair or something other than the bed to sit on. There wasn't one. The bed was made up of a few mattresses on top of each other and there was a big trunk suitcase for his clothes, also my new suitcases. There were pictures on the walls, lots of pictures, but no chair. I looked at the throne; there was no way I was going to sit on that!

I nearly jumped out of my skin when there was a knock on the door! Mana opened the door and quickly closed it behind him. "You scared me!" I whispered as he came in and sat next to me.

"Weren't you expecting me?" he whispered back sitting beside me. "Anyway why are we whispering? We are married now; we no longer have to whisper or hide." He leant over and kissed me on the cheek but I pulled away. "What's wrong?" he asked, worried.

"Your mum's outside the door listening to us!" I whispered.

Mana laughed at me so I told him what his mother had told us. I felt at ease with him and wasn't shy about bringing up the subject of me losing my virginity and the fact that we had to show everyone the white blood-stained cloth. Mana listened patiently and after I'd finished babbling on he took my hand.

"I won't hurt you; I promise you I will do nothing without your permission." He then got up off the bed and went over to the throne; he tugged at the sheets and ripped the white cloth off it.

The cloth had been tucked nice and tightly into big pillows, but now all those pillows had fallen down in a heap, it was no more a throne! "What are you doing?" I gasped. I couldn't believe my eyes; he had just destroyed the throne! He then took the sheet and laid it on the bed spreading it out, and as he patted the sheet down I couldn't help admiring how handsome he looked in his wedding outfit. He had a long brand new white zenna on and his hair had been freshly cut.

"There, if we do anything today we will do it here and we will take our time. You are my wife now and I'm the only one that has a say in what you do, with your permission of course my love! Therefore, if we choose we can stay in this room all day and all night!"

Mana playfully grabbed me and pushed me down on the bed and we started play fighting. I was trying my hardest not to laugh out loud, worried what his mum would be thinking stood outside. I was sure this wasn't the sound she was expecting to hear! After about an hour of playing, cuddling and kissing we got serious and started to talk again about what needed to be done.

I told him I wanted to get it over and done with; it wasn't something I wanted to worry about every morning when I woke up. My only fear was not bleeding; I told him that although I was a virgin I couldn't help but feel scared that things would go wrong for me. Mana held me close to him and kissed my head, and then he told me that I was the best thing that ever happened to him in his life. He told me that from the first moment he set eyes on me his heart was taken and he knew we would be together. He said that he would never let anything come between us and if I didn't bleed he would cut himself with his own knife and stain the cloth, as long as it meant that we would be together forever. I believed he meant ever word of what he said.

As we lay on the bed I finally told him it was OK for him to go ahead, and he gently pushed himself inside me, but the pain was too much so I screamed in agony and pushed him off. Mana jumped up, distraught because he had caused me pain.

"I'm sorry my love, I'm truly sorry!"

But I wasn't listening. Kneeling on the bed I looked down on the cloth and noticed a tiny little bit of blood.

"Oh my God! Blood! I bled!" I squealed in delight.

The look on Mana's face was that of pure delight, full of love. "Turn around for a moment!" I beckoned with my hand for him to turn around, and as he did I took the cloth and wiped myself carefully. I wanted to see if I could get any more blood. "The more the better," I thought to myself! There was a little more, and after I'd finally finished getting ready I stood up and told Mana he could turn around. He looked the proudest man in the world as we both folded the cloth ready to hand it over.

As we got ready to hand over the cloth he couldn't stop kissing me and telling me how beautiful I was. He now had to go and re-join the men for their celebrations, and I would have to get ready to unveil for all the women of the town. At least now I could hold my head up high and know that the worst was over!

Mana knocked the on the door and within seconds his mother stepped inside. She took the cloth from Mana. "Mother there's not much, it's very little!" he said, concerned.

"Every girl is different my son, we only need a drop!" she reassured him as she carefully unwrapped it, as though it held precious diamonds.

As soon as she saw the blood she let out a whistle and as soon as she did, so did the other females from outside; you could hear the whistles far into the distance. She looked over at me and smiled, blessing Allah for giving her such a beautiful daughter-in-law. Just as she was about to leave, she told Mana to get ready while she prepared the water.

As soon as she stepped outside the room the whistles got louder and louder. The blood stained cloth was being shown to Mana's family and friends. Not knowing what his mother meant when she said she was preparing the water I asked him. He explained to me that every time a man and women were intimate they had to have a full wash because they had become unclean. This was a religious thing. When his mother called him out to have his wash, he kissed me goodbye and told me he would wash and go straight to his celebrations and wouldn't be back until the evening.

As soon as he left the room Yas came in and closed the door behind her, pouncing on me as I was sat on the bed, a big smile on my face. "Ugh, you dirty bugger, his mum's out there passing around your blood! You OK Moo? Did it hurt? That was quick! What happened?" She had a ton of questions for me and I tried to answer them all, but Mana's mother came back to tell me my water was waiting.

"Why do you need a wash?" Yas asked, looking confused.

"Maybe it's because I'm a dirty bugger! Tell you when I get back," I laughed.

I was hidden under a blanket when I was escorted into the bathroom because nobody was allowed to see me and the house was packed with people. The main room was already overflowing and the hallway was full, I'd never seen so many women at a gathering before and they were still coming! The bathroom was big; it could have fitted at least 20 people in it, a big change from Granddad's. The floor was cemented with a hole at the far end and a huge bucket of water waiting for me on the side. I quickly washed and went back to the room where I was helped to get into my wedding dress. My make-up, tiara and veil were fitted and I was ready to go.

I felt relaxed and the happiest I'd been in a long time, with my sister by my side we enjoyed the celebrations together. Mana came back earlier than expected that evening before all the women had left. His mum called me and escorted me to my bedroom.

"I'm sorry my love, I couldn't stay away from you any longer. I don't want to go back and sit with them anymore," he moaned.

I didn't want to disappoint him but I wasn't going to leave Yas alone with all those women, it was too early and she was only here for a few more days. Anyway, he had snuck out of his celebrations and his guests wouldn't be happy when they realised he was missing! Like earlier today he was going to be escorted back with all men dancing, singing and firing their guns. He knew he had to go back, so he stayed for a while then showered me with kisses and compliments before leaving and going back to his guests.

I was really happy to see everyone go; although the day had gone the best it could it was long and exhausting. Dad came after the guests had gone to congratulate me on my wedding and even though he didn't come right out and say it, I knew he meant the fact I'd bled. He didn't stay long and that was the last I saw of him that night. Loads of guests stayed because they were from out of town and were relatives, therefore would be staying for a few days. That meant Yas would be sharing a room with some of the other women, but she was fine with that because everyone was friendly and happy.

This time when I heard Mana was being escorted back home

the only thing I felt in my stomach were butterflies! I had nothing to fear anymore. I was terrified of having sex again because it hurt so much, but I knew he would never pressure me or hurt me. That night we stayed up until early hours of the morning chatting about everything and anything. We didn't whisper and we didn't hide. We laughed and joked and sex never came into the conversation because he didn't try or pressure me, but the best thing was, we didn't have to do any of this by candle light, because Mana's house had electricity!

The next morning Mana's mother knocked on the door to let us know our hot water was ready. We hadn't long fallen asleep and I just wanted to crawl back under the covers.

"You go first," he said playfully, pushing me out of bed.

"But we didn't do anything! Why do I need to wash now, why can't I wash later!" I sulked; covering my head with the sheets while slumped at the edge of the bed.

"You can't let them know we didn't do anything! We are newly-weds! They will have me seeing a witch doctor and taking all sorts thinking there's something wrong with me! Trust me my love, we will wash morning, midday and night if that's what it takes to shut my mother up!" Mana started to ruffle my head under the covers until I got up and agreed to go and wash.

As the morning went by, Mana was in and out of the bedroom. He and Yas got on like a house on fire and all three of us chatted in our room as he popped in and out. His mother would always come and tell him to go and get back to his own celebrations, but no sooner had he left than he would be back again, trying to sneak past his mother who was in the kitchen.

The celebrations would last for three days and whilst they went on, the men would be down the street in his uncle's house, because this house was full of women. He was only supposed to be allowed back to sleep or change his clothes. That day after dinner Mana came back to the house to talk to me; I was alone in my room. He told me his cousin had spotted my sister when she arrived with the wedding convoy and had asked who she was.

When Mana told him she was my sister he asked if she was spoken for. Mana said his cousin was called Abdul Kareem and was around his age. He said he had told him it was love at first sight when he saw Yas, just like it was for him when he first saw me. He told me Abdul was willing to do anything to marry Yas and if she agreed we would always be able to visit each other whenever we wanted. He told me Abdul would never break his promise; he would vouch for him because they had grown up together like brothers and he trusted him at his word. He also said that he was in university studying politics and that he would soon be travelling the world and he would take Yas with him.

Mana wanted me to speak to Yas and ask her to see Abdul. He said he would set it up so that Yas could see him stood talking to Abdul Kareem outside the window, that way she could at least see what he looked like. Mana left the room as Yas was coming in, a grin on his face.

"He can't stop smiling can he, poor thing doesn't know what he's got himself into!" she joked.

"Ha ha, funny! He's smiling about you, not me," I said as she sat next to me.

I told her about Abdul and everything he had promised but she didn't look happy. I felt uneasy in myself. It felt as though I'd become like the others, trying to sell her off to the first man that came along. I tried to make her understand that if she looked at Abdul and didn't think she could ever live with him as his wife then she must immediately say no!

To my surprise she agreed to see him, and Mana set up the time for them to be stood outside the window. Mana was back and forward all afternoon and finally he was stood outside the window with Abdul Kareem. Abdul was stood as if he was posing for a photo! Moving from side to side, holding his head up high!

"Look at the size of that nose!" I burst into giggles at my sister's sarcasm.

"Don't be horrible, he's not bad, I think he's OK," I said as we both looked him up and down.

I could see Mana anxiously stood beside Abdul, pretending to talk to him while waiting for me to give him the signal to tell Abdul to stand down from his posing!

"He's shorter than me, look at that nose, and what's with the hair?" Yas sounded uncertain.

I had noticed the hair but didn't say anything! He had really thick wavy hair that just didn't suit him, he also had a long pointy nose, but he wasn't bad looking.

"Do you know what? I want to talk to him." I nearly lost my balance when she spoke!

"You were just telling me how much you hated him! Make up your bloody mind," I sighed.

Yas explained she was merely picking out that he wasn't her type of lad but she could tolerate living with him if he gave into her demands, which she would put to him if he had the balls to meet. Yas didn't believe Abdul would have the guts to meet her face to face in secret before marriage. I gently tapped the window and ran to the door to speak to Mana to pass on Yas's demands, then came back in; now we would wait for his answer.

Mana came back within minutes to tell us Abdul agreed to meet Yas in secret, he said for Yas to set up the time and place and he would be there! That afternoon as we sat in the gathering I asked Yas what her demands were going to be for Abdul, but she refused to tell me, she wanted it to be a surprise. We had set up the meeting for the next day when it would be quieter. Many of the guests would have gone home by then and the plan was for Mana to sneak Abdul into our room. His family members were in and out of the house all the time so nobody would suspect he was here for us.

The next day the plan went ahead and Abdul was snuck into our room without anyone seeing him. Yas had insisted Mana and I stayed in the room with them. Abdul was nervous as he sat down and we could see that his skin was much fairer closer up, and his hair a dark brown and not black like most Yemenis. We all made idle chit chat for a few minutes before Yas came to her demand.

"If I agree to marry you I want everything you have already promised and one thing more!" She looked straight at Abdul when she spoke.

"Yes OK, ask me what it is you want and if I can give it to you then I will." You could hear how nervous Abdul was when he spoke.

"I want you to find a house and allow the four of us to live together," Yas said.

I was gobsmacked! Only Yas could think of something this genius! But surely he would never say yes, and what would Mana say? I glanced at Mana but he was looking at Abdul waiting for him to respond.

"Yes, I'm OK with that as long as my cousin is?" he said, looking at Mana.

"Yes, yes, I'm good with that idea," Mana agreed, looking at me for approval, but I was already nodding for him to say yes!

"But I won't lie, it won't be straight away, it will most probably be next year because I am in university at the moment and can't afford it. Until then you can both visit every month, maybe more, you have my word," Abdul said anxiously. Yas told Abdul she would let him know her answer before she left.

"This is shit," Yas said after they left. "We should be at home in England, hanging out with our mates having fun, not trying to sort out who we need to marry so we don't end up as sex slaves for the rest of our lives!"

I wished I could have told her something to make her laugh at this point, but I couldn't think of anything. She was right, but we weren't home and we both knew she had to make a decision fast. She looked at me, her face full of concern. "Do you trust him?"

I'd only met Abdul for the same amount of time that she had, but I'd known Mana for longer and I trusted him. "I don't know Abdul yet but I can tell you this Yas, if Mana says he's a good man then I believe he's a good man, and I believe he will stick to his word and maybe one day he could take you home, back to England!" We both sat in silence for a while.

"I know I will never fancy him or love him, but I'm going to do it because it's going to happen to me anyway. I'm going to be married off to someone sooner or later, and it's going to be someone I don't want to marry. You never know, he might even take me back to England! At least this way I'm living with you even if you are a moo cow!" she joked. I picked up a pillow and threw it at her.

"Piss off Yas! You haven't called me that in ages!" I giggled, picking up another pillow.

"Moo cow, moo cow!" she taunted, as we started throwing pillows at each other, but were interrupted by Mana's mother who once again came back to the room to check he hadn't snuck back to see me.

"Good, good!" she said, looking around the room, totally ignoring the fact that there were pillows thrown around the room. "He would sit here all day with you if you let him!" she said, closing the door.

Within seconds of her leaving, Mana came back; he opened the door and quickly popped his head around. "Quickly my love, I'm in a hurry! Any news?" he asked, out of breath. He had run all the way.

"Are you kidding me? You've been gone all of five minutes!" I tried to sound angry, but my voice was too soft and Mana giggled as he apologised.

"Sorry my love, but my cousin is also a man in love and I'm trying to help him."

Yas cut in, "OK! OK! Tell him I said yes!" she said impatiently. Mana, who had until then only had his head around the door, stepped in and closed the door behind him.

Looking at me he gasped, "Did you say yes?"

"Don't look at me I didn't! I'm already married to you, but she did!" I smiled, pointing at Yas. Mana rushed over and cupped my face with both his hands, he kissed me gently on the lips while Yas looked on, pulling a disapproving face.

"Yes, my love, you are my wife! My heart! My life and my everything!" Then he looked over at Yas and gave her the biggest smile. "Thank you, thank you sister, he will treat you as his queen!" he promised her, rushing out the door.

The wedding celebrations came to an end and it was time for Yas to go home. We said our goodbyes, not knowing what the future had in store for us. If our plan worked and Abdul got to our family in time then we would soon be together again, but if someone else asked for her hand in marriage before he did we could be separated forever.

As I watched Yas get into the jeep to go home I saw a group of men waiting to get a lift in the same jeep; I smiled to myself when I saw Abdul also waiting in the group. I thought to myself how difficult it would be for them on that journey. They would not be able to look or speak to each other because the jeep was packed with other people including Dad. Hopefully Dad would get to know him and that would make it easier for Abdul once he went to ask for Yas's hand in marriage.

Once everyone left I got to know Mana's family better. He introduced me to all his family and some friends, both male and female! He didn't try and hide me when his male family members were in the house; Saada and I were allowed to walk around freely if they were there.

Mana was kind and funny and always did everything he could to make me happy. He took time off teaching after the wedding to be with me but while off work he helped his father in his shop. His father's shop was up the road from the house and it was a proper little shop, as shops go! His father was called Ahmed, he was tall and slim with grey hair, and he was a quiet and gentle man who was always smiling.

He would always praise his sons and speak nicely to Saada. He would leave the house in the morning to go to the shop and only return to eat dinner and sit for a bit before returning to the shop. Saada would always have a bucket of hot water ready for him at night when he came home; she would sit him down and take off his shoes then bath his feet in the water while she sat next to his feet, rubbing them in the water as they talked about the day's events.

Mana had a little brother called Hameed who was 11 years old and the spitting image of Mana; he adored his big brother and Mana would sit and teach him in the evenings and even tried to teach me some Arabic. Mana also told me that the photos in his room were of his older brother Mahmoud who had died when he was younger.

Mahmoud had died in England where he had been studying. He died suddenly; he had previously been in good health. They were told he started to vomit blood and days later died, they never had answers to why he suddenly died.

Mana told me that although he was very young when his brother died, his mother never fully recovered and till this day they would find her crying in her room. Mahmoud was around 18 years old when he died. Mana said that he had wanted to go and study in England but his mother had refused to let him go out of worry that something would happen to him. Now he was happy that she had said no, because if he had gone he would never have met me.

Saada and I got on really well; she was kind to me and fussed over me as we did the house work together when Mana was at the shop. The house had running water and electric and although we still had to cook everything on the big clay oven every morning, they also had a tiny gas stove that we could use to heat water or cook on when we needed to cook something quickly.

Mana was forever in and out of the house, he said without me he couldn't breathe and he needed to come back to see me. Saada would chase him out of the house and send him back to his dad. "You're going to wear the poor girl out! She won't want to see you anymore!" she would yell at him. He would bring me sweets and chocolates from the shop. I had an endless supply in our room but he just kept bringing more. One day Saada caught him bringing more.

"No more sweets, she's going to get so fat you won't love her anymore!" she joked.

"I couldn't care if she was the size of the house, I will love her until the day I die!" Mana laughed as he rubbed my tummy and I jokingly pushed his hand away. But the atmosphere quickly changed when Saada burst into tears!

"Mana, never talk of dying!" she wept, tears pouring down her face. Mana rushed to his mother.

"Forgive me mother," he begged, kissing her head over and over again, "I promise I will never talk about death again!" At first I didn't understand why she was crying. But then I remembered Mahmoud. I quickly went over and hugged her.

"I'm sorry," I said starting to cry. I could understand her pain; even though her son had died so long ago she could still feel the pain when the simplest of words reminded her of losing him. I could also feel the same pain when I remembered Issy, and right at that moment I remembered her.

"Oh my sweet child, you have nothing to be sorry about, it was my son and his silly choice of words," she said, wiping away her tears. We both told Mana off for making us cry and sent him back to the shop. It was nice to finally be with a family that loved each other and showed each other affection. Now all I needed was confirmation that my sister was also going to be OK!

That news came within days. Abdul sent news to Mana that he and his father had gone to ask our Dad for Yas's hand in marriage:

they had agreed! No date had been set because Abdul needed to take time off from his studies but the deal had been made. I wished I could have been there for Yas to give her support, she would have needed me on that day and although I knew Farouse would have been there for her I couldn't help but feel that I had let my sister down by not being there. At least now I knew that soon we would be able to visit each other whenever we wanted, and in time we would even be living in the same house!

About a week or so after our marriage, Mana told me we were going for a picnic. He had told me before about the waterfalls that were up in the mountains not far from the house. He told me I would have to wear my sharsharf until we got to the mountains but once there he said I could take it off and walk free. He told me to wear something nice and straight away I thought about my English clothes hidden in my suitcase. I showed him first because I wasn't sure if he would be OK with the top because it was a crop top and it showed my belly, but he loved it and told me to wear it.

We set off for the afternoon and Saada told us to make sure we got back before it got dark. The mountains were beautiful! I could hear the waterfall in the distance and I could smell the water and the fresh grass. There wasn't anyone else in sight so I took off my sharsharf as soon as Mana told me it was safe; he didn't have to tell me twice!

I was so excited at the thought of walking around free again. I took off my head scarf and let my hair down, straightening out any tangles, and then I rolled up my jeans so I could walk in the water without getting wet. I could see him admiring me as I folded up the clothes I'd taken off and passed them to him to put in the bag he was carrying.

The mountains were rocky but green, with little trees sticking out the sides of them the further up we went. He held my hand and guided me alongside him through the streams of water that were coming down from the mountains. We kissed and giggled, feeling completely free while splashing each other with water from the stream until finally we came to the waterfall. I'd never seen a waterfall before and I couldn't help but feel the beauty as I looked around. We sat down on a rock and he put his bag down, it was a big bag and when he opened it and pulled out what was inside he showed me a little blanket amongst the food and water. He pulled me close to him, "How would you feel about spending the night with me up here?" he asked, stroking my hair.

"When?" I asked, unsure when he meant.

"Now, tonight, we've got enough food and water." He pointed at the bag.

"Your mum will have a heart attack if we don't go home," I said, worried.

"Well, no she won't, I told my dad that we might be staying up here tonight so if we don't go home he will deal with Mum, don't you worry. Well, what's your answer?" He was anxious for my reply.

"Can we go swimming?" I asked, with a naughty look in my eyes.

"My love, you can do anything you want to do!" he said, standing up. Mana had a huge smile on his face as he removed his outer clothes and jumped in the water!

He squealed from the coldness of the water and then pretended to drown to get me to jump in and rescue him. I removed my clothes leaving just my underwear and jumped in after him. We played in the water for ages, swimming back and forth underneath the waterfall. We ducked each other under the water and pretending to drown each other and then pretended to give each other the kiss of life! The afternoon went so fast and before we knew it night was upon us, so we put the blanket on the grass and lay down.

Since our wedding night Mana hadn't attempted to have sex with me again. We discussed it after I lost my virginity and he told me he never wanted to put me through that pain again and that he wouldn't bring it up again until we were both ready. He had kept to his word since that day, and although he had cuddled up to me every night he hadn't attempted to have sex with me. That night at the waterfalls we had sex, and although I found it painful I tried not to show the pain in my face. I loved Mana and I knew he loved me, and would do anything to make me happy. Even though I wasn't ready for marriage, or a sexual relationship, it had happened and now he made me happy. I was willing to do anything to keep my marriage to him a happy one.

We had been married for just over five weeks when Mana needed to go back to work so he kissed me goodbye that morning and off he went. He was going to work in a village not far away and would only be back on Fridays. I hated the thought of him being away and so did he. We had spent every moment together since our wedding and now I would only get to see him once a week.

On top of all of this it was Ramadan, the holy month of fasting. All Muslims are required to refrain from food and drink and intimate contact from sunrise till sundown every day for one month. I didn't understand anything about this and found it boring. The people were miserable and grumpy and I felt guilty every time I was caught eating or drinking, even though I was told I was OK to do so.

I hadn't been back to Dad's for my family celebrations after my wedding because it had been arranged that I go after Ramadan, at Eid. Mana was going to allow me to stay with Yas for a week. I'd missed my sister terribly and wondered how she was coping without me; I was looking forward to spending time with her.

Mana had only been gone one day when he returned, telling us he didn't feel well and needed to be home with his family. At first his mum didn't believe him, saying he had come back to be with me, but then I found him in the bathroom curled up in pain. I tried to comfort him, thinking it was just a bad stomach ache but then he started coughing, and when I looked at his mouth I saw blood!

"Oh God no! Please no!" I silently prayed. Then I started shouting at the top of my voice for Saada but she didn't hear me, so I ran out of the bathroom to find her. She was outside talking to someone by the door; I just grabbed her hand and dragged her behind me.

"What's this, child?" she asked, upset with me for dragging her away without explanation, but I didn't know what to say, she needed to see for herself.

"You need to come quickly!" I cried, my voice shaking. She tried to tell me to calm down but just as she spoke I flung open the bathroom door! Since I'd left to get her Mana had got worse, he had vomited blood, lots of blood! He was slumped on the floor up against the bathroom wall. His legs were out straight in front of him and his head tilted down to his chest with blood all down his white zenna. On the floor next to him was a pool of blood, as if someone had spilt it from a bucket.

Saada let out a chilling scream as she ran to her son and scooped him in her arms. "I'm sorry mother," Mana's voice was weak as he tried to communicate with his mother.

"Fetch his father, quickly!" Saada ordered me. I ran out of the house as quickly as I could. People were looking at me as I ran down the street because I wasn't wearing my sharsharf.

"Quick! It's Mana!" I was out of breath and sobbing but I didn't need to say any more. Ahmed was sat with his best friend; as soon as they saw me they both left the shop unattended and followed me to the house. I could hear Ahmed praying as he ran behind me but when we got to the house he was not prepared for what he was about to see. Mana had been sick yet again and his mother was covered in his blood because she was cradling him in her arms.

"My son, please God protect my son!" Ahmed prayed as he walked over to Saada.

"Give him to me," he gently asked her as he knelt down beside her and tried to take Mana from her arms. Saada was rocking back and forward, singing to him as if he were a baby, and Mana was in her arms barely awake. He looked weak but he was looking up at his mother.

"Please Saada, just let them take him," I begged her.

I didn't know where they were going to take him but I knew he couldn't stay on the bathroom floor. Saada wasn't thinking or listening as Ahmed and his friend took him from her arms, she just continued to rock back and forth, unaware that they had taken him away from her.

Mana was carried out of the bathroom by his father and friend and as soon as they got to the front door people saw them carrying Mana and ran over to help, loading him into a nearby jeep. Ahmed told me he was taking him to a nearby hospital and said he would send a car to come and get Saada and me as soon as he knew what was happening.

I went back to Saada who was still on the bathroom floor. She was in shock from everything that had happened and as soon as I went to her and touched her it was as if she had just woken up from a trance. She looked at the pool of blood on the floor and started screaming, and then she started rolling around in the blood, scooping it up with her hands and washing her face in it while crying uncontrollably.

I sat next to her and sobbed, pleading with her to stop, telling her that he would be OK because he had been taken to hospital and the doctors would fix him, but she kept saying it was Mahmoud all over again. I tried my best to reassure her it wasn't, Mahmoud was a long time ago and things were different now, because doctors could do much more.

Mana was taken to Sanaa Hospital. He was in a very bad way and a car was sent for us within hours to join them at the hospital. It was late at night by the time we arrived and the hospital was full with his relatives from Sanaa, including Abdul Kareem. I was only allowed to see him for a few minutes because he was asleep. He had lost a lot of blood and the doctors didn't know what was wrong with him. He looked as white as a ghost, and as I sat with him I prayed to God that he wouldn't take him away from me.

I wasn't a religious person, but I made so many promises to God that night that if he gave me Mana back I would become a good Muslim girl and never disobey him again. I sat and kissed my husband and held his hand before I was told I had to leave.

Abdul offered to take me to his family home that night, but I asked him to take me to Nebat's because I needed to be around people I knew. Mana's mother was staying at Abdul's and she was with people she knew.

Nebat had no clue what was happening when I turned up, but as always she was loving and supportive. I hardly slept that night but sometime during the night I managed to fall asleep because when I woke up early in the morning Dad was knocking on Nebat's door. Someone had arrived late last night from Sanaa to the village and told him the news of Mana's illness; Dad had got a lift to the city on the first ride so he could be by my side. I was happy to see him, and as soon as I did I ran up to him and started crying as he held me and comforted me, reassuring me that Mana would be OK.

Just after breakfast Abdul Kareem came to Nebat's house to give us a lift to the hospital; on the way he told us that Mana had improved during the night and that he was now sat up, chatting and laughing. He said that Saada had been to visit and was happy to see her son better and had now gone back to get some sleep.

My heart skipped a beat when I saw Mana sat up in bed. I was still in the corridor waiting to go into his room because it was full of men and I wasn't allowed to enter until they had gone. I just wanted to run in and hug him, but I'd promised God I'd be good if he let him live.

"Thank you God, thanks!" I kept saying under my breath over and over again. "I promise to be good, I promise I will!"

I could see Mana looking over at me and looking around at his guests, looking bored and pulling faces when they weren't looking at him! I was shaking my head at him to stop being silly and to be patient but he kept rolling his eyes until Abdul caught him doing it!

"OK everyone, I think it's time we let him get some rest," Abdul said, nodding at Mana. Everyone said their goodbyes and left.

Dad came over to me. "He's all yours, be gentle with him and I will be back at lunch time." Then he kissed me on the head and left, and as he walked off I wondered why he couldn't show this side of himself more often.

I sat with Mana all morning and was really happy to see he was feeling much better. He was still very weak, he had vomited a lot of blood and the doctors still had no idea where it was coming from, but at least for now it had stopped and he was feeling better. We laughed and joked and even had a little kiss. I wasn't allowed to see him in the afternoon because I'd been given the morning with him; the rest of the day was for his family and friends. Although I didn't want to leave, I knew I couldn't be selfish. I kissed him goodbye and told him I would be back first thing in the morning.

The next morning Dad had gone to the market to buy some things to take back to the village with him; he was leaving after our visit with Mana. Abdul had come early to take us to the hospital and we had been waiting for over an hour for Dad, but something inside me told me I needed to go to the hospital, and quickly! I told Abdul we needed to go and although he didn't want to leave without Dad, I insisted.

When we got to the hospital I knew something was wrong because when we walked in I saw a group of Mana's relatives stood together in the hallway; as soon as they saw us one of them came over to Abdul and took him aside. I saw the blood drain from Abdul's face and I went to walk down the corridor to Mana's room, but Abdul ran after me.

"Please Muna come with me, please, I'm asking you." He was choking up. I could hear his voice shaking when he spoke. I pulled away from him as he gently guided me down an empty corridor.

"No! No! What's wrong?"

I had my veil on, but as I spoke I pulled it up over my head and pulled down the scarf that covered my face. I could feel the heat covering my body and I was struggling to breathe. I knew what was coming.

"Just tell me where he is?" My body started to tremble as tears started to roll down my face, but I wasn't screaming or making a noise. My heart was thumping so hard against my chest it felt as though it was going to explode! Abdul just started to shake his head crying.

"I'm sorry, he died this morning." I started shaking uncontrollably for a few seconds, and then I stopped.

"Where is he? I need to see him!" My voice was demanding. I couldn't leave without seeing him.

Losing Issy was the hardest thing in my life that I'd ever had to deal with. But not being able to say goodbye to her or go to her funeral was just as hard. I knew I wouldn't be able to go to Mana's funeral, but I needed to say goodbye.

"Muna, I can't! You are not allowed because you are a woman," he said apologetically.

"Stop telling me what I'm allowed or not allowed to do!" I shouted at him. "Please Abdul, I need this," I begged.

I fell to my knees and started to cry out loud so Abdul immediately lifted me up, begging me to stop. Then he told me he would take me to Mana if I promised never to mention it to anyone. I agreed.

Mana was alone in a part of the hospital kept for dead bodies. Not a morgue, but a resting place for a few hours until they are buried. He was wrapped from head to toe in white with only his face showing, like a mummy. Abdul told me I could only have a few minutes with him because if I was caught he would be in great trouble.

I knelt beside him and silently wept. If Abdul hadn't led me to his body I would never have recognised him as Mana. I wanted to touch him but I felt scared, he didn't look the same. He looked as white as the sheets he was wrapped in and he had little bubbles on the sides of his mouth. I was about to wipe them away, but at that very moment Abdul came back and told me I had to hurry and leave with him. As I stood up to leave I looked at the man that made my life so happy for such a short time and I struggled to understand why he was taken away from me so suddenly.

He was yet another loss in my life that I would have to overcome, only by this time my heart was feeling too weak and I wasn't sure I could.

As Abdul begged me to hurry, I wiped away my tears and then I kissed my hand and placed it on Mana's forehead. A shudder whipped through my body as my hand touched his forehead and I felt his skin. He was cold, very cold! "Goodbye Mana," I said quietly as I turned away and left the hospital.

Dad was waiting for us at Nebat's house when we returned from the hospital; nobody had told them the news. I hadn't cried since I left the hospital, but he knew as soon as he saw us that something was wrong. My veil was up over my head and I hadn't covered my face with my scarf since leaving Mana's side. He looked at me and saw the dead lifeless expression in my eyes and then he looked at Abdul and demanded an explanation. Abdul struggled to tell him of Mana's death, his words cutting off as he spoke.

Dad immediately grabbed me, wrapping his arms around me tightly to comfort me while telling me he was sorry and that everything would be OK, but I didn't respond to him. I had nothing to give back and I didn't want support from him or anyone, I just stood there like a zombie.

Nebat didn't need an explanation when she saw me. She rushed over to me and helped Dad guide me inside. I could hear them fussing around as I sat in Nebat's room but I didn't speak to anyone or want anyone to speak to me. I didn't feel as though I was in my own body. I could hear myself breathing really heavily and my head was pounding as though there were people smashing hammers across it; my eyes felt like lead. It was a struggle to keep them open and I didn't know whether I wanted to sleep or not, so I just curled up in a ball in the corner and closed my eyes.

I listened to Dad and Abdul debate on whether or not I should go back to Mana's house or Dad's house. Abdul was saying I was still Mana's wife and should be allowed to go back with Saada and his family and grieve as his widow. Dad said I now needed to go home with him and start afresh.

Chapter Ten
The Pregnant Black Widow

Nebat helped me into the jeep a few hours later. She had insisted on coming with me back to Dad's house, saying she wouldn't allow me to make that journey alone with just Dad by my side. She insisted I needed her for moral support. I sat next to her in the back seat, we sat in silence as I rested my head on her shoulder, and she held me, with Dad turning around every now and then to ask her if I was OK.

When we pulled in to the village I heard Dad tell the driver to go to his father's house. He was talking to Nebat, telling her that it would come as a shock to everyone to hear what had happened because no one would have heard yet! It was early evening by the time we arrived and because it was Ramadan everyone was busy cooking the food to break the fast. Yas was over at Dad's house with Amina but she had heard the car pull up and looked out and saw me get out of the jeep supported by Nebat.

Gran was first to see me. She came to welcome me with smiles but Dad stopped her and told her what had happened. As soon as she heard the news she started crying loudly, slapping her head with her hands, which brought Farouse from the kitchen to the door who joined in with the crying as soon as she heard what happened.

I didn't react to anyone crying; even when they tried to hug me I didn't have the energy to hug anyone back, until Yas ran out of Dad's house and straight over to me.

"Moo, what's wrong? Why are you here? Why is everyone

crying?" She looked around at everyone confused, and then she looked at me. Without knowing why, she started crying.

"Moo, say something to me please!" I was looking at my sister and as much as I needed to hug her and speak to her I couldn't move or speak. I felt numb.

"Mana died this morning, so let's help her inside the house," Dad told her.

"No! Please tell me it's not true!" she cried, but Dad gave her a sharp look.

"Yas! Just do as you're told for once and let's get her inside, please." Yas put her arms around me and helped me upstairs, straight up to the guest room.

I sat down in the corner and just curled up while Yas sat beside me and put her arms around me.

"Please speak to me Moo!" she begged. I could see how worried she was for me.

"I can't, Yas," I told her, "Not at the moment. If I speak I'm going to cry and if I cry I won't stop. I think my heart's breaking." I could feel my tears welling up but I stopped. I knew I mustn't cry whatever happened. I wasn't strong enough to cry, my mind and body felt weak as if I was dying. Yas understood.

"OK then, you let me know what to do and I will do it?" she said. I didn't have to think because I knew what I wanted, or didn't want!

"I'm not going downstairs to sit with anyone; I need to be left alone, please, Yas." I looked at her and she could see how badly I was struggling to keep it together. Yas promised me she would sort it out and keep everyone away from me and she did. That night Yas and I stayed upstairs alone. I could hear people downstairs coming and going; I also heard her arguing with Gran and other people outside the room, but she refused to allow them inside to see me.

It was early hours of the morning when I finally broke down. Yas was asleep next to me and I was sat up because I couldn't sleep. I couldn't breathe so I opened the window to get some fresh air and as I sat at the window I looked over to the house where Mana used to live when I first met him. I imagined him sat at the window and I just started to cry uncontrollably. Yas heard me crying and jumped up from under her blanket; when she saw the window open she grabbed the handle and closed it, and then she held me as I cried.

I cried for hours. My body was shaking while my sister cried with me. She begged me to stop but I couldn't. I wasn't just crying for Mana, I was also crying for myself and my sister and all our dreams, the dreams we had made together, that had now been buried along with my husband.

Mana had given me an escape from this life with my family. An escape from these slums we were living in and the hard gruelling labour that I had to endure every day. He had been loving and kind to me and his family had given me respect and also treated me with love and kindness. Together we had made plans for the rest of our lives, and in those plans was my sister. We had made plans to get my sister away from this life so that she, too, could live close to us and in time we would be together again. Now that Mana was gone I didn't just lose him, but I'd also lost the chance of living with her.

On top of that I was the one who talked my sister into agreeing to marry a man she would never love. I knew in my heart that Abdul was a good man, that he would always respect and love Yas and would never harm her. But I also knew she would never love him, and would therefore live a loveless marriage as long as she was with him.

Even if we tried to get Yas out of marrying Abdul now it would be too late because the deal had been done. I'd lost everything and felt I had nothing else to fight for; I now had to await my fate, which was once again in the hands of my father and his family.

My heart was breaking in more ways than imaginable and nobody at that moment, not even my sister, could help me. Yas did her best to try and help me but it was difficult for both of us. When Issy died we both felt the same pain and we grieved together, but with Mana's death it was something she couldn't help me through. I could see how hard it was for her watching me hurting and not being able to comfort me, but I felt that if I allowed her to come close I would break down and sink into a hole, one I would never be able to pull myself out of.

Yas came to me so many times, begging me to speak to her and to let her know what I was thinking. She asked me to cry and lean on her shoulder but I couldn't. I curled up in the corner of the room and drifted in and out of sleep.

One day blended into another. After a while, people would come and go and talk to me but their voices would sound as if they were miles away because I was in my own little world blocking them out, until one day Yas broke down. She was so worried about me it was breaking her heart and she couldn't stand it anymore.

"Moo, please! I'm really worried about you, you're not eating or speaking and I'm scared I'm losing you," she cried. I'd been curled up in the same corner since I came back from Sanaa and I knew she was right. I had to pull myself together. Mana was gone and he wasn't coming back. But the pain was too much!

I sat up and held her hand. "I promise you're not losing me, Yas, but I'm in a really bad place that I don't understand right now, I'm really scared to cry or speak to anyone." My voice was faint and weak because I hadn't eaten properly for days. I couldn't even lift my head without feeling as though I would fall over. Yas hugged me.

"But I'm not just anyone, I'm your sister and I'm all you've got and you're all I've got," she cried.

I knew I was going to be OK in time because I had my sister by my side, and I knew I was going to pick myself up and carry on with my life, but I still needed time. I sat up and gave her a cuddle.

"I will be OK in a few days, Yas, you just need to let me deal with this in my own time, but you're not going to lose me!"

"Moo, promise me you'll come back to me soon," she begged as we hugged.

"I promise you I will, Yas."

It was about a week before I started to talk to people again. I hadn't cried since my breakdown that day with Yas at the window and I still didn't feel like I could cope with crying. I'd put on weight since marrying Mana, even though since his death I'd hardly eaten anything. Yas and I were sat upstairs with Nebat one morning when Yas turned to me.

"Moo why you getting so fat? You don't eat much!" I shrugged my shoulders at her.

"I don't know, maybe it's because I'm not well?" Nebat looked me up and down.

"When did you have your last period?" she asked. I tried to think back but I couldn't.

"I don't know, why?" I asked, confused why she was asking about my periods.

"Muna, you could be pregnant!" she gasped. I looked at Yas who looked even more confused than me.

"No I'm not! Anyway, what's my period got to do with getting pregnant?" I asked.

"Yeah, what's her period got to do with it?" Yas asked. Nebat explained to us that if a girl misses her period it means she could be pregnant. I couldn't think back to when I had my last period but I knew that since being married I hadn't had one. Nebat called Gran and told her and then Gran called for Dad.

Nebat went on to tell me that if I was pregnant with Mana's baby then that changed everything. If Mana's parents wanted to take care of me and the child then they could, all they would have to do is agree to financially provide for both us for the rest of our lives. However, she told me that this very rarely happened in Yemen, usually the baby would be allowed to stay with its mother until a certain age before it's taken off her and given to the father's family so that the mother can remarry.

Although the thought of being pregnant at 13 terrified me, I was praying that I was pregnant. I didn't know anything about being pregnant or having children but I felt in my heart that Mana's family were good people and would take care of me if I had his child. I would rather live as a widow forever, bringing up my child, knowing that I was close to my sister, than spend another day with this family of mine!

I could hear my grandparents arguing with Dad downstairs about me. Obviously I was a pain in the backside to them but I didn't care, I was going back to Mana's home! Word was sent to Mana's family straight away and although I was happy that I was carrying Mana's child, I couldn't help but worry that his family wouldn't want me, they would only want my baby.

The next night I became ill and woke Yas up during the night. I was hysterical and was sobbing. I'd had stomach pains since I'd gone to bed but hadn't thought anything of it. Now I was bleeding and my trousers were covered in blood, I didn't know what to do! Yas went down stairs and woke Nebat who told us I was having a miscarriage, but we didn't have a clue what she was saying until she put it plainly. I'd lost my baby and now it was coming out! The miscarriage sunk me back into silence.

The next day I crawled back into my corner where I cried over the miscarriage, and then I wiped away my tears and stopped crying. When people spoke to me I would look through them and not at them. This became my way of coping.

My grandparents were furious with me, yelling at me and calling me a liar, saying that I'd lied to them from the start about being pregnant just so I could go back to Mana's house! It was then that my grandmother said I'd done it because I was worried nobody else would want to marry me because I'd caused my husband's death! She said I would now be known as the 'Black Widow'.

Although we had no clue what a black widow was, Yas was fuming with Gran for calling me names and threatened to rip her head off. Nebat had to calm Yas down, telling her Gran always said silly stuff when she was upset. Dad was more worried than angry. He had sent for Mana's parents and he now had to explain to them what had happened.

Saada turned up two days later. It was early afternoon and when she came I was upstairs, curled up in the corner of the room, just as I'd been most of the time since Mana's death. She asked to see me straight away, not wanting to speak to anyone else before me. When she came in Yas and I were alone, so Yas gave her a hug and left. Saada and I hadn't seen each other since Mana was in hospital when he was still alive.

I looked up at her but I couldn't move. I could already feel my heart starting to break; she looked like she had aged a lifetime. She came and knelt beside me, wrapping both her arms around me, covering me with her body as she rested her head on my head. I could feel all the strength I'd held on to to stop myself from crying melt away, and I started to cry with uncontrollable rage! We cried together for what felt like hours, our bodies shaking with anger as we silently cursed the God that took Mana away from us.

When our tears finally dried up she lifted my face and looked at me, wiping my face with her hand to dry my tears she asked me, "Are you carrying Mana's child?" My eyes started to well up again.

"I was told I was pregnant because I didn't have my period but now I'm bleeding, so I think it's gone. I'm sorry!"

Saada held me and we cried some more, while all the time she kept telling me I had nothing to be sorry about. She told me she would find a way to take me home with her because I'd made Mana's life the happiest he had ever been and she would always be grateful to me for that. Saada told me she had a plan, but needed to speak to Dad before me; then she kissed me lovingly on my forehead and left the room.

Saada spent time downstairs with Dad and my grandparents, and from what Yas told me it was a heated discussion. Saada was trying to convince them to allow me to marry her younger son Hameed. She promised them it would merely be a marriage of convenience as he was Mana's brother and these marriages are not unusual in Yemen. Many women are married off to their husband's brothers if he died, but this is if they have children and they want to keep the women in the family to raise the children. She promised no sexual relationship would ever take place and once Hameed was old enough he could pick another bride for himself. She purely wanted me as her daughter. An hour or so later she came back. I could see from her face that things hadn't gone her way.

"I'm sorry, my child, I have tried everything with your family but they won't let me take you." She gently touched my face with her hand. "I never had a daughter but if I had I would have wanted her to be just like you. I would gladly take you today and love you as my daughter, but your family won't let me. I want you to know that if you ever need me, I will always be here for you, and so will my family."

Once again we cried as she said goodbye. Mana had been such a happy part of my life and his family, especially his mother, could have been a good family to me. I wondered why it was that every time I had a chance of living with a good family, something or someone was intent on ripping it away from me…!

What I did know was that although I loved him and couldn't

imagine life without him, Mana was now a part of my life that was gone forever. Nothing I could say or do would bring him back and I needed to forget him if I ever wanted to survive.

Nebat went back to Sanaa the next day and I was moved back with Dad. It was coming to the end of Ramadan and everyone was getting ready to celebrate the small Eid. Muslims celebrated two Eids. There was one at the end of Ramadan, and one around two months later. Eid was like a Christmas where everyone would get dressed in their best clothes but instead of giving presents the men would go from house to house and give money to children and women of their family. Although I was still suffering from losing Mana, I'd learnt that I had to deal with any pain I was feeling and move on.

I told myself that nothing good could come out of dwelling over something that had happened in the past; I was sure that if I was strong enough to deal with the loss of my mother and sister then I could overcome anything else that came my way.

I knew I would only hurt myself if I thought about him so I put him to the back of my mind and carried on with my life. Any time I caught myself glancing at his window, I would quickly distract myself so not bring back any memories. Soon I found myself thinking of him less and less.

Chapter Eleven
What Really Happens
When a Girl Says "No"

Back at Dad's house it was work as usual. Granddad had given Dad most of his land by then so Dad was spending more time than ever in the fields. When he was at home his temper was scary! He would lash out at Amina on a regular basis, beating her so badly that some days she could barely walk! If we tried to stop him he would turn on us, telling us to stay out of it!

The first time I saw Dad beat Amina scared me so much I didn't recognise him! He was like a man possessed. He had been asleep all afternoon and when he woke up he was in such a bad mood as usual. He would always take his food for the night and go to the fields, taking along with him food for the dogs. But this day he complained she hadn't made enough food for the dogs and he just went berserk!

He hit her over the head with an old paint tin that he had been carrying in his hand to take the dog's food to the fields, and then he continued to punch and kick her! We tried to stop him but in the course of doing so got a beating ourselves; not as bad as Amina! She was left battered and bruised. Yas would stand up for herself more than Amina and I would, but even she would still get a slap or punch when dad was like that. Yas and I used to secretly plot to gang up on Dad and beat him up, but we never did. We knew if we did we would be severely punished, if not killed!

Yas got married a few months after Mana died. Just like me when I got married, she didn't want to leave me, but she had no choice. Dad agreed I could go with her to Abdul's house until her celebrations were over. Abdul's family were nice and even though she didn't want to marry him she knew she was better off with him than with our family!

He had two sisters and two brothers. The youngest brother Mohammed was in Germany studying, but the others were at the wedding and all of them adored Yas. Yas was a bag of nerves that day, I'd never seen her as nervous as she was when I sat with her until Abdul came to be with her. Just like I was, she was terrified of losing her virginity.

After I left her with Abdul, I sat in the other room biting my nails waiting for something bad to happen. It seemed like forever, but finally I heard the whistles from the women in the hallway and my heart started racing once I realised my sister was in the clear, the whistles meant she had bled!

I cried tears of joy when I finally got to go back into her room and see her. She was happy it was over and she could now get on with whatever she needed to do to stay safe. She told me Abdul had vowed he would do everything in his power to keep us connected not only because he loved her, but because it was a promise he had made to Mana on his death bed. Mana had made Abdul promise that no matter what happened to him he would look after me for the rest of his life.

Yas looked beautiful in her wedding dress and Abdul's family were so proud to have her in their family. They ran around her, just like Mana's family had done with me. Even though Abdul and Mana were cousins Mana's family didn't come to his wedding. They sent their best wishes and apologised, saying they didn't feel ready to celebrate.

On the last day of the wedding I was sat with Yas and Abdul's family in their living room when I was told I had a visitor. My heart nearly broke again when a lady walked in and lifted her veil; it was Saada. She ignored everyone and came straight to me as I got up and hugged her and immediately burst into tears. We both hugged and cried for a while, as did the rest of the women in the room. It was difficult for anyone not to cry.

Saada had lost two sons to an illness she knew nothing about and although their deaths had been years apart, the strain was obvious in her face. After we cried, Saada apologised to Yas and her mother in law Ghania for ruining their celebrations, then she sat next to me, where she held my hand kissing it over and over again. She stayed for about an hour, whispering to me that she had only come because she had heard I was at the wedding and she wanted to see me. That was the last time I ever saw her.

Before I left to go back to the village Abdul promised me that no matter what happened or wherever I ended up he would never stop me from seeing my sister. He promised me he would treat her like his queen and he would give her everything he could within his power; he promised he would never hurt her.

I believed him and although I hated the fact that I was leaving my sister with a man she didn't love, I could see that he would do his best to make her happy. His family adored her and Yas got on well with his sister, who was around the same age as she was. I knew she was safe; Abdul had a house in the city of Sanaa where he was still studying English, Psychology and Politics. Yas wouldn't have to do hard labour, like she would have done if she had been married in a rural village. At least she was now away from our family and the slums of our village; neither Dad nor his family would ever be able to hurt her again.

It was hell living without Yas, especially living in Dad's house by myself, and I realised how awful it must have been for Yas whilst I was away with Mana. Farouse was in Granddad's house and although we saw each other every day she was over there and I was at Dad's.

Dad's temper got worse with time by the day, and I was terrified of him so I tried to stay out of his way as much as possible. When he came home in the morning to sleep, Amina and I would tiptoe around the house, too scared to make a noise in case he woke up. If he heard us doing chores or talking he would wake up and slap, punch or throw whatever he could find at us! He became unbearable to live with. I couldn't wait for him to wake up and leave to go to the fields just so we could get some peace and quiet.

It wasn't long after Yas got married that I heard rumours about men asking for my hand in marriage again, and I was terrified! Farouse would tell me every time she would hear something, because these men would go to Granddad's house to speak to him rather than Dad. Every time I saw a stranger at Granddad's door

I would wait for Farouse to let me know what was said, but as far as she could tell Granddad was waiting for someone with money!

One of those men who visited Granddad's house was a newly arrived Yemeni from Japan. When Farouse and I first saw him we were coming back from the fields carrying water on our heads and he was sat at the door of a newly built house on the edge of the village that faced towards the fields; it was his house!

He watched as we walked by and we discussed who he could be. We hadn't seen him before in the village and he was dressed in a suit. Not the usual wear for Yemenis! He was thin and short and not at all good looking and he had a presence about him, but not a very good one!

His name was Ahmed Bin Ahmed and when he visited Granddad's house I held my breath, scared of what I might hear, but it wasn't me he was interested in, it was Farouse. My heart broke when she was telling me the news but she wasn't sad she was getting married, in fact she had been waiting for this day for a long time. She was just happy that she wasn't being married to a man that would take her out of our village, because this way she could be close to her family for support. She was also happy that she had a brand new house that had just been built. The only thing that concerned Farouse was losing her virginity.

Since arriving in the village, we sisters had played some cruel jokes on Farouse! We were all young and naive but she was extremely naive and didn't know anything about anything. When we arrived in the village she hadn't even had her first period and when she did, a few months later, she had woken up with blood on her trousers and no clue to what it could be!

We had told her that her virginity had burst whilst she was asleep and she had completely freaked out! She cried for ages while Gran was in the fields and we let her cry! She had done something to piss us off the day before and we were getting our own back. Although we later explained to her what it was she never truly believed us, even after we had gone to Gran and asked her to explain to Farouse about periods. Many periods later and Farouse still somewhat believed her virginity had burst that night!

Farouse also had lots of young female friends who had told her many horrific stories about stuff that had happened to them on their wedding nights at the hands of their husbands. The cruel and inhumane ways they were forced to lose their virginity. The thought of marriage didn't scare Farouse; she believed she would come to love her husband in time. It was just the thought of losing her virginity.

Farouse's wedding was planned and so was Yas's family gathering. It was decided that they would take place at the same time. As the wedding plans went ahead so much was going through my head. My heart was breaking for Farouse, knowing how scared she was, and I was worried for myself knowing that my only friend was going so I would have no one left to turn to. The only good thing to come out of this was the fact that my sister was coming back and she was staying for at least a week!

Yas arrived the first day of Farouse's wedding. As she arrived fireworks were let off, gun shots and whistles filled the air to welcome her home. I ran to the jeep to welcome her back and couldn't stop smiling or chatting to her as we ran upstairs! Nebat had come with her in the same jeep and although I was happy to see her too, all I wanted to do was chat to Yas. She looked OK and promised me that Abdul and his family treated her well, but she still didn't think she could ever love him.

Whilst I tried my best to spend time with her I was now the only female in the house doing all the chores. We were at our grandparents' house and I was being ordered about and being shouted at constantly by Dad and our grandparents to do everything, and found myself with little time for my sister. I could see Yas hated it as she watched me being shouted at, but she was married now and had to act in a certain way. She couldn't do much to protect me from my troubles in the village anymore.

Farouse was taken to her husband's house early evening; because she was married to the same village, she would spend the night with him and lose her virginity that night. We wouldn't see her again until the next day, which would be the day she would reveal herself to the village. That night, as Yas and I sat together, we prayed that she would be ok.

The next morning we knew things were not OK when Ahmed's mother came for Gran; the conversation didn't sound good and then Gran went off in a hurry towards Farouse's new home. We all sat anxiously waiting for Gran to return. Every bad thing that could go through our minds did and not knowing what had happened we dreaded the worst: that she hadn't bled.

By the time Gran came back we were all waiting at the front door. "Where's Farouse?" I snapped, looking behind her, but Gran quickly ushered us back inside.

"Go inside all of you! What on earth are you doing stood out here? Farouse is with her husband where she belongs!" Gran said, walking quickly upstairs. We all followed her wanting an answer, we could tell something was wrong by the way she was behaving so I nudged Nebat to encourage her to speak up; she was Gran's favourite and best to ask!

"Is everything OK? You look worried," she asked, putting her arm on Gran's back. We listened on as Gran told Nebat that Farouse had refused to allow Ahmed to touch her. This was causing great concern amongst his family and they had threatened to take measures to force her if she hadn't allowed him by the end of the celebrations.

Nebat now looked more concerned than Gran, which in turn made us worry, so we demanded an explanation. Nebat told us that she was worried that Ahmed could force Farouse into having sex with him by raping her, and that he could be as violent as he wanted because she was his wife!

We had dinner at Farouse's husband's house that day along with the rest of the village. We spoke to Farouse and she didn't seem worried about not doing anything with her husband before the end of the celebrations. She told us that he was OK; she said he had told her he would wait until she was ready. She told us she hated his mum, saying she was a witch and looked at her with evil in her eyes! Maybe Ahmed wasn't the problem, maybe it was his mother?

Farouse looked gorgeous in her wedding dress that Ahmed had brought from Japan and it fitted her beautifully. The afternoon went well and as we left she told us she was going to try and allow him to touch her again that night. The next morning we found out that when her husband tried to touch her, Farouse started screaming and wouldn't stop.

When we went to see her that afternoon she looked scared and told us she couldn't do it. She said she knew it would hurt because all her friends had told her so and she was scared. We tried to comfort her but we could tell that nothing we said or did could reassure her that everything would be OK. After the third day we would find out just how cruel Yemeni culture could be towards young girls who said no.

On the fourth day Al Mouzayna was brought back into Farouse's house, accompanied by another woman most females referred to as 'The evil witch doctor'! Together they took Farouse away in a jeep, accompanied by Ahmed and his mother. We were told they were taking Farouse to hospital to find her some medicine to help her relax a little bit because she had become hysterical every time Ahmed tried to touch her.

They returned a day later, but we weren't allowed to see our cousin for a couple of days. When we finally saw her she looked as if she had been beaten, she was full of bruises. We hugged and cried together while she told us how she had been taken to a house where she was held down by those women and her mother-in-law. They stripped her naked, then tied her to a chair where Ahmed raped her to prove her virginity, and then he raped and beat her over and over again until she agreed never to disobey him again!

Farouse looked different; her innocence had been taken, and her spirit broken! When Ahmed's mother came into the room offering drinks, I looked into her eyes and saw the evil that Farouse had spoken of. I tried to understand how one female could do that to another. This woman had daughters of her own! Did she not worry that the same thing could happen to them?

When we left, Yas and I spoke about how lucky we had been up until then with the men we had married. Mana was gone, but at least I wouldn't have the fear of losing my virginity with the next man I was sold to. Yas was lucky that Abdul had been OK with her on her wedding night.

Once again we discussed our future and what we could do to ensure we stayed safe and together. Yas told me about Abdul's younger brother Mohammed, who was due back from Germany soon and looking for a wife. She wondered if I would see him and see if there would be a connection between us. I didn't have to think about it; straight away I said I would. Yas said she would do whatever she could to get me to Sanaa when he came back so that we could meet.

Once again we wept as we said our goodbyes, and held on to each other for as long as we could before we were pulled apart. I ran behind the jeep shouting out to her how much I already missed her. I blew her kisses as the jeep pulled away from our front door, praying that I would see her again soon.

It had been five months since Mana died when Dad called me to the room one day saying he needed to speak to me; my legs turned to jelly. I was convinced he had sold me again, but I was wrong. He had been sent word from Abdul that Yas wasn't well and wanted me to go and look after her for a few days. I was over the moon; I loved going to the city and getting out of the village. I was sure Yas was OK; this was just her way of getting me to Sanaa!

When I got there Yas hadn't been that well, but said she had played up that she was worse than she was just to get me there. She wanted me to meet Mohammed. Abdul had told his brother I was coming and he was expecting me, although none of the other family had any idea what was going on. We had to be careful not to be seen talking together because although we would pass each other in the hallway going in or out of rooms, we were not allowed to speak. It was difficult because Abdul's house was small and the rooms very close to each other so we couldn't sneak into a room and talk. However, they did have a garden full of lovely trees so one evening whilst everyone was sat inside, Mohammed and I snuck out under the trees to talk.

He was tall and slim with darker skin than his brother and not at all shy, the total opposite of Abdul! We chatted really quickly, trying to be quiet if we thought someone was coming so they wouldn't spot us under the tree. He told me he would allow me to do whatever I wanted and treat me just as well as Abdul treated Yas. That was good enough for me, so I told him I would agree to marry him, and he said he would arrange to come and speak with Dad as soon as he could!

I stayed with Yas for a few more days and then had to go back to the village. I was skipping with joy in the knowledge that

Mohammed would soon come and propose and I would soon be with my sister again.

The day after I got back I heard the devastating news that would change my life forever! Mohammed was too late; there was nothing he or I could do to change anything. Dad had sold me to the son of one of the wealthiest men in the Yemen.

Chapter Twelve
The Wealthy
"Muhamasheen"

His name was Ziad Nasser and he was 18 years old. He lived in one of the nearby villages with his extended family and he was coming to see me the next day. Dad sat me down with my grandparents when he told me. I felt as though he had punched me in the stomach!

I knew as soon as he started to talk that there was nothing I could do about it. Dad told me he had turned down another man that same day that was also rich but was known to marry and abandon his young wives after a while. Dad went on to tell me he had refused many men since Mana died, because he was waiting for the right one. He said Ziad was different because he was wealthy and came from an influential family with status and power!

My grandparents kept saying I should feel grateful to be marrying into such a family. Ziad hadn't been married before and usually young men like him only married virgins, but Ziad was adamant he wanted me.

I didn't argue or even talk. After seeing what had happened to Farouse I knew I couldn't win, no matter how much I argued. After they had finished describing what was going to happen to me I left them and carried on with my chores, waiting for the next day. The following day Ziad and his father came for dinner at Granddad's house.

Farouse was with me at Dad's house; she and Amina were peeping out the window trying to get a look at Ziad. I was sat next to them in the room and they had the window slightly open and were

179

taking it in turns to peep out so they wouldn't get caught looking. Although I wanted to know what he looked like I felt drained, cut off from all my emotions. I could hear them as they whispered to each other and it didn't sound good and then Farouse suddenly turned to me.

"I really think you need to see this," she said, pulling me up because I didn't want move. "I mean it, quick before he goes in!"

When I looked at Ziad I couldn't see what all the fuss was about. He was tall, athletic and very smartly dressed. His shoes were shiny considering he had been walking on dirty dusty roads. He had on black suit trousers that looked like they had just been ironed and his white shirt looked brand new, with the sleeves slightly folded up. He also kept patting down his afro hair that was cut very short.

"What am I looking for?" I asked, confused.

"He's black!" Farouse gasped.

Not knowing what was wrong with his colour, I had to ask. "What's wrong with black? Most Yemenis are black!"

Farouse was quick to point out that I was wrong; most Yemenis are dark, not black. She said Ziad looked African black and that wasn't something they ever saw, not in the villages anyway. She said she had never seen one before, only heard of them. African Yemenis or 'black Yemenis' as she called them, do not mix with what they called 'pure Yemeni' because they say black Yemeni have a difference in culture and pure Yemeni believed they were beneath them.

She told me that they referred to these as 'Akhdam' meaning servants; they were also referred to as 'Muhamasheen'. I was told that they lived as outcasts in Yemen, living in isolated communities that are garbage filled slums!

I assured both of them that I had no problem with the colour of his skin; I actually thought he looked rather nice; it was the whole marriage thing that I didn't want and had a problem with.

I was anxious when Dad came over after dinner with Ziad; he walked him into the room and introduced us. Ziad shook my hand very gently, not saying a word, and although his skin was dark I could see he was blushing. Once Dad made sure we were OK he left saying we had around 20 minutes together. Ziad looked kind of shy but arrogant at the same time, as if he was confident in himself and the way he looked, but not good with people.

He looked around the room as if to admire our house but I could tell from his face he wasn't really impressed. Our house was a dump, what was there to be impressed about? He looked at me and smiled; his teeth were the whitest I'd ever seen! I looked away from him while he looked at me. I could feel his eyes on me and it made me feel very uncomfortable. There wasn't much I wanted to say to him or ask him.

Although I tried my hardest not to, I couldn't help but remember the day Mana came with his family, he and I were put in this very same room for what everyone thought was the first time we met. We laughed and giggled together that day and we made plans for the rest of our lives, now today I was here with this man and it didn't feel right! I didn't know or want this man but he was going to be my husband and there was nothing I could do about it. I turned and looked at him.

"Do you know my name?" I was being sarcastic but I didn't know what to say. Ziad laughed.

"No I don't, maybe you could tell me?" he joked.

"I'm sure you'll find out sooner or later. Why did you want to marry me?" My voice sounded angry because I was, and he could tell.

"Have I said something wrong?" Ziad was smiling when he asked me the question and he didn't sound worried. But if he was waiting for an answer he wasn't getting one. I just stared at him.

"You're a tough one, aren't you; OK, this is why I picked you. My aunt saw you many months ago at a wedding and told me I had to marry you because you are very beautiful, and she is never wrong about anything!" He smiled again, waiting for me to say something nice.

"Do you do everything your aunt tells you to do?" I carried on staring at him, right in his eyes, but he looked away.

"No I don't!" He was getting defensive but he didn't raise his voice. "But I don't have a mother and she raised me so I trust her! Anyway, she knows what I like and don't like and in your case I think she chose very well, she told me you were very beautiful and she was right! So once again she hasn't let me down." Ziad looked at me and smiled. I couldn't really argue with him after he was sat there telling me how beautiful I was. I wished I had someone I could trust like a mother as much as he trusted this woman to pick out his wife.

We started a proper conversation and I tried to be less angry with him. I asked him if he had any brothers and sisters and he told me he did but he really didn't know them because he spent most of his time travelling abroad. I told him I had a sister who lived in Sanaa and who I wanted to visit as much as possible. He said it shouldn't be a problem because at the moment he was working in Sanaa, not abroad, but he would make no promises to how often I could visit.

Ziad obviously took pride in his appearance because he wore a gold watch and gold rings and although I was sat across from him I could smell his aftershave. I asked if he spoke English, he said he didn't but he spoke French and African.

He said that his family owned a lot of shops and houses in Yemen and abroad and were very rich. He told me that he would be sending my suitcases in a few days' time. He said it would be full of clothes and jewellery but if anything was missing that I needed or wanted I should let them know immediately and he would have it sent to me.

After he left Farouse and Amina came in, all excited to find out what we had talked about. I had nothing to tell; unlike Mana, I felt nothing for Ziad.

Yas came for the wedding, which took place a week later. Just 6 months after Mana had died. We were both devastated that things hadn't worked out the way we planned. It seemed no matter how hard we tried, things didn't go our way. She looked thinner than the last time I saw her and it hadn't been that long ago. She hadn't been well for a while but now she had found out she was pregnant; I was so sad for her because she looked frail and she couldn't eat or drink without bringing it back up. Her beautiful smile had gone and, although my heart was breaking because I was being sold, I tried to put on a brave face for her.

I told her Ziad looked OK and that he was good looking and I told her I didn't think he would stop us from seeing each other. I tried to convince her and myself that I'd be OK, but I didn't know that I would. I kept telling myself if Yas could live with a man she didn't love then so could I! As long as Ziad treated me well and with respect then I would be fine!

We were both now married. Yas was pregnant and we were being separated on different sides of the country with no means of communication, so it was now up to us to keep in contact by any means possible.

I kept smiling throughout my wedding. There wasn't much more I could do! The suitcases arrived from Ziad and just like he said they were packed with the most expensive of dresses and materials available. There was lots of gold. It was custom for the groom to send at least one piece of gold if he could afford it. The richer the groom the more gold the bride would receive, and Ziad proved his wealth! All the family wanted to see the necklaces, bracelets and rings he sent. They had never seen so much gold! They couldn't understand why I wasn't excited to see all the gold, but nothing could take away the pain that Yas wasn't coming with me to Ziad's house, or the fact that I didn't know when I would see her again. It could be months, maybe years, and the not knowing was the worst part.

The day I left to go to Ziad's house was heart wrenching for both of us. We hugged and wept and begged each other to do whatever it took to stay in contact.

"Please let me know when you have your baby," I sobbed as we hung on to each other, not wanting to let go.

"We will see each other before then," Yas promised.

"I know," I sobbed, "I'm just saying; remember how much I love you."

"Love you too, Moo," she replied as I was taken away.

Ziad's village was about 20 minutes from ours and as we came to the edge of the village it seemed as though the entire village of men were waiting for his convoy. All I could see were rows of jeeps full of men firing their guns and letting off fireworks. Dad was sat with me in my jeep, but he was of little comfort to me as my stomach turned with nerves.

The village looked bigger than ours and the houses got bigger and higher the more we drove into the village. As we drove closer to the house we went up a steep rocky hill that made the jeep shake from side to side, and as it turned a corner it rocked to its side as if it was about to turn over! I held on to the edge of the seat and held my breath, scared we were going to end upside down, but then it gradually steadied back up and carried on around the bend.

The whistling had started as soon as we entered the village from women who were on their rooftops joining in the celebration, and carried along as the jeeps did. The closer we got to the house the louder the whistles got, as did the gun shots.

When we pulled up to the house at the top of the hill I realised that even in the slums and the most remote rural areas of the world, people with money still had the biggest houses! We pulled up to a huge house at the top of the hill overseeing the rest of the village. There was a big dirt drive for the family jeeps, a drive that was also used by the neighbours who were also rich. Our jeep was the only one from the convoy allowed to pull into the drive and as soon as it did, the women swamped it to usher me inside. Dad quickly said his goodbyes and disappeared to celebrate with the men.

My heart started to beat really fast. With the sharsharf on and the veil over my face I could feel myself heating up as I was taken into the house and up the stairs, while surrounded by dozens of women whistling all around me from all directions! I started to sweat as I was rushed up floor after floor, and by the time we got to the room on the top floor I was so hot I turned to the lady who was holding me the closest.

"I need to take this off now!" I was tugging at my veil.

"No you can't, not yet!" she whispered.

The room was full of women and I really didn't want to start my married life on a bad note by ripping off my veil. "Please, I can't breathe, I need to take it off!" I begged. She whispered something in the ear of a second lady next to her and they announced they needed the room cleared.

Within seconds the room was empty of all but the two ladies that had cleared the room. I ripped off my veil and my sharsharf and threw them to the floor and I heard them say something at the same time but I ignored them. I had been made up before leaving our village so my face was full of make-up.

"You have to hurry and put this back on!" The second lady said to me anxiously handing me my veil from the floor, but I ignored her and continued to cool down, picking up a book from the window sill and fanning myself.

"Just as you said Ayesha, she's perfect for Ziad, the others are not going to like this, she's more beautiful than I thought! Marsh Allah, Marsh Allah! Ayesha, put her cover back on quickly!"

She was speaking to the lady who had helped me up the stairs and helped clear the room. I looked over to the other lady. "So you're Umie Ayesha?" I asked, smiling.

She was the lady Ziad trusted like his mother and called 'Umie', which meant mother. It was nice to know I had picked the right person to ask for help and that she had helped me when I needed her.

"Yes that's me and this is my sister Sofia, now hurry up and cover yourself before anyone sees you, it's bad luck until we get the bochor and unveil you in the right way!" Bochor was used in all occasions not just to make something smell nice, but also to ward off the 'evil eye'.

No longer had she finished speaking than the door flung open and about three women tried to walk in, with dozens more stood in the hallway. It took a few seconds for everyone to realise I was unveiled with the sisters screaming at everyone at the door to go back out, whilst at the same time trying to cover my face by throwing my sharsharf over me!

The women quickly retrieved and shut the door behind them but not before they and many of the women in the hallway had seen me. Umie Ayesha and Sofia were convinced something bad was going to happen to me and spent the next few minutes praying whilst I put my sharsharf back on! Once my sharsharf was back on, I sat in the room with them while the other sisters and family members came in and we were introduced. The others were not allowed to see my face and at the time I didn't understand why. I'd always thought sisters and close family were allowed. But later on I would find out why.

They brought me dinner but left me alone to eat what I could. After that I was left alone to wait for Ziad. I could hear them bringing him from the edge of the village; they had driven him all the way down there just to drive him back in a blaze of gun fire and whistles.

Although I was no virgin, this was Ziad's first wedding and it was a big one! The whole village had been invited to a feast and the food had to be cooked in several houses because the village was big and there was so much food! Everyone was grateful and most of them worked for Ziad's father, or wanted to.

I heard the convoy outside the front, singing and dancing for ages before Ziad came up into the room. When he finally came into the room I wasn't scared but more nervous. I didn't have the life and death situation of my first marriage but more a how-is-this-man-going-to-treat-me? situation.

Ziad barely acknowledged me. He asked me if I was OK and then he lay down in the corner of the room and stretched out on a mattress that was made into a bed. I sat in silence, thinking to myself if I didn't speak time would go quicker! I was happy when Ziad said he was going to rest for a while because he wasn't used to all the noise. I sat across from him in total silence for what seemed like hours but I'm sure wasn't, while he nodded off and then woke up.

When he got up he moisturised his hands and face and combed his hair, and then he sprayed himself with aftershave. Just before he went to leave he came over and attempted to kiss me, but because it was unexpected it went awkward and I pulled away from him. He didn't seem to care. "See you later!" he said as he left the room smiling and whistling. As soon as he left Umie Ayesha and Sofia came back in to get me ready for my unveiling.

They fussed around getting me ready, but when Sofia went to comb my hair she gasped in horror as if she was going to have a heart attack! "Oh dear, sister look, she's caught the evil eye!"

Her sister stood up from what she was doing and put her hand to her chest, also gasping. "What?" Umie Ayesha demanded to know what she was ranting on about and Sofia pointed out that I had many white hairs on the crown of my head; therefore I'd been looked upon by a jealous eye.

Yemenis strongly believe that if you look upon a thing of beauty you should always say 'Marsh Allah'. The old Yemenis say that if you look upon someone with jealousy and do not say 'Marsh Allah' then you are wishing them bad luck. Ziad's aunties believed that someone had seen me when the door opened a few hours earlier, and now all of a sudden I had gone grey! They believed one or more of the women that looked at me when the door opened had looked upon me with jealousy. They were discussing taking me to see a 'medicine woman' as soon as the celebrations were over to get 'the curse' broken. They decided in the meantime they would use some of their brother's hair dye!

I tried my best to convince them there was no such thing as the evil eye and the white hair was just grey hair that I'd most probably got from years of stress. Seeing the grey hairs did come as a shock to me too, because I'd never seen them before and I was barely 14 years old! The sisters were having none of it and Sofia took a bunch of keys from her sister and ran off, returning moments later with a little match box-sized clump of black powder, a small metal tin with water in it and a twig of a branch! They mixed a tiny bit of powder and water into custard-like paste using the twig as a spoon.

I sat in silence as they covered the few grey hairs I'd collected over the years from people scaring the death out of me! As they did I wondered what this woman would be like that was going to 'break the curse', if she would have to touch me in any way, or if she would want me to do any weird stuff. This started to worry me more than meeting Ziad had; I put it to the back of my mind because, after all, there wasn't anything I could do about it.

With my hair dyed, washed, my wedding dress and make-up redone, I was escorted into a huge room next to the one I'd been sat in. Umie Ayesha walked in front of me with the bochor, twirling it around in circles as she chanted some words I didn't understand while the women whistled. They stared at me, trying their best to see behind my veil before I was sat on the throne at the head of the room.

Once I was sat and my wedding dress spread out as wide as it could be to look perfect, the whistles got louder and my veil was lifted! I had a horrible feeling in my stomach as all the women stretched their heads to look at me. Those that were in the hallway pushed each other forward to get a look at Ziad's English bride.

The room was as long as I could see and packed full of women. The middle of the floor was a sea of bodies with hardly any space to move once I had been seated, and they were all staring at me!

Once the staring and gossip had died down, the women made way for dancing in the middle of the floor and the celebrations continued until early evening. When the sun started to go down I heard a big noise come from outside. It sounded like a powerful lawn mower and then all of a sudden the lights came on. I was happy as I thought to myself, "At least they have electricity in this village."

When all the guests had gone, I was surprised to see lots of women left in the house. I thought maybe they were family guests staying for the wedding, but later I found out they also lived in the same house! After everyone had gone I was taken back into the room I'd been in before; this was now my room. Dad came in quickly and said he was leaving but promised to come see me in a few days.

I looked around my new room; it was the top floor room and it had big glass windows with shutters. When opened not only did they look over the village but also miles and miles of hills and mountains in the distance. The room wasn't huge, but a good size, and was kitted out with brand new mattresses and cushions and had a beautiful brand new rug that covered the entire floor. There was no bed, just a mattress on the floor made up into a bed that Ziad had laid on earlier.

There was a big stereo on the window sill with cassettes next to it, lots of them! There were lots of bottles of creams and toiletries all around the other window sills and a few books. Ziad's clothes were neatly folded and hung over pillows in the corner, not a crease in them! I made my way to the cassettes and got excited when I saw there was lots of English music.

Ziad came in as I was looking through his music collection. He closed the door behind him and then came over to where I was stood and picked up a few cassettes. "There's only a few I don't want you to touch but you can listen to the rest," he said as he sorted through them and put a few to the side.

"Why, what are they?" I asked, pointing to the ones he had moved.

"My favourite, I've had them for years so I don't want you

breaking them, you can have the rest, you'll like them!" he said, sitting down.

The rest of that night with Ziad wasn't good or bad. When we had sex there were no emotions or feelings between us. He didn't attempt to kiss or cuddle me. It was just sex, and I was glad once it was over.

The celebrations continued for three days and it was a huge do! I couldn't wait for it to be over because there were so many women in the house; I wanted to get to know who was who! Ziad kept telling me not to trust anyone except Umie Ayesha and Sofia, and I didn't understand why because he wouldn't tell me. Ziad didn't talk much. He liked to sit and listen to music when he was in the room, which was fine by me because he had some good music. I started to explore on my own and find out who was who.

There was always someone willing to gossip! The house was five storeys high and housed three generations of his family. The first person I met was Ziad's grandmother Dobia; she was his father's mother and head of the house. She adored Ziad because he was her first born grandson and as soon as she met me she told me she felt a connection between us.

She was a very old lady who always sat in the same spot in the corner of a room on the second floor. She always had a blanket over her legs, and as I sat and chatted to her I noticed that every-body who approached to speak to her would kiss her on her head, or touch her knee with their hand and then kiss the hand they had touched her with, or both!

Dobia was a big lady who was waited on hand and foot. If she needed to move to go from room to room she would be aided by two women who held her either side. She had taken the title of 'head of the house' after her husband had died just a couple of years earlier. Although Ziad's father, Nasser Ziad, was officially head of the house, being the first born son, he didn't live in the village and everyone knew nothing got done without his mother's permission. Dobia was known for her gentle nature and kind heart.

She had two living sons and four living daughters. Her eldest daughter Ayesha was a widow and now lived back home to take care of her mother and her brother, Nasser Ziad, paid for her financially. The other three daughters were married, two into the same village who were called Sofia and Noriya, and Funda who was married in Sanaa. The other son Ali and his wife, also called Dobia, lived in the same house.

Ali had a daughter from an African woman that he had brought back from Africa and was now living with him in the house, her name was Viyza and she was around 8 years old. She was also dark skinned like Ziad, another of the so called 'Muhamasheen'. Although she was Ali's daughter, his wife didn't look after her; his sister Ayesha did. Ali's wife was really pretty with fair skin and greyish eyes. Although grandmother Dobia only had five children, her late husband had many more living under the same roof; so did wife number two!

Wife number two was the total opposite of Dobia. She looked evil and would sneak around the house hiding behind doors like a witch and was always listening to people's conversations and gossiping. She was about 20 years younger than Dobia and thin with a really red face. Her name was Humayrah and from the moment I saw her I didn't like her! She had one daughter called Nashida, who was a young widow in her late 20s with a son about four years old.

Humayrah had three sons called Hussein, Ahmed and Mohammed who all still lived in the house. Mohammed lived there with his very tiny petite young wife, who only looked about 12 years old! She already had a baby boy and was again pregnant. The other two were still not married, although Ahmed was engaged. Then there was also wife number three!

Wife number three lived with her son and daughter in a tiny mud house that was joined to the side of the main house. She had married the grandfather only a few years before he died and was so hated by the family at the time she was not allowed to live in the main house. She was only in her late 20s when I met her. That meant he must have married her when she was very young, and he was really old because in a picture Ziad showed me of him before he died he looked like my Granddad! Her name was Ulfah and she had a daughter about eight years old from her first husband who had also died, and a son around two years old called Abdulla from Ziad's grandfather. At the time she married the grandfather, she was apparently known for trying to find a rich old man to marry!

That's why the family said they didn't like her; they felt she was the one who had taken advantage of him in his old age. Since his father's death, Nasser Ziad was the main provider for Ulfah and her children. He made sure they needed for nothing and Dobia and her children had become more accepting of Ulfah. Humayrah and her children still hated her and refused to speak or acknowledge her. Humayrah's children would walk past their little brother when they saw him playing in the street, refusing to see him as their little brother!

I soon realised that none of the family got on; although they tolerated each other and pretended to be nice to each other because they lived in the same house, you could feel the tension! Dobia went on to tell me the reason the sisters believed I'd been looked upon with jealously from Humayrah and Nashida when they had opened the door and seen me the day of my revealing.

She told me that months earlier, Ziad's family had approached another wealthy family that lived nearby and asked for their daughter's hand in marriage for Ziad. She said they had been turned down because the father had said she was spoken for. I was told this young girl was beautiful and well sought after; her father was also a judge in the courts of Sanaa.

A while after, Humayrah approached the family for the same girl for her son Ahmed and her father agreed. Ziad's family was furious because they believed they had been turned down because Ziad was black. They vowed to find a girl younger and more beautiful, that's when Umie Ayesha saw me. She believed her mother-in-law was jealous that I was more beautiful than her future daughter-in-law. After hearing all the gossip about this family I'd been married into, I began to worry that I was going to have a hard time fitting in. I wasn't wrong!

A few days after the wedding Umie Ayesha and Sofia took me to see the medicine women. I was hoping they had forgotten all about my grey hair since it was now dyed black and looking OK, but they were adamant I needed to have 'the curse' lifted! We were driven into the city of Rada'a which was about 15 minutes away. I was told it was to be kept a secret from the rest of the family; if anyone asked where we had been we should tell them we went shopping.

The medicine woman was a little old lady and we visited her

at her house, which was a little mud house down a back alley. She sat me down and searched my hair, rummaging through it as if she were looking for lice, while the sisters told the story of what happened on my wedding day, and how my hair had turned white from the evil eye! Of course she agreed with everything they said, praising them for being so vigilant and bringing me to her so quickly! She mixed some horrible smelling herbs in a cup of water and forced me to drink it while they all sat and watched, making sure every drop was gone from the cup before I handed it back. Then she wrapped a bunch of other herbs in a little tiny round cloth and said I needed to carry them on me at all times. They stank! But Umie Ayesha shoved them down my top and into my bra, making me promise I would keep them on me at all times to keep me safe from the evil eye! I promised her I would, if this was all I had to do to keep them happy then I was willing to do it. Even if it did meant I'd stink!

There was never much communication between Ziad and me from day one. He would wake up in the morning and listen to his music while he got ready to go out. Then he would spend ages perfecting his look, matching his clothes to his shoes then his watches to his chains because he always wore a chain around his neck and one on his hand. On the other hand he wore his watch, and he loved his nice watches. He would moisturise his skin all the time and comb his hair every time he came back to the room. He had short afro hair and he had an afro comb that he carried with him everywhere.

If I wasn't busy that morning helping with chores, I'd just sit by the window and listen to his music, watching him dance along while he got ready. I was allowed to sit at the window as long as I wasn't hanging out; it looked over onto the kitchen that was separated from the house and directly opposite our window that was also above the front door.

One morning about a week after we got married, whilst he was changing his clothes he took a big pile of money out of his pocket. "Here, that's for you!" he said, handing it to me. I leant forward and took the money out of his hand. It was so much money!

"How much is it?" I asked, trying to count it myself.

"Oh, around three thousand!" he replied as he carried on getting ready.

"Do I need to do the shopping or something?" I thought maybe I had to do food shopping now that I was his wife. Why else would he give me so much money?

"It's your money do what you want with it, I don't know! Don't women like to buy gold or clothes? Do what you want with it, I don't care!" he laughed. I sat for a few minutes and thought. I'd never seen so much money before but now I had it in my hands, and he's just told me I could do whatever I wanted with it.

"Can I send some to my sister?" I held my breath and looked to the floor, not wanting to hear his answer, and then found myself surprised when he did.

"If you want to, I don't care!" he said, as he carried on dancing to his music.

Ziad would usually go to the city of Rada'a in the morning or just wander down into the village and hang out at the many shops that were down there. He would always come back around lunchtime with something for me, Umie Ayesha and his grandmother Dobia. I told him I liked to draw so he would bring me pencils and pads and bring us cakes or sweets. He didn't talk much to the others in his family; he would just walk past them with his head down. Even with his uncles, he would always give one word answers and try to leave the house quickly to avoid them, or dash in and out of the room when he knew the coast was clear!

I tried my best to laugh and joke with him but I never got far. He preferred his own company. He would give me presents and money for no reason almost every day, but when I tried to have a conversation with him he would put his music on and lay back and close his eyes. When it came to sex he would just take what he wanted and I wouldn't dare say no after seeing what happened to Farouse! There was never the slightest emotion between us. Sometimes he would be rough but not aggressive, and as soon as he finished he would push me aside and not want to speak, and that became our relationship.

The week after the wedding I was taught the chores of the house, and there were a lot! There were so many people living in the house that the wives took it in turn to do chores. It was done by rota. One day one would cook and the others would clean and do other chores, or take care of the animals, or have a day off.

They had many animals, including cows and bulls that needed to be fed by hand. We would have to wrap and tie straw, hay and dry bits of sugarcane together and sit to hand feed them. They would have to be fed twice every day! The family had the means and the money to have water delivered in a huge water truck that would pull up to the drive and then empty the water by hose pipe into big huge water tanks that were beside the house. One of the chores was transporting water from those tanks to other parts of the house.

There was a second kitchen in the house that was sometimes used when all the men were away working abroad. It was on the top floor and smaller than the kitchen outside. It had a huge water tank in it and we had to make sure it was always full so that we could use that water for drinking and bathing.

The big lawnmower noise that I had heard on my wedding day was an electricity generator. We were the only house in the village at that time to have one; they would turn it on at sundown and turn it off at bedtime.

The day I had to do the cooking was the worst; although I'd been taught basic cooking at Gran's house, this was completely different! Ziad's family were rich and they expected everything to be perfect! Umie Ayesha was my mentor and although she wasn't supposed to, she helped me through everything and openly favoured me over her sister-in-law Dobia. Ayesha also helped me with my language because although I'd learnt so much and could speak really good Arabic by then, I was still making a lot of mistakes.

The other family members were taking delight in constantly pointing out all my little imperfections. She could see I was getting frustrated with the others constantly laughing at me; I was really trying to bite my tongue because I didn't want to snap at anyone so soon into my marriage and I didn't know how to argue well in Arabic. I had heard Ali's wife and Mohammed's wife a few days earlier have an argument and they really went at it! I wouldn't have known how to argue like that!

My first argument was a disaster! It was the second time of

doing my cooking chores and I'd been up since 4 am with Umie Ayesha by my side helping me cook. I had to make about ten breads in the clay oven and that was just for breakfast! At breakfast the men had their breakfast served in their rooms by their wives and then we all sat in the room with grandmother Dobia to eat our breakfast. Ali's wife kept making fun of the shape of my breads, pointing out that they were funny shaped and not perfectly round like they should be, they were fat at certain ends and thin at others and not nice and smooth all the way through.

Umie Ayesha and grandmother Dobia were defending me, saying how well I'd done, but the others sat around laughing with Ali's wife. I could feel my blood starting to boil as she picked up yet another piece of bread and ripped off a fat lumpy piece from the end and held it up to show everyone! I started to think of what I could say back to her to defend myself but I couldn't think of anything! Then I remembered all the swear words Farouse had taught us. I leant over and snatched the bread out of her hand throwing it down on the plate.

"If you don't like it go fuck yourself! You fat ugly whore!" I screamed.

I immediately knew I'd said the wrong thing when I could see everyone struggling to swallow their food and all eyes were on me! I looked around at everyone; I could see the look of satisfaction in Humayrah's eyes knowing that I wasn't so perfect after all!

"What? She started it!" I sulked.

Ali's wife turned to her sister-in-law. "Are you not going to say anything?" she demanded.

"Muna, say sorry!" Umie Ayesha looked at me but I just stared at her, my head held high in defiance. "Now!" She raised her voice and I could see she was disappointed with me.

I stood up. "Soorrrrry!" I teased stubbornly, pulling a childish face while staring at Dobia, and then I turned and stormed out of the room and ran upstairs to my room where Ziad was eating his breakfast.

I could hear them arguing as I left the room and I knew I'd need to go back down and finish my chores but I needed to get out of there. As I ran into the room and slammed the room door behind me, Ziad could see I had tears in my eyes. I was angry with myself because I couldn't stick up for myself properly and I'd let Umie Ayesha down.

He asked me what was wrong so I told him what had happened, but he just burst out laughing! He said he thought I'd stuck up for myself pretty good and that Dobia had it coming because he didn't like her anyway. He told me to take no notice of them and just stick with Umie Ayesha; she would teach me everything I needed to know.

It wasn't long after I got married that I got pregnant, but this time I just felt different and I couldn't explain why. After a while I was being sick and showing signs of pregnancy, so the sisters decided to take me back to see the medicine women to make sure I was OK. The old lady touched my tummy and confirmed I was expecting. She made up yet another bag of herbs and sent me on my way. I was so happy and dying to get news to Yas to let her know.

Not long after I found out I was pregnant, Ziad's Uncle Mohammed came back from shopping in Rada'a; it was early afternoon and I was sweeping at the front door. He told me he had bumped into Dad in Rada'a, Dad had invited him back to our village where he had given him ghat as a present. While there, Dad asked him to pass on a message to me. My sister Yas had lost her baby; she had a miscarriage!

Mohammed looked shocked when I burst into tears and ran off. I ran upstairs to the room and straight into the arms of Umie Ayesha who was sat with her mother. I told her what her brother had said and asked her to explain to me what a miscarriage was? I told her my sister wasn't just a little bit pregnant but she was really pregnant, she had a hard belly when I last saw her! She asked me how pregnant Yas was and I told her a few months before I got married.

"Oh the poor child," she said. "Well, it means that her baby came out too soon and it wasn't meant to be!" But that wasn't what I wanted to know.

"No! I still don't understand. Would it have hurt?" I asked. I was still confused as I continued to cry.

"No, she wouldn't have been in pain; it would have just come out," she said, trying her best to comfort me.

I tried to think back to when I thought I was pregnant with

Mana's baby and I was told I'd lost it. I was in pain but maybe that was just a bad period like Gran had said and I wasn't really pregnant. I was sure I remembered hearing once that having a baby was like sneezing, and sneezing didn't hurt! So Yas wouldn't have been in pain!

That night Ziad told me he was going to Sanaa the next day for work. I begged him to take me with him; he said he couldn't because he was going to be busy, but he promised to take me another time. He did promise to take a letter and some money to Yas from me. I sat down to count the money to send to Yas. I had a few thousand rials, which was a lot of money. I decided to split it between Yas, me and Nebat and with mine I would ask her to buy me gold from Sanaa and keep it with her for when we saw each other again; if she wanted to she could wear them. I started to write the letter on some paper that Ziad had bought me from the market.

Dear Yas. I'm very sorry about what happened to you, they told me your baby fell out of place!

The next time I saw Yas was a few months after my wedding at my family gathering. Yas told me she thought she was pregnant again. While I didn't suffer that badly with pregnancy Yas did, and she looked terrible!

She would refuse to eat in fear that she would bring it back up, and because she wasn't eating she had become so thin. Abdul's family was doing everything they could to support her but nothing worked.

The biggest and best news that we heard since arriving in Yemen was that our sister Nebat, who hadn't been able to conceive since she had been married, was now pregnant! She put it all down to Yas and me, saying that we sisters had brought her good fortune and that she would never be able to repay us.

Yas and I spent as much time as we could together. We knew this was a one-off occasion that brought us together, so we snuck out of the house to our mountain. I told her all about Ziad and his dysfunctional family and she told me about Abdul and his. They treated her well although financially it was a struggle. Abdul spent most of his time studying in college and she was helping him with his English studies as well as doing her chores.

Yas told me about the day she lost her baby. She said she was in a lot of pain and ran up to the roof in Gran's house holding on to her tummy and crouching over in pain. It was just after my wedding and she was still in our village. On the roof she said she felt something come out of her and when she looked she saw something small. She described it looking like a small lizard with tiny hands and feet but without the tail. She said she and Gran buried it on the roof under a load of dirt. Yas and I stayed on the mountain and chatted for a while before we made our way back to the village.

I was only allowed to stay at Dad's for two days because Ziad was going to Africa in a few days, and I was needed back to see him off. It was never easy saying goodbye to Yas but we always knew we never had a choice.

We would beg each other to stay in touch and promise to write. We held on to each other hugging, and would always have to be pulled apart. Granddad would even threaten never to let us see each other again because of how long it took us to say goodbye! Whichever one was driving away in the jeep, the other would run behind blowing kisses and waving, shouting how much we loved each other. My heart would break every time I said goodbye to my sister and I'd swear to myself I'd never lose touch with her.

Chapter Thirteen
The Scorpion Bite

Ziad had been taken away from his African mother not long after she had given birth. His father brought him back to Yemen, where his mother Dobia and her daughter Ayesha raised him. He was sent to boarding school in Paris when he was very young where he stayed; only returning to Yemen for short holidays.

Ziad had two younger brothers and two sisters. The girls lived with their mother and father in Sanaa but the boys, Ali and Hussein, lived away from home. Ali and Hussein were in Paris studying just like Ziad had when he was younger; they only returned for short holidays. After leaving boarding school Ziad travelled the world, working with his father in his businesses before settling in Africa where he had been working before coming home to marry me.

His father owned properties and businesses in Paris, Switzerland, Africa and Yemen. He had shares in Hilti, the company that made tools and owned the one and only tele-communications company in Yemen. He also had shares in many other businesses, one of them an oil company. Nasser Ziad was a very well-known and ruthless businessman, feared by everyone who knew him!

When he came to the village everyone would fuss around him, following him around and making sure everything was perfect as if he was some kind of king. He didn't come often, but when he did all the wealthy men of the village would be invited to a feast at our house. A cow would be slaughtered in our back yard and we would all have to come together and cook.

He would hand out money to all the women while they kissed his hand and praised him. Ulfah, his father's third wife, would even go as far as falling to her knees and kissing his feet! I didn't hate Ziad's father, he hadn't done anything bad to me, but I also didn't fear him like everyone else did. I thought he was arrogant and rude, I would just take his money and say a quick 'thank you' and smile. This was to the dismay of all the sisters who would tell me off for being rude!

Nasser Ziad had now decided that Ziad, who was his first born son, was to be in charge of all his assets in Africa. He owned many properties and shops with many workers and Ziad now needed to go to back to Africa to be in charge. Other family members and many villagers were also working for Nasser Ziad in Africa. Humayrah's sons Hussein and Ahmed were both there working for him.

Ziad was to leave that week and was trying to convince me to go with him. He was telling me that over there I wouldn't have to lift a finger, they had servants that did everything. As tempting as it sounded, I couldn't go; Ziad was going to be gone for many years!

When he first told me he was leaving to go to Africa I only thought he was going for a few weeks or months. But when he told me he could be gone for at least two years maybe more, I was shocked! I told him I couldn't go with him because I couldn't leave knowing that I wouldn't see my sister for that long.

It wasn't really Ziad that wanted me to go to Africa with him but his father; he had told Ziad that the whole purpose for him getting married was for him to have his wife by his side. Although Ziad wasn't happy he said he understood, and promised he wouldn't stop me from travelling in his absence to visit Yas. Usually when husbands are away the wives are not permitted to travel unless it's an emergency. Ziad left instructions with his grandmother and Umie Ayesha to allow me to travel to Sanaa whenever it was suitable. Ziad left for Africa when I was around two months pregnant with my first child.

Life became really difficult after Ziad left. I was made to give up my luxury top floor room and move into the room downstairs with Dobia and Umie Ayesha. This room was also the room that was used for gatherings and every other occasion, so privacy became impossible. Wives were allowed their own room but there weren't enough rooms in the house for me to have my own. The room we had been staying in was Nasser Ziad's room and now it was to be cleaned and locked! The house was split into sections for wife number one and her family, and wife number two and her family.

Our side of the family had bigger-sized but fewer rooms. It was a strange setting because although they were divided in so many ways, they still ate together and sat together as if they were one big happy family, but behind the scenes they hated each other!

After I got married I was told every day to wear my make-up and gold from when I woke up until I went to bed; I would also have to change my clothes twice a day. As soon as Ziad left I was made to pack away all the gold, clothes and make-up and lock them in my suitcases where they would stay until he returned. I was only allowed to pick out a few of my worst dresses and trousers that I was allowed to wear.

When he was there the work I'd been doing was minor house chores; as soon as he was gone I was made to do both house and field work. Ziad's family owned a lot of land, way more than Granddad ever had, and it was harvesting time! Although Umie Ayesha still favoured me over everyone else and supported me in every way she could, she had her own work to do.

I would rise at 4 am every day to start my chores, and if it wasn't my turn to stay at home and cook or clean I would go to the fields with the others and work until the sun went down. Whoever was on cleaning duty would bring us breakfast then lunch to the fields so that we wouldn't have to come home. At harvesting times there were no days off for anyone and harvesting came around a few times a year. It always felt as though once we had finished picking one thing, another was ready to pick!

I was about five months pregnant when I finally got to see Yas again. Although I had sent a few letters with Ziad's uncles when they went to Sanaa and was over the moon when she had sent me one back, I hadn't seen her since my family gathering and I was missing her like crazy! Umie Ayesha was going to visit her sister Funda, who lived in Sanaa, and who had just had a baby. She was going to be gone for a week and I begged her to let me go with her, and after a lot of begging and crying she finally agreed!

Funda was lovely, just like her sisters, and after staying with them the first day her husband dropped me off outside Abdul's house the next afternoon. Yas had no idea I was in Sanaa and when I walked in we both jumped up and down in delight and then rushed into her room to catch up.

After I took off my sharsharfs I looked at Yas as I rubbed my tummy. Although I wasn't very big I was much bigger than Yas; she didn't have any bump at all! I leant over to rub her belly, joking around.

"Where's your belly? Look at the state of me, I look so fat and you don't even look pregnant!" Yas stopped me from touching her belly and held my hand.

"That's because I'm not, I had another miscarriage!"

We sat down and once again I listened to my sister as she told me how she had lost yet another baby about a month earlier. She said Abdul had been taking her to see doctors because he's getting worried about her health and the fact that she keeps losing her babies. One doctor gave her injections that she had to take every day for a few weeks.

I was so upset. My sister was going through such a bad time and I knew nothing about it because we lived so far apart, but then again even if I had known, what could I have done to help her? We tried not to let the sad news ruin the fact that we had managed to stay in touch and we tried to enjoy our time together. It was on this visit that Yas told me she had been able to send a letter to Uncle Jim back home in England, and she had received a reply!

She had convinced Abdul to allow her to contact him and now he had written back, saying he was going to save money and come over to the Yemen to visit. She told me she hadn't said anything bad in the letter because she didn't know if it would get read before it got sent, but she just wanted to make contact.

That afternoon we both sat and wrote a letter to Uncle Jim and our families back home. We told them all our news, trying not to sound like we were complaining, Uncle Jim was wise, and we knew he would come for us. We spent the rest of the afternoon hopeful.

We always had fun together, giggling like little school kids and running back and forward from her room to the main room where the rest of the women were. Abdul's family were nice people and would let us get on with it as long as we respected the rules of keeping covered from any men who were in the house eating ghat or visiting the family.

I was allowed to visit Yas a few times while I stayed in Sanaa, but soon had to go back to the village. We said our goodbyes as always, but this time we knew that we would see each other soon because I would have my baby!

It wasn't long after coming back from seeing Yas that I was whisked off to see the medicine woman once again. I was having really bad nightmares about my baby being taken away from me. I couldn't remember the exact dream but my baby was being ripped from my stomach in my dream and when I woke up I had scratches all down my back and chest. When I told the sister of the dreams I had more than once, and showed them the scratches, they freaked out and immediately took me to see the old lady! I knew I'd made the scratches myself because I was always scratching since becoming pregnant, especially in my sleep, but once again the sisters believed there was more to it and off we went!

The old lady really made some potions that day! She made us sit in a dark room and started chanting some stuff that I didn't understand while throwing these potions she had made around the room! Then she sacrificed a chicken and drained its blood and left it on a plate in the room while we all went into another room. Then she made another wrap for me to carry. She told the sisters that dark forces from the other side wanted my baby but because she had sacrificed the chicken I was now protected!

I didn't believe in dark forces or any of the old ladies' talk but the visit really freaked me out! I was so scared of losing my baby; this baby meant so much to me because it was the one thing that nobody could take away from me. It was one person I could love as much as I wanted without the fear of losing.

Ziad sent me stuff every time one of the workers came back from Africa. He would send me money, clothes and perfumes from the shops they owned over there. Every time he sent me money I would put some in a letter and send some to Yas. Ziad's uncles were always going to Sanaa and they would take it for me. Whatever money I had I would split it, some for her and Nebat and some to buy gold for me. Gold was expensive but I could see the other wives buying gold and I knew it was good to put it aside. Maybe one day I would need it!

When his uncle Ahmed came back he sent me a huge suitcase full of baby clothes! The clothes were so expensive and nice, all the women from the family wanted to see them because they had never seen such nice baby clothes. There were clothes, blankets, bibs, washable nappies, talcum powder, creams, hats, even little shoes for when the baby got bigger! Usually babies are wrapped in sheets until they can crawl but our baby would be dressed from the day it was born!

Ahmed had come back to get married, he was marrying the girl that Ziad was refused before me. She was tall and beautiful, much taller than Ahmed and her name was Sofia. She only lived a few doors away from Ziad's family home and the wedding happened a few weeks after he got back from Africa. Even though the wedding was huge, it was nothing compared to our wedding. I could tell that the family was not happy with the fact that Ahmed had married the girl that had been refused to Ziad; not that they cared about the girl anymore, but it showed that they had no loyalties to each other.

The sisters helped with all the arrangements and didn't let their disapproval show, and for the first time I was on the other side of the family that took home a virgin at a wedding. Once Sofia and Ahmed had spent time together in their room Humayrah proudly came into the room where all the sisters and female family had been called to see the 'white cloth.' I was horrified to see them all pass it around and inspect it one by one and as someone went to pass it to me I respectfully said 'yuk' pushing it away to get it passed to the next person before it was handed back to Humayrah. Then she took it to another room, this time for the male members to inspect!

It was about two weeks after Ahmed's wedding that Mohammed's wife went into labour with her second child. Warda was really young and although she kept saying she didn't know how old she was, she looked younger than me and she was tiny!

She was skinny and petite and although she was pretty she wasn't the prettiest out of the wives, but I got on well with her. She kept herself to herself and didn't stick her nose into other people's business, but she could stand up for herself if she needed to!

Mohammed was really tall and because Warda was tiny she barely came up to his chest. Mohammed was an Imam, a preacher at the village mosque; he was Humayrah's oldest child.

Humayrah was away in Sanaa with her daughter when Warda went into labour, leaving the sisters to take care of her. She went into labour during the night and it lasted until the next afternoon. That day was my day to do the cooking so I was home, leaving me to help them with Warda. Umie Ayesha had kept me out of the room, saying that I needed to do my chores and that they could cope without me. As time went by I could hear Warda screaming and couldn't understand why she was making so much noise!

Sofia came out of the room and told me to go in with her; she said I needed to see what giving birth was really like. When I entered the room I saw Warda lying on her back, she was obviously in a lot of pain. Umie Ayesha got up straight away and escorted me back out of the room, arguing with her sister this wasn't the right time for me to be seeing someone giving birth because I was heavily pregnant myself with my first child. She said it would scare me. Sofia on the other hand felt that I needed to see what really happened during child birth; she felt I had unreal expectations about child birth because I kept going around telling everyone that I was going to 'sneeze' and the baby would fall out! Sofia won the argument and I was allowed to witness my first birth!

I was told to sit beside Warda and hold her hand, which was uncomfortable because as she kept twisting and turning she wouldn't let go of my hand, instead she would twist me with her! She was having contractions at the time, which meant absolutely nothing to me. I listened to her scream in pain over and over again, and listened to the sisters telling her to push with nothing happening, so I thought what the hell! I put my face close to her ear and quietly told her to sneeze, maybe that would help? With that she grabbed my hand and bit me! We both started screaming! She was trying to push her baby out while I was trying to break free of her bite! Unfortunately for her, I broke free first!

"She bit me!" I screamed, looking at my hand. Thankfully she hadn't broken the skin because she had bitten the fat bit.

"That will teach you a lesson!" Sofia said, laughing. Umie Ayesha gave her sister a disapproving stare.

"Don't be so cruel, she's just a child, she knows nothing about childbirth. Why do you think I didn't want her in here?" she said angrily.

Warda started screaming again cutting off the argument. As she screamed she grabbed the top of my arm and started squeezing. For such a little girl she was strong! But this time I kept my mouth shut while she delivered a little baby boy!

My visit with Yas came sooner than expected. Nebat had her baby and it was a little baby boy. She had finished her period of rest in Sanaa and was now going to Dad's house to show off her little baby, but we also had another reason to go to the village.

One of our uncles had come back to Dad's village and we were all called to a family feast to meet him. His name was Salah; our family hadn't really spoken of him much. They had always spoken about Uncle Ahmed, our youngest uncle who was studying abroad but not Salah. He was the black sheep of the family and for many years hadn't been allowed back into the family home. We were never allowed to know why, but now he had talked things through with the family and was welcomed back!

I was heavily pregnant and was due soon but nobody knew my due date and Umie Ayesha really didn't want me to go, but I insisted. I didn't care about Salah or anyone else, all I cared about was that I was seeing my sister!

Everyone was already at Dad's house when I got there. Yas and Farouse were at the front door waiting to welcome me. Nebat looked the happiest I'd ever seen her with her little baby boy, whom she had named Neshwan. Farouse looked happy, although I could never imagine how she could be happy with a man who had done what her husband had done to her.

Then I sat down with Yas, who told me she was pregnant again. She had become pregnant straight after her last miscarriage. I could see the pain in her eyes. She told me she was fed up and was scared of losing another baby and she wished she had never become pregnant! She had begged Abdul to allow her to take birth control but he refused, saying he believed she would have a healthy baby soon and he wasn't willing to give up until she did.

Although I did my best to comfort her, I could never imagine the pain she was going through because I'd never experienced it myself, and would never wish to. I remembered how worried I was when I was having the nightmares that something bad would happen to my baby and I prayed every night that my baby would be safe, but nothing I'd felt could feel the same as what she was going through. She had had two miscarriages and now she was worried at the thought of having another. I felt so guilty. I was happy that my baby was OK and nothing had gone wrong in my pregnancy, but how could I feel such happiness that my baby was OK when my sister was in so much pain over her babies?

Dad came in to welcome us to his house and as I looked at him, I couldn't have hated him more! It was his entire fault that Yas was in so much pain because he was the one who had brought us to this country and put us in this situation. I'd always despised my Dad for what he had done to us but for some reason I always wanted his approval and yearned for his love. He had destroyed our family, and now he was causing the same pain to his new family.

Amina was half the woman she was when she first married Dad. She had come to the village full of life and fun, but now she hardly spoke and when she did you could see the pain in her eyes. Her daughter Samira was also at the house at that time, we had met her a few times and got on well with her. She was very young and very beautiful; it must have been heart-breaking for her watching her mum being abused by our father. Dad never physically abused Samira, but he never hesitated to beat her mother in front of her and that was just as bad!

Every time Dad spoke to Amina, you could see her flinch in fear as if he was going to hit her. She had fled to her uncle's house many times to get away from his violence, but she would always be sent back because Dad would go and pay what was called 'binding money'. This is a fee paid to the female's family if she has been severely beaten by her husband. If the husband paid the fee he could have his wife back and it didn't matter whether or not she wanted to go back. It was up to her family.

Uncle Salah looked a lot like Uncle Nasser but I got on well with him. He was quiet and didn't have much to say but he was never horrible to us. Nobody liked him much and it was at this time that we found out it was because he was a member of a group called 'The Muslim Brotherhood', a group opposed to the regime of the government of the time. Although he and Uncle Nasser were both in groups that fought against the government, Uncle Nasser was thought to be fighting for something totally different to his brother and they didn't get on!

While Uncle Nasser had been welcomed to sneak back into the village under the security of darkness and keep contact with his family, Uncle Saleh had endured many years of being made an outcast by everyone. Even Dad didn't like him much and kept his distance from him. He refused to allow him to work in the fields with him, but then Dad had become cruel and nasty to everyone. Dad didn't like anyone anymore.

I went into labour in the middle of the night, I'd been woken hours earlier by something crawling up my right arm and then I felt a sharp pain that made me cry out! I smacked whatever was on my arm, crushing it with my hand then flinging it across the room while shaking in fear. We were all asleep in the same room and as I screamed everyone woke up and started lighting candles and searching to see what had bitten me.

"It was a spider! I know it was!" I cried over and over again. I'd always been terrified of spiders and now my arm had started to swell very slightly at the sight of the bite. "I've been bitten by a poisonous spider!" I sobbed, thinking I was going to die.

"I found it!" Nebat shouted out from across the room.

When she brought it over and examined it she could tell straight away it wasn't a spider. It was a tiny white thing and I'd crushed it enough to injure it but its tail was still wagging. "It looks like a scorpion!" she said, crushing it to death. That made me cry even louder, scorpions were very poisonous in Yemen! "It's a baby one, it wouldn't have done much harm, all we need to do is cut the poison out!" she said, trying to calm me down.

"Cut what?" I gasped in horror!

Nebat had done nothing to calm me down; in fact, she had terrified me even more. Gran was called from next door to cut the site of the wound which had swollen very slightly. She was cursing me for being such a stupid girl and letting myself get stung, as if I'd invited the scorpion over to play! She was also not happy with me for constantly crying like a baby while she sliced me with one of Dad's old razor blades.

Gran made about six cuts, sideways, up and down; all I knew was that they were deep and painful! As she was tending to me Nebat was busy crushing garlic, getting it crushed as smooth as she could to push deep into the wound once Gran had finished cleaning it. Yas sat next to me all the time, holding my other hand and telling me to be brave; I could tell she was just as scared of losing me as I was of dying. Gran sucked on the wound, spitting out any blood that she collected in her mouth. Then she took the garlic, pressing and rubbing it as deep as she could into the cuts she had made, before wrapping the wound up as tight as she could with strips of old sheets! After I was all bandaged up, the candles were put out and we were told to go to sleep, but I couldn't!

As the hours went on I could feel the pain in my stomach and back getting worse and the fear that the poison and gone through my body was terrifying me. I crawled over to Yas.

"Yas I think I'm dying!" I cried, shaking her to wake up.

Yas sat up. "Don't be stupid, Moo, why do you think that?" she whispered.

"I've got really bad pains in my stomach and my back hurts, I think it's the poison," I cried.

Yas woke Nebat up and told her what was happening. Nebat told me she thought I was in labour, once again a very tired and very unimpressed Gran was called in! My labour was slow so the only two that panicked were Yas and I. Yas was worried about me, and I worried about myself!

The contractions only happened once every few hours but I didn't know anything about labour; even though I'd seen Warda give birth all I knew was it hurt and there was lots of blood, nothing else!

The next morning the decision was made to take me back to Ziad's house to give birth there. Abdul was also at the village because he had come with Yas, so he and Granddad volunteered to drive me back home. I'd hoped to stay at Dad's house to give birth because at least I would have Yas with me, but I wasn't allowed. I was shoved in the back of a jeep with Abdul and Granddad while some stranger drove us back home.

The journey was uncomfortable and on the way I had a contraction, but nobody cared. Granddad kept asking Abdul if he was OK because the ride was bumpy, but I wasn't asked if I was OK! As we came to the rocky turn in the corner in Ziad village I slid off the seat to my knees, holding on to the car seat as I had yet another contraction, while Granddad shouted at me to get back up and sit on the seat! I ignored him and as we pulled up to the house I was still on my knees, holding on to the seat.

I was left with Umie Ayesha as Granddad and Abdul went straight home. Straight away she went on about how she should have never let me go, what if something would have happened to me! She got even more upset when she saw my arm bandaged up!

My labour went on all day and through the night and all the next day. The contractions were slow, long and painful and when nothing happened by the second night the decision was made to take me to the hospital in Rada'a. The hospital was horrible. It was small and dirty, and as we went into the room where I was told I was to give birth, I was horrified to see nothing but a long thin wooden table with no pillow or blanket on it. Surely I wasn't going to be asked to lay on that?

The midwife came into the room; she was really fat and middle aged and scared me as soon as I saw her. She had a tone to her voice that made you never want to argue with her; she ordered me to take my trousers off and lay on the table!

I turned to Umie Ayesha for support but she told me to do as I was told, so I did. I climbed onto the table and lay back but it was the most uncomfortable I'd been since going into labour. The table was barely wide enough to take my body and I was wobbling as if I was going to fall off! I rested back to put my head down but I couldn't, it caused me too much pain to stretch my body out so I sat up and got down off the table.

The midwife immediately shouted at me, making it clear that if I didn't do as I was told she would slap me! She ordered me back onto the table where she dipped her hand into some water before doing an internal examination, which was so painful and uncomfortable. I lay back on the table and Umie Ayesha tried to tell me to stay calm and do as I was told, but as she did I had another contraction which felt much worse than all the rest! I got up and slid down off the table screaming in pain, but just as I did the midwife slapped me across the face, really hard, ordering me to get back up on the table!

I started screaming abuse at her calling her every name I could think of, telling her if she touched me again I would rip her face off and much more! I could hear Umie Ayesha apologising on my behalf but I just carried on screaming the place down until the contraction was over. This carried on for several hours and I refused to get back on the table... in the early hours of the morning I gave birth to my beautiful baby boy, Tarek.

Chapter Fourteen
Losing a Child

Tarek was born on the 11th of April 1980. Since the day I became pregnant I'd prayed for a little girl. I wanted to call her Ismahan, Issy. She could never replace my sister, but I would tell her how much her aunty was loved and why she took her name.

When they told me I had a boy I had one second of disappointment, but when I saw him, I could never begin to explain the love that filled my body the second I laid eyes on him. He was the most perfect being on the planet and he belonged to me!

"Pass him to me," I begged as Umie Ayesha wiped him down. She told me to be patient but I couldn't! I'd watched them cut his cord, which had already made me cry because I was convinced he was in pain. Now he was screaming the place down and I wanted to hold him so that I could comfort him. I tried to get up to take him off her but I couldn't move; I was still in a lot of pain and I didn't realise there was more to be done after the baby had come out!

"Stay down and stay still!" she shouted at me, gently pushing me back in the position I was in while handing me my baby to shut me up. "Here take him, but be gentle." Tarek was covered in blood and other stuff and I didn't have a clue what it was, but that didn't stop me from covering his body with kisses.

"I love you soooo much," I sobbed over and over again.

The midwife told me to stay still while she removed my placenta. The placenta is an important part of a ritual after a women's birth and they needed mine intact. Mine was extremely important because they needed it for a special occasion.

Umie Ayesha didn't need to show me anything about being a mother; it came naturally to me from the moment my baby was born. Tarek became my whole world. My child was a piece of my heart and I felt every breath he took. When he was in pain I felt his pain, and when he smiled I smiled with him.

When we got back to the village Sofia and Noriya were waiting to escort me upstairs like an old woman! I'd never felt better and could have run around the village, but it was custom that if you had a baby you got treated like a queen for 40 days, which was fine by me! I was taken upstairs and put in the opposite corner to grandmother Dobia and covered with a blanket while my baby was laid beside me, and that was where I was to stay.

Umie Ayesha had carefully wrapped my placenta and brought it back home with her. Usually it was buried to ensure the mother is able to get pregnant again but because mine was in perfect condition and I'd become pregnant so soon after getting married, mine was considered good luck. Sofia had been married for over 20 years and had been unable to get pregnant. It was believed that if she ate a healthy placenta she would become pregnant, so Umie Ayesha handed her my placenta.

The family were over the moon I'd given birth to a son for Ziad, and although they weren't over the moon with the name they soon came to love it. Tarek Ziad was the name of a great warrior and it was Ziad's choice to break tradition and not name him after his father or grandfather. They were just happy it was a boy and not a girl; boys are loved much more than girls in Yemen and if you have a son it's a sign that God is giving you love and wealth!

Tarek became the apple of Umie Ayesha's eye and grandmother Dobia and her daughters adored him. He resembled the family and they were happy that although he was slightly dark, he wasn't as dark skinned as his father! He was a big baby and weighed over ten pounds! He was healthy and took to breast feeding straight away with no problem from either of us. Umie Ayesha came and fed him cows' butter as soon as we got home from the hospital and fed him twice a day. She said it would make him strong and healthy because it was fresh from our cows.

She also showed me how to wrap him up to make sure he slept well; she would wrap him with a sheet really tightly like a mummy, leaving no room for him to move or wriggle. Then she placed him in a baby basket that was made from cow's skin and shaped like a huge handbag with long strong straps. She then hung him up on a thick metal pole that was nailed to the wall opposite to where I sat; she told me if he cried I was not allowed to pick him up because he would get used to it! I was told I would soon have to go back to work and leave him home with her, and she wouldn't have time to look after him. She handed me a long piece of string that was attached to the side of the basket and showed me how to rock the basket, banging it against the wall to put him back to sleep if he cried. Then I was told I was only allowed to pick him up if he needed feeding or changing.

Yas came to visit me the next day with Dad and Abdul. Dad and Abdul said a quick hello before going off to eat ghat with the men and Yas came and spent the afternoon with me. She sat next to me that afternoon as the room filled up with women coming to congratulate me on the birth of my son. We sat and chatted all afternoon pretending nobody else was in the room but us, while I showed her my beautiful baby.

Although Yas was hurting that she had lost her own babies she was truly happy for me that my baby was healthy. I was allowed to cuddle Tarek and show him off to my sister for a while that afternoon before returning him to his spot on the wall, where he slept peacefully for the rest of the afternoon. Yas left early evening and I wasn't allowed to leave my spot in the room to say goodbye to her at the front door as usual, or run after the jeep blowing her kisses. When she kissed me goodbye I begged her to take care of herself and write to me, and I promised I'd visit her soon. We both cried in silence that day, trying not to show our tears in front of the room full of women.

Things were different now; we were no longer the young sisters who struggled to be apart. Although being away from my sister broke my heart, we had become accustomed to the fact that nothing we did or said would change the fact that it would always be this way. We knew we would continue to fight to stay in touch whenever possible, but we were now becoming young mothers who were about to enter a struggle to keep our own children safe and alive.

Tarek was the light of my life; if he stayed asleep for more than a few hours I would rush over to his basket and poke him to wake him up. I would always get caught and get told off for waking him up, there were always chores that needed to be done, no time to play with my baby.

I wanted to change his clothes all the time, show him off to everyone in his beautiful clothes that his dad had sent him, but Umie Ayesha would always cover him up in a blanket, worried that he would catch the evil eye because he was so healthy and well dressed. He was a big strong baby who never cried and was always smiling, but when he got to about six months old he got a bad fever.

He woke up one afternoon crying, and we knew straight away something was wrong because he was always so good. The sisters tried to cool him down and I left them to get on with it because I had no idea what to do. They had sent for the jeep to take us to the hospital but it was already in Rada'a, so we had to wait for it to come back. In their panic to cool him down they decided to use an old ancient remedy.

Sofia rushed outside and got a chicken, where they proceeded to slaughter it, ripping out its guts and then placing them on the crown of Tarek's head, before placing a woollen baby hat over his head and tying it up! As I looked on in horror, they reassured me this would suck out any fever from his head.

Hours went by before the jeep turned up and we finally got to take Tarek to the hospital. His condition hadn't got any better and he was starting to break out in red blotches. When we got to the hospital we waited in the corridor for our turn to see a doctor. It was packed and I was so scared for my baby I was pacing up and down the corridor trying to settle Tarek who was crying in my arms, when suddenly I heard someone speaking English and I realised it was a doctor. I thought to myself, "If I speak to him in English he will see us quicker." So I walked up to him.

"Excuse me, are you a doctor?" He turned and looked at me; I was covered in my sharsharf.

"Yes I am, how can I help?"

"Please, my son is really sick, will you see him?" I begged, showing him Tarek, who was wrapped in my arms.

To my delight the doctor escorted us to a room. He asked if I was English because my English was so good. I told him I was but I was now living here, then I shoved Tarek in front of him! In any other circumstance I would have chatted for England but my son was ill, and I wasn't really up for chatting.

He didn't question me any more, but he started to examine Tarek, asking questions about his health. He spoke in English, to the sister's dismay because they couldn't understand the conversation, which meant they couldn't butt in, but I was happy to be in charge of the conversation for once. Being in charge of my own son was something I rarely got to do, and it was all going so well until he went to remove his hat!

"I can do that!" I said quickly as he went on to untie Tarek's hat, but I was holding him tightly and he was whining. I looked over to the sisters in panic. "The chicken guts," I mouthed, but they were clueless to what I was saying, and it was too late!

When the doctor pulled Tarek's hat off his head and the guts fell out he got the shock of his life! He jumped back, quietly mumbling something under his breath, going on to joke that he had thought it was Tarek's brains! Then he looked at me, shaking his head in disbelief that I could put such a thing on my son's head!

I quickly pointed at the sisters, "I swear it was them! I had nothing to do with it! You have no idea the stuff they get up to!" The doctor found the funny side in telling me Tarek was suffering with chicken pox, but I'd never felt more embarrassed in my life!

My son recovered well and a few weeks later I was summoned to Sanaa to Nasser Ziad's house because he wanted to see his grandson. Nasser Ziad had been down once to visit and see Tarek and gave us money and gifts. The family said this was a good sign because it showed that he loved him. He was married to a Lebanese woman and had two daughters by her and they were all stunningly beautiful. She was very westernised and didn't cover when she went out, and they had a huge beautiful house with everything an English home would have. Being inside the house you would never know you lived in the Yemen, and when she went out she had all the freedom to do as she pleased, she even drove a car!

Nasser Ziad looked at Tarek maybe twice during our stay and complemented me on his health but didn't kiss him or pick him up. Most of the evening he talked about Africa and told me how nice it was out there, and how I should have gone with Ziad when he left. It felt like he had only wanted me to go to his house so he could convince me to go to Africa and be with Ziad. I sat and listened but said very little, not wanting to say the wrong thing. I stayed with them for one night and it felt strange to sit at a table again and eat with a knife and fork! I didn't want to get out of the shower that evening; she had soaps and shampoos of all kinds! I couldn't get to sleep being in a bed again; it was because I didn't like being comfortable knowing that it wasn't going to last. The next day I was driven by his wife to Funda's house where I was told I could stay for a week and visit my sister.

Yas was over the moon to see us when we turned up at her door, but she was unwell again. She had been back and forth to the doctors but they still didn't know what was wrong with her. We sat and played with Tarek all afternoon but I could see she was struggling. She was pregnant once again and she was still suffering from vomiting. I was allowed to visit her every afternoon until I went home.

She had the weirdest cravings; she craved dirt, red dirt from the ground, and black crumbling coal from the fire! Abdul's family were tending to her every need, almost smothering her out of fear that she would lose this baby too. She would beg me to take her outside the house gates for a walk. "Please, Moo, just up and down the road!" I would always manage to talk Abdul's mum into letting me take her for a walk, promising that I wouldn't let any harm come to her. She would walk with me slowly to the end of the road where a huge pile of red dirt lay besides an abandoned building site. Then she would slowly lower herself, reaching her hand out from under her sharsharf while grabbing a handful of red dirt. On the way home I would laugh at her while I listened to her licking the dirt from her hand under her veil, as if it was the most delicious thing she had ever tasted!

I always hated going back to the village after being in the city. Although I tolerated the women in the house I wasn't close to any of them, except grandmother and the sisters. Humayrah had always hated me and it was because she hated Ziad; although she would never come out and admit it, the sisters told me it was because he was black. They said she felt he had no place in the family, even though he was Nasser Ziad's son he was also Muhamasheen.

She also disliked Ali's daughter Viyza, but she was much more verbal towards her. She didn't racially abuse Viyza outright because that would show she was also racist towards Ziad, but she told her how useless she was and how ugly she was. After all, she was just a girl, and she was only Ali's daughter, not Nasser Ziad's son!

Soon after Humayrah's son Ahmed come back from Africa, she had started spreading rumours about Ziad's behaviour over there. She told the other wives that he was drinking alcohol and taking drugs and that he was bad tempered, she also told them that he was seeing other women.

Word got back to the sisters, who decided to tell me about the rumour. They told me not to worry about it because it was just Humayrah starting trouble, they said she had spread these lies about Ziad for many years. I believed the sisters because Ziad had never treated me badly and I saw the way Humayrah treated Viyza! I decided to put the rumours behind me. If Ziad was drinking I wouldn't be happy, but when he was here I didn't see any sign of it, and he was always shy, not bad tempered. If he was seeing other women in Africa I really didn't care because I wasn't there and as for drugs, I didn't know what drugs were!

Ziad returned early from Africa, he came back when our son was around ten months old. We returned to the top floor room and he was his usual shy generous self; he adored Tarek. Although he was happy to play with his son Ziad never liked to get dirty, so unless his son was looking clean and perfect he wouldn't pick him up. He would take him down to the shops with him and show him off to everyone, he was proud to have a son! However if Tarek cried for his father to pick him up when Ziad didn't want to, Ziad would ignore him or sternly tell him to be quiet. Ziad's affection towards his son or anyone else was on his terms, and only his terms!

I became pregnant straight away when Ziad came back from Africa. It was also this time that Yas was due to give birth to her baby; because Ziad was doing work in Sanaa with his father I was allowed to visit Yas and was with her when she went into labour. She was extremely weak by this time, and after three days of hard, long labour at home, she gave birth to a little girl who she called

Nasseem. We were over the moon with joy that day with Yas's beautiful little baby, and although Nasseem was tiny and fragile, with long jet black hair and big black eyes, she had the face of an angel, and I'd never seen my sister look happier.

Ziad went back to Africa when I was around two months pregnant and once again my life went back to hard labour in the house and fields. I would have to leave Tarek with Umie Ayesha when she was home, but if she was also working in the fields that day then I would have to strap his basket over my shoulder and take him with me to the fields. There was always a tree to hang him on! When he woke up I would strap him to my back with a sheet while I worked.

I continued to write to Yas, who in turn wrote back and told me that Nasseem was unwell and had been for a while.

When Umie Ayesha finally went to Sanaa and allowed me to go with her I was anxious to go and see Yas and her little girl. Nasseem was still tiny; she hadn't grown much since she was born. Her belly button was hard like a lump and she cried constantly, but she was stunningly beautiful and still looked like a little angel and she was still the apple of her mum's eye.

Yas had taken her to see lots of doctors to try and find out why she wasn't growing but they told her there was nothing wrong with her. Even though she fed like a normal baby she didn't gain any weight. Nasseem cried day and night and although Abdul's family helped her, Yas was her mother and I could see she was struggling. I tried to help while I was there but time went so fast and within a few days I was taken back to the village. I didn't see or hear from her again, until I gave birth to my second baby.

When I went into labour I was in the fields working. It was the middle of the afternoon and Tarek was strapped to my back. I untied him and handed him to Umie Ayesha, asking her to take him for a while, not realising I was starting to have contractions. As the afternoon went on I told her I was in pain and we headed home.

My labour went on into the next day and night, and just after midnight on 1st January, 1982 I gave birth to my precious little girl. Ismahan Ziad. Issy was small compared to Tarek; her features were like mine but her skin darker like Tarek. She had loads of black curly hair and huge dark eyes. Nobody wanted me to call her Ismahan, they wanted me to call her Dobia after her grandmother, but I refused. She was my daughter and Ziad had given me permission to name her after my sister.

Yas came to visit the day after Issy was born. I was tucked up in my corner full of joy that I had my little girl at last, ignorant to the pain that my sister was in. Yas sat next to me and congratulated me on the birth of my daughter.

"Where's Nasseem?" I asked, excited to see her.

Yas told me she had left her at home with her grandmother, but I could tell there was more to it. She looked tired, thin and frail, and although she insisted everything was OK I knew my sister. The room was full of women at the afternoon gathering, but I couldn't help notice Yas kept putting her hand down her top. She looked as though she was sniffing a cloth she had tucked inside her chest.

"What's that?" I asked, trying to look down her top, but she pulled away. I could see she was trying not to cry.

"Where's Nasseem?" I asked again, but this time I had a knot in my stomach, I knew something was wrong; I could feel it.

"Please, Moo," she begged, fighting back tears, "I'm not allowed to tell you anything, if I tell you I will get into trouble!" she whispered.

"Let's go to the toilet," I said, standing up and holding her hand to take her with me. I made an excuse that I needed the toilet and that I wasn't feeling well so I needed my sister to take me. Once inside Yas broke down, sobbing uncontrollably.

"Please tell me what's wrong, is Nasseem ill?" I pleaded with her to tell me, putting my arms around her as I started to well up with tears.

"I was told I could only come and see you if I promised not to tell. If they find out I told you I'm in deep trouble, you just had a baby!" she sobbed.

I was crying with my sister because I could see she was in pain, but up until that moment I didn't know why.

"I'm fine, Yas, and I promise, whatever you tell me I won't tell!" However, what she was about to tell me nearly ripped my heart out.

"Nasseem died a while ago." she wept.

I felt as though someone had stuck their hand inside my chest and was slowly ripping my heart out, twisting and squeezing it. I struggled to breathe and my head started spinning. My sister had lost her only child, Nasseem was no miscarriage; she was nine months old. Yas was warned she could only visit me if she didn't tell me of her loss, because I'd just had a baby!

This was not Abdul's choice but my family's and Nasser Ziad's. They decided between themselves not to tell me when Nasseem died because they knew it would affect me too much, and could affect my unborn child! It wasn't us they were worried about, or my precious daughter, they thought I was having another son!

We sat together on the cold toilet floor and hugged each other as we sobbed uncontrollably, until Yas made me stop and pull myself together. She reminded me of the time when Mana died, when I had to deal with my grief alone because nobody else could understand the pain I was going through.

She pulled out the cloth that was down her top; it was Nasseem's dress and it still had Nasseem's smell on it, she said she kept it with her at all times to remind her of what she once had. She told me Nasseem was her child, and although she knew I loved her and wanted to grieve for her I had to stay quiet, because if I left that toilet and told anyone I knew of her death we would never be allowed to see each other again. Our family would surely find a way of keeping us apart if they found out we had disobeyed them! I knew my sister was right, Nasseem was gone, and we could never bring her back, but the pain my sister was going through left an ache in my heart that tor me to pieces.

We left the toilet and walked back through the crowded room hand in hand. I was unsteady on my feet and felt faint, but my sister explained to the women that I wasn't feeling well. Instead of me being allowed to support her when she lost her child, she now needed to support me.

For the rest of the afternoon we tightly clung onto each other's hand underneath my blanket in my corner. As the afternoon went by we glanced at each other from the corner of our eyes, too scared to give each other full eye contact, and too scared to speak to each other, just in case either of us broke down.

It seemed with every loss we incurred, our grief got worse. With Mum we were too young to know about grief, so we will never know how we coped. With our sister we were not allowed to grieve in peace, but at least we were allowed to comfort each other and cry out loud. I needed to grieve for Mana alone, but I got through it with my sister's love and full support. Now with the worst loss of all, the loss of a child, I wasn't even allowed to hold my sister, or be able to comfort her through her grief!

We sat grasping hands, letting the other know how much we loved each other; our bodies were trembling and screaming from the inside, but we grieved Nasseem in silence, in fear.

Chapter Fifteen
I Never Wanted
to Marry You

Issy was around six months old when I was told I was being sent to Africa. Umie Ayesha told me the rumours about Ziad were true and that his father had made the decision that I should go and be with my husband. She told me that although Ziad's behaviour had been out of control, once I was there he would be different because I could sort him out. She told me I would need to be a good wife to him and that I would be gone for a year at the most.

I begged and pleaded not to go but the decision had been made, his uncle Ali was going to Africa in the next few days and I was being sent with him. I would need to go to Sanaa straight away and have a passport processed; I was also allowed to visit Yas and say goodbye. She was pregnant once again. She was pregnant when Nasseem died but hadn't known it at the time. Our contact had become less and less and when she did write to me she didn't tell me about her pregnancy because she believed she would lose it anyway and didn't want to upset me.

There was little I could do to reassure her that this time things would be different but I tried, telling her it wouldn't always be this way for her, and she would be OK. But the strong argumentative tomboy sister I once had disappeared the day she got married, and continued to fade with every child she lost; my sister had no energy to fight for anything anymore, she was just surviving.

I told her why I was being sent to Africa, what Ziad had been getting up to. We both knew there was nothing I could do to change anyone's mind. Nasser Ziad had made the decision and there was nothing I could do about it, but there was one thing about going to Africa that gave me hope: I was getting a new passport!

We discussed the possibility of what I could do if I could hold on to my passport once I got to Africa. I knew Ziad travelled a lot so maybe he would allow me to travel with him, or maybe he would take me to England for a holiday? If not, I'd by that time bought enough gold to amount to something, the possibility of running away and going back to England was never far from my mind.

Yas also had a bit of good news: Abdul had finally finished university and was now working in government, with the president of Yemen! Abdul told Yas he owed all his good fortune to her because she was the one that helped him get the high grades that got him the job with the president. He was now going to be making lots of money and travelling all around the world taking her with him, just as he had promised. Could our dreams of going home finally be coming true?

Then there was Uncle Jim. He had stayed in contact since his first letter, he had tried to come over but had been in poor health. He had just sent word that he would be coming soon and promised that he would never stop with his quest to find us. We both knew we would do everything in our power to get back home to England, with or without our husbands' help!

Saying goodbye to Yas was one of the hardest things I ever had to do. I knew it would be at least a year before I would see her again, maybe more.

She was pregnant again and the thought that something could go wrong, without me being there, troubled me, but even when I was there I wasn't allowed to comfort her. Nasseem's death showed us just how apart our family had kept us. We always knew that once we got married we would be separated, but the reality was hard to take; she was my sister, a piece of my heart that was missing. We promised to stay in touch and find each other wherever in the world we ended up. I knew she meant it; I could always depend on her because we are sisters!

When we landed in Africa it was early evening. I held on to my passport as we checked in, sliding it into my bag as soon as we came out of the airport. Ziad's uncle sat with us in the car that had been waiting for us outside the airport. He chatting away as he pointed out all the buildings in the city of Bangui, Central Africa, telling me what was what.

I got on well with Ali; it was his wife that I didn't see eye to eye with! Africa looked beautiful with bright lights that filled the city. "That's ours, and that one's ours and that one!" He was proudly pointing out building after building as we drove past.

Ziad didn't meet us at the airport, but he was stood outside a big row of shops as we pulled up. As soon as we got out the car he picked up Tarek, swinging him around, and then he turned to Issy, who was in my arms.

"Pretty little thing!" he said, pinching her cheek, which was all she got, but it was more than I did. He simply nodded at me and said, "Hello," then turned his attention to two males stood beside him, their heads bowed as if they dared not to look up. He spoke at them in a demanding tone and in a language I didn't understand, but I knew he was telling them to get the suitcases from the car.

They bowed to Ziad as they hurried to the car, and then Ziad turned around and walked over to some steps that were in between two shops. He ran up them with his son in his arms, beckoning us to follow. At the top of the steps was a long round circular balcony that was the entrance to around 15 flats. The balcony overlooked a huge courtyard that was also where they parked their multiple cars.

Ali stayed downstairs while Ziad led us into a big beautiful flat, showing us the living room which was big and full of brand new furniture. It had a brand new multi-coloured carpet on the floor, with a big settee and a glass coffee table next to it. A lovely oak table and chairs with a vase and flowers in the middle of the table was to one side, and a TV in the corner of the room next to a big cabinet that had a stereo and cassettes on it.

The whole length of the living room had long beautiful curtains that covered glass balcony doors, which opened up and joined onto the rest of the flat, but also overlooked the street. Out on the balcony were a table and chairs, which I was told I could sit on and relax whenever I wanted to!

In the living room next to the table and chairs was a door. It led into another room which was our bedroom that had an en suite bathroom. It had a big double bed with brand new white bedding laid out on it, a beautiful white cot resting in the corner for Issy. The carpet was fluffy and off-white, and there was a big white wardrobe in the corner. The bedroom also had huge glass doors that led to a balcony looking onto the street, and on this balcony were also table and chairs. Tarek ran around excited to see his new home, but I was also excited! "Do you like it?" Ziad asked.

"I love it! It's gorgeous!" I said, excitedly exploring as I opened the wardrobes and ran in and out of the bathroom. I was so excited! A toilet, a shower, a bath tub! I could have jumped up and kissed Ziad at that moment, but I knew he wasn't the kind of man who liked that kind of behaviour, especially with people around, and the men who had brought up the suitcases had just entered the room.

As they put the cases down I approached them to say thank you, but as soon as I did they fell to their knees and bowed their heads! Ziad said something to them and they stood up, and with their heads bowed they walked out of the room, backwards, shifting their eyes sideways so not to bump into anything on their way out.

"What the hell was all that about? All I did was say thanks!" I asked Ziad in shock. Ziad laughed and told me I should never thank them or treat them kindly. He told me they were his 'servants' and they were there to do as he told them to do. He said if we treated them kindly, they would take advantage of us. He said I should make sure they bowed to me every time they entered or left the room and if they spoke to me without permission that I should let him know and he would punish them.

He also said I was not allowed to lift a finger while in Africa; I would have a nanny, a cook, a cleaner, and a driver! Although I didn't tell Ziad at the time, I had no intention of treating anyone as my servant. I was more than happy to have help from anyone while in Africa, but I knew I would be treating everyone as kindly as I possibly could.

Once Ziad finished giving me a lecture about his 'servants' he grabbed Tarek to show him his room, which was detached from our flat; it was right next door but it was a single room with its own door. Although Tarek's room was beautiful with a brand new bed, a TV and the carpet the same as our bedroom, I didn't like the fact that it was detached from our flat. Tarek was just over two years old and I didn't like the thought of him sleeping alone. However I knew I wouldn't be able to do anything about it. At least I knew Tarek was a good baby and a good sleeper, he hardly ever woke up!

After Ziad showed us around we went back into the living room and sat down, and then he called out to the servants who came into the room. With their heads bowed they shuffled along, and once they got in front of us they dropped to their knees awaiting Ziad's instructions. Ziad introduced me to them in their language, telling them I was their 'mistress' and they were to obey me. I'd never felt more uncomfortable as they shuffled over to me, kissing my hand as if I was some kind of queen! I told Ziad I never wanted them to do that ever again, but he just laughed at me and carried on to tell me their names.

He had nicknamed the older one Matata which meant trouble maker; he said he was fond of him because he had been the family cook ever since he was a child. Matata had worked for Nasser Ziad for over 20 years; he also said that if I needed anything I should ask Matata because he knew everything. The other one was younger and his name was Danso. Once he finished the introductions he ordered them to go and bring us our food, and once again they left the room in the same manner as they entered.

After we finished eating Ziad told me he had work to do. He said he would be gone most of the night and not to wait up for him. He said he would sleep in one of the other flats so that he doesn't wake me up! I didn't question him because I was tired, it had been a long day and all I wanted to do was cuddle up to my children and go to sleep. It also meant that Tarek could sleep in the bed next to me if Ziad wasn't coming home.

Ziad went through his usual routine of getting ready; he always took forever perfecting himself and the fact that he had a bathroom and shower only made him take longer! Once he left I took the children and we cuddled up on the bed and fell asleep.

The next morning Ziad was nowhere to be seen so I took my time playing with my children in my room, bathing them in the bathtub that they had never seen before. Tarek jumped up and down on the bed and I allowed him, but all the while making sure he didn't dirty or damage anything, everything was so clean and new! After they were washed and dressed we went for a wander outside the balcony that overlooked the courtyard and I bumped into the servants. As soon as they saw me they bowed their heads and fell to their knees.

"No! No!" I said calmly, trying not to freak them out while helping them up one by one and shaking my finger, trying to let them know I didn't want them to do that. Matata could speak a little Arabic so I explained to him that I didn't want them to fall to their knees for me, but he said if 'Patron' saw them, meaning Ziad, then they would all get punished, even lose their jobs! I told him this would be between us, so when Ziad was around they could do it, but I wasn't like Ziad.

The way I saw it we all needed to treat each other with respect and kindness. I asked him to quietly talk to the other servants on my behalf and let them know how I felt. Matata translated to Danso but I could see Danso was struggling; it was as if he had never been treated with kindness from an employer before! Danso shuffled away smiling, but bowing his head and walking backwards until he was out of sight!

Matata and I continued to walk along the balcony as he pointed out which flats were vacant and which were occupied. He also pointed out the flat on the far end and told me that was the flat Ziad slept in, said he hadn't come home until early hours of the morning because he was working. He told me he usually slept until late afternoon but if I needed anything I was to ask him. I asked him if he would post a letter for me if I wrote one to my sister in Yemen, he said yes and agreed to take it to the post office. I wrote a long letter to Yas telling her all about my new beautiful house and how happy I was!

Later on that day Matata came to my room and introduced a young girl to me who looked in her late 20s; her name was Ayoka. Ziad had hired her as my nanny. Ayoka was lovely and although she didn't speak Arabic or English and we had no way of communicating, that didn't stop us from getting on. The children took to her straight away and we became instant friends. Ziad woke up late afternoon and after he showered and had some food he spent a few minutes with the children. Then he sent Ayoka off with the children while we spent time alone.

Ziad always treated me as though I was a chore, something that needed to be ticked off his 'to do list', and when he was done with me he would always get up and leave. Later he would spend hours getting ready to go out, telling me not to wait up and that he would sleep in the next flat. I just wanted a quiet life so I never questioned him even though I had a gut feeling he was up to no good! This became a daily routine for Ziad, until one night about three weeks after we arrived in Africa, I made a terrible discovery!

It became a routine for me after putting the children to sleep to sit on a balcony at night; Ziad was always out so I would sit alone. In the daytime the front balcony was nice, I was allowed to sit and watch people go by as long as I acted respectfully and didn't hang over, so I would sit way in the corner and just enjoy being able to do so. However, at night the front balcony was lit up by the street lights so I would prefer the back balcony.

On the courtyard balcony at night I would take a chair and hide in the corner. My privacy was protected by the balcony stone wall that had beautiful flowers and plants all along it. I was able to sit in silence and watch people as they come and go between the gaps in the wall and plants, and they couldn't see me! It was extremely quiet and peaceful, and it gave me a sense of freedom to sit outside by myself, something I wasn't allowed to do in the Yemen! While I sat I would often nod off and then wake up later and go back inside.

On that night I woke up at around midnight and as I woke up, I picked up my chair to take it inside, when I heard voices coming from the flat a few doors up. It was the flat that Ziad slept in and it was Ziad's voice, and a female. I made my way over to the flat and realised the reason I could hear them was because the door was ajar they were laughing and making lots of noise, so I tip-toed inside. The flat had a small narrow entrance that led into the living room and as I entered the hallway I saw female clothes on the floor, then I saw Ziad's clothes. My heart started racing and a voice in my head told me to turn around and leave, but because of my stubbornness I carried on walking. I came to a complete standstill as I entered the living room and saw Ziad and a female completely naked having sex on his settee! For a few seconds I froze, and as my heart pounded against my chest I could feel the rage building up inside me! They hadn't noticed I was stood there at this time and I could see a bottle of whiskey and glasses on the coffee table next to them, and then he looked at me. He shoved her off him, throwing her to his side.

"What are you doing? Get out!" his voice slurred, full of rage, while he staggered to his feet, he was drunk!

The female just stared at me, slouched on the settee not even attempting to cover herself! I stayed silent for a few seconds while Ziad struggled to regain his balance, I couldn't find the right words to say! Then I turned and ran from the flat, but as I did I stopped and picked up both their clothes, grabbing what I could, which was almost everything, slamming the door behind me!

As I ran down the balcony towards my flat I could feel tears pouring down my face as I threw their clothes over the balcony into the courtyard. I ran into my living room and sat on the settee, resting my face in my hands I cried. I wasn't jealous of what Ziad had done but I was angry! I didn't love him and I was under no illusion he loved me. He had never once told me he loved me since the day we married, I was purely his trophy wife, but I was furious that he could do this to me!

I knew Ziad was no angel when it came to his women because I'd heard the rumours more than once about what he was like. While I was in Yemen he could do as he pleased because I was not here to see it, but I was here now, so why did he have to carry on behaving like this? Why was I brought to Africa if this was what he wanted to do and why did he have to humiliate and embarrass me like this?

I was crying out of pure rage and frustration when the door flung open and Ziad staggered in with a towel wrapped around his waist. "Where are our clothes?" he demanded, making his way over to the settee towards me.

"Get lost, you can go and buy your girlfriend some new clothes! You have enough money!" I responded sarcastically while wiping away my tears. Ziad came over to me with a grin on his face and yanked me up off the settee by my arm.

"Don't mess with me, bitch! Give me my clothes!" he threatened while squeezing my arm. My whole body was trembling with fear but I refused to give in and, with defiance written all over my face, I put my face up to his, and with gritted teeth I confronted him.

"How dare you do this to me? I'm your wife!"

Ziad pushed me away from him and let go of my arm, then he punched me with all his force in my face, sending me crashing to the floor. Blood started spurting from my nose as he repeated his demand.

"Where are my clothes?"

I gave in like a coward, as blood sprayed from my mouth; "In the courtyard," I choked. I couldn't argue with him anymore, I could barely hear or speak from his punch because my head was spinning.

As soon as he left the room I tiptoed into the bathroom as quietly as I could so not to wake the children. Blood dripped from my nose onto the brand new bedroom carpet and I silently cursed him as I thought to myself how difficult it would be to get blood out of that white carpet!

My face was red and swollen and my nose wouldn't stop bleeding, so I took a towel and went back into the living room and lay down on the settee trying to stop the blood. After a while my nose stopped bleeding, but I knew it was broken; I could hardly breathe and it was swollen and looked crooked. I sat there and tried to straighten it but the pain was too much. I sat and thought about what had happened, wondering if I had done anything to make Ziad behave this way towards me when suddenly, Ziad came back into the room.

He was still wrapped in his towel, only now he was holding a bottle of whiskey with two glasses. Ziad came and sat next to me and placed the whiskey and glasses on the coffee table and as I got up to walk away he pulled me down, forcefully telling me to sit back down. I sat down; too scared to move as he poured whiskey into both glasses. "Drink!" he demanded, handing me a glass.

I looked at him, then the glass. "You know I don't drink, I hate the stuff!" I said pulling a face and wondering why he had offered it to me in the first place. At first I thought maybe he was trying to make peace with me, but it became evident he wasn't as soon as I refused! Ziad yanked my head back by my hair, and as I struggled

231

to try to release his grip he held the glass to my mouth.

"If you don't drink it willingly I will pour it down your throat!" he threatened.

I knew he meant what he said; I'd never seen him look so evil. The look in his eyes scared me, and once again I could feel myself shaking with fear as my eyes filled up with tears. I hated myself for feeling scared, for feeling weak. "Why are you doing this to me? What have I done to upset you?" I pleaded. Ziad looked at me, no emotion in his eyes as he let go of my hair.

"I need you to learn how to satisfy me. I want a real woman in my bed not a child, now drink!" he said coldly.

His words made me angry; if he had wanted a real woman then he should have married one. With a mixture of fear and anger raging through my body I screamed at him.

"It's not my fault you married me when I was a child! Why didn't you marry a real woman if that's what you wanted?"

Ziad didn't want to hear any more. He took the glass and shoved it in my hand. "Drink!" he demanded again. With raging anger I took the whiskey and gulped it down in one go! Not realising how strong it was I started coughing and heaving, struggling to catch my breath.

Ziad started laughing whilst he refilled the glass and handing it to me again, "Drink!" he demanded again, but this time I refused. He tried to persuade me to drink the whiskey, telling me it would make things easier for me if I did, but again I refused. The first glass had made me feel sick and my throat felt as if it was on fire.

He went on telling me how he never wanted to marry me but he had no choice, he would have chosen a real woman if he could have, someone who could satisfy him the way he wanted to be satisfied, but now he would teach me what he really liked. Ziad then picked up the glass of whiskey and gave me one last chance to drink it, but when I refused he got angry and raised it in an attempt to smash it in my face.

I raised my arm to protect myself and the glass smashed into my elbow, digging into my skin and cutting me as it smashed to pieces. While blood poured from my arm, he dragged me off the settee into the middle of the sitting room. As I viciously wriggled and kicked to try and escape his grasp I kicked the beautiful glass coffee table, smashing it and breaking it into pieces, but he carried on dragging me through the glass as I begged and pleaded with him to let me go; he was big and strong and I was no match for him!

All I could think about were the children who were asleep a few feet away. I begged and screamed as quietly as I possibly could. I had never in my life felt this much physical pain. I had pieces of glass stuck in my body and blood pouring from my wounds, but I had to stay quiet, I couldn't allow my children to wake up and witness this.

"Please Ziad, the children, don't do this, please they might wake up." He just kept telling me to shut up, telling me I should have done as I was told and everything he was doing was my fault!

He leant over me, punching me on one side of my face then the other. I clawed at him, trying to fight back but I could feel myself getting weaker and weaker as he ripped my clothes off. I could hear myself faintly cursing him. "You bastard! You bastard!" He grabbed my head and slammed it repeatedly on the floor until I passed out!

I woke up a few times whilst Ziad was raping me, but I felt paralysed, I couldn't move or speak. It was as if he was a beast and it wasn't me he was raping. I closed my eyes and drifted back into unconsciousness.

When I finally came around Ziad had left me on the floor, soaked in my own blood. I lay there for what seemed like forever looking up at the ceiling, my mind blank from any thought, unable, and not wanting to move. I finally picked myself up and quietly made my way into the bathroom, closing the door behind me so not to wake the children as I sat in the shower and washed away the blood that covered my whole body.

Ziad had viciously raped me and he had done so without fear of leaving his evidence behind! I picked out the pieces of glass that were stuck in my body, thanking God that although my wounds were bad they did not look life threatening. My body was covered from head to toe in marks and cuts from where I had struggled over broken glass and where he had beaten and raped me.

I thought about cleaning up the blood and mess in the rooms, only because I didn't want Tarek to see it when he woke up, but he was going to see me, and I didn't know how I would explain this to him. The new white carpet in the bedroom was full of blood drops, but I had no energy to clean it, so I sat in the chair in the corner of the bedroom and silently wept as I looked at my children, and thanked God they hadn't woken up during their father's vicious attack.

Until this night I didn't have any bad feelings towards Ziad, although I'd never loved him, I'd respected him for treating me kindly. This night had changed everything; Ziad wasn't the man I thought he was. He had become like a vicious animal and he had the nerve to blame me because I was a child bride, and didn't live up to his expectations! I knew I had to protect myself and my children from this man; yes he was their father, but he was evil, and I didn't know whether or not he was capable of hurting them.

It was early hours of the morning and the sun was up when I finally fell asleep on the chair, dreading the day ahead. Ayoka knocked at the bedroom door early morning because she could hear Issy crying, even though I hadn't; Ziad had damaged one of my ears and it affected my hearing. When I went to move from the chair, the memories of the night before came flooding back. I could hardly move because I was in so much pain so I called out for her to come in, and as soon as she saw my injuries she rushed over to help me.

She knelt by my side and held my hand, I could see the pity and concern in her face as her eyes welled up with tears. Although we didn't speak the same language we managed to communicate, and I asked her to take the children and keep them away from me because I didn't want Tarek to see me in pain.

Tarek woke up and tried to jump on me wanting to play, but I told him he couldn't because Mummy had fallen down the stairs and hurt herself.

Ayoka took the children from me but came back a while later with Matata, telling me she had left the children with Danso and now they wanted to help me. They argued between themselves for a while because Ayoka wanted me to go to the hospital but Matata was worried what Ziad would say. He said we should wait for Ziad to wake up before taking me anywhere because he couldn't tell the driver to do anything without Ziad's permission. He said he was never allowed to wake him up unless it was a real emergency.

I was helped into bed, where I stayed for the rest of the day while Ayoka treated my wounds and told me she felt that I had broken ribs. My nose was broken, my jaw was badly swollen and I could barely talk or swallow; my face alone looked like a huge black and blue football! She cared for the children away from me for the rest of the day, while Danso cleaned the blood off the carpets and cleared away the broken glass from the coffee table.

Ziad woke up late afternoon and walked into the bedroom totally ignoring me as I lay in bed battered and bruised; he went straight into the bathroom and continued singing whilst he showered. When he came out he looked at me with a grin on his face.

"What's wrong with you?" he asked sarcastically, while sitting on the edge of the bed next to me and pulling the bed sheet off me.

I struggled to speak as I pulled the sheet back up. "Get lost Ziad! I'm not playing your pathetic games anymore; you can go and do whatever you want!"

"Good!" he said, standing up. "Well, maybe next time you will do as you're told. Now, where are my children?" he mumbled, leaving the room. I never went to the hospital, most of my injuries healed slowly over time.

Chapter Sixteen
Please Don't Hurt
My Children!

Issy became sick a few months after we got to Africa. She was always a small baby but healthy, however once we arrived in Africa she was always picking up infections. She had a fever and her whole body had swollen up within hours and she became worse around early afternoon, but nobody wanted to wake Ziad to ask him to take us to the hospital.

I barged into his flat and found him asleep, next to the same women I'd caught him having sex with the first time he had raped me, but I didn't care. I woke him up and he was furious with me, cursing and shouting at me to get out of the room, but I refused until he gave me permission for the driver to take Issy to hospital.

When we got to the hospital Abu, the driver, took us straight in and introduced us to a doctor. As soon as the doctor heard I was Ziad's wife, and Issy was his daughter, we got the royal treatment and Issy was rushed into a private room and hooked up to an IV injection. Although the doctors had no clue to what was wrong with her, Issy's condition was critical and when the doctor told me there was a chance she wasn't going to make it my whole world felt as if it was falling apart.

I sent Abu back to get word to Ziad because as much as I hated him he was still her father, and if she was going to die then he needed to be here with us. When Abu came back and told me that Ziad had told him he was going out, but would try and pop in later, I was devastated! Ziad had chosen his lifestyle over his own daughter. I didn't care how he treated me, but I did care how he treated my children. Abu could see I was upset.

"Not to worry mistress, I will stay with you," he kindly offered, but I knew only too well that if he stayed away with the car he would get into a lot of trouble. I thanked him and sent him back, asking him to ask Ayoka to stay with Tarek because I wasn't coming home that night. I told him I needed her to make sure she kept him away from his father when he returned drunk that night.

Issy made no improvement during the night and the IV in her hand became so swollen they had to take it out of her hand and cut open her leg, and then hook it into a vein just above her ankle before stitching it up. It broke my heart seeing her lying there in the hospital bed lifeless, while her father was out not giving his daughter a second thought!

Ziad stumbled into hospital in the early hours of the morning drunk, hurling abuse at the doctor that was treating Issy. I sat next to my daughter in silence, too embarrassed to speak as he warned the doctor that if his daughter died he would sack him. He drunkenly bragged about how he owned the hospital and most of Africa, and then he left without even looking at his daughter or speaking to me.

After Ziad left I apologised to the doctor, who told me that I didn't need to apologise on Ziad's behalf; he said they were used to his ignorance. I asked what Ziad meant about owning the hospital and he told me that although he didn't own the hospital, Ziad's family donated a lot of money to the hospital, therefore received top privileges in the hospital, and most of Bangui. The doctor told me that although there wasn't much he himself could do about it, he was becoming tired of Ziad and his behaviour.

That night as I slept next to my daughter in hospital I had a terrible nightmare. I dreamt that I was bathing her in the bathtub back at the flat and as the water emptied she was being sucked down the plughole with the water. I was screaming in my sleep as I struggled and struggled to pull her out, and when I awoke I was still struggling to pull her out. I couldn't go back to sleep that night too scared of what might happen to her in my dream if it came back!

Over the next few days, the IV in her leg became so infected it left her with no flesh around her ankle and a deep scar for life, but she pulled through. She stayed in hospital for a week. Her father didn't visit her again after the first night.

I'd written a few letters to Yas and spoken to her on the phone, but I decided not to tell her what Ziad had been doing to me. I knew how badly it would affect her especially so late into her pregnancy. When she finally told me she had a baby girl who she had called Ghania after Abdul's mother, I was over the moon! Ghania was healthy in every way possible and she had no problems growing like Nasseem had.

I knew Yas was busy now that she was the wife of a diplomat, but I needed her help. One afternoon I rang her from my flat. I didn't do it too often because Ziad had warned me not to use the phone, but I needed to speak to her. I didn't go into full detail but I told her that Ziad was drinking and seeing other women, that he was becoming violent and that I was in trouble; I told her I wanted to come back to the Yemen.

Yas knew things must have been bad for me to say that I wanted to come back to Yemen, but she told me not to. She told me that Uncle Jim had visited her in Yemen; there was nothing he could do for us anymore because now we had children of our own. She said if we ever wanted to go back to England we would have to leave our children behind unless their father gave us permission to take them.

Yas reminded me that I had my passport with my children on it and told me to try and see if I could get a ticket and escape, anywhere, as long as it wasn't back to the Yemen. Both Yas and I knew we would never leave the Yemen without our children, even if it meant that we were being abused for the rest of our lives! We had grown up without a mother and would never allow that to happen to our children, but we had also lived in Yemen, and come to realise that if we allowed our children to grow up there, then they would be abused just like we had been!

I knew I couldn't go out and look for a ticket because I wasn't allowed out alone, and I'd begun to lose trust in Matata; I was starting to suspect that he told Ziad what the other servants got up to so that he would look good, but I trusted Ayoka.

I could see in her eyes that even though she was terrified of Ziad, she hated him enough to help us because she loved me and the children. I always gave her extra money and gifts because I knew she was poor and I loved the way she protected and looked after my children; I knew she would help me.

One day I sat down with her in my bedroom and showed her my passport. Once again we communicated as we always did and she understood me when I told her I needed a ticket to run away. Ayoka was excited when she took my passport and looked at it, laughing as she made sounds like an airplane flying high, until she looked at the date, my passport was only valid for six months, and the expiry date had passed.

I wasn't able speak to Yas on the phone anymore because Ziad had violently beat me with it during one of his vicious attacks, after he found out I'd used it to call my sister. His attacks had become more frequent, more violent, and I was spending more and more days held up in bed.

I'd also sent loads of letters to Yas through the post office with Matata but had no reply, and Ayoka told me she suspected they were given back to Ziad. This was because Nasser Ziad part owned the post office in Bangui, something I'd never known before! I was stuck.

Unable to communicate with my sister I had no hope of getting out of Africa, or letting her know how much trouble I was in. Ayoka told me she might be able to send a letter for me through the post office. She said the people at the post office didn't know her, therefore they wouldn't suspect the letter was from me. I wrote two letters, one to Yas, and one to Dad, both addressed to Yas asking her to pass Dad's on to him.

I'd sent Dad letters before but he never sent me one back so this time I begged him to come for me or to at least send me a passport! I knew he was violent and cruel himself, but I was convinced once he knew that Ziad was hurting me he would come and rescue me, after all I was his daughter!

Ayoka took the letters and went to the post office, and later she happily returned and told me she had sent them without anyone suspecting. A few days later when Ayoka didn't turn up for work I asked Danso where she was. He told me Ziad had found out she had sent a letter for me through the post office; he said she had been badly beaten but he wouldn't tell me by whom. I was devastated! I asked Danso to help me contact her but he refused because he was too scared. So was Abu, and Matata insisted he didn't know where she lived.

Ziad and I argued about her because I knew he was behind it, but he denied knowing the reason why she didn't turn up for work. A new nanny was brought in, but we didn't have the same bond as I did with Ayoka.

Ayoka and I would play with the children and she would hang out in my room with me and listen to music. I would lend her make-up and jewellery and she was the one who tended to my wounds every time Ziad raped and beat me. Losing her was like losing a best friend.

It seemed like any company was better than no company after Ayoka left, so when a couple of strangers turned up on my door one day wanting to come in I was open for discussion. First of all I didn't know how to talk to them; they were talking French, the language that most people spoke in Bangui after the native language. Although I'd learnt a little French I couldn't speak well so I told them that I couldn't understand them. They were showing me leaflets, something to do with God, but I didn't have a clue what they were saying. "English! I speak English!" I said as they babbled on.

That was the first time I'd ever met a Jehovah's Witness! One of them pulled out a little leaflet from his bag, it was in English and I snatched it from his hand as if it was precious, because to me it was. I hadn't seen an English book in years! He told me in broken English how he would be back tomorrow with someone who could speak good English.

"Make sure you do please, they have to be female or I will get in trouble and bring books, lots of books!" I pleaded.

I wasn't religious and never would be, but I hadn't been allowed to read English books since coming from England, so the thought of being able to sit down and chat to someone in English for a while put a smile on my face. That night I sat on the balcony and read the little leaflet. It was a story about Jehovah and the last days

240

on Earth, how heaven was such a lovely place. I had no idea who Jehovah was, but I was sure I was about to find out!

The next day two females turned up with lots of small leaflets, and one big book, the Bible. All I wanted to do was to sit and chat but they were there for a reason, to spread the word of God! If I wanted them to continue with their visits then I needed to start studying the Bible, which was fine by me, because I had nothing better to do in Africa!

That's when I started studying the Bible as a Jehovah's Witness. I didn't do it because I believed in God or wanted to; I did it because I wanted the English books and English conversation. They visited me twice a week and even when Ziad found out he just laughed at me, but allowed them to visit because they posed no threat to him.

At first I didn't take the lessons they offered seriously, but when I started to realise they could offer me a way to escape Ziad, I became engrossed in Bible studies. Jehovah's Witnesses were not scared of Ziad or Nasser Ziad's empire, because they had their own empire. The only thing they feared was God. So when they told me I could take my children and leave Ziad and join them, I was willing to do whatever it took!

They told me as long as I passed my Bible studies and pledged my life to God I would be under their protection. I could walk out of my life with Ziad and there was nothing he or anyone else could do about it, but it was hard work, and it would take years because I had to read and learn the entire Bible! I was willing to do whatever it took to escape the life we were in.

I was promised my children wouldn't have to become Jehovah's Witnesses; once they grew up it would be their own choice. There was a lot in their beliefs I didn't agree with, a lot in religion itself I hated, but I didn't hate it as much as the life my children and I were living! I figured once I'd escaped Ziad, I could most probably escape them. I was willing to try!

Ali, Ziad's uncle, had been living in one of the flats since we both arrived in Africa; I hardly saw him around because he worked long hours and turned a blind eye when he saw me black and blue. Now his wife Dobia was arriving in Africa to live in the flat next door, and although I'd never got on with her in Yemen I was happy she was coming. I was lonely and needed company.

When Dobia turned up we put the past behind us and started getting along, she brought me a letter from Yas, the letter Ayoka had posted did get through, Ziad must have found out too late! Yas told me Dad was sorting things out, and for me not to worry. She also told me she was pregnant again, and she was going to England for a holiday.

Although she was happy about going to England the news was also sad, because Yas told me she wasn't planning on running away once she got there, she couldn't live in England knowing I was still suffering. I knew Yas and I had planned to escape one day and get back home, and I wished I could have contacted her to tell her to take her chance while she could, but I also knew nothing I could say would change her mind.

Dobia told me that Umie Ayesha had heard the rumours about what Ziad was still doing over here and wasn't happy. Maybe Umie Ayesha did think she knew what Ziad was up to, but she didn't know the whole truth, nobody did! I didn't tell Dobia the whole story, just that Ziad beat me; it was embarrassing, humiliating and degrading, and I could never fully speak to anyone about the real horrors of what Ziad did to me when he raped me, not even to my own sister.

By the time Dobia arrived, Ziad had left me alone because I'd found out I was pregnant. First of all he didn't care and the abuse carried on until I started to get big, then he told me I disgusted him and he left me alone.

When she arrived I was around seven months pregnant and my belly was huge! It was a miracle the baby had survived in the first place after the abuse Ziad put me through. I'd gone to the hospital a few times through my pregnancy for check-ups because of complications and the doctors had seen the bruising and commented, but I'd always made excuses, even if I did tell someone, nobody could help me.

I was about two weeks into my eighth month when I was rushed into hospital after Ziad beat me. He had come home drunk as usual and I was in the kitchen getting something. I'd had problems with my pregnancy because I was constantly being sick and the doctors told me I had too much fluid around my baby and the baby didn't have much room to move around. Ziad was arguing and I tried to walk away from him but he pushed me to the floor and started kicking me. I tried to curl up to protect my baby the best I could but I was huge, then after a few kicks he walked off, leaving me in agony on the kitchen floor.

I went back to my room and stayed up until the next morning in pain, and then I went and woke Dobia and told her what had happened. She immediately got the driver and rushed me to hospital. After I was examined the doctor told me I needed to be induced because my baby was in distress. I wasn't in labour at the time, but he was worried Ziad may have damaged the baby and it was safer for both of us for labour to be induced as soon as possible. Dobia went back to tell Ziad what had happened. I knew he wouldn't care but he still needed to be told because he was my husband, but just as I thought, he was asleep and didn't care. She told the nanny to take care of the children as I wouldn't be home that night, Dobia stayed with me in hospital as the doctor started my labour.

The doctors monitored me throughout my labour, they told me all the way through that it was going to be difficult as my baby failed to turn, and I was in labour until the next afternoon.

Sadig was a breach baby; he was born on 8th September, 1984. Dobia screamed in horror whilst he was being born, backing up against the corner because she feared I'd given birth to a beast!

"It's nothing to worry about," the doctor told her as he wiped the hair from his eyes, "It's just hair!" Then he quickly showed us Sadig who was covered from head to toe in a carpet of jet black hair!

My baby was rushed away to a private room, where he was placed in an incubator. Ziad didn't come to the hospital when his son was born. I was the one who decided to call my baby Sadig because it means 'truthful' in Arabic.

Sadig was allowed home after three days, and even after everything his father had put him through while he was still in my womb, he was a beautiful, big and strong baby.

The abuse started within weeks of me giving birth to Sadig. I was drained of energy and couldn't understand why he couldn't leave me alone and go to his other women. I wasn't what he wanted, yet he took pleasure in torturing me. In the past he would get ready to go out, then tell me to be ready and be waiting for him when he got back, which would be early hours of the morning.

Most nights I would hear him bring other women back to his flat, but I would sit on the settee waiting in fear for him to finish with her, and then come for me. I never once heard him beat them, they would always leave laughing as they bid him farewell on the stairs. It was only me he enjoyed abusing and degrading. He would bring the whiskey with him; I hated it but it numbed the pain so I would gulp it down, the quicker the better! I didn't plead with him anymore because I didn't want to give him the satisfaction of knowing he was hurting me. He tried his best to get a reaction from me, I could see it with every punch, kick, degrading and despicable thing he did to me that he wanted me to beg him to stop, but I didn't, I wouldn't. I knew no matter how much I begged he would never show me mercy.

When the abuse started up again I couldn't take it anymore, Sadig was only a few weeks old and not sleeping well so I'd asked Dobia to have him for the night. I made the excuse that I wasn't feeling well, but in reality I knew that Sadig would most probably wake up while I was being abused, and I wouldn't be able to go and comfort him. Ziad turned up and started insisting I drink the whiskey but I told him I didn't need whiskey for him to rape or beat me anymore; I was immune to his pain.

"Just get on with it," I insisted, "Nothing you do to me can hurt me anymore!" I was so wrong!

Ziad stared at me and coldly said, "Well that's not true is it? There is one thing I could do to hurt you!" My heart started racing as he stood up and headed for the bedroom where the children were sleeping. I tried to run after him but he kicked me in the stomach taking my breath away. I continued grabbing at his clothes whilst being dragged behind him into the bedroom.

"Please!" I begged, "I'm sorry, I will do anything you want, anything! I promise!" However, I knew he wouldn't stop; he yanked Tarek from his bed, pulling him by his arm and throwing him from the bedroom into the living room.

As I tried to grab hold of our son Ziad punched me again, sending me crashing to the floor of the bedroom as he took the key from the door, pulling it behind him and locking him and our son in the living room.

I could hear Tarek crying as I crawled over and put my eye to the keyhole. He had turned the key so I could see through and I could see them, he was yelling at his son for crying, and then suddenly he punched him. I heard Tarek scream and it was as if someone was slowly sticking a knife though my heart!

"Ziad, stop! That's enough! He's your son! You're scaring him, he's just a child!" I pleaded with him through the keyhole, sobbing while slapping my head over and over again! Why? Why? Why was I so stupid? Why couldn't I just do as I was told? I hated myself for allowing this monster to do this to my baby!

I didn't know what to do. I thought about going and waking Dobia and her husband but I knew they wouldn't be able to protect us from Ziad tomorrow night, or the night after, we were alone in this fight.

"Tarek, baby, it's OK!" I tried to sound calm as I talked to Tarek through the keyhole. "Daddy's just playing a silly game, please don't cry baby, just do as Daddy tells you."

I watched Ziad as he lifted Tarek and placed him on the dining table next to the flower pot; he was warning him to sit and be still, not to move or fall asleep unless he told him to while he lay on the settee.

I was hopeful, I knew once Ziad laid down he wouldn't get back up, he never did, he would soon be asleep! Tarek was weeping, but quietly out of fear from his father. I opened the balcony door and ran over to the living room balcony; I was praying the balcony door would be open even though I knew I always locked it. I tried the other door that led to the courtyard balcony but Ziad had locked that one as well, I went back and sat next to the keyhole. With Issy fast asleep I sat with my eye up to the keyhole for about ten minutes, whispering to my baby to be brave, but how could I tell my five year old child to be brave, when I was terrified myself?

I felt, and was, helpless, as I watched him struggle to stay awake because his father had told him he had to. Tarek sat in total silence until finally I could hear Ziad snoring and I knew it was safe to do something, so I finally convinced him to move off the table.

He was terrified, shivering. I convinced him to come over to the door and quietly take out the key and pass it to me under the door. I quietly opened the door, I picked him up and placed him on the bed while I locked the door from inside the bedroom. I then went to hold Tarek in my arms, to comfort him, but his father had done more damage than I'd realised. He had punched him so hard in the shoulder he had dislocated it, his shoulder was drooping, hanging and swollen, he couldn't move it!

I gently picked him up in my arms and ran over to Dobia's room where I tapped gently on the door, fearful that I would also awake Ziad. Ali answered the door; he was shocked to see me holding Tarek in my arms and at first thought he had fallen out of bed. Dobia went and got Issy and brought her back to her flat while I told Ali what Ziad had done to his son. He was furious and wanted to go and drag him off the settee and confront him, but we persuaded him that at that moment Tarek needed help, we needed to go to the hospital; he could deal with Ziad later.

Dobia stayed with the children while Ali took us to hospital, it was heart-breaking to see what Ziad had done to his own son. Because of his age, Tarek was put under general anaesthetic to have his shoulder fixed; we returned from the hospital the next afternoon.

Although Ali had a word with Ziad he convinced him it was all a misunderstanding, something that got blown out of proportion! Ziad thought it funny that his son dislocated his shoulder. He refused to take the blame or apologise to his son, he thought that if he bought him lots of presents Tarek would forgive and forget, but Tarek had seen too much.

When we first moved to Africa Tarek adored his father; he would run up to him when he saw him come home, and he would cry when he left. Tarek was very young but very clever, he was in private school in Africa and the short time we lived there had learnt to speak French and African, and although he wasn't fluent, he could get by. He woke up many mornings and found me black and blue and unable to move from my bed, and although I tried my best to make excuses for my injuries, there are only so many excuses one can make to a child before the truth becomes apparent!

Tarek started to cling on to me and fear his father; he hid when he saw him coming, and cried when Ziad tried to pick him up!

One afternoon, after Ziad had shouted at his son for being a 'mummy's boy', Tarek took a box of matches from the kitchen and went into his bedroom and closed the door. He set fire to his bedding while he was sat inside. Danso smelt the fire and opened the door, the bedroom was on fire and Tarek was curled up in the corner. Danso ran through the flames and grabbed Tarek!

I was in Dobia's flat with no idea what was going on outside. We heard loud voices and ran out to the balcony to see what was happening; smoke was everywhere and there were people running around, and then I saw Danso running towards me with Tarek in his arms.

"Tell Daddy I don't want my bedroom or toys anymore!" Tarek told me when Danso passed him over. I was crying with joy as I cuddled and kissed him; he was OK, but I knew his father would be furious with him.

The bedroom was totally ruined, burnt; Ziad had gone out at the time but I knew he would be back soon and I was terrified of what he would do to his son. Dobia decided to take him to one of her friends' houses. She had been to Africa many times and had more freedom than I did, and she had friends outside of the flats. She took all the children and left, she promised that if she came back that night she wouldn't bring the children back to my flat or let their father know where they were. She would leave me alone to deal with Ziad.

Ziad came back around 8 pm to get ready to go out and found out what had happened, as I thought he would be he was fuming and came looking for his son to punish him. We started arguing and I thought that because he was still sober and hadn't been out drinking at that time, that maybe I could talk some sense to into him. I tried to explain to him that his behaviour towards his children was becoming out of control, and that it was affecting his relationship with them. I also told him Tarek was seeing what he was doing, and that was why he set fire to his bedroom and toys, because he was angry with him. But Ziad didn't want to listen.

That night Ziad beat me so badly he left me nearly crippled. When Dobia came back from her friend's, hours later, she found me on the floor semi-conscious. She had left the children with her friend. I was rushed to hospital where my neck was put in a brace, my arms and legs in casts; I had multiple injuries and I stayed in hospital for a week.

By some miracle I found out I was pregnant and the baby was unharmed! I suppose it had become instinct to curl up into a ball when Ziad beat me, maybe this had saved my baby.

The next day Ali came to the hospital, he told me that he had spoken to Ziad and made it clear to him that if he touched me or the children ever again he would send word back to Nasser Ziad. Although I was hopeful that this would be the last time Ziad abused me or my children, I knew in my heart that there was nothing Ali or anyone else could do to stop Ziad; he wasn't someone to reason with. This latest attack was proof of that. The only person that could save me and my children was me!

When Ali's mother became ill he decided to take his wife and go back to Yemen. Grandmother Dobia had been ill for a while but now it was her final days and he wanted to be with his mother.

Dobia and I had become close during her short stay and I would miss her terribly. I wrote yet another letter to Yas and one to Dad begging for help. I knew this one would get through; I'd written many letters with family members and men who worked in the shops that came and went to Yemen, but I never really knew which ones got through. At least I could trust Dobia to hand this one to Yas herself, she had seen with her own eyes what Ziad was doing, some of it anyway, and she didn't like it!

After Dobia left I survived like I did before she first arrived, alone. I protected my children the best I could while Ziad carried on with his abuse whenever and however he felt like it!

When Sadig was nine months old the nanny left a big pot of boiling coffee on the cabinet table, while Sadig was just learning to walk. He was a big, chubby baby. He pulled the coffee over himself from his head down and was rushed into hospital with horrific burns; the skin on his ear, shoulder and chest melted off and he was in hospital for weeks having treatment. Of course his father was asleep when it happened but gave us permission to use the driver, but Ziad never once visited.

When I was eight months pregnant with my fourth child, Dad finally turned up in Africa. I was so happy seeing my father had finally come to my rescue! I had no idea he was coming but I had noticed a big change in Ziad's behaviour for a few weeks. He hadn't raised his voice or finger to any of us, and although I was always the optimistic, as soon as I saw Dad I knew Ziad had known he was coming, he just didn't tell us.

Instead of coming to rescue us, Dad and Ziad became best buddies. Ziad would take Dad out and show him around, he bought him new clothes, a watch, told him he could choose whatever he wanted from the shops to take home as presents! Ziad behaved like the dutiful son-in-law and loving husband in front of Dad, and nothing I said made any difference!

Dad called me a trouble maker, he said I always had a big mouth; he said I should listen to my husband and do as I'm told! Ziad told him there was no need to take me back with him; because once the baby was born we were both going back. Dad stayed for a few weeks and left, without me. I was in my last month of pregnancy when Dad left, I weighed under eight stone.

Ziad turned up at the hospital in the early hours of the morning while I was in labour; he was drunk, swaying all over the place and hurling abuse at the staff. I was in a private room and there was an empty bed in the room, he eventually climbed into the bed and fell asleep. When the doctor turned up he asked me if I wanted him removed, but I said no, leave him alone, he's not bothering me. The hospital was a small one and I'd been there many times from injuries and so had the children; the staff had all seen what Ziad was really like and had become tired of his behaviour. Although most of the local staff was scared of him, some of the doctors were foreign and didn't fear him.

On 1st October 1985, I gave birth to my beautiful little girl, Dobia, she weighed over 10lb.

When he finally woke up Dobia had been born and was asleep in the cot next to me, he came over and looked at her.

"That's not my baby! She's too ugly to be my child! Tell the doctors they must have given you the wrong baby, and don't come home till you have the right one!" Ziad wasn't joking; his voice was mean and cruel.

"She's the splitting image of you, so if she's ugly, so are you!" I shouted after him as he left the room.

I wasn't lying, Dobia was the splitting image of her dad and that was OK, because I'd always said Ziad was good looking, it was his heart that was ugly!

I wanted to call her Yasmin after my sister but Ziad refused, his grandmother had just passed away and he had insisted if it was a girl she be named Dobia.

It wasn't just the staff at the hospital who had become tired of Ziad's behaviour, so had his father. Ziad had become a burden and an embarrassment to his father and the family. Nasser Ziad had built his empire out of hard work, he didn't throw away his money and he was both feared and respected. Ziad wasn't working in Africa; he partied all night and slept all day. He wasted money on drink, drugs, and women, and he was making a lot of enemies in Africa because of his temper and arrogance.

He was firing good workers when they had the nerve to stand up to him, and the last one was his uncle Ahmed! When Ahmed returned to Yemen and told them that Ziad had fired him, Nasser Ziad was furious and demanded we go back to Yemen! I was over the moon, but Ziad refused to leave Africa.

Jehovah's Witnesses helped me wrap up the one book I'd been studying for years with them in hope to access their help, The Bible was also a book that was banned in Yemen. I wanted to smuggle it back to allow me to keep up with my studies, so I ripped off the front and back hard pages and replaced them with newspaper. They told me they had people working undercover in Yemen and gave me contact details for them. In 1986 I was escorted back to the Yemen, with my four children.

Chapter Seventeen
Disowned

When I landed in Yemen I got through the airport with my Bible without any problems. Yas and Abdul were there waiting for us. I'd been gone for over three years and it had been absolute hell being away from my sister. As we held on to each other I didn't want to let her go, we had a lot of catching up to do! As always I could count on Yas to be direct with me.

"What's wrong with your face, Moo?" she asked, touching my cheeks. Ziad had knocked out some of my teeth leaving my face looking collapsed, and my cheeks sunken.

They took me to their house where I would stay for a few days before travelling to Dad's house, where I would stay until Ziad got back from Africa. Ziad had told me to stay at Dad's house because he was having problems with his family and he didn't want us going there until he got back.

It was nice sitting with my sister again after all those years. It was like we had never been apart; in fact it felt as though we had a stronger bond. We both had different strengths and we fed off each other.

We got to know each other's children; she had two children by then, Ghania and a little boy called Amar. Our children played together for the first time. They bonded instantly and loved each other and squabbled just like we did when we were kids. It was great to watch them while Yas and I told each other almost everything about what had happened in the time we had been apart, good and bad.

We talked about our children and their births, first teeth, their first steps, first illness, the first words they ever said, their habits. We also spoke about our marriages; I told Yas what I could about mine, while sparing her the gory details of what I knew would really break her heart.

I only told her what I knew she could handle. She told me about hers and I'm sure she did the same, we both knew the other had struggles and secrets we would never share out of sparing the other the pain.

She told me about Uncle Jim's visit to Yemen. She said he had been devastated to see what had happened to us and told her how he had tried everything he could before we left to stop us from leaving. She said he was upset I was away and he didn't get to see me, and was worried about the way I was being treated.

Yas told me about her visit back home to England, how all the family was so excited to see her, and how upset they were when she told them she was returning because she couldn't abandon me. We cried when she told me that Uncle Jim told her he was the proudest dad in the world because of the way we stood by each other, and were always there for each other.

She also told me about Dad's new wife Viyza, she had given birth to a baby boy called Abdulla weeks earlier. Viyza was from a family of thugs who ruled the village with their thuggish behaviour. They were not a good or wealthy family and nobody liked or respected them, but they were the only family willing to allow their daughter to marry Dad after what he had done to Amina. Most Yemeni men would prefer their loved ones to stay alive, no matter how hard handed their husbands ruled his house.

Dad had divorced Amina after nearly killing her. Her family had finally had enough, and that time refused to return her to him. Dad had beaten Amina unconscious, then he threw a bucket of water over her to bring her around, he then dragged her into the kitchen and stuffed her semi-conscious body into the clay oven and tried to set fire to her! Yas said it was only because her clothes were wet from him throwing water over her that he couldn't set her on fire! When he went off to get more petrol to pour over her she managed to flee the house and escape him!

Not long after that he divorced Amina and remarried a young

girl called Viyza; apparently Dad hadn't laid a finger on her because he was scared of her brutal brothers and what they would do to him if he did!

Our sister Nebat had four children by then, all born within months of my children. Yas said Nebat was a rock to her when I was away and was always loyal and kind. She was always there to guide her through the tough times and show her what was needed from her to fit in perfectly in the Yemen society. So much was expected from Yas being the wife of a Yemeni diplomat, and Yas's health was poor at times, but Nebat was there for her, just as a big sister should be.

Farouse had two girls by now, and was living in Sanaa with her husband and his horrible mother; Yas told me that although Farouse put on this front that she was always happy and OK, she knew it wasn't true, she could see that her husband was a nasty, brutal man!

Our youngest and most educated uncle, Ahmed, had come back from abroad and got married. We had met Uncle Ahmed very briefly in Aden when we first came to Yemen; he was flying off to Russia at the time to go to university. Back then I didn't even know he was our real uncle because everyone was introduced to us as uncles when we first arrived!

He was back and had married a young girl who was from outside the family and all the local villages. Her name was Azeza, and she was also one of the very few educated Yemeni girls I'd ever met.

While I was staying with Yas, Nebat and Farouse came over to visit at the afternoon gatherings, along with many other women, including Azeza. She wasn't what I was expecting, given that my uncle was considered a catch, but there was something about her that made me like her. She was friendly, and seemed kind and interesting. She spoke her mind in a very quiet, gentle, diplomatic way, while moving her hands as if to hold an audience, or gain your attention. Uncle Ahmed had insisted in choosing his own wife, saying he wanted an educated wife, a wife with a brain, not a slave. Azeza was purely his choice, not his family's.

It had been many years since I'd sat in a gathering but it didn't feel uncomfortable. Yas and I had both become accustomed to what was expected of us to blend in if we wanted to be good mothers. Whilst we sat in that gathering and watched our children play, we knew we had a bigger struggle than ever to save our children from having to one day do the same.

A few days later I hugged and kissed my sister and her children goodbye as I set off for Dad's house. This wasn't a journey I was looking forward to. It was going to be just me and my children at Dad's village, all my loved ones were now in Sanaa. I knew as always that Dad would show me very little love once I arrived at his house, but I had nowhere else to go.

Any hope I had of finding help to escape were once against destroyed; I'd tried a number of times while in Sanaa to contact Jehovah's Witnesses on the number I was given by my friends in Africa but it failed, the number was a dead line. Yas had been furious with me about the whole Jehovah's Witness thing and smuggling the Bible in Yemen, saying I could have been arrested, and she was right, but I was desperate, I still was, and with my Bible safely in my bag I would never give up. I didn't enjoy reading the Bible, I couldn't make heads or tails of it, but it kept me up to date with my English!

Viyza was waiting for us as we arrived; she tried to put on an act that she was happy to see us but I could see straight away she didn't want us there. She was much younger than Dad, she looked in her late 20s, and there was something about her that made me wary of her, I just didn't trust her! She was short and thin and although quite pretty, she had a devious look about her!

Abdulla was cute, and I could understand Dad's excitement for his only son, he had always wanted a son. Abdulla was doted on by everyone, and it was made clear from day one that he was the only child in that house that was to be shown any love from anyone, as far as my family were concerned my children didn't exist. They were ignored when they spoke , pushed aside when in the way, and shouted at when they made a noise.

It was so different being back at the village with my children. The last time I'd lived at Dad's house I was alone, it was hard even back then, but in many different ways. I had no clue as to what lay in store for us.

Dad took Tarek to the fields to work with him the next day, he was only around six but that was old enough to do a hard day's work. I knew Dad was ruthless and moody with my son, and it broke my heart every day sending him off with my father, but that was what young village boys did, and my son was no different.

I would make sure he was fed and give him what scraps of food I could to tuck into his pockets for the long day ahead, and then I'd send him off with a quick kiss on the head. Tarek was a crazy boy and always doing silly things, but he was strong and healthy, and he was a kind boy with a good heart. He loved his brothers and sisters and would always protect them if he thought danger was around the corner, he acted so much older than his age!

Issy was my little helper. She would run around and want to do everything with me, she would copy everything I did and attempt to pick up her younger brother and sister to look after them, but she was tiny and they were both so big and heavy! Issy would drag them along and play the big sister in any way she could.

Sadig and Dobia were still toddlers and just played outside, they didn't have toys, but they had the sun, stones and dirt and that would keep them busy all day!

Viyza did very little; she took little care of Abdulla and spent most of her time on her sewing machine. She made clothes for the women of the village and many women from other villages. She made good money from her work and although she loved her son, she was ruthless and would never spend a penny of it on him or her house keep. Viyza had a daughter from a previous marriage - she was about eight and lived with Viyza's mother in our village - and any money she made she hid it away or gave it to her family.

The house chores rested on me. I would wake at dawn and my children would awake and follow me silently around the house as I cooked and cleaned, I did it all without complaining. There was no use in complaining about anything because when people don't care about you, they don't care if you complain or if you are unhappy!

Viyza was just as cruel as Dad; she became pregnant again within months of having Abdulla and while I was living with them she gave birth to a little girl who Dad called Ismahan. Viyza showed Ismahan no love or affection, everything was about Abdulla.

As time went by I realised why I didn't take to her, she was a liar and would blame any mistake she made on me and my children. She complained that my children ate too much and made too much noise, and if she misplaced anything or broke anything she would deny it, putting the blame on us. Dad would never listen to anything I had to say.

He told me many times that as far as he was concerned I was nothing but a burden to him and so were my children, he just wanted us gone, and the sooner Ziad came and took us the better. I told Dad when I came back from Africa that I didn't want to go back to Ziad and Dad's reply was, "Fine, give him his kids back and you can remarry." That was the end of that discussion!

He had a vile temper and would explode at the slightest thing, and Viyza never once came under attack from him, it was always me and my children. Dad would scream at us for anything and everything and my children would cower from him just like they did their own father, but up until then he hadn't laid a finger on them.

Even though I hated living with Dad and his wife, I hated the thought of going back to my husband more. I never heard from Ziad or any of his family while he was in Africa, although there were many rumours going around about his conflict with his father. I feared the day that Ziad would come back, knowing that sooner or later I would be returned to the monster that had nearly killed me so many times.

Ziad turned up around a year later. Dad was over the moon to be finally getting rid of us, he couldn't wait to send me back with my husband. I tried to plead with Dad not to return me but my pleas meant nothing to him. He told me everything that had gone on between Ziad and I was my fault because I was stubborn with a big mouth. He told me to obey my husband and keep my mouth shut! He sent me back without hesitation.

Unknown to me Ziad had got into so much trouble in Africa we were no longer welcomed back into the family home; his father had disowned him. When we arrived back in his village we were taken to a house next door to his family home where we would live alone. The house was empty; it had nothing, not even a blanket.

Ziad had come back from Africa with no money and no means

to support us, he had spent all his money on what he loved doing most, and now because of his behaviour, we had been banished from the main house; it was his children and I that would pay for his wrong doing.

The house was big, it was a three storey high building made from mud and old stone. It had a small old stable that had been built on the side of the house by the front door; all that was left of the stable were broken bits of crumbling walls. Straight in front as we opened the front door were big dark stables, to the left were the stairs; they were dark, steep and bendy.

There was no electricity in this house, although most of the bigger villages had electric by then. The room on the middle floor was so badly damaged it was uninhabitable and therefore closed; only the top floor was safe to live in. On the top floor there were four rooms, to the left was a small kitchen that had a clay oven and a tiny cemented piece on the floor by the outer wall with a hole and a pipe that went outside, that was my sink. Straight ahead was a long room with loads of little wooden windows that opened up and looked over the village and the front door, also the back of the house. Next to that was a big long toilet that had a hole on the floor right at the other end, and to the right of the stairs was a little room that also had a few wooden windows that overlooked the back of the house, all of these rooms were joined by a tiny hallway that was on the top of the stairs.

The long room became Ziad's room where he slept alone, calling me only when he wanted to satisfy his needs, while the small room became the room where I would sleep with my children.

Although Ziad had dishonoured his family name, my children and I had done nothing wrong so the sisters didn't push us aside. As soon as we got there they came over and gave me a few things to keep us going. They told me Ziad's father was furious with him and wanted them to have nothing more to do with him. However, Nasser Ziad had a soft spot for my son Tarek, therefore he would allow them to give us a little help.

The sisters and Ulfah were the only family that spoke to us and I soon understood how Ulfah must have felt when she was banished by the family. I was looked upon as if I was the one who had done wrong, not only by the family but by other people of the village. I was ignored when I walked through the village; people would turn away from me to avoid speaking to me.

I soon realised how difficult life would become in the village being made an outcast by everyone. Once considered an import-ant member of a rich family and able to gain access to everything available to the Ziad family, we were now unable to even share the same water as them. I needed to fetch water from the wells that were miles away in the fields, while Ziad's family had theirs deliv-ered next door by the truck load. I also wasn't allowed to collect food or crops from their many fields in the harvest times.

Ziad would wake up every morning as usual and go through his daily routine of grooming himself to perfection, and then he would head off down to the village, or head into Rada'a where he would always find a way to make a bit of money for himself. He could never find money for his children's food, even though he would always come home with plenty of ghat and alcohol for himself. Because he had been banished from the family nobody would give him work. Everybody was too scared to employ Nasser Ziad's son without permission from the big man himself, and that was never going to happen! Ziad's father wanted him to suffer for the embarrassment he had caused him; he wanted him homeless and penniless to teach a lesson to anyone else that ever dared to cross him!

It was then the years of collecting gold showed me its use. I started selling my gold piece by piece, to buy food for my family.

I tried to stay out of Ziad's way the best I could; I realised very soon after moving to that house that the space we lived in was small and there was nowhere to run or hide, so I did as I was told, when I was told. Although his brutal abuse continued towards me, it was not as vicious as it was in Africa, just different.

His behaviour towards his children depended on his mood that day, sometimes he would take them into the village for a walk with him, and then other times he wouldn't even speak to them. He would ignore their sibling fights on some days, and then on other days he would threaten them and hit them. We were always on edge with him, not knowing what the day would bring. All I could do was shield my children from their father when he turned nasty, and give them as much love as I possibly could. What worried me the most was I had no say into what happened to my children's future and would never be able to protect them from their fate in Yemen.

Tarek was put into the village school but Issy wasn't allowed; as far as everyone was concerned she was just a girl, and education wasn't important for her. As far as her father was concerned she would be ready for marriage in a few years. I became pregnant not long after Ziad came back from Africa with my fifth child, it was inevitable. I'd asked for birth control many times but Ziad would laugh at me or just ignore me. It was a huge difference from the last time I was pregnant in the village with Tarek and Issy. Everyone was so happy for me then; this time nobody cared, in fact they looked upon me as if I had done something wrong by getting pregnant, but from the second I realised I was pregnant I knew I had to protect my baby.

It was when I moved back to Ziad's village that I first met Thahaba, another one of the sisters that I'd never met before. She was really a niece of theirs from grandmother Dobia's older daughter. Thahaba, who was from a Sudanese father, had married and lived away from the family, and had only come back when her grandmother Dobia died. She had grown up calling her grandmother 'mother' and her aunts 'sisters' because her mother had died when she was very young.

Thahaba was kind and generous and had a good heart, she was one of the very few who still spoke to me and we got on great; I was soon going to her with all my problems. I didn't tell her everything, but I could run to her house when things got too much for me. She had a small mud house at the bottom of the hill where she lived alone, she was divorced and had a small son called Mohammed who lived between her and her ex-husband. She was financially supported by her family from her father's side.

Although she was young and beautiful she had refused to remarry and was not giving in to any pressure from her mother's side of her family. She didn't get on much with Nasser Ziad, but refused to tell me the real reasons why, saying it was just sibling squabbles. Thahaba was the one I went to with my problems; aside from Umie Ayesha, she was the one person in the village who I could rely on not to let us down if I needed a shoulder to cry on.

Umie Ayesha had always been there for us and she was always bringing us little things, but there was only so much she could do. Ziad's father had put a limit on what help she could and couldn't give us. I knew she adored my children and I could see that being apart from them broke her heart just as much as it did theirs. She would find little chores for Tarek to do, that way she could pay him money and say it was because he had done work for her.

One time she asked Tarek to take the donkey from her house down to her sister's house, which was around a mile through the village. She told Tarek to make sure the donkey didn't run off, it was a wild donkey and the slightest thing scared it. Tarek set off, wrapping the donkey's strap and tying it to his wrist.

Halfway into his journey something spooked the donkey and it took off, dragging Tarek behind it through the gravel and dirt roads, but Tarek held on, not wanting to untie his strap in fear of losing the donkey! The donkey had taken the route many times before and knew where it was going, so when it got to Noriya's house it stopped. However Tarek had been dragged behind it for a while and his face and body was scraped and bloodied with wounds full of gravel and dirt from the roads.

Noriya cleaned him and patched him up the best she could before mounting him back on the same donkey and bringing him back to Umie Ayesha. Tarek wasn't upset that he was hurt, he was just so proud of himself. "I didn't let the donkey go!" he told her with a big smile.

Chapter Eighteen
Forbidden Love

Yas moved to Rada'a with Abdul while I was in that house. Abdul had become high in the ranks of government now and was in charge of the City of Rada'a. He commanded a large number of soldiers and had an army that escorted him everywhere, a driver that took Yas everywhere, and he was well known for his kindness and generosity, yet Yas was still in a loveless marriage. She was loyal to Abdul and stood by him in everything he did, she tried her best to love him, but couldn't.

Yas's chores became more gruelling every time Abdul got promoted. Every day she would have to wake up and cook for all of Abdul's solders. That would range from cooking for a few dozen to a few hundred; sometimes she would only be given a few hours' notice that more guests were coming. Yas was also pregnant; Abdul had refused to give her any birth control and this wasn't going down well with her. She had lost so many children over the years and didn't want to go through with any more pregnancies, she was grateful for the living children she had. She also said that he never spent time at home with the children; he was always working, so why did she need to have more? Yas was tired and I could see it on her face.

It was a blessing for us both with her being closer; she would visit me sometimes when she wasn't so busy with her chores. Sometimes she would send us their driver and we would go and visit them, our children loved playing together.

Ziad didn't mind because every time we came back from my

261

sister's house we came back with a car full of food, boxes of tinned food and sacks full of flour, sugar, and rice. I didn't tell Yas but Ziad started stealing our food and selling it down at the village to feed his addiction. At first he started off only taking one or two boxes or sacks, leaving us a bit of food to get us through, not because he felt sorry for his children but to feed himself. We would argue over him taking them and I would always end up getting hurt, punched, slapped, kicked or shoved to the side.

One time he had taken everything, leaving us with absolutely nothing. I would usually make the cement from the flour Yas would give us and any soup from milk or meat that Ziad would bring home, if he ever did! Some days I would make rice then other days we would just eat bread and foul. I would always try and do something, even if it was just bread and tea.

One day we had nothing. I didn't have flour, rice or foul because he had sold everything and I was at a loss with what to do. Thahaba knew what Ziad was doing with our food, the whole village knew because he was selling it to them, so she took the children and told me to have it out with him. I hadn't told her how bad Ziad's violence could get, she had heard rumours but I'd told her he had stopped since we got back from Africa.

I'd put up with so much from Ziad and kept quiet, not wanting to antagonise him out of fear that he would become violent, but he was now starving us for his own selfish reasons and I'd had enough!

That day he came back from the village at lunchtime with nothing but a frozen chicken. The chicken was wrapped in a clear plastic bag that was sealed, and the wrapper had a little extra bit of thick plastic on the end that could be used as a handle. He walked into the kitchen and placed the chicken on the cold clay oven.

"Where are the children?" he asked, half-heartedly. I told him they were having dinner with Thahaba and he made a joke about, "more food for him," as he walked into his room whistling.

I looked at the chicken and could hear Ziad playing his music, chuffed with the fact that he had sold all our food, but was kind enough to have brought us a chicken; he could see no wrong with what he had done!

I knew I was going to get a beating, but I was stubborn and

wanted to have my say. I also knew that my children were safe, so I took a deep breath and I picked up the frozen chicken, which was still in its plastic bag. I could feel the anger boiling up inside me and I hated myself for feeling this way because I knew what was coming! I was going to say something he didn't like and I was going to get hurt, but I couldn't stop myself. I placed it on a metal plate and walked into the room where Ziad was.

When I walked in he was stood with his back to me looking for something on the window sill; he didn't think to turn to look until I placed the plate near where he usually sat. He turned around thinking that I'd somehow, within minutes, cooked up a meal from nothing, and he was genuinely taken by surprise to see a frozen chicken on the plate!

He stood there rubbing his mouth as he laughed. "Oh, you didn't just do that?" he said under his breath, shaking his head from side to side. It was the look on his face that sent shivers down my spine! "What's this?" he asked, in a tone that dared me to speak.

Though I was terrified I was also fed up, and I had a big mouth! "That's all you brought home, isn't it? I didn't see you come home with anything else in your hand, so that's your dinner!" I stood there in front of him, my head stuck up as high as I could to defy him. I could feel my legs starting to tremble because I knew he was going to hit me. I was expecting it, but I didn't want to cower away from him, not this time.

Suddenly he bent down and picked up the chicken by the handle of the wrapper, and I thought he was just going to hand it to me as he straightened up, but instead he swung it and hit me across the side of my head with such force, the frozen chicken flung out of his hand, and I went crashing to the floor! The force of the blow affected my hearing because he had caught me on my ear and all I could hear was whooshing noises.

As I lay on the floor, dazed, flashing lights darted across my eyes and I struggled to pull myself together. Ziad reacted as if he hadn't done anything wrong. He sat down and started shouting at me, instructing me to pick up the chicken and go and cook it if I wanted to avoid further punishment. He was yelling that I needed to be quick about it because he had ghat to eat! I struggled to leave the room, my eyes were blurry, my head was spinning, but I picked up the chicken and stumbled out of the room, trying my best to hold my head high, refusing to cry in front of him.

I'd stopped crying many years ago from any physical abuse Ziad or anyone else felt they had the right to inflict upon me, but in private things were different. As soon as I got to the kitchen my tears started to flow, and as much as I tried to hold them back I couldn't! It wasn't the pain, but frustration that made me cry. I knew Ziad would never change; in fact he would only get worse! I was in tremendous pain but I still felt defiant and in that mood I decided I would cook the chicken, but it wasn't going to be for him! I was taking it to the children!

I took the chicken and gently tiptoed down the stairs and out the door, and then I ran as fast as I could through the village to Thahaba's house! My head was still throbbing with pain when I arrived, but the sight of my children made the pain disappear.

They were playing outside when I got to the door and when they saw me approach they ran up to me calling out, happy to see me. I didn't have any visible injuries so they were clueless to what had happened, but I was worried their father would come looking for me so I took them inside and told them they needed to play inside for the rest of the day.

I told Thahaba what had happened and she insisted I stay the night at her house; she said if Ziad came for me that I was to stay inside, and she would deal with him. I hardly slept, quietly sat on her roof most of the night, waiting for Ziad to get drunk and come and cause a problem at her house, but he didn't come.

The next day Thahaba insisted we stay again, but late afternoon her half-brother Anwar arrived from Sanaa to stay with her, and although they both insisted we stay it was the first time I'd ever met Anwar and even though he seemed nice, Thahaba's house only had two small rooms. Against both their wishes, I returned home early evening.

Ziad wasn't home when we got back but he returned late that night; we were in our room when he got back and he didn't say a word to us as he walked past our room and went straight to his room.

In the early hours of the morning, when he was drunk, he

came into our room and yanked me out of bed from my sleep; he dragged me into his room where he viciously beat and raped me. I stayed silent throughout the whole ordeal knowing my children were asleep just feet away.

The next day I stayed inside, too embarrassed to leave the house because of my injuries, and when Thahaba came to visit me early evening she was horrified. She refused to allow us to stay in the house with Ziad and took us back to hers; Ziad was out at the time.

Thahaba was such a good friend to me and that didn't stop when her brother arrived, when I arrived at their house they were both so angry that Ziad could do something so horrible. I'd never told Thahaba of all the things Ziad had done to us in Africa or since we had been back. I hadn't told anyone, I never would.

Thahaba was outspoken and not scared of Ziad, and I knew she would give him a piece of her mind when she saw him, but up until then I'd tried to stop that from happening by not telling her or allowing her to see the real Ziad out of fear of repercussions. Now I'd given up, Ziad would abuse me whatever I said or did and I needed help. Thahaba was the only person in the village who was not scared of Ziad or his father, and who was willing to help us.

That night at Thahaba's house after I'd put my children to bed I myself couldn't sleep, I was worried that Ziad would come to the house once he was drunk and cause her problems. I knew he wouldn't dare touch her, but he could be loud and embarrassing when drunk and I didn't want to put her through that. I quietly snuck up to the roof. Thahaba and Anwar were asleep in one room and my children and I in another. I'd sat for a while next to the window in the room where we were sleeping, but I couldn't see much from any of those windows, whereas from the roof I could see the path from all around, so if Ziad was to approach the house I would see him coming.

It was a full moon and it was so quiet outside you could hear a pin drop, so I sat in a corner and rested up against the wall, and then if I heard a noise I would discreetly peer over the edge to check it wasn't Ziad.

Suddenly Anwar appeared from the roof door, he had to duck

down to get through the door because he was so tall. "I thought I heard someone up here .Why are you up here?" he whispered, sitting down right next to me.

I told him why I was up there; in return he told me he couldn't sleep either so he would sit with me for a while. I didn't feel uncomfortable sitting with Anwar even though he was somewhat a stranger, even though he was sat extremely close to me! Earlier that evening we had all sat together in the room downstairs for hours chatting, he'd even played with my children.

He told us he had come to stay in the village to work in the school as head teacher, which meant he was going to be Tarek's head teacher. Tarek had taken an instant liking to him and they hadn't stopped chatting all night. As we sat there on the roof he laughed at me a lot; although I was fluent in Arabic I would still make mistakes, because in some words there is a different way to speak to men and women!

We joked around and because he was learning English he thought English was a difficult language to learn.

We sat and debated on whether Arabic was harder to learn than English, I thought Arabic was, whereas he thought English was! As we joked around he would nudge my shoulder in a friendly way, and to me it seemed like the most natural gesture, however it wasn't, not in this country!

Every now and then someone would walk by and we would just look at each other and fall silent, quickly checking over the edge to see it wasn't Ziad; with the full moon we could see everything so clearly.

Once the person had passed by we would sit back down and go straight back to our conversation, as time passed we were sat so close to each other I could feel the side of his body next to mine. We didn't talk about anything upsetting; all we talked about were languages, books, drawings and silly things. He didn't ask me anything about Ziad and it felt as though I'd known him for ages. There was one thing that felt new to me, and that was the attraction I felt for him.

As he spoke I felt myself admiring him, he was tall, around 6'4" and muscular with big shoulders.

He had black afro hair and although his parents were from

Sudan he had olive skin with green eyes. He had high cheekbones and his nose was long and thin with slightly big nostrils, and he had a small mouth with a thin top lip and a fuller bottom lip. His face was strong but kind and when he smiled his eyes lit up and when he laughed he made a chuckle sound that made me smile.

I knew I had feelings for him from that very first night, and by the end of the night I felt he had some sort of feelings towards me.

He was sat extra close to me, not something men and women did in Yemen, but it felt natural, and there was something in the way he playfully nudged me with his shoulder while he laughed. I could see it in the way he looked at me when we spoke, and it gave me butterflies in my stomach.

Before we knew it the sun was coming up and we decided to go back in, and as we got to the bottom of the stairs we mimed good-night to each other as we disappeared into our separate rooms to catch a few hours' sleep. I for one couldn't sleep; he was on my mind.

The next morning we all woke up around the same time and gathered in the kitchen to make breakfast. Anwar and I had not long gone to bed! Thahaba wasn't like the other women in the village, she didn't wake up in the morning and make her own bread in the clay oven, and although she had a clay oven she very rarely used it. She had a little one ring gas cooker that she cooked on. While we sat and cooked the foul Anwar went off into the village to buy bread from a shop that sold ready-made bread.

We all sat around and ate together as Anwar and I tried to avoid eye contact; neither of us mentioned the night before, and once breakfast was over Anwar took Tarek with him to the school, whilst Thahaba and I stayed in and cleaned up. School was over by lunchtime and as we all sat around and ate dinner I found myself glancing over at Anwar, and I would catch him looking at me. We would both quickly look away only to catch each other doing it again a while later.

Thahaba was one of a few women I'd ever known to chew ghat and that afternoon she and Anwar chewed ghat while I sat and played with my children in the same room, we all laughed and joked and my children looked relaxed and happy but I knew it couldn't always be this way. I would have to go home to their father and it would have to be soon. As much as I liked the way I was feeling towards Anwar, I knew nothing good could ever come of it.

That night after I'd put the children to sleep I told them both I was leaving in the morning. Thahaba tried her best to convince me to stay while Anwar stayed silent. He bowed his head and looked at the floor but would glance up at me every now and then. I could see in his eyes that he wanted to say something but he knew he shouldn't intervene. Thahaba was Ziad's family so she could have her say, but he wasn't our family; it would have been disrespectful for him to speak.

Later that night after everyone was asleep I went back up onto the roof, and although I told myself I was there because I was worried Ziad would turn up, I also knew I wanted to spend time alone with Anwar. I knew it was wrong and that nothing could come of us but I just wanted to have one last night with him, just a nice happy night like the night we had before. I sat on the roof, jumping at every sound I heard, hoping that the next sound would be Anwar coming in from the roof door. Finally he appeared, crouching over as he made his way to where I was sat.

"What you doing up here?" I asked as he sat next to me. My heart was racing and I had the weirdest feeling in my stomach and I couldn't stop myself from smiling, however, I tried to act calm.

"You are a guest in our home, we can't have you sitting up here all alone!" he joked. "What if you need something? Anyway, I'm here to rescue you just in case someone climbs onto the roof and runs away with you!"

As he smiled I nudged him with my shoulder and he started to chuckle; that made me smile even more, his chuckle was cheeky and silly at the same time. Then suddenly his mood changed, and his voice saddened.

"It's nice when you smile, sometimes I see sadness in your eyes and it hurts me."

He was looking at the floor as he spoke. I looked at him but didn't speak; the full moon provided light and I could see how sad he looked even though he wasn't looking at me. As I looked away I saw him look up at me.

"Look at what he's done to you! Nobody should do that to someone they love!"

Once again I didn't answer, and we both fell silent for a while, then the silence was broken by a sound from the street and we both peered over to check who it was. After the passer-by was out of sight we sat back down and the conversation changed to a different subject, and once again we laughed and joked until the sun came up.

It was going to be harder than ever for me to leave and go home, and although I knew I had to go, I was fighting against the urge to want to see this man more, he made me feel happy, even if it was wrong! Once again we parted in the hallway with a quiet goodnight to catch a few hours' sleep, and the next day, after Anwar took Tarek to school, I made my way back home.

Ziad was nowhere to be seen when I arrived, and later on that afternoon when Umie Ayesha came around to see the children she told me he had gone to Sanaa the day before; he told her he was doing work and would be gone for a week or so. Ziad was always doing one dodgy deal or the other, but I was happy just to have him gone because it meant that I could have some peace and quiet!

This wasn't the first time Ziad had taken off to Sanaa without telling us; some days he would say he was going to Rada'a and not come back for days or even more, and then he would say he had been in Sanaa working. I knew he was selling alcohol because he would hide boxes of it in the stables of our house and sell them from there. Ziad was involved in a lot of things he shouldn't have been involved in, but I knew better than to question him on his business.

When he did come back he was in a good mood because he had made himself some money. This was typical of Ziad's behaviour, he didn't mention what happened before he left or ask me where we had been, he didn't care, and I didn't care that he didn't care! As long as he had money in his pocket he didn't care what happened to any of us, but within days that money was gone, he had spent it on himself, and once it was gone he was back to see what he could sell from the house.

It wasn't long before Yas found out that Ziad was selling the food that she gave us; she and Abdul were furious! I begged Abdul not to say anything to Ziad but he confronted him. Ziad denied everything and said I was lying. However, Abdul knew better than to believe Ziad, he'd been told by many people who'd seen Ziad selling the food in the market and gone back to inform him. Ziad didn't stop selling our food, instead he would leave us a little and sell the rest of it, and although I'd lie to Yas and tell her he'd stopped she knew I was lying, but she'd never questioned me. She knew things were difficult for me and she also knew that if I could've stopped Ziad taking the food I would have, so alongside the food she would give me extra money, and tell me to hide it.

Months passed by so quickly and Ziad left me alone the heavier into my pregnancy I got. He never could stand being close to me while I was heavily pregnant and he spent most of his time in Sanaa.

In the meantime I spent more and more time over Thahaba's house getting closer to Anwar, until one day he finally told me how he felt.

Ziad was away in Sanaa and I was in my last month of pregnancy and staying at Thahaba's. She had gone off to visit her sister for a bit that afternoon leaving Anwar and I alone in the house. The kids were outside playing and Anwar came and sat next to me with a book in his hand, asking me to help him read it. We sat shoulder to shoulder reading the book, laughing as we always did, when suddenly he quickly kissed me on the lips! I didn't pull away or kiss him back, not because I didn't want to, but because it all happened so fast.

"Sorry!" he said, worried, as he looked away. I had a smile on my face as I nudged his shoulder with mine.

"Why are you sorry?" I said quietly. "I'm not!"

Anwar's eyes lit up as he looked back at me. "Really? I didn't think you wanted me to kiss you!"

I could see his chest moving up and down because he was breathing heavily, he was nervous. I looked into his eyes; he had the most beautiful green eyes that lit up when he smiled.

"I'm worried about what could happen if we did fall in love and

270

act on those feelings, what could happen if people found out?" I told him, but he just took my hand and kissed it.

"It's too late for me; I'm already in love with you! I have been from the first night we spoke on the roof, all I need to know is do you feel the same way about me?" he asked, holding my hand to his chest. I nodded my head.

"Yes I do, but I'm worried," I admitted.

He put his arms around me and pulled me closer to him. "I promise you, I will never disrespect or hurt you or your children, or give you reason to worry, what we feel for each other is not wrong and nobody will ever find out from my mouth, this has to do with us and the children."

He held me close and we sat in silence until we heard a noise on the stairs. Thahaba had come back early, so we took the book and I carried on teaching him English as we always did when she was around.

We tried to carry on as normal, but from then on Anwar and I couldn't hide the way we glanced at each other from across the room, we couldn't look away from one another when our eyes caught the other's stare. Now we would stare into each other's eyes and smile, only breaking eye contact if we feared we would get caught. On the roof at night we snuggled up to each other and stole the odd kiss.

I stayed for a few more nights but things were about to change once more; Ziad was back from Sanaa, he was broke and he wanted money!

That night I'd put the children to bed and Thahaba, Anwar and I were sat up chatting in their room, when suddenly there was a bang on the door; it was a heavy bang and I knew straight away it was Ziad! We all looked at each other as Anwar went to stand up to open the door. "No, I will go!" Thahaba insisted as she stood up. The banging continued while she made her way downstairs.

It was a small house and there were only a few stairs from the front door to the room that we were sat in, so we could hear the conversation clearly as she opened the front door to Ziad. He was drunk, but not too drunk that he couldn't hold a conversation, or know what he was doing or saying, and he was being rude, demanding to see me! As I stood up to go downstairs Anwar put his hand out to me.

"You don't have to speak to him, she will get rid of him," he said.

I knew I had to. "I'm OK!" I said, as I walked towards the door. "He will only come back later if I don't speak to him now."

At the front door as Thahaba told Ziad off for being rude and a bully, she too tried to convince me that I didn't have to speak to him, but I assured her I would be OK, so she walked back upstairs leaving Ziad and me alone on the doorstep.

Not wanting him to wake the children with his shouting I stepped outside and pulled the door, only leaving it slightly ajar. "What do you want?" I asked sternly. I wasn't scared of him as we stood there face to face, even though I knew he was unpredictable, especially when drunk!

Ziad was demanding that I give him money, and when I told him I didn't have any he said he knew my sister gave me money, and he wanted it. I told him once again that I didn't have any, but even if I did I wouldn't give it to him, because any money my sister did or didn't give me was for my children!

Ziad then grabbed me by my throat and started squeezing really tightly. "Just give me some money!" he breathed in my face. I didn't cry out or make a noise. Even though he had his hand tightly around my neck I could still breathe. Realising I wasn't going to give in to his commands he squeezed once more. "I want you and my children home tomorrow!" he told me in a threatening tone before letting me go, and then he punched me in the face, making me stumble backwards onto the front door, before he quickly walked off.

Thahaba came running down when she heard the noise from me falling back onto the door. As soon as I gained my balance I quickly locked the front door, realising Anwar was behind her, heading down the stairs. I could see anger in Thahaba's face when she saw blood dripping from my nose, but the look in Anwar's eyes was something different; he looked hurt, like a man who wanted revenge!

"I'm going to kill that bastard!" he raged, heading for the door. Thahaba turned around and blocked his path as he tried to storm past her.

"No you don't! What are you going to do?" she demanded to know as she shoved him back up towards the top of the stairs.

She tried to calm him down, placing her hands on his shoulders and looking him in his eyes. "I'm not stupid my brother! I know how you two feel about each other, so I know why you're so angry, but this isn't your fight! If you go after him you will only make things worse for her." Thahaba then turned and looked at me but I hung my head in shame, I couldn't look at her knowing she had found out about Anwar and me.

"Don't look away from me! You need to speak to him if you want to stop him from getting killed!" she told me in an angry tone.

"She's right," I said, looking up, wiping the blood from my nose with my sleeve. "There's nothing you or anyone else can do or say that will change him, so why bother?" I made my way back upstairs as Thahaba escorted an angry Anwar back into the room, and I made my way into the kitchen to clean myself up and check that the children were still asleep.

Thankfully my children were good sleepers who slept through most things, but as I looked at them I couldn't help but feel sad. Being at Thahaba's house didn't just make me happy, it also made them happy. Here they didn't have to worry about their father's unpredictable behaviour; however I knew we would have to go back home tomorrow.

I could hear Thahaba and Anwar talking in the other room about us, she didn't sound angry with the fact that Anwar and I were in love, just concerned that nothing would ever come from our love. I for one knew she was right, but I didn't know how to switch off my feelings towards him.

Later that night on the roof Anwar and I snuggled up to each other, he cupped my face in his hands and kissed my injured nose. "I can't understand how any man could do this to someone they love?" His voice was full of pain and despair.

"Ziad's never once told me he loves me so maybe he doesn't?" I sighed.

"How could he not love you? You're funny, kind, caring, and you have given him these beautiful children, what else could he want in a wife?" he asked.

I looked at him and pulled a sad face. "Oh thanks!" I joked,

"You left out beautiful!"

He pulled me closer to him squeezing me gently. "You are very beautiful and you know it! But I have to be truthful and say you're not the most beautiful women I've ever seen!" He chuckled when I elbowed him playfully. "But you have beauty inside and out, and that is something I have never seen before, it's also why I love you!" he told me, kissing my forehead lovingly.

His demeanour changed as he carried on. "I know you don't want to be with him so why don't you leave him?" he sighed. I knew Anwar was right.

I told him I didn't want to be with Ziad, and maybe I could have walked away from him, but where would I go, and to what cost?

If I had a family that loved me and cared for me then they would have helped me by now and provided a safe haven for me and my children, however I didn't have that. Every time I went to my father for help he hurt me and my children. My father had told me point blank that to stay with him, I would have to give my children back to Ziad's family so that I could remarry; he would never accept me with my children. I had nowhere else to go, and I would never leave my children alone.

I told Anwar about my past, how I'd come from England, and about the loved ones we had lost, what my father had done to our family. Anwar listened, and although he wasn't happy about me staying with Ziad he said he felt he understood why.

He told me a bit about his family, and how although they were religious and followed certain cultural beliefs, he and his family grew up with no pressure into getting married. Salwa, his younger sister from his mother's side, was an airline stewardess in Sanaa and under no pressure to marry, even though she was in her early 20s. He told me how he would always support Thahaba so that she could look after her son, and never have to remarry unless she wanted to. He said that Thahaba had promised to keep our secret, and that I should never worry because she was a person who always kept to her word, we could trust her.

Though we didn't talk about it we both knew that there was never a possibility of us being together, both religious and cultural beliefs in Yemen would never permit us making a life with each other. That night we snuggled up and counted the stars until they disappeared in the sunlight, realising that every single moment we had together was precious.

When I went into labour Ziad was away in Sanaa. I'd been in labour for two days and two nights, it was slow and painful, and I was drained. Although I had Umie Ayesha and Thahaba by my side I wanted to be with my sister.

I'd never been able to be with Yas at any of my births and this was a one-off chance for me, so on the third morning I sent word to Yas and she sent me a car! Yas was in Rada'a, a 15 minute drive from our village, and when I got there it was mid-morning and her house was in chaos. Abdul had just told her that on top of her usual 30/40 odd soldiers she always cooked for on a daily basis, he was expecting around 50 more coming from out of town. This was a regular thing that happened for Yas, she would usually get a few hours' notice to cook for an army of soldiers without any help, and it was taking its toll on her. My contractions were slow and far apart so I went straight into the kitchen to help cook dinner.

My task was to make the cement with pans the size of actual cement mixers full of boiling hot water, and wooden spoons so big I could hardly grip them. I did my best to mix the flour and boiling water together into a smooth doughy paste-like mixture, transferring pot after pot to the floor and sitting down so that I could press my legs against it while mixing, and at the same time screaming when my contractions came along! With Yas busy running around sorting out everything else she left me alone to get on with whatever I wanted to do, so I filled pan after pan and carried on mixing the cement, not realising I'd made enough to feed the actual entire army!

When dinner was over, and with the help from a local neighbour, I gave birth to my beautiful, healthy fifth child. I had another son, who his father insisted on naming.

Nasser Ziad was born on 12th February, 1988.

At the time I couldn't understand why Ziad was so insistent on naming our son after his father, especially since his father had disowned him and we hadn't spoken to Nasser Ziad since coming back from Africa.

Nasser Ziad would often send his sister, Umie Ayesha, to ask me if I would allow Tarek to go and visit him in Sanaa, but I would always refuse. I had a bad feeling about him. When Nasser Ziad came to the village he would only ask to see Tarek, and in my opinion that was wrong and cruel of him, because I had four other children who were also his grandchildren.

I could understand that Tarek was favoured because he was the first born son, but Nasser Ziad had shown no interest in my other children and I couldn't understand why; they were all his grandchildren, and he needed to show them all affection, not just the one!

Umie Ayesha told me that Nasser Ziad wanted me to give him my son so that he could send him abroad to boarding school; again I refused, maybe my son would get a better education abroad but he would also be away from us, his family. If I allowed him to go and be brought up by his grandfather he would most probably grow up like all the other men in his family: mean, cruel and violent! That was something I could never allow to happen!

I thought Ziad was trying to get back into his father's good books by naming his son after his father, but in reality that was never going to happen; Ziad was driving his father and his family further and further away with his behaviour. He was still taking our food and selling it, still beating me, sometimes also succeeding in taking away from me the money my sister gave me.

It wasn't long after I gave birth to Nasser that Ziad's temper showed just how volatile and dangerous he could be, and how lucky my children and I had been up until then to still be alive.

It was mid-morning and Ziad had gone down into the village to buy some ghat; it was a rare occasion when Tarek and Issy had gone with him. When they came back the children told me that their father had been arguing with a man and then he hit the man. They told me the man then fell to the floor and didn't get back up. Ziad laughed when I asked him about it, saying it was all the other man's fault, dismissing the notion he had done anything wrong!

Later that afternoon after Ziad had gone out, Umie Ayesha came around, she was deeply concerned telling me that the man Ziad had punched was now in hospital, and in a very bad way. They had argued because Ziad owed him money, and when the man told Ziad to hand over his watch as payment for the money Ziad punched him in his head, and the man fell, hitting his head.

Three days later the man died from his injuries, and though I knew there would be consequences, Ziad didn't care!

The night the man died, when I dared to bring up the issue with him he turned on me, reminding me never to ask him, or question him about anything that he did. Knowing that there would be backlash from the village Ziad woke up and left for Sanaa the next morning, leaving me to face everyone.

Too worried to leave the house to face the villagers I kept Tarek from school and the children inside, and when Thahaba came to visit me the same day she found me black and blue from the night before. She tried to convince me to go and stay with her but I refused; I'd already started to pack my things. I told her I was leaving to go to my father, maybe now seeing what Ziad had done he would offer us help.

I wrote a letter and asked her to pass it on to Anwar, although I wanted to see him I couldn't bear for him to see me battered and bruised once again. That day I left for Dad's house, hoping that this time my father would welcome my children and me into his home, and offer us refuge.

Chapter Nineteen
The Evil Stepmother

Dad wasn't happy when I arrived; although he took us in, he made it clear that if Ziad came back for me he wouldn't hesitate to send me back! Once again he told me that if Ziad didn't want me anymore but wanted his children, that he could have them, and I would have to remarry.

All I could do was pray that Ziad wouldn't turn up at all! A few weeks later, to my surprise, Thahaba turned up at Dad's house. I was over the moon to see her and even happier that she had brought me a letter from Anwar. She said he had become really upset after I left and couldn't carry on working; therefore he had given up his job and left the school, but was now working in Rada'a at the hospital as an accountant and wanted me to try to go and see him. I told her there was no way I could go to hospital unless I was at death's door; even then it was doubtful that I would get taken. It wasn't as if anyone cared enough about me, or my children, to seek us treatment if we became ill.

She stayed for a while and then left, leaving me with my letter, and once she was gone I went straight to the toilet to read it; it made me smile and cry at the same time. He was upset with me for leaving without seeing him, angry with himself for not being able to help me; he questioned what I would do now, where I would stay in the long term? I smiled when I read how he referred to my children as "our children". He didn't ask how "my children" were, but how "our children" were. He begged me to go and see him, telling me he couldn't live without me.

I sat on the toilet floor, holding the letter close to my chest for as long as I could before I had to get back up and carry on with my chores, and then I tucked the letter down my top. This wasn't a letter I could leave around in my box with all my other memories, but it wasn't a letter I was going to get rid of either!

I stayed with Dad for about a month before Ziad showed up. I begged Dad not to return me, but Ziad paid him some money, and I was given back to my husband.

It was then I realised Dad would never offer me any love or support of any kind, ever! Growing up I'd always yearned for his love, hoping that one day he would open his heart, but now I needed to face reality because it was never going to happen. Ziad had actually killed a man with one punch but my father was still willing to give me back to him, even though he knew I was being beaten by him every day. My father didn't care for me, he most probably never had.

Ziad became smugger than ever that he could do as he pleased with me because he knew that my father didn't care, and although I tried my best to stay positive, it was difficult. I think that was the first time I'd actually felt defeated, squashed!

I felt as if my head was going to explode, so I would lock myself in my room for hours and cry until I couldn't cry anymore. It took me a while but I managed to pull myself together. I knew I had to be strong for my children and I knew I wasn't allowed to fall apart, because if I did, who would protect them?

I didn't dare question Ziad anymore, but I'd heard that blood money was agreed between Ziad and the dead man's family. I had no idea how he could afford to pay this because blood money was a huge amount of money, and I knew Ziad didn't have any.

I tried my best to stay out of his way; I hated everything about him, his smell, his smug face, his voice! I'd started getting headaches while I was still in Africa from the smell of his aftershave; I could smell him when he came up the stairs and I would start to panic, because once I'd smelt his scent or heard his voice I knew we were in danger.

My time with Anwar became less and less, he was working in Rada'a at the hospital and Ziad was home a lot, which meant I couldn't go over to Thahaba's much, but every moment Anwar and I spent together was cherished. He would become angrier with Ziad every time he saw a bruise on me, which became almost every other day. As soon as one injury healed, I had another. All he wanted to do was protect me, but I'd made him promise he wouldn't interfere. I knew it would only end in disaster; Anwar had no right to defend me, so if he did it would only bring suspicion upon us.

When Yas and Abdul came to visit they would become more and more concerned. Yas would hold on to me, hugging and crying when she left, knowing that she was leaving me behind with a monster! Yas hated Ziad with passion for what he was doing to us, and when everyone else would be polite to him, she would refuse to speak or even look at him.

Abdul also hated him, but he knew that if he got involved he would go up against my family, also the elders of both my village and his own. I wasn't classed as Abdul's family, even though he was married to my sister.

I was stuck, with nowhere to run to, and no one to turn to for help, I couldn't even protect my own children. I'd never felt so helpless or abandoned in my whole life.

Tarek was around eight when I heard the rumour; their father was so desperate for money that he was going to sell him to his grandfather, Nasser Ziad, to pay off his debts.

When I confronted Ziad about this rumour, he didn't confirm or deny it, he told me the children belonged to him, so he could do as he pleased with them. He laughed while he told me Issy would also bring him a nice sum of money, and then he beat me so badly I could barely walk the next day.

The next morning he left for Sanaa and I sent Tarek to Rada'a to ask my sister to come for me. She came straight away; she loaded all our belongings into the back of the jeep and drove us away to her house. It was then that Abdul decided that he was going to get involved, he and Yas talked things over and they refused to allow me to return to Ziad.

A few days later, after Ziad found out what had happened he went to Dad, and Dad turned up at Abdul's house alone, demanding we go home and furious with Abdul for interfering, but Abdul refused to allow me to go anywhere!

Abdul had broken all the rules by interfering in another man's business, but he stood his ground and refused to allow Dad to take me. However, Dad wasn't happy that Abdul had got involved and returned with the elders of our village. Abdul still refused to allow me back into Dad's care unless he promised not to return me to Ziad. With all the elders listening to what Ziad had done to me over the years, Dad had no choice but to agree to look after me and my children. I was handed back to my father and taken back to his house.

Finally I was away from Ziad, but nothing was ever meant to be easy for us, I knew things would never be easy living with Dad; he was just as cruel and unpredictable as Ziad, but in different ways!

I thought that if I kept my head down and my children away from him then he would leave us alone, but I was wrong. As usual I was the main worker in the house but that never bothered me. Tarek worked hard in the fields, he was such a mature, strong boy for his age and Issy was a mini me, she wanted to do everything with me. Issy would always have one of her siblings attached to her hip in her attempt to play big sister! Dobia and Sadig were good quiet children. Dobia was such a strong healthy child who never moaned or cried even when she really hurt herself. I remember one time she fell head first onto a rock and hit her forehead so badly a piece of the rock broke off and became lodged in her forehead! There was blood everywhere and it took me hours to squeeze and pick the piece of stone out of her head, but she didn't say a word! Sadig was the quietest of my children; he hardly ever made a sound. He loved drawing and would spend hours outside in the dirt with a twig drawing pictures on the ground. Nasser was a good healthy baby who gave me no trouble and would just feed and sleep.

My little sister Ismahan latched on to me from the moment I got there; her mother never showed her the slightest bit of affection, all her affection went on Abdulla, and that was only when she could be bothered!

Viyza was pregnant again by this time with her third child, but she wasn't at all maternal. She would rather sit on her sewing machine all day and make money than spend time with her children; even when they were ill, she didn't care. The only time she came out fighting for her children was when Abdulla claimed that one of my children did something wrong, and that was all the time.

Abdulla was only a few years old but Viyza was already teaching him that violence and cruelty towards females was OK, he was growing up believing that because he was a boy, he could do whatever he wanted.

Viyza absolutely hated it when I moved back home. Although it was a huge house she felt as though the house had become too crowded for her, and she didn't hesitate in letting her feelings show this time around. Once she found out that Dad had agreed to look after me and not return me to Ziad, she picked every opportunity to point out to him what a mistake he had made by burdening himself with other people's children. She didn't care that I was his daughter and my children were his grandchildren.

It was awful living with them both. Dad never wanted us there from the beginning, but with his wife giving him more grief over us being there, that just pushed him over the edge, and he took out every bit of his anger and frustration on me! Dad would go to the fields almost every night to guard his ghat, and he would return in the morning to sleep, telling my children and me that if we made any noise that woke him up there would be consequences!

Tarek would have to go and work in the fields and I would have to tiptoe around the house doing my chores. The children would play outside in the scorching heat in fear that if I allowed them inside Dad would hear their voices and wake up. Viyza would sit in her room and sew; it was strange how her children could run up and down the stairs to her, but Dad would rarely shout out for them to be quiet, however if my children entered the house when he was asleep, he would wake up and go crazy with me and them, lashing out at me to keep them quiet.

When he woke up, usually early afternoon, he would eat his food and go to the fields once again, but those few hours he spent at home he spent shouting and ordering me around. He would never ask his wife to do anything, it was always me, and he would lash out over the slightest thing, his dinner not being made on time or the dogs not having enough to eat.

It was also a struggle not being able to allow my children to play freely while my brother was allowed to do whatever he wanted, and it was equally heart-breaking to watch Viyza give Abdulla affection, but when her own daughter cried for her mother, she would get pushed away. Abdulla would smack and hit his sister and never get told off for doing so, but if she cried from being hit by him, she would get shouted at, or even smacked again by her mother for crying!

I was forever trying to keep my children away from my brother in fear of them fighting, worried of what would happen if one of my children dared to fight back or lay a finger on my brother! If Dad was ever home he would never interact or chat to us when Viyza was around, he acted as though he was scared of what she might say or do.

At night I would sit quietly with my children and Ismahan would come and sit with us in the corner of the room, and while she and my children would draw or look through my box of endless pieces of scrap paper, I would sneakily read my Bible.

Months passed and by this time Viyza had given birth to another son called Zain; just like she did with her other children, she paid him little attention. If she wasn't on her sewing machine she was at her family home; she and I just didn't get on, she didn't want me there, and I didn't want to be there!

We couldn't sit down and talk or have a laugh and joke about anything, and this put a huge strain on us as a family. I tried my hardest to stay out of her way and keep the peace but it never seemed to work. I'd become a huge burden on my family, and so had my children.

I longed to get away and I would dream of being rescued, dream of running away, but one day blended into another and time passed me by.

Yas visited us a few times and although she had asked Dad to let me go and stay with her, he refused. It wasn't as though he didn't want to get rid of us, but he had to hold onto his pride in front of everyone, he had to show that he was taking care of his family.

Even though he and Abdul had spoken, he was still a little upset with him for interfering in his business. Dad wasn't one to let go of a grudge easily, and it hadn't been that long since Abdul had stood up to Dad because of me! Yas could see I was still unhappy and questioned me why, she asked if Dad was still hitting me, but

I lied again and told her he wasn't; I could see how worried she was about me but I could also see that she herself wasn't well. Her health had declined in recent years and although Abdul had taken her to see many doctors, nobody could tell them what was wrong with her. She had three children by now, Ghania, Amar and she hadn't long ago had another little boy called Hameed. The children she had were beautiful and healthy, and she was hoping that now Abdul would allow her to take birth control. It was on one of her visits that she saw just how bad Dad's violence was getting towards me, and how he nearly turned on her!

Our cousin Farouse had given birth to a son, and had come to the village for her family gathering. Everyone was gathered at Granddad's house for dinner, including Yas and Nebat, but Dad was asleep at his house. He had been arguing with Granddad over something and refusing to go to dinner, so we were going to put dinner aside for him for when he woke up.

Dad woke up before dinner and came over to Granddad's front door and started yelling for me to go home. Although his wife was also at Granddad's house, it was me he wanted to go and tend to his demands. I went home and he started yelling at me to quickly heat up some water for him to wash, so I went up to the kitchen and tried to start the small gas cooker that they had. While I was struggling with it he came into the kitchen and yelled at me to hurry up, saying he also wanted me to go and get him his dinner from Granddad's house!

When I finally got the cooker started I turned to Dad to try and convince him to come and eat dinner with us all over Granddad's, but he took this as me taking sides with them against him. He started slapping me around the head, over and over again. Whilst I was pleading with him to stop I could hear Yas calling my name from the bottom of the stairs, so I tried to get away from him by running out of the kitchen, but he grabbed me and punched me in the stomach, sending me hurling down the stairs, right to the feet of my sister who had come looking for me. Yas picked me up.

"What did you do to her?" she screamed at Dad, who was stood at the top of the stairs, but he came storming towards her, his fist clenched as if to punch her.

"Go on, try it! You'll see what you get back!" she warned in a tone that made him step back.

Dad lowered his fist. "You had better get your husband and go home!" he raged at her, but Yas was defiant.

"I will go home when I'm good and ready! And if you ever lay a finger on my sister again, I won't be responsible for what I do to you!" she threatened.

Dad pushed past us both as he stormed down into his room. "You're both going to end up like your mother!" he shouted, disappearing into his room. As we walked down the stairs hand in hand, Yas asked me why I lied when I told her Dad wasn't hitting me any more

"This is my life now, so I just need to get on with it," I told her, and then I asked her what she thought Dad meant when he said we would end up like Mum?

"Take no notice of him Moo, you know what he's like, he's just talking crazy!" she said, trying to reassure me.

When we got to Granddad's house Yas approached Viyza. "If your husband wants dinner, or anything else, then you better get up and go and do it for him, because my sister is not your slave!" she told her before she sat down. Viyza didn't answer Yas back, she didn't dare! Yas had a different status than I did with my family, and everyone else. Yas was the wife of a much respected diplomat and she held the same respect from everyone who respected him. I on the other hand was the wife of a disowned man and had no respect from anyone.

That day after my sister and everyone else went home, I went back to Dad's house; Dad was at the fields and Viyza ignored me, but that was nothing new from her, we only ever spoke when absolutely necessary.

That night I couldn't help but wonder why, over the years, my sister and I had given up fighting for ourselves. We would fight for each other, and we would fight for our children, but we had given up on ourselves. Our dream of ever going back home to England looked like just that, a dream. I'd talked to my children about England so many times, told them that one day I would bring them home with me. It had been almost 14 years, and although this was always a dream of mine, maybe I needed to stop dreaming; but if I did, what else would I have to dream about?

I was almost happy when my brother injured himself, needing hospital treatment. Dad was busy in the fields and Viyza was busy sewing, so I was chosen to take him to the hospital. I tried not to sound too excited as I put my sharsharf on, while Abdulla screamed his head off because he had fallen on glass, cutting his leg open. It was a bad cut and it obviously needed a few stitches, but I wasn't concerned with my brother, I was going to see Anwar!

I didn't need anyone to look after my own children because they looked after each other; they may have only been children themselves, but they had grown up looking after one other. Sat in the back of the jeep on the way to the hospital Abdulla sulked on my lap, but all I could think about was Anwar, was he still working there? It had been months and anything could have happened.

Once we arrived I got to reception and instead of booking Abdulla in I went to look for Anwar's office. I'd never been to his office before but Anwar had told me precisely where it was! I knocked on the door then waited; my heart skipped a beat when I heard his voice. "Come in!" Only my eyes were visible but he recognised me straight away.

"Muna!" He couldn't help but show his excitement as he jumped out of his seat, but I was worried he may say something, so I held Abdulla slightly higher in my arms. "I need a doctor for my brother," I said straight away.

Abdulla may have only been a child, but he was not someone we could trust. "Yes of course, you wait here," Anwar said as he rushed out, squeezing my arm as he went past me.

Within moments he returned with another man. "This man is going to look after him until I get some details from you, OK?" Anwar was nodding at me to convince me to hand Abdulla over to the other man.

"Go with the doctor," I told Abdulla. I knew the man wasn't a doctor, but I needed to reassure my brother who was still whining.

Once they left the room Anwar closed the door and grabbed me, squeezing me so tight I could barely breathe. "Hey, hey calm down a bit!" I joked.

"No I can't, let me see you," he said, pushing me back and pulling my face scarf down.

"I never thought I would see you again, thank you God, thank you!"

He started kissing my face all over, then hugging me, then kissing me again, until I made him stop.

"Stop it! I need to talk to you!" I said, pushing him playfully away while he tried to kiss me again.

"Don't be so cruel!" he sulked. "I need to hold you, and to kiss you and look and you, I need to smell your scent, I need as many kisses as I can to last me for as long as it takes, because I don't know when I will see you again, we don't need to talk here!"

He reached into his pocket and pulled out a letter. "I have carried this with me every day since you left, wishing, and praying, that you will walk through that door, it says everything I need to say for now!" He placed the letter in my hand, and I quickly put it down my top.

"I'm sorry, I didn't write you one," I said with a frown, but he just looked at me with a sad face.

"Is that because you don't love me as much as I love you?" he sulked.

"That's not true, it's because you have more time on your hands than I do, anyway, I don't have much time now because I have to see to my brother, so, tell me, what have you been doing?" I asked. Anwar grabbed me and held me close to him again.

"I'm not talking about me; tell me about you, what are your plans? Are you going to get a divorce? Are you planning on staying with your father?" He carried on with his questions until I let out a big sigh.

"What else can I do? I have nowhere else to go and I haven't heard from Ziad."

He sat me down and sat next to me, and then he told me that nobody had heard from Ziad since I left, and they didn't think he was coming back. Then he tried to convince me to go to Sanaa, he said he would help me find work and he would support us in any way he could. He told me that I should learn to be independent from everyone, and said that if I did, it would mean that we could see each other until Ziad divorced me.

I told him that although that sounded like something I would love to do, it wasn't something my family would allow me to do. I knew my family, and I also knew that if I ever tried to leave, my father would track me down, and kill me!

Then he told me that he himself had been offered a good job in Sanaa, but up until this time he had refused because he was waiting for me, convinced that eventually, I would turn up to see him. He said that now he had seen me he was going to take the job and hoped that soon, I too would go to Sanaa, so that we could be together.

With time passing quickly and my brother awaiting treatment, we said our goodbyes and I took my brother to see the doctor. He had his wound stitched up we went back home.

Once home I read the letter from Anwar, he was begging me to run away with him so that my children and I could have a better, free life, telling me how strong a person I was, and how much he loved me.

Anwar's letters, his words, they made me fall more and more in love with him. I wished I had the strength to make that choice, or was given the rights to choose what I wanted to do. I wanted to be with a man like him forever, someone who could love and respect me, love and respect my children, allow us freedom, allow us our own choices in life.

It was around a week later when we needed to take Abdulla back to the hospital, his wound was opening up and was weeping, and once again I was chosen to take him. As before I went straight to Anwar's office, but I was heartbroken to find him gone. I was told he had left, and although Anwar had told me of his intentions to leave I had no idea he meant so soon!

Abdulla was seen by the doctor and found to have glass in his wound, they had stitched his leg up with glass still in it; I found myself feeling guilty, if only I'd paid more attention to my brother's injuries on the day rather than putting my feelings for Anwar first, then I would have noticed the doctor not doing his job properly!

As I cradled Abdulla in my arms and he clung on to me while they unstitched his wound to clean it, I felt a slight connection with my brother for the very first time; he was merely a child, and it was not his fault the way he was behaving, it was the fault of the people who were bringing him up, and the culture that he was being brought up in! I knew that in reality my brothers and sister were also the victims of the culture they were born into, just as my children were.

When we got back from the hospital it was in the afternoon and Dad had gone to the fields for the night, and Viyza was sewing away at her machine. When she heard about Abdulla's leg she went berserk at me, blaming everything on me, she said that if I'd been looking after him properly in the first place he wouldn't have fallen and cut his leg, and why didn't I notice before now that the wound wasn't healing? We got into a huge argument. I did feel guilty about not paying attention at the hospital, but I told her Abdulla was her son, not mine! It was not my duty to look after her children, and if she loved him that much, she would have been the one to take him to the hospital, not me. I also told her that a good mother would have noticed before now that his wound wasn't healing!

Viyza got upset and stormed out of the house, saying that she was going to stay with her family for the night, but she told me she wasn't taking her children. She had no choice but to take Zain because she was still breastfeeding him, but she was leaving the other two with me! I was happy to see the back of Viyza for the night, but terrified of what Dad would do to me once she told him what I'd said to her.

That night, although I had seven children to look after we had lots of fun, we made as much noise as we wanted and ran around the house, even Abdulla, who would usually have his guard up when his parents were there, joined in our games and had lots of fun.

The next day Dad had his breakfast and dinner sent to the fields for him because he was busy with work, so I didn't see him until the afternoon. When he did come home he was chewing ghat and was in a mellow and calm mood, I was sure he had spoken to Viyza because he hadn't asked about her or mentioned her, so I found the strength to approach him and try to put my side of the story across. He was sat in the main room with his children; my children were outside playing, so I asked if I could talk to him.

"Of course, come and sit here," he said in a surprisingly good mood, while tapping the floor beside him. There was a time when I yearned for those moments of love and affection from Dad, but now I was older and somewhat wiser to his charm. I was merely here to put my side of the argument across, even though he still terrified me.

"Viyza and I had an argument yesterday." My voice was trembling and my mouth was drying up. Dad seemed unfazed, as though he already knew.

"What about?" he asked in a blank tone while he carried on playing with Abdulla.

"About Abdulla, I think she doesn't show him enough affection, especially when he's ill." I knew I was pushing it telling him these things, but I had to say something to defend my argument with her.

Dad looked concerned. "Are you saying she doesn't care?"

I just wanted to tell him exactly what I thought of her, but I knew I couldn't, I wasn't free to talk, to tell him that I thought she was devious, manipulative, cold hearted, unloving, selfish, back stabbing… the list goes on! But I couldn't say all these things; I knew I had to be careful what I said. I knew in a few days' time once he had spoken to his wife he would turn on me again!

"She should have checked Abdulla's wound ages ago but she's instead blaming me, she's too busy on her sewing machine, all she thinks about is that machine!" I said angrily. As soon as I spoke I waited for Dad to lash out and hit me, after all, I'd just insulted his wife, the mother of his children, but instead he looked at me with a hint of a smile.

"You care for Abdulla, don't you?" he asked, looking into my eyes.

"Of course I do Dad, he's my brother!" I insisted.

Dad smiled, "Well, you have a point about Viyza, I'm sick of her bloody machine, so as far as I'm concerned she can stay with her family, you can take care of your brother and sister, they will be safe with you!"

We sat together and chatted a little more, it was nice to see Dad relaxed when my children came up and played in the room. It was a rare occasion when he would allow my children to play inside if he was home.

That evening after Dad had gone to the fields, the children and I played games again and drew drawings on my scraps of cardboard and paper, then I laid them all down and told them children's stories from what I remembered being told to me when I was a child. I told them the story of Jack and the Beanstalk, I didn't have any books, but I remembered the stories in my head.

It had been a good day for us, Dad had been in a good mood, and the children had all gone to bed smiling. The next morning I was up bright and early to cook breakfast. Tarek took Dad's breakfast to the fields with him on his way to work, and I carried on with my chores and looking after the children. Dad was due home for lunch so I was busy in the kitchen, when suddenly Viyza turned up with one of her brothers.

She was furious that Dad hadn't gone around begging for her to come home, and she had come back to pack some clothes to take back with her, but that wasn't all she wanted; she was taking Abdulla!

Viyza knew that by taking Dad's favourite son she would provoke a reaction from him, she also knew that he would take out any anger on my children and me!

"Tell your father I'm taking his sons, if he wants to see them he knows what he has to do!" she demanded, dragging Abdulla down the stairs; he was crying because he didn't want to go with her.

"What about Ismahan?" I asked.

"I don't want her, you can keep her!" she snapped in her cold hearted voice, and then she ordered her brother to pick up her sewing machine and follow!

I couldn't hide the fact that I hated her just as much as she hated me; she was a rare breed in the Yemen and not in a good way. Most females were kind, good hearted, or at least had some decency in them, but Viyza didn't; her heart was made of stone, and that showed in the way she treated her own daughter, the child she gave birth to!

Ismahan started to scream while grabbing hold of her mother's dress as she was leaving the house, but Viyza just loosened her grip and pushed her away.

"Go to your precious sister!" she hissed at her daughter, shoving her in my direction. I ran over and picked Ismahan up to try and comfort her, but she was screaming to be with her mother. I knew Viyza was heartless but I was stunned at how cold she was being towards her own child.

"You're a heartless bitch!" I shouted after her as she walked away. "Does Ismahan mean anything to you?" I followed her out the door.

"I'm not telling Dad anything you said because I'm not your slave! If you want to speak to him, then you can go and find him yourself!" I screamed at her, but she quickly walked off totally ignoring both Ismahan and me, dragging Abdulla along with her.

As I held Ismahan in my arms I thought about what was going to happen to me once Dad got home; he was going to be livid with me for allowing her to take Abdulla, but what was I supposed to do? I tried to block it out of my head and carried on cooking dinner, knowing that there was nothing I could do to change the outcome of what was about to happen to me! Sure enough, about an hour later, my stomach turned when I heard Dad's voice calling out for Abdulla as he walked up the stairs; his voice got louder as he got closer to the kitchen, so I went out and faced him.

"Viyza came and took him but left Ismahan!" Once again my voice was trembling with fear.

Dad looked at me, disappointment filling his face. "I will deal with this later, just get me my food and then I'm going to sleep!" His voice said it all, once he woke up, I was in big trouble!

Dad ate his food and then went to sleep, and as soon as he woke up, around 7 pm, I was surprised when he left the house without a word. When he came back about an hour later my children and I were all upstairs ready for bed, they were huddled around in the corner of the room drawing, and I was reading my Bible. When I heard the knock on the door I ran downstairs, my heart was pounding as I opened the door, and to my surprise Dad was stood at the door with Abdulla in his arms.

"Hello!" I said to Abdulla, a big smile on my face, but before I finished saying it Dad had swung his arm and hit me with the back of his hand across my chin. Although I'd been hit harder it still hurt, and because I wasn't expecting it I stumbled a bit! I knew Dad had taken Viyza's side again without listening to me, and I was so angry with him for it.

"Now what have I done?" I shouted. I couldn't hold back my anger, and my voice was demanding an explanation.

"You make life so difficult for me don't you? You always have!" Dad was fuming as he stormed past me. "What did you say to Viyza?" he demanded to know as he made his way up the stairs with me behind him insisting I hadn't done anything wrong. Dad stormed up the stairs and into the room where the children had been drawing, but by then they had heard Dad's temper and they were all cowering in the corner of the room, with Tarek hugging them together in a protective circle. Dad looked over at the papers on the floor next to them.

"Get up, you little bastards!" he shouted at them. They didn't move but had started to cry with fear.

"Books! Books! Books!" he continued to yell. "You're just like your bloody mother, you remind me of her so much! I can't take it anymore!"

I could see his whole body filling with rage as he put Abdulla down and stormed over to my box of papers. "Well, no more!" he yelled as he started tearing at my precious books and papers and ripping them to pieces.

The box of papers not only had my scrap papers in it, but photos of my sister Issy, Yas, and my children, and also letters I'd kept over the years from my family, and so many other little things I'd kept as a reminder of years that had passed. I screamed in terror as I ran over to stop him, but Dad pushed me aside and onto the floor, and then he turned and kicked me in my thigh. As Dad went to kick me the second time Tarek shouted out at him and ran towards me to protect me.

"Leave my mum alone, stop hurting her!" he cried.

As Tarek tried to cover my body with his own, Dad went to lash out at him, aiming for him with a punch. "How dare you speak back at me!" he threatened as he lowered his fist at him, but I saw it coming, and as I pulled Tarek out of the way and into my arms I caught the blow myself. As I held on to my son Dad turned back to the papers, gathering them all together and shoving them into the box, making sure he didn't leave any behind, as he continued to ramble on like a mad man.

"That's all you ever do is bury your head in these bloody books, well no more!" he growled as he marched out of the room, the box tightly in his grasp. Once Dad had left the room, Tarek looked up at me.

"Don't worry Mother, I will protect you," he whispered as I held on tightly to him.

With a choice as to whether I should run after my father and try and save my life's worth of memories, or look after my terrified children, I chose to stay; I knew that if I'd chosen to follow, someone would have been hurt. Dad had always been this spiteful, cruel, and hurtful towards me, and now he was going to repeat the same behaviour with my children.

A few minutes later I could smell smoke coming from upstairs, and I knew Dad was burning my papers, but again I chose to stay put and comfort my children. I knew I wouldn't have been able to stop him from doing what he was doing; he was angry with Viyza not me, but he couldn't vent his anger out on her, because he was a coward.

I stayed with the children until he came back down and took Abdulla, and then he went and locked himself in his room. Later that night after everyone was asleep I snuck upstairs to see if anything had survived the fire, but Dad had put everything in the clay oven and made sure they had turned to ashes. He was a cruel man in so many ways!

That night it was as though I'd lost another loved one. I sat beside the oven and quietly wept until I couldn't cry anymore. Dad had taken so much from me, and he kept on taking. Deep down I knew I had to put a stop to him hurting us anymore, before one of my children got hurt standing up for me. As I reached down my top I pulled out the letters from Anwar; I hadn't taken them off my body since he gave them to me. I knew I needed to find him, and be with him. I went back downstairs and lay down by my children, hoping that somehow, someway, a miracle would happen that would allow me to get away from my father.

The next few days Dad spent most of his time at the fields. Abdulla was back with his mother, but Ismahan was still with us. When he did come back home he would have Abdulla with him and they would totally ignore Ismahan. Abdulla was cruel towards his sister and I could see so much of Dad in him, even though he was just a child! I tried so much to just love him because he was my flesh and blood, my brother, but Dad and Viyza made that so hard by the way they treated him and paraded him in front of the other children.

Ismahan would cry when Dad left with Abdulla in his arms to take him back to his mother, but Abdulla would shout at her and tell her that her mother didn't want her because she cried too much. My children and I would hold her and tell her she was the sweetest little thing ever, she didn't cry for nothing, she was a sweet girl who was lovely and kind and we all loved her. Unfortunately for Ismahan, my little sister's fate had been decided the day she was born as my father's daughter. She was merely a girl, unloved and unwanted. She would be sold, just like we were; it was just a matter of time.

Chapter Twenty
The Marble Step

It was late 1989, and my escape from Dad at this time came in the form of my uncle Ahmed, whose wife was pregnant and needed someone to look after her. Uncle Ahmed told Dad that his wife Azeza wasn't well, and had been told to take rest until she gave birth; he managed to persuade Dad to allow us to go and stay with him in Sanaa until his wife gave birth. Azeza had family of her own who could have gone and looked after her if she needed it, but Uncle Ahmed had his own reasons for wanting us to go.

Once I'd taken my little sister to my grandmother so that she could look after her until her mother decided to pick her up, we were on our way, and I couldn't wait to be out of the village, and away from Dad! Later, Uncle Ahmed explained that he had heard Dad was mistreating us, and he wanted to offer us his help. He said his wife wasn't as ill as he had made out, he told me he would keep us with him for as long as possible. I thanked him for his help and told him I would do everything I could to help him and his family. I barely knew Azeza, but what I had seen and heard was good.

Once in Sanaa we settled in to Uncle Ahmed's flat, it was tiny compared to the houses in the village. This was a two bedroom flat in a block of flats, and there were going to be nine of us living here now. Azeza was lovely and did everything she could to make us feel welcome; she was around four months pregnant and already had a little son called Hisham. Their house was only five minutes' walk from my sister Nebat's house, and that afternoon she turned up with her children. It was great seeing her and catching up properly, but I missed Yas.

Yas wasn't in Sanaa or Rada'a any more, she was now in a city called Dhamar. Yas and Abdul had moved again because of his work, once again he had moved up in his rank in government and because of his promotion they had to move house and city. They were now living in a beautiful huge mansion in Dhamar, however, although this promotion gave Abdul a higher paying job and a better title, it also meant more responsibilities for Yas, and my sister was becoming more and more unwell.

I was seeing less and less of my sister, but every opportunity we could spend together we would. As soon as she found out I was in Sanaa she sent word via her mother in-law that she was coming soon to visit me in Sanaa. I couldn't wait.

My children had always been used to playing outside in the street, which was something Dad made them do when we lived with him, and in the villages that's what children did anyway, but in the city they couldn't do that. Uncle Ahmed lived on a main road with lots of traffic so they weren't allowed outside, and that became difficult at times. I would send them over to Nebat's house on most days to play with her children, because she had a huge gated garden and they could play outside.

Azeza was a lovely girl and we got on great, she was lucky that her family had allowed her to be educated, something that is very rarely seen in Yemen! My uncle was also well educated and had a very well paid job, he would be gone all day at work and I would make sure that Azeza didn't need to lift a finger; I wanted to make sure that I gave them no reason to want to send me back to Dad, no reason to complain.

I yearned to call Anwar; I knew his brother's number, I had it imprinted in my brain, and I knew he was in Sanaa, but fear stopped me! The fear of being found out, fear of letting my uncle down, fear of being sent back to Dad, fear, fear, fear!

Every day, since I arrived in Sanaa, I wanted to pick up Uncle Ahmed's house phone and call Anwar. I wasn't allowed to use the phone, but surely once wouldn't hurt, they wouldn't know! One day, a few weeks after I arrived, while Azeza was visiting the doctors, I finally picked up the courage to make the call.

"Hello!" came the sound from the other end. My heart started beating, he sounded so much like Anwar.

"Can I speak to Anwar please?" I said quietly.

There was a gasp, and then, "Muna, is that you?"

My heart skipped a beat. "Who is this?" I asked, needing to be sure! Anwar started giggling and I knew for sure it was him. "Anwar, it's you!" I was smiling, all excited.

"Where are you?" he asked. I told him quickly where I was and why I was there; I also told him I couldn't talk for long because I wasn't allowed to use the phone.

I was the one who did the food shopping from the market, so we arranged to meet up a few days later at the market; I told him I would have Tarek with me so he would recognise me, because I would have my veil on.

We said our goodbyes, and I got back to my chores. I was happy, I couldn't stop smiling, I was over the moon with joy knowing that soon, I would see the man I loved.

The day came that I would go to the market and meet Anwar; I didn't tell my son that I'd arranged to meet him, I would pretend it was a coincidence! I knew I was putting pressure on him and it did worry me; however I knew that Anwar was someone that Tarek also loved and respected, and I knew that Anwar loved and respected my children.

The market was crowded and I was hot and sweating, covered from head to toe in my sharsharf; not only did I have to cover my face with a scarf, leaving only my eyes visible, but on top of that I had to wear a veil to cover my whole face. We were there to buy groceries, but I was more interested in the crowd, I was looking for Anwar, and soon I spotted him!

My heart sank as he made his way through the crowd and came closer; I could see he was limping, struggling to walk, and I just wanted to run over to him and help him, and then I saw the crutches! Tarek spotted him the same time as I did. "Mum, it's Anwar, look!" he said, running over to him, hugging him and throwing his arms around him to help him walk over to where I was.

"What happened to you?" I asked. I felt as though I wanted to cry before he even spoke.

"I just had a little accident," he replied, ruffling Tarek's hair.

"How's my son?" he asked Tarek.

Tarek started telling him how we had been living at his Grand-dad's and how we didn't like it, but now we are staying with my Uncle who is nice. He went on to tell him how much he'd missed him. Anwar told him he missed him too, and then he suggested we go for a walk away from the market because it was so crowded, and I agreed.

We walked and talked, and after I kept asking and asking he finally told us why he was using crutches; he had been in a car accident a few days after my visit to the hospital, that was why he had left his job so quickly. He had broken both legs, and his hip, and had to have them put back together with pins and screws, and he had only just started walking again on crutches.

I was devastated that I hadn't known and couldn't do anything to help him, but as usual, Anwar was all smiles and didn't want to talk about himself, he wanted to know about the other children and wanted to see them. I told him it would be too risky for me to bring them to the market; Tarek could keep a secret, but they were too young.

He told me Thahaba and Umie Ayesha was in Sanaa now, and would love to see me and the children, if I would go and visit. I told him they would need to visit me first at my uncle's flat; other-wise I knew I wouldn't be allowed to visit them. We didn't spend long with him because I didn't want to get into trouble, but I told him what days we came to the market, and told him if things changed I would try and call him again.

Tarek hung on to him when it was time to leave and didn't want to go, but Anwar promised to see him again, then he secretly passed me a letter, which I quickly put down my top! We got home and nobody was suspicious that I'd done anything wrong; as soon as I could I went and read the letter he gave me. He was begging me to take the chance now that I was in Sanaa to run away with him, asking me to put my faith in him to help me and our children if we needed him.

What Anwar didn't understand is that I did have faith in him to do right by me and my children, I knew he loved me with all his heart, but I needed to write to him and let him understand that I would never run away with him in Yemen, and why. Although he loved me he didn't understand my fears; if we ran away and hid in Sanaa, or anywhere in Yemen, but then got caught, it would mean instant death for us, and that would mean my children grow up without a mother, just like I did. There would always be a possibility that we would be found. I had too much family, so did Ziad, and they would never let me just run away without trying to find me; it wasn't safe to even try. That night I sat down and wrote Anwar a letter.

Finally Yas came to Sanaa and it was great to see her and her children, she stayed for a few weeks at Abdul's family's home which was close to Uncle Ahmed's house, and we saw each almost every day. She and Nebat would come over to visit me or we would all go to Nebat's house, it was good to be able to sit with my sisters and watch our children play without me having to worry about anything other than being with my sisters.

Yas was thinner than ever, the doctors still had no idea why she was so frail or why she was in so much pain, so she carried on with the task of looking after Abdul and his army of soldiers, who followed him wherever he went.

Yas was still in contact with Uncle Jim who she had stayed with on her last visit to England. Uncle Jim was always calling and writing, anxious not to lose contact with either of us and wanting to stay up to date with our lives. Time with Yas always went by so quickly and before I knew it she was gone again, she went back to her life, and I back to mine.

Nebat was a tower of strength for me at my time at Uncle Ahmed's house, just as she was for Yas when I was in Africa; she would always take my children to her house knowing that the flat was small and crowded, not wanting for us to put extra strain on Uncle Ahmed or Azeza, who was having a particularly hard time with her pregnancy.

I carried on with my regular visits to the market to see Anwar, and after he read my letter he stopped asking me to run away with him; he said he wasn't giving up on us, but he would find another way for us to be together. We would always exchange letters at the market because it was difficult to say certain things in front of Tarek. His letters would always make me smile because he would always write love poems and silly drawings, with lots of kisses. Those letters would always stay down my top, they were becoming a little bundle by now but I couldn't take the risk of hiding them somewhere else!

Anwar's hip hadn't healed as well as it should have. The surgery he had done was not good, and he ended up with a metal rod sticking out from the flesh on his hip. The doctors insisted it had been cut and filed as close to the bone as it could be, but told him his bones had grown around the metal rod that they had planned to remove and there was nothing they could do but leave it as it was! It was constantly infected because it was an open wound and he was left with a permanent limp. He didn't have enough money to find anyone else to do surgery for him, so until he could find some money, he was left in pain.

I didn't receive a visit from Umie Ayesha or Thahaba until Azeza gave birth to her little daughter. Although nobody else knew they were coming, Anwar had already told me in advance that they were going to turn up at an afternoon gathering, and use the birth as an excuse for their visit. My children were over the moon to see Umie Ayesha, and she was to see them; there was no denying how much they loved each other, it was the circumstances of the family problems that got between us seeing each other. She spent most of the afternoon kissing and cuddling them, while Thahaba and I caught up on all the gossip.

Ziad still hadn't been seen or heard of since I left, but that wasn't something that interested me; although I would have liked a divorce from him, that would have left me open for Dad to sell me on again, so I was OK as I was - and he was a bad father to my children, so I had no interest in having him back in their lives!

Umie Ayesha was now living in Sanaa in her Brother Nasser Ziad's house, taking care of him when he was in Sanaa. His wife had moved back to Lebanon, she always spent a lot of time in Lebanon, and he didn't spend a lot of time in Yemen because he travelled abroad a lot with work.

Umie Ayesha was also in Sanaa because there was fighting going on between certain tribal groups and the government. The fighting had been going on for a while and there were troops in and around Ziad's village, and lots of other towns and villages nearby. She told me about a beautiful hilltop Nasser Ziad had once bought for Ziad and me, and told us he would build us a house once we came back from Africa, but it never happened once they had the falling out. Now the hilltop had now been taken over by the troops, it was apparently full of tanks.

In Sanaa we didn't hear or see any fighting, but when people came to Sanaa from the villages they would talk of hearing bombs and gun fights going on in the hills and mountains all the time.

Thahaba was also now living in Sanaa with her brothers Anwar and Jabil; she now also had her son Mohammed living with her on a permanent basis, and both her brothers helped her provide for him. Anwar's sister Salwa, who was an air hostess and travelled a lot, also stayed with them when she was in Sanaa. They were also awaiting the arrival of Anwar's mother from Sudan to join them in Sanaa.

I visited Thahaba once while I was in Sanaa; it was when Anwar's mother arrived from Sudan. Anwar was sat in a side room while I was there, and though I didn't get to see him he passed me a note with Thahaba. Anwar's mother was a lovely, kind and gentle lady, who made it very easy for me to like her from the moment we first met. She had no idea about my relationship with Anwar, and at the time had asked Anwar to get engaged to his cousin; although she didn't insist, it was something she was hoping he would think about. Anwar told her he had no interest in marrying his cousin, or anyone else at that time, however, his mother was desperate for him to marry, but she wasn't pushing him. That note that Thahaba passed to me was the last contact I had with Anwar for a long time.

A few days later we got a phone call from Abdul asking if I could go and spend time with Yas in Dhamar, he said she wasn't well and needed someone to help her with her chores. Uncle Ahmed decided I was allowed to go and stay with her for a few weeks, he insisted I was to return to his house once Yas no longer needed me.

When we arrived at Abdul's house Yas was tired, she had so much to do as the wife of a diplomat and sometimes things were just too much for her, but she wasn't ill, she was lonely. Yas also had something she wanted to discuss with me. She told me she had made friends with a girl called Sofia, an English girl who had come to the Yemen willingly to marry a Yemeni. Sofia had told her that there was a place in Sanaa called the British Embassy where they could help me get a passport and help me go home to England. Yas said Sofia told her that if I told the Embassy my story, they could also help my children.

Yas and I discussed the possibility of me escaping first, and then she promised she would follow once I was there, and only if I was there. I promised her I would sneak out and go and find the Embassy once I was back at Uncle Ahmed's house.

Yas's house was lovely, with marble hallway floors and huge beautiful rooms; we settled in straight away, and she and Abdul made sure my children had everything they wanted. My children and I didn't have a care in the world for the first couple of weeks, until one day my youngest son Nasser had an accident that would change his life forever.

The children loved running up and down the hallway on the marble flooring, sliding and skidding across the floor while they laughed, it wasn't often they were allowed to play freely, making as much noise as they wanted without repercussions. Nasser was 18 months old, he was a bright little boy who had been walking since he was just nine months old, and he was learning to talk and had no problems whatsoever.

There was a tiny marble step in the hallway, and one horrible day Nasser slipped, banging the back of his head on the corner of the step. I heard the other children screaming for me and I ran from the kitchen to find Nasser lying on the step, his eyes were rolling back and he was making a funny noise, grunting, and then he fell asleep.

I picked him up, not knowing what had happened to him. I cradled him in my arms, rubbing the back of his head and kissing him telling him everything would be OK, not realising or knowing that he had suffered serious damage. He woke up as I carried him into the room and sat down with him, cradling him as if he had just fallen over and bumped his head like any other day. As time went by I realised Nasser had bumped his head badly: he was turning yellow and was throwing up, his cry wasn't a normal cry, just a moan, and he kept drifting in and out of sleep.

Yas called Abdul, who came home straight away, and we took Nasser to the hospital. The doctor checked him over and said he couldn't find anything wrong with him. No X-rays were taken, or blood tests done. The Doctor said he was fine and gave him a course of antibiotic injections, which he showed me how to do myself because he said I would have to be the one to inject him. I took Nasser home, but his condition never improved, and he continued to drift in and out of sleep for days.

From that day on Nasser's walking became unstable, he had to learn to walk and talk all over again, he suffered fits, and his behaviour changed. Unknown to me, Nasser had suffered a brain injury.

A week later I was returned to Uncle Ahmed, but within days Dad started nagging that I needed to go back to the village. I tried my best to find a time when I could sneak out of the house to go and find the Embassy but was never able to go. I will never know why Dad wanted me back other than to be their slave, because neither he nor his wife wanted me there.

Uncle Ahmed did everything he could to keep me with him and avoid sending me back to Dad; he made out that Azeza was ill, then that his children were not well and they needed my help, but Dad insisted.

We were about to go back to the village when we received terrifying news that Nebat's husband had been involved in a car accident, and was expected to die.

Nebat was at the hospital when Uncle Ahmed and I arrived; we had gone together because we were told that Nebat was pulling her hair out at the hospital and nobody could calm her down. Uncle Ahmed knew that as sisters we had become extremely close, and he knew that Nebat needed me. We rang Yas before we left for the hospital and told her what was going on.

The hospital was filthy, the floors and corridors were full, and there were people everywhere! On the ward there was row after row of old hospital beds full of sick, dying men, wrapped up with blood stained bandages! Nebat was at the far end of this huge long ward, she was on the floor beside Ahmed's bed, tugging at her headwear, pulling her hair out, while she wallowed in grief.

There were people beside her but they were not trying to reassure or comfort her, they were trying to adjust her headwear so her hair wouldn't show; to them, this would be shameful!

I quickly made my way over, I'd seen Nebat like this before, when Issy died, and I knew that nobody could unclench those fingers when she gripped them like that! I sat next to her and put my arms around her holding her close, whispering in her ear that it would be OK. I told her I was there now, and that Yas was on her way. As soon as she heard my voice she let go of her hair and hugged me, crying uncontrollably.

Ahmed was in a coma. From the time of his accident he was kept on a main ward, hooked up to a machine, and put on an IV drip. He was six foot two, or taller, and his legs hung over the edge of the bed; he just looked uncomfortable lying on this tiny bed. His body was full of blood stained bandages in an attempt to cover his injuries, and his head was just huge. We couldn't tell his eyes from his nose, or his nose from his lips! The doctors said they didn't know what was wrong with him, but they gave him antibiotics, and were waiting to see if he would wake up.

Yas arrived within hours and we both stayed with Nebat; now it was our turn to support our sister.

Dad arrived the next day. Word had spread fast about Ahmed's accident because Ahmed was very much loved, and although he wasn't a rich man he was kind, loyal and funny. Both Nebat and Ahmed were loved by everyone; people came from far and wide to show their support to both of them after his accident.

Nebat had struggled through the years; she and Ahmed were building a new house in Sanaa. They had started building it after we first arrived in Yemen, and were in the middle of doing so when this tragedy happened. Ahmed was a carpenter, and his workshop was a garage on the side of his house. He was the main builder with their new home, with Nebat helping him. They had little money and Ahmed's work was their main income, now he was in hospital they would be cut off from any income.

We all knew that Dad would be of no help to her, or her children. Dad had barely acknowledged Nebat since he came back to Yemen and back into her life all those years ago; he treated her as if she hardly existed. He only really visited her if he was visiting Sanaa and needed somewhere to stay, or if it was a family occasion, for example if she gave birth. All we could do was pray that Ahmed would wake up and be ok!

A few days after Ahmed's accident Dad tried to make me go back to the village with him. This caused a huge argument between us. I was still scared of Dad but I was becoming more and more frustrated with him, and this frustration was giving me a bit more courage to answer him back. I'd been at Nebat's side since Ahmed's accident and wasn't prepared to leave her; she needed me now more than ever.

Uncle Ahmed stepped in once again and told him I should be allowed to stay and look after my sister's children while she cared for her husband. Dad backed down and left without me. I moved in with Nebat and we spent our time between the hospital and her home, while Yas stayed at her in-laws and came over every day to help us out.

It was difficult for Nebat because at the hospital she would have to be nurse for her husband or he would be left in his own filth every day. There was no one to care for those in hospital; patients were left to die in their beds if their relatives didn't go in to care for them.

Ahmed was in a coma for many weeks before he regained consciousness, and when he finally did, we realised how badly injured he was. He had suffered horrendous brain damage, and that was something doctors in Yemen didn't understand, or treat!

Ahmed didn't recognise anyone and his behaviour became uncontrollable! He was paralysed down one side of his body and he couldn't speak, he also had no control over his bodily fluids. On top of all this Ahmed was lashing out at everyone, he didn't know what he was doing so we couldn't tell him to stop.

As soon as he woke up Nebat was told to take him home, there was no place for him in hospital any more, as far as the doctors were concerned he was as recovered as he would ever be!

We were all devastated for Nebat and her children. Not knowing what her future held we tried our best to run around and help her with Ahmed, after all, he was her husband, and her children's father. We helped her to carry him, toilet him, wash him, feed him, exercise him, teach him to walk, talk… It was like having a giant baby with a violent temper, and with Nebat less than five feet tall, this was never going to be easy for her! Nebat would cry herself to sleep every night, but wake up every morning with a fresh smile and a positive attitude.

After about a month Yas had to go back to her life with her husband. Although she tried to stay, she wasn't allowed; she had her own house to run and Abdul was extremely busy and needed his wife at home to support him. Yas travelled back and forth as much as she could and sent food and money to keep us going, while I stayed with Nebat for many months.

While I was there we taught Ahmed so many things, he became calmer, and although he still had many outbursts they were further apart; we learnt how to talk to him and eventually calm him down. We sometimes walked him to the toilet and Nebat would wash him alone instead of the two of us having to hold him or wash him. He learnt to eat his food with a wooden spoon made especially for him, although not great, he did it himself! His speech was very slurry, but he was getting there; his progress was slow but ongoing, and we knew never to give up!

For the first few months while at Nebat's house I had no contact with Anwar. I knew I had much more to do than think about myself. My sister needed me and so did my son. Nasser was still very ill and looking after him was difficult, especially with Nebat's husband now needing so much care. My other children would always care for their brother and play with him, which made things so much easier for me.

When I finally started contacting him again we decided to meet at a different market not too far from Nebat's house. That's when I first saw the Embassy; it was huge and had a big British flag hung above it. Anwar laughed when I said I thought it was the president's house, asking me why id thought the president of Yemen would have a British flag hung outside his house.

I told Anwar my intentions and he told me to go for it, he said I needed to do whatever was best for me and my children. I would go to the market with my children and walk past the Embassy like a snail, listening to the people talk English as they came in and out. It took me a while to pluck up the courage to go past the gates, or talk to somebody. I always thought I would get arrested for trying, or told to go away, or anything other than yes, we can help you.

I would stand outside the Embassy and tell my children that British people worked in that building, and that they made passports for people to go on airplanes to England. My children must have thought I was crazy because they had no clue what I was talking about! I'd always spoke to them about the dream of one day going back to England, but that's what it always had been for me, just a dream. It was a day when I had my two girls with me, and I was hanging around outside, when I first met Karen, an Embassy worker.

Karen approached my girls, who were closer to the gates than I was; although my children had very little, I would always comb their hair and dress them as best as I could, they both had beautiful, long curly hair!

"Look how lovely you both are!" she said, touching Ismahan and Dobia on their heads and speaking in broken Arabic. "Marsh Allah, you have beautiful daughters!" she said, looking over at me. I realized she must have thought I was Yemeni because I was wearing my sharsharf, so I replied in English.

"Thanks, they are beautiful, aren't they?" Karen looked at me, surprised.

"You speak excellent English! Where are you from?" she asked. Not knowing what to say, I hesitated for a second.

"Are you from here or are you married to a Yemeni, as I am, are you just living here?" she carried on, and this time I didn't hesitate!

"I'm English, I've been here since I was 13; my father brought me and my sisters here and forced us to get married…" just as I was about to carry on talking, someone called Karen's name from a window inside the building, telling her she needed to hurry up and go inside.

"Listen," Karen came closer to me, "if you need any help, I work here, if you ever need me, just come to the gate and ask for me, my name is Karen, what's yours?" Without hesitating I replied.

"Muna, my name is Muna!" I could see Karen was in a rush, she was still being called from inside the Embassy.

"OK Muna, I have to go now but it was nice to meet you, please come back and see me, see you again soon, bye!"

With that Karen was gone, and I was left stood outside the Embassy gates not knowing what to do. I knew that British people worked in the Embassy and that British people got passports from the Embassy, but I had no clue as to what help Karen could offer me. I dreamt endlessly of going back to England, but I also knew that just because Karen had been kind enough to speak to me and offer us help, that didn't mean that she could actually help me. I had no money, no passport, and most of all, I had my five children.

I went back to Nebat's and decided that for the time being I needed to try and put my meeting with Karen in the back of my mind; at this moment in time my sister still needed me. While Nebat struggled with finding their next meal and caring for her husband, I tried to help her by keeping her house in order. Nebat struggled with money and depended on hand-outs from Yas, my uncles, and her mother's side of the family.

Dad told her he was struggling and couldn't help her financially; he complained that he was losing work because of the conflict going on around the villages. We had been hearing more and more about conflict going on in the outskirts of our villages, and how this was having an impact on certain people, and how they went about their lives.

Dad had still been sending messages for me to go back home, but Uncle Ahmed had managed to put him off by telling him I was still needed at Nebat's house; however I knew it was only a matter of time before I got sent back to the village. I'd spoken to both Yas and Anwar about my meeting with Karen; they were both supportive, and convinced me go back and speak with her and see if she could help me get a passport to go back to England. I was all ready to go and speak to her when suddenly we got some dreadful news; Dad had disappeared!

Chapter Twenty One
Dad's Confession!

We were all in a state of panic; we were told that he had been picked up from the fields while he was working, and driven away by a jeep full of soldiers, but nobody knew where he was, or why it had happened!

Within hours of being told the news I was on my way back to the village, apparently Granddad had insisted I go back, saying I was needed to give support to Dad's wife and children. With all the male members of my family now backing Granddad, I had no choice but to go back to the village. I was devastated; it was as though forces were against me. Every time I thought I was closer to finding a way out, I was dragged back to the village, and into the clutches of my family.

With many of our family members working in government positions we soon found out that Dad was suspected of having information that the soldiers wanted, and they were willing to go to any lengths to get their information! They had kidnapped him, and he was being held in prison and being tortured. Everyone knew that my uncles, both Nasser and Saleh, had ties with groups that fought against the government. Uncle Nasser was part of a Tribal Group who opposed the President Ali Abdulla Saleh; they wanted unification of the North and South of Yemen. Uncle Saleh was part of a group called the 'The Muslim Brotherhood', who also opposed the president. But Dad wasn't like them, he was just a farmer.

Since being back Uncle Saleh had married one of his younger

cousins, it was a very quiet celebration because although he was allowed back in the village, he was not liked much. His wife, a young girl called Jalelah, still lived with her mother because Uncle Saleh didn't want her living with his family. He never stayed for long in the village, and when he was gone we would never know where he was, or what he was doing, or when he would be back.

Uncle Nasser had also secretly married a young girl from our village and taken her with him to Aden; he would also be gone for long periods of time, and only came when he had business to attend to, and we never knew where he was, or when he would come back.

We were told that there were now talks between tribal leaders and the government that could mean an end to the conflict and fighting, and that meant Uncle Nasser would be able to openly come back and live wherever he wanted, with no need to hide away in the mountains anymore. However, the agreement hadn't yet been made and the soldiers had found out that Dad was related to my uncles. They suspected that he was either in on their fight or had information; either way, they had him and were not giving him back.

I'd come to hate my father for the things he had done to us over the years, but the thought of him being in prison and tortured broke my heart, I couldn't understand why they took him.

The months that Dad spent in prison were hard; Viyza and I didn't see much of each other because she spent most of her time at her family home. That made things a little easier for me. I didn't like her and didn't want to be around her, and I spent most of my time at Granddad's house.

Granddad spent most of his time travelling between the village and Sanaa trying to secure Dad's release, he found it difficult and frustrating and was only given very little information. We would hear the odd explosion in the far distance, which would let us know that fighting was still going on somewhere. We would also see the odd military tank drive through the village heading to some unknown destination, but in reality we had no idea of what was really going on.

We had no idea where Dad was being held, only that he was still alive, or at least that was what we were being told. We knew that people in prison got treated badly at the best of times, but this was a military conflict which was even worse. Prisoners being tortured were lucky to make it out of prison alive.

Most people were kept in prison until a family member paid a back handed payment for their release. If the crime was a bad crime, or you had no one who cared about you, people would stay in prison to rot and die, without even a trial! If a family member didn't bring your food then you were lucky to get one meal a day. Prisoners slept on concrete floors with no blankets and used anything they could find as their toilet, they had no access to water unless given to them, and that was very little.

Many months later, with the help of family members who were forming a new government, he was handed back to us. Dad had always been a thin man, but when he came out of prison he was skin and bone. They had pulled out his finger nails and toe nails. He told us they would hook up electricity to his genitals to shock him, these were a few of the terrible things they did to him. He couldn't walk for months from the injuries to the soles of his feet!

He was frail, and couldn't do anything for a long time. He would have terrible nightmares and wake up shouting and sweating, and although Viyza would tell everyone what hard work Dad had become for her because he was a temporary invalid, it was never her that took care of him, but me, his daughter.

Dad would never go to hospital for treatment even before his imprisonment; if he cut himself badly he would treat himself, with a needle and thread! So just like always, he and I took a needle and thread and stitched up his deep wounds ourselves.

Yas came as often as she could, she sat with Dad and helped as much as she could, and Dad would sit and talk with Yas, more than he did with me. She wasn't a burden on him like I was, and in his own way he respected the fact that she was now the wife of a diplomat.

For a while Dad and I got on OK; he knew he needed me, his wife was useless and I was the only person who was there to give him support. It took him a long time to recover but after he was well enough he managed to go back to work in his fields. Dad knew that if he didn't go back to the fields he wouldn't be able to provide for his children.

Within weeks of Dad recovering and returning to work, he went back to being his nasty self, and if possible, worse. I could understand Dad having a hard time because of him being kidnapped and tortured, I could understand his mood swings, his lack of sleep, and his lack of appetite; after all, he had been through a lot over the past few months. However, I'd been through much worse in my life.

I'd been kidnapped and tortured for many, many years, not just months, emotionally, mentally, sexually and physically abused. I'd hoped that Dad would have changed after his ordeal; after all, I'd cared for him and nurtured him back to health even after everything he had done to us.

Dad always felt like he had the right to take his anger out on me whenever he had a bad day, and since I was a child he had gotten away with it, but I was a mother now and I was becoming wiser and stronger, and things were about to change.

Once again I tried my best to put up with Dad's anger towards me; it was as if I triggered a switch in his brain when he looked at me, and I couldn't understand why. He was constantly hitting me and I could feel myself ready to snap, it was as if a volcano was building up inside me, waiting to explode, but I tried my best to stay in control. I knew the risk I would be taking if I let my anger out; with no friend in the village to run to for protection, and nowhere to go, I knew Dad would kill me if I went up against him!

I felt so isolated and I was too worried to say anything to Yas. Abdul was very high in power by now and Yas had so much going on with her own family, it seemed every time she saw me I had problems. It was unfair for me to keep burdening her.

I knew sooner or later I would have to stand up for myself, but I didn't know how. With every day that passed I was feeling as if there was something more that I needed to do, something more that I should be saying. However, I did nothing, and said nothing, until things turned so bad one day that Dad not only took his anger out on me, but also on my oldest son Tarek.

From the day my first child was born, everyone knew that if you wanted to hurt me, the only way you could really do it was to hurt my children. I'd become immune to physical pain when inflicted on me. But I wouldn't stand for anyone to inflict that same pain on my children.

Dad was well matched up when he married this wife; they were both as bad as each other because in my eyes Viyza was an evil woman, cruel in so many ways! We hardly ever spoke; even though we lived together we would sit in different rooms. When Dad was home and awake she would eat with him, and I would eat with my children, if Dad was asleep or in the fields she would eat alone. She sat on her sewing machine every day and went crazy if anyone interrupted her, even her own children. She was a very cold hearted woman who didn't seem to care if she saw others in pain. She reminded me so much of Farouse's mother-in-law, and I'd seen what she was capable of! Viyza would always blame anything that went wrong on me or my children, and on this particular day she had hidden the huge metal key for the front door just to teach me a lesson, because someone interrupted her sewing!

I knew it was her that put it somewhere because I'd seen it in her hand earlier that day. When Dad woke up from his sleep around mid-afternoon, Viyza told him that my children had lost the key; therefore she would not be able to lock the front door when he went to the fields that night. She told him she was going to take her sons and stay with her family until I found the key, and then she went off, leaving Dad furious with me and my children for causing her to leave.

With Dad going into an instant rage I frantically searched for the key. I knew it was somewhere upstairs because that's where I'd seen her with it, and I finally found the key hidden high up in a gap in the kitchen wall, too high to have been put there by a child!

No matter how much I tried to reason with Dad, or tell him that she had done this on purpose, he refused to listen, ending up with him brutally attacking me in front of my terrified children, and his own daughter, who by this time were cowering in the corner of the room.

As I covered myself from his blows I heard Tarek scream, then he launched himself at Dad, waving his arms and kicking out at him while screaming at him to leave his mother alone. Dad immediately turned on Tarek, cursing him for having the nerve to stand up to him, slapping him and grabbing him by the scruff of his neck as he dragged him out of the room.

I ran after Dad and a struggle took place over Tarek, but with all my other children now hanging on to me in fear, Dad managed to win and drag my son downstairs and out onto the street, where he took the key I'd recently found, locking the door behind him from the inside.

Dad and I continued to struggle while he dragged me back upstairs and threw me into the room; we were all sobbing and shaking with fear and I was terrified Dad would attack the rest of my children; he was acting like a caged animal and his rifle was never far away from him. Dad carried on ranting like a madman, screaming at us, telling us if any of us opened the door for Tarek, he would kill us all. Telling me he wasn't going to the fields that night; he was staying home to make sure my bastard of a son never stepped foot in the village again.As soon as Dad left the room I opened the window and looked outside. Tarek was hiding behind the stable wall. My heart started to slowly break as soon as I heard his voice.

"Mother, are you OK?" he called out quietly.

"Yes, son, we are fine! Quickly, come under the window quickly!" Tears were pouring down my face but I tried to stay calm, I couldn't believe what was happening or what I was about to ask my ten year old son to do.

I reached down my top; this was where I kept anything I needed to hide from Dad. I pulled out all the coins I had, it wasn't much at all.

"Listen carefully, I need you to do something very brave, I know you can do it because you are strong, and brave, and you have shown me just how brave you are." I threw the money out the window.

"Take this money and quickly make your way to the main road, stop the first jeep you see going to Dhamar and find Aunty Yasmin's house and stay with her, she will look after you, can you do that?" It was as though his answer took forever and I could see Tarek looked worried.

"I can't leave you alone with him, I will get help and come back for you!" he promised, tears starting to form in his eyes.

"No, no, you stay with your Aunty, I promise I will follow you in a few days, I promise; I just need to get some things ready first, please promise me you will go now and take care of yourself. I love you so much." At this point I could hear the other children behind me crying out because their brother was leaving and I burst into tears.

"I promise you we will be OK but I need you to do this for me, please!" I begged; tears were pouring from my eyes but I was trying to stay strong. Tarek promised me he would go, and he started picking up the coins, but as I was talking Dad came back into the room, and when he saw me at the window he went crazy!

"Is that that bastard son of yours? Close that window now!" he screamed at me, but defiantly I hung out the window as far as I could.

"Run, as fast as you can, run and don't stop until you get there, I love you so much my son," I shouted after him as I watched him run away from the window, and out of my sight.

My heart felt as though it was crumbling into a thousand pieces while Dad tugged at me, pulling me in from the window, and pinning me to the ground with his knees pressed on my chest, all the while cursing my child.

"Who does he think he is? I feed the bastard, take care of him, and he thinks he can just turn on me! He will never enter this village again; I will make sure of that!"

All of a sudden he let go of me and stormed out of the room, and down the stairs. I felt my heart fall into my stomach thinking he was going after my son. I scrambled to my feet and ran behind him, screaming at him to stop, but stopped myself when I realised he had gone next door to my grandparents' house.

He banged on the door until Farouse looked out the window; she herself had been staying at Granddad's because of problems in her marriage. Then he started shouting at her that if they allowed my son entry to their home, ever again, there would be consequences. Gran followed Dad back to our house to try and reason with him, and get him to go after Tarek, or at least allow her to send someone after him and return him to her house, stating that he was still a child and shouldn't be left alone. Dad was having none of it, sticking by his word, that my son was no longer welcome in the village.

I'd spent many years in Yemen, and all through those years I'd had tragic, terrifying, and horrific things happen to me and my sisters, but that night at Dad's house was by far the worse night of my whole existence.

My heart told me that my son had made it safely to his Auntie's house. I knew he was strong, brave, clever and determined, but there was that niggling thought in the back of my mind that kept reminding me of the dangers that were in the hills and mountains that led to the main road. Tarek would have to walk many miles through dangerous hills and mountains that hid deadly snakes, scorpions, and spiders!

He had left a few hours before the sun went down, which meant he would be walking in the dark; he had no light, he had no food, or water, and he was alone. Being without my child was something I couldn't handle, because besides my sister, my children were the only reason I'd put up with years of abuse at the hands of their father, and mine.

If my child had survived his journey, I knew I could never allow what happened this day to ever happen again. I couldn't allow Dad, or any other human being, take my children away from me. I made up my mind that night that I was going to run away, I just needed to do it safely so not to put my other children a risk.

True to his word, Dad stayed home that night. I didn't sleep, but neither did he. I could hear him marching up and down the stairs to the roof, and back down to his room. All night I lay awake trying to devise a plan to escape, but as yet I couldn't think of one. All I needed to do was get to Rada'a, and from there I could get a lift to any city or town, but I couldn't work out how to get there.

Nobody would give me a lift out of the village without Dad or Granddad's permission, and if I tried to walk out of the village I would be seen and caught before I ever made it to the road. I would be killed and my children would grow up without a mother. I had no money left and I knew it would be difficult, but I also knew my mind was made up; I was leaving, all I needed now was a safe plan.

As soon as the sun came up I made breakfast, I wasn't going to give Dad any idea of what I was up to, so I had to try and stick to the routine. Dad had his breakfast and went to sleep and soon after that Viyza returned with her children. She was so smug and happy when she found out Dad had kicked Tarek out.

I decided I couldn't stay in the house with her and told her I was taking my children and going to stay at my grandparents' for the day. On any other day I wouldn't have done that, but my cousin Farouse had been staying with Gran for a few days and today was her last day, so Gran had already asked me to go and have dinner with them.

Gran could see how unhappy I was; if it was just me Dad had beaten she would have stayed quiet, but Gran was sometimes kind to my children and she didn't like seeing very young children get hurt. While I sat crying with Gran and Farouse they tried to reassure me that Granddad would talk to Dad once he got back from Sanaa and sort things out to get my son back. Granddad was in Sanaa having talks with Farouse's husband over his treatment of my cousin, collecting money so that Farouse's husband could have his wife back. I knew by now that my Grandfather wouldn't care about us.

I didn't tell them I'd sent my son to my sister's; as far as they knew Tarek had gone back to his family in his father's village. I loved Farouse with all my heart but since she got married we had barely seen each other, I think in her whole married life I only ever saw her at certain gatherings, when she was permitted to come. I couldn't tell her about my plans to take my children and run away.

It was early afternoon when Dad woke up. I was still over Granddad's house sat with Farouse, Gran and a couple of other female relatives who had come to see Farouse because she was leaving to go back to her husband later that evening. All of a sudden, Izzy came running upstairs with her little brother Nasser who was just over two years old. Nasser was crying and she was scared because, she said, Nasser had been fighting with my sister Ismahan, and Abdulla had gone to tell his mother!

Nasser was still weak, he had been since his accident, and Ismahan was bigger and stronger than he was, but nobody was allowed to touch Viyza's children, or argue with them, especially when she was sewing. Even though they were just children fighting, and nobody had been hurt, I knew there was going to be trouble. I braced myself for what was to come, but I could never have imagined what was about to happen! Nasser had calmed down very quickly after I kissed and cuddled him, and had started playing again with the children in the room, when suddenly Dad barged into the room; Viyza had woken him up to tell him.

"Where's that little bastard?" he raged, his eyes searching the room until he spotted Nasser, who looked terrified. "How dare you touch my daughter?" he yelled, heading towards him. I instantly jumped up but couldn't stop Dad as he lashed out and punched Nasser in his face!

I reached out, grabbed Nasser and managed to stop him from hitting the ground from Dad's punch, but as I looked back around I saw Dad once again raise his hand to hit Nasser, who was by this time screaming in pain and fear. I could hear the women telling Dad to stop, but by that time something inside me erupted, I was in pure rage, the volcano inside me that I'd tried so hard to keep under control finally erupting. I looked at the face of the monster stood in front of me and I flipped!

Dad had always been a chain smoker, who walked around with a cigarette hanging from the corner of his mouth, and that day was no exception. As Dad tried to reach out to hit my son again I shielded him behind me, and then for the first time in my life, I turned on my father.

With all my strength I grabbed him by the neck and pushed him away from my child, pinning him up against the wall by his neck, with my other hand I flattened the cigarette against his face, and then yanked it from his mouth. While I stared in his face I could see his utter shock and disbelief that I was doing what I was, he was taken by surprise. With gritted teeth, I threatened him.

"Don't you EVER touch my children again!" But just as I finished my words, Dad punched me full force in my stomach, and as I fell to my knees. I heard my children scream, and when I turned my head, I saw them run towards me.

"Stay back! Get away from me!" I yelled at them, which must have been the first time I'd ever yelled at them like that. Izzy grabbed her siblings and immediately pulled them back as they cried out to me in terror, and then I saw Farouse pull them back to protect them. I could hear Dad cursing and threatening me, telling me he was going to send all my children back to their family, take them away from me! Knowing my children were being kept away from me by Farouse, I was ready to fight. I immediately pulled my flip-flop off my foot, and jumped up.

The worst humiliation for any Arabic man is a shoe in the face, and Dad was about to get mine! I jumped up and slapped him full force across his face with my shoe, then as my children cheered on, I started throwing punches at him, some missing, and some hitting. I'd never been in a fight before, not where I'd fought back like this, and I didn't know how to fight, but I did remember all of the things that had been done to me in the past, and now I was fighting for my children!

All I could think about was what Dad had done to Tarek the day before, and what he had just done to Nasser.

I knew he was much stronger than I was; however the fact I was fighting back had taken him by surprise! He had become accustomed to me sitting back and taking abuse from him; this was a side neither he, nor anyone else, including myself, had seen before.

I could hear the women screaming in horror, shouting at me to stop what I was doing, but it was a distant sound, there was something else going on in my head, something I could never explain.

Both Dad and I were throwing punches, but I couldn't feel his, and somehow I managed to grab hold of his collar, then I tugged his head towards me and head-butted him as hard as I could! I don't know what damage it did to him, but the blow dazed me a little; however I continued to fight. I managing to grab him and wrestle him to the floor where I jumped on him scratching at his face, slapping him, punching him.

I just wanted to hurt him in any way possible; I could see the blood on his face but I didn't stop. I could feel my heart beating in a very strange way, but again, I didn't stop. I started screaming at him, telling him how much I hated him, and how I wouldn't let him hurt my children like he had hurt me and my sisters in the past. Tears rolled down my face as I fought him, not from pain, but from another feeling, a feeling I couldn't identify with. I could feel someone tugging at me from behind, and then I heard my grandmother's voice begging me to stop.

"Muna, stop! Stop! That's enough!" But I didn't. They couldn't pull me off him and we kept on fighting. Then Dad managed to put his hands around my neck and started squeezing.

I kept on clawing at his face but his grip got tighter and tighter, and I could feel myself struggling to breathe, but I carried on fighting. It felt as though the fight went on forever, but I refused to stop, until finally, all the women that were in the room dragged me off him.

Gran and Farouse held on tightly to me as I struggled to stand up, still lashing out with my arms, kicking out with my legs that felt like jelly, my heart was pounding.

Dad got up off the floor, blood all over his face; the look of evil in his eyes could not cover the humiliation he had just suffered at the hands of a woman who had dared to fight back! I knew if I ever fought back there would be a heavy price to pay, but Dad's next words left me numb.

"Today, I'm going to kill you the same way I killed your mother!"

After that he rushed out of the room, but the words he had just threatened me with lingered behind him. For many, many years I'd known my father was capable of nasty, evil things, but the death of my mother was something he had always denied. I stood there in a daze, with what had just taken place between Dad and I, and now his words.

I'd always wondered what happened to my mother, but I'd never known what to believe. I'd thought maybe she did just disappear and run away from Dad. One thing I never believed until this day was that my father murdered her!

I was in a state of shock, a state of disbelief, when all of a sudden Farouse screamed when she saw Dad walked back into the room carrying his rifle aiming it straight at me. It had only been minutes since he left and I was still stood in the middle of the room trying to reassure my children that I was OK. Gran was still shouting at me for what I'd done, cursing me, telling me it was all over for me, telling me I would never be forgiven for attacking my father! When she saw Dad she jumped in front of me, placing herself between me and the gun, and for the first time in my life Gran stood up for me!

"You will have to kill me first Ali, before you kill her!" she told him, spreading her arms out to protect me.

Dad looked at her as if to warn her to move, but when she refused he yelled at her, "Move! I won't hesitate to pull the trigger! Now get out of my way!" But again Gran refused, standing her ground.

"Go ahead son, if you want the blood of your mother and daughter on your hands then so be it!" Dad realised she wasn't moving.

"You foolish woman! You can't protect her forever, she's dead! Do you understand me, dead!"

With that he stormed out, leaving a room full of terrified women and children behind, but none of them were as terrified as I was.

Dad didn't come back that afternoon, and for the rest of the day my children stayed close to me; they were terrified by what had taken place, and cuddled up close to me not wanting to leave my side, and there was no way I was letting them out of my sight!

Gran cursed me constantly all afternoon for what I did to Dad, she told me to thank my lucky stars Granddad was away in Sanaa, because he would have given me a beating too! Farouse was chuffed I'd given Dad what he had coming to him, and wished she could have joined in. She couldn't stop smiling, and also got a telling off herself for encouraging my bad behaviour! However, everyone was missing the big picture.

According to Dad, he had killed my mother, and he was now going to kill me. I for one believed every word he had said! There was no way Dad would let me get away with humiliating him like that in front of all those women; I knew I had to act, and I had to act quickly.

Farouse was leaving to travel back to Sanaa later that afternoon, she told me she would be sure to inform Uncle Ahmed I was in danger, and ask him to come and help me. Although I appreciated her help, I knew I wasn't going to hang around and wait for anyone to come to my rescue anymore. I asked her if she had any money she could give me, telling her I needed it to send to Tarek because he was all alone. Farouse gave me a little money, it wasn't much but it would come in handy. Before she left she also went to Dad's house to get my clothes.

Gran had gone and spoken with Dad beforehand, telling him that I was staying with her for a few days, she told him everyone needed to wait for Granddad to come home and sort out the mess

I'd created. To me, this was the perfect opportunity to run away; with Granddad away, and us being away from Dad's house, it was now or never. Later that evening, once Gran had gone to sleep and left us alone, I gathered my children together.

"Do you all want to go and find your brother, and escape all these horrible people?" I whispered.

"Yeah!" Their eyes lit up as they screeched with joy.

"OK! But you must listen to everything I tell you, everything, or we can't go, and it's not going to be easy."

My children promised to listen and follow my instructions so I told them the plan of escape. They were just as eager as I was to escape the clutches of the monsters that made our lives a living hell! I sat them down and explained to them what was needed for us to escape. We would leave that night, taking the same journey I'd told their older brother to take; we would walk through the same hills and mountains until we came to the road. I told them the journey out of the house and the village would have to be silent, no matter how tired, hungry or thirsty they became, they couldn't complain or cry.

Izzy would have to help me carry her younger brother if the others got tired so I could carry them. From the road we would make our way to the pick-up stop in Rada'a, where the cars gathered to take people to the towns and cities, where we would attempt to hitch a ride to Dhamar, to my sister's house. Then, we would pick up Tarek and continue to Sanaa, to the Embassy.

That night I made the children sleep until early morning, when I knew the village would be quiet, and we would at least have a few hours lead before anyone found out we were missing. When the time came to wake them up they were as quiet as mice whilst I put on whatever clothes they could wear; I didn't want to carry extra luggage unless absolutely necessary. I strapped Nasser tightly to my back before we made our way downstairs, then quietly out of the house, before I pulled the door shut behind us. It was eerily quiet as we quickly made our way out of the village, holding hands and hurrying, but not running, while I constantly checked around to make sure no one was watching us!

Although it was dark, we knew our way out of the village and towards the hills that took the short cut to the road, but once out of the village I couldn't make out which way to go: I was stuck! It was too dark to see properly, and each hill looked the same, I'd never taken the route before, I'd only ever left the village by jeep on the dirt road!

We quickly made our way towards the dirt road so that we could follow the track that would lead us to the main road. This route would add ages onto our journey, but at least we wouldn't get lost! We walked for hours, staying way out of sight of any vehicles that would come along the road, but close enough for me to know we were on the right path. I didn't want us to be seen before we got to Rada'a town, we had a better chance of blending in once in the town, the last thing we needed was someone spotting us leaving a village on foot.

Izzy and I took it in turns carrying Nasser who slept on our backs most of the way; she wanted so much to show me that she was there to help me, but I could see in her eyes how terrified she was. Sadig and Dobia, although tired, didn't complain, and when Izzy carried Nasser, I would take it in turns to carry them. It was an extremely hard journey, we constantly had to look out for, and dodge, snakes and scorpions, and with every step I took I wondered how or even if, my son had made this journey by himself.

As we walked through the darkness I would catch myself silently searching the bushes and space around us with my eyes, praying to myself, that I wouldn't come across a body.

We were still walking as the sun came up, and I became nervous that we would get caught, so I took the decision that instead of going to Rada'a town, we would go straight to the main road and try and stop a jeep further up on the main road. We weren't too far from the road, and my feelings were, if anyone was looking for us, they would go to the pick-up stop in Rada'a.

Just before we got to the road I stopped and put my sharsharf on, and gave the children what food and water we had. We got to the main road early morning, and by that time there were loads of trucks and jeeps already on the road, and luckily for us there were a few parked up. Usually, it would be a male who would approach the jeep to discuss transport, but I had no choice. With my veil down, and my children by my side, I approached a man sat in his jeep.

"Are any of these jeeps going to Dhamar?" I asked, as casually as I could.

Without even looking at me the man pointed to another jeep. "That one." We hurried over and I approached the man sat behind the wheel.

"Are you going to Dhamar?"

The man turned and looked at us. "How many of you?" he asked.

"Me and four children." I was nervous, but I tried not to show it in my voice as I waiting for him to ask about my husband, but he didn't.

"We are leaving now, so climb up!" he ordered, before shouting out to the crowd of men stood at the side of the road.

Not believing our luck I quickly bundled my children into the jeep, completely taking over the back seat as we squeezed together. "Dhamar! Dhamar!" The driver shouted out until the jeep filled up with men. I'd paid the driver what he wanted and we were off to Dhamar; the children slept all the way there, they were exhausted. I kept my veil down throughout the journey so not to attract any attention from the men that filled the back of the jeep, and who I'm sure were wondering why I was travelling alone!

Once in Dhamar we were dropped off in the market; I had no clue where Abdul's house was, but once I asked a shop keeper he quickly pointed me in the right direction, as Abdul was a well-known government figure. It was midday when we finally arrived at Yas's door; the children were hot and tired, and they hadn't eaten or drunk anything since early morning. I banged on the door, half expecting someone from the village to be waiting for us inside!

When Yas's oldest son Amar opened the door, his eyes lit up, "Mother! Mother! It's Auntie Muna!" he shouted, running back inside full of excitement, leaving us to follow.

Yas came rushing to the door. "Oh my God! You look knack-ered! Who did you come with?" she asked, looking behind us, but I ignored her question.

"Please tell me Tarek is here?" I begged, my eyes started to fill up with tears, but just as I finished asking her the question, Tarek came running towards me.

"Mother! You made it!" he squealed in delight, running towards me with his arms open wide. I fell to my knees and held on to my son, we were both crying with joy as I kissed him and thanked God for keeping him safe for me. Those two nights I'd spent away from him, not knowing whether he was dead or alive, wasn't something I ever wanted to go through again. I knew what I needed to do, what I wanted to do, and now that I'd taken those first steps into securing our freedom, nothing, and nobody, was going to hold me back!

Abdul was at work when we arrived, so while Yas and I fed the children, I quickly brought her up to date on what had happened over the past few days. She was shocked, but proud of me for finally standing up to Dad. She was horrified when I told her of Dad's threats towards me!

After we fed the children, she sent her driver to call Abdul home from work, telling him it was urgent, and that she needed him home for family matters, at the same time telling me she needed to speak to me without the children.

Yas then told me of a horrifying confession Dad made to her after he had been released from prison by government troops, just months earlier. While visiting the village Yas had spent time with Dad alone and had had a disturbing conversation with him. He admitted to killing our mother, telling her the gruesome details of what happened that day. She said she was talking to Dad about her visit to England and about her desire to one day return to England forever!

She said Dad was upset with her, and was trying to discourage her, telling her that her place was with her husband in Yemen. He told her that if she continued her quest to return to England she would end up like our mother, dead! When she asked him what he meant by saying that she said he started crying, saying that he had killed her. Yas said after his initial confession of killing her his tone changed, she said he started mumbling a lot, making out it had all been a terrible accident.

He said it was the night before Mum's birthday and they had been arguing over her birthday plans; he said Mum was holding a knife at the time. He said in the argument there was a struggle, and he 'accidently' slit her throat.

He told her after that he panicked and had to get rid of her body, so he cut her up into pieces and rolled her in a carpet to hide her.

He told her the next night while we were in the house he got rid of her body. He sat us down in front of 'Top of the Pops' which was a programme we always loved to watch at the time. Her body had been kept somewhere in the house but that night he carried her body out of the house, and later took her to a place he worked part time, called Llanwern Steelworks. There he burnt her body, and then he said he collected her ashes and later buried them into a house wall he was working on, somewhere in south Wales.

Yas said that although she believed part of his story, at the time she didn't know whether or not to believe everything. She said it was the way he talked. She believed he killed mum, but not the way he said it happened, or that he burnt her.

Dad had just been through months of torture, and his state of mind was fragile. She thought maybe he was just trying to scare her from ever trying to return to England at first, that's one of the reasons why she didn't tell me; she also didn't tell me because she felt I had enough to deal with, and didn't need any extra pressure, however now she felt it was time I knew.

Although it was a lot to take in, Yas and I finally believed Dad had killed our mother. The story he told about it being an accident was untrue, Dad was a monster; we had all seen how brutal he could be. He did try and kill Amina!

I believed that every horrible thing he could do, he would. After Dad's attack on my children, and his threat to kill me like he had killed our mother, Yas agreed with me that I could never come face to face with Dad ever again, it was too dangerous! It was time for me to try and seek help from the British Embassy, and she was about to put my case to Abdul.

Abdul arrived back home and was taken straight into a room by Yas while I waited outside. I was anxious, because although I knew Abdul was a good man, I also knew I'd overstepped the boundaries by attacking my father. When I was finally called into the room my whole body was shaking with nerves. I respected Abdul's opinion, and really needed his help, but I also knew that whatever he said it would make no difference to my decision. I was going, and that was that!

I sat down opposite Abdul. "Let me just start off by saying, I wholly disapprove of your actions in attacking your father, which was wrong and disrespectful! However, I can't stand by and watch anyone get treated this way, it's inhumane, and needs to stop right now!" Yas looked at me and smiled.

"He's going to help you," she said, looking at him. "Aren't you?" She was demanding an answer!

Abdul looked reluctant. "As much as I can, and without anybody knowing!" he said with a frown.

"We have to go today; they are most probably already on their way here looking for us," I said anxiously.

"Calm down!" Abdul said in a stern voice. "Where are you going to go today?" he asked, looking at us both, but he could see the urgency in our faces. "OK but we need to find you a place, give me an hour at least!"

With that Abdul stood up and said he needed to make some calls, he told us he would be back for dinner in an hour. Once he left Yas tried to reassure me everything would be OK, she promised she would never let Dad, or anyone else, ever hurt me again, but I was convinced Dad was about to burst through the door and shoot me!

When Abdul returned he told me he had spoken to his parents in Sanaa, and that they had agreed that from tomorrow, I could stay with them for one night. He said he hadn't told them the real story, just that I was staying the night and that I would be gone the next day; it was up to me to make sure the children stayed quiet about everything.

He said once I'd been to the Embassy he would arrange further help for me, but until then, I would need to stay the night with them in Dhamar. Just as Abdul left the house, the house phone rang, and their son Amar answered it, I nearly died when he shouted out to his mum that his Granddad Ali was on the other end of the phone!

Yas went to the phone, putting her finger to her mouth to tell all the children to stay quiet, as I ushered them into a room and closed the door behind them. I heard her greet Dad with a joyful voice, pretending all was well, so not to give away that she knew anything was wrong. After a short pause she changed her tone and sounded concerned, telling him she hadn't heard from us, and asking him what had happened, begging him to inform her as soon as he had any more information.

"I think he bought it!" she said, looking hopeful, once the phone was down. "He didn't mention the fight, he just said you disappeared for no reason, and he's worried about you and the children, what an idiot! Making out this was all your fault!" I was worried, if Dad started going around telling people I'd run away for no reason, he would have everyone searching for me!

The next morning the driver was ready and waiting to take us to Sanaa, and the children were happy but anxious about the journey we were about to take. I'd told them the night before how dangerous the whole situation could be.

If we made it to the Embassy, and they agreed to help us, then we would be OK, but if we got caught, then my children may never see me again. The only two who really understood anything were Tarek and Izzy, and they told me they were with me all the way, and would do everything they could to help us escape.

From then onwards Yas and Abdul told me they would not be able to talk openly to me ever again; they told me how to contact them because they would not be able to contact me. I hugged my sister and her children goodbye, and although I didn't know when, or even if, I would ever see her again, my departure felt different from ever before.

I was scared to death of what I was doing, but for once in my life I felt as though I was doing something right. I was now on the run!

We arrived at Abdul's family home before lunch and his family were friendly and welcoming; Abdul had told them I was going to my Uncle's house the next day, so they didn't ask questions. That day we rested at Abdul's family home, in the knowledge that Dad would never expect us to be there, and therefore, it would be the last place he would look.

Chapter Twenty Two
Not Without My Children!

I was up bright and early the next morning; I'd washed the children's clothes the night before and put them out to dry so they had something clean to wear. Yas had given us extra clothes of hers and her children's, but they were different ages so not much fitted. We hadn't taken anything from Dad's house because we couldn't carry anything, but none of this mattered to us any more, because our lives were about to change.

After the children were fed we said our goodbyes and set off. Abdul's family thought we were walking to my uncle's house, when in fact, we were off to the Embassy! It took us around 20 minutes to walk there. I had Nasser strapped to my back and the other children were helped along by their older siblings.

Although my mind and heart felt strong, my body felt weak. I was petrified of what could happen. My family knew so many people in government who could track us down, and I wasn't sure if any of them had contacts within the Embassy, but I was sure of one thing: what I was doing was right! I was finally standing up for myself and protecting my children from having to suffer the abuse that my sisters and I had suffered. I was also standing up for my right to return to my country of birth!

When we arrived at the Embassy the workers were starting to arrive, so I stood back and watched, hoping to see Karen walk in. My children stood close to me as the gates opened to allow the workers in, some were Arabic and some English, but Karen wasn't amongst them.

Once they were all in, the soldiers took their places on either side of the gates to stand guard; it looked like the Embassy was open for the day. I approached a man making his way towards the gates, he looked English, carrying a briefcase as though he was going into work, and with my heart beating so hard against my chest I thought he could hear it, I asked him a question in English.

"Excuse me; do you know a lady called Karen who works here?" He looked at me in a strange way because I was speaking English, and then answered in a polite tone, oblivious to my nerves. "Yes! But she won't be here yet, however she will be in later."

As I turned to walk away the sound of another man's voice turned my legs to jelly. "Muna, is that you?" I felt my children grab onto my sharsharf in fear as I slowly carried on walking off, pretending I couldn't hear him while my children scuffled along close to me. I felt as though my legs were going to give way, a voice in my head was screaming, "Please God no, no!" Then he spoke again.

"I'm so sorry, I didn't mean to scare you; you just reminded me of a young girl I knew a very long time ago, she was married to a cousin of mine who died, his name was Mana!"

My heart stopped beating for a few seconds by the mention of Mana's name. I'd never spoken about Mana to my children, or the fact that I was married before I married their father. I turned around and looked at the man; I'd seen his face before, but I couldn't place him.

"I'm sorry," I said, my voice trembling, "I don't know your name; I'm surprised you remember me."

I was still looking at his face, trying to remember him, but I was also worried. If this man had recognised me from all those years ago when all he could see were my eyes, I was in real danger!

"My name is Mohammed," he said with a smile. "We did meet a few times, but it was a very long time ago, I was very close to Mana and he never stopped talking about you. Can I help you with anything?" he asked. I was hesitant. Although Mohammed looked friendly I'd become nervous because he had recognised me; I was uneasy.

"No! No thank you, I'm here to see Karen but she's not in yet, so we will come back later," I said, turning to leave. Mohammed was quick to stop me from leaving.

"Karen will be in at any moment, please come in and wait for her; are these children yours? They look like they could do with a nice cold drink," he said smiling. I looked at my children and realised I needed to start trusting people, I was here at the Embassy, and at this moment in time we had nowhere else to go, so I accepted Mohammed's offer and he escorted us past the soldiers, and into the Embassy.

It felt strange being taken into an English-owned building, where I could hear people speaking English. The women were dressed in trousers and tops, and although long sleeved and covered, they were still dressed in English clothes. I felt myself yearning to get back the days when I was allowed to wear what I wanted, and speak the language I was born to speak!

Mohammed took us into a room where he sat us down on some chairs, while he went off to get drinks for the children, and when he came back with the drinks he was accompanied by Karen, who had just turned up for work. She looked excited to see me.

"I'm so happy you came back!" she said, coming over and sitting beside me.

Mohammed told us he would see us again soon, and then left us alone while I introduced Karen to my children. Then I went ahead and told her a brief story of my life, dating back from my mother's murder, to the present day. Karen wiped the tears from her eyes as she listened to me.

"I promise you, I will do everything I can to help you get home, but I have to let you know, it won't be easy! First of all we have to prove your British nationality, but that shouldn't be too difficult if you left England on a British passport, or can tell us where you were born?" Then Karen's face changed. "Then we have your children, they are not British, and cannot leave the Yemen without their father's permission." My head started to spin as I digested Karen's words.

"No! No! I'm not going anywhere without my children! Not without my children!"

I started to cry and Karen put her arms around me, reassuring me that she would speak to the British Consul, who would find a way to help us. She told me that she was his secretary and trusted him because he was a good man who helped people in bad situations, and she believed he would help us.

Karen went off to speak to her boss while we waited in the room. In that time, my children asked me about Mana. Wiping my tears I told them the story of how I met Mana and how he died.

After about 30 minutes she came back and took me into another side room away from the children. Then she told me that her boss felt it would be too difficult to get my children out of Yemen without their father's consent; he asked her to try and persuade me to travel back home alone.

He said once back in England I could generate media attention, then return to the Yemen and shame my husband into handing over my children. I wasn't shocked by what Karen was asking me to do, but rather more hurt; how could anyone ask me to leave my children behind? From the way she was speaking I didn't feel as though she was trying to convince me into going home alone, she was merely giving me advice.

I told her under no circumstances would I ever allow my children to go back to the life I was subjected to growing up in Yemen. I would never abandon them, even for a short amount of time. I would rather we all die than allow them go through the abuse my sisters and I had been through.

I couldn't allow my sons to grow up amongst family members as brutal as their father and mine, who would teach them their values? I also couldn't allow my daughters to be subjected to sexual abuse, emotional, physical and mental torture, at the hands of their future husbands, the way I had by their father, and mine. Going home without my children was not an option I would ever consider!

I also told her that I'd run away from my family, and had nowhere else to go from here; I was being hunted, and our lives were in danger. Karen then told me she understood, and told me to understand that it wasn't something she herself would do, however it was something she was told to ask me to consider. She then went back to her boss while I went back to my children. Shortly after she returned and sat with us.

"We have a lot to do, and we can't promise anything, but we are going to try!" she said with a big smile.

We discussed my returning to the Embassy the next day to complete paperwork, and giving them the information they needed to get started, but then I realised I had nowhere to go. With Karen's permission I was allowed to use the Embassy's phone to call Yas, and wary of the fact that Dad could already be at her house, I waited for the voice at the other end, it was Amar her son, who immediately called his mum.

Yas told me Dad had been out looking for me, he called her house again the night before asking if I was there, and told her he was coming to her house today, she told me to be careful and stay out of sight. I updated her on what was happening and she told me they had found me a place in Sanaa where I could stay for a while. It belonged to Abdul's cousin who was going away at the time and said we could use his outhouse to live in; Abdul trusted him not to say anything, so he said we would be safe.

While we waited at the Embassy the keys was dropped off to us by Abdul's cousin, and then Karen came back to me with even more good news. "What could you really do with right now?" she asked, a big grin across her face; I'd no clue to what she could be referring to, so I gave up. Then she informed me that a nursery that took care of the Embassy's children in Sanaa needed extra help, and she had spoken to her friend the owner about giving me a job, I couldn't have been happier! For the first time in my life, it looked like I would have a job, where I would be the sole provider for my children; I would never have to rely on my father, or their father, ever again.

Karen drove us to our new home, or 'safe house' as we called it; it took us a while to find it, and on the way Karen told me a bit about her own life. Karen was married to a Yemeni, whom she had met and married in London. She told me she loved him at first, and moved to Yemen to be with him because of his work as a pilot; now she has two children with him, a boy and girl.

She couldn't leave him because her children loved their father so much, and he was a good father to them, even though she was profoundly unhappy. Her children were getting the best education, and were not being abused, they travelled a lot and she told me her husband would never force them into marriage. She was sad when she told me her husband knew how unhappy she was, and would hardly allow her any alone time with her children, in fear that she would kidnap them! She also told me that although she was unhappy, all she cared about were her children, so as long as they were happy she would continue in her marriage.

I told her I thought she was brave, and I could feel how much she loved her children, because she was sacrificing her own happiness for theirs, that was the sign of a good mother! I could see the sadness in Karen's eyes while she told me her story, and I could feel her need in wanting to help us. I knew she would do everything she could to make it happen!

We turned off the main road in Sanaa and drove down a dirt road, right to the end house that was well away from all the other houses. As we pulled up to the safe house I looked at these big red rusty metal gates.

"Well, at least we have privacy!" I said with a smile, looking at the high walls that surrounded the house. I got out of the car and unlocked the gates with one of the keys, then waited for Karen to drive in before I locked it behind her. The garden was big, with plenty of room for the children to run around and play as freely as they wanted, and the gate and walls were high enough to ensure nobody could see inside.

The kids jumped out the car, they were full of excitement as they ran around the garden. This was to be our very first home, where we would be entirely alone to do whatever we wanted, and it felt good!

In the middle of the garden was a single storey house. I was told that Abdul's cousin, when home from his army job, lived on one side, and we would be staying in the outhouse. We were all excited to open the door and see our new temporary home; the outhouse was a part of the house that was still under construction, and it wasn't even half finished!

The door opened onto a very dusty dirt corridor that had four doors off it. The door immediately to the right was a small room with a concrete floor, it had one big window that overlooked the garden from the road side, and a small square window high up on the gate side of the house. The room straight ahead was slightly bigger and also had a concrete floor, and a big window that overlooked the garden; this room had a few mattresses and blankets thrown on the floor, as though they had been left for us. One of the rooms was the bathroom, it had a rusty tap hanging from the wall, and a hole in the floor, and the fourth room was the kitchen. As I entered I looked up to see only half of the roof had been built so far, the floor in the kitchen was also unfinished, and it was dirt. But none of this mattered, this house was our safe house, and I didn't care how bad it looked, all I cared about was the fact that it was safe!

There was a basin and a single tap that hung from the wall in the kitchen, and to my surprise there was running water, although I couldn't tell where it was coming from! There was a single camp stove in the corner, with an old black kettle, and a few cups and pots, and hanging from the ceiling was a light bulb. Just out of curiosity I pulled the cord, and then jumped for joy as the bulb lit up!

"We have electricity!" I yelled, running outside to tell the kids.

Karen looked on as my children and I jumped for joy at the sight of our new home; for us, this was perfect, a step closer to freedom!

Karen left us with instructions on what to do the next day. Before she left she offered me money for food, but I reassured her that my sister had already taken care of us. Yas had given me enough money to last at least a week, and I knew we would manage somehow, we always did.

My children and I soon became familiar with our new home as we cut branches from the tree outside and made a sweeping brush, we cleaned and lay the beds, ready for our first night alone. We had stopped at a shop on the way back from the Embassy, and got enough food for the night. After their food the children played happily for the very first time in their lives, free to just be children, free from any fear whatsoever.

The next day we went back to the Embassy; it was going to be a long day and I'd told the children to expect to be bored, but they were all excited to be going back to the building where they had been the day before, so they could play with the toys! The only one of my children I worried about was Nasser; unlike my other children, I couldn't leave him alone for long periods of time with anyone. Since his accident he had become unpredictable, he needed more attention than his brothers and sisters did at his age, and I couldn't explain why.

We didn't need to hang around at the gates because the soldier from the day before recognised me as soon as I asked for Karen, and let us straight through. Karen welcomed us and showed us to the play area where the children happily played, while Karen prepared the forms we needed to fill out. She had asked if it was OK for Mohammed to help out with the forms, I said it was OK, if I needed to trust anyone it would be someone related to Mana!

I found it difficult to give her the information they needed, starting with whether or not we left Britain on a British passport? Where I was born? Even my mother's maiden name had left my memory. I was a child when I left England and couldn't remember much, I'd buried my childhood memories a long time ago; it was a way I dealt with my pain, to forget certain things.

Then there were my children. None of my children had birth certificates, and although I'd memorised their dates of birth, they were never issued with birth certificates, not to my knowledge anyway!

There was also the identity of which family I was married into; I was sure this would worry the Embassy, my father in-law was not a man to be messed with! Mohammed smiled as he asked, "Just tell us which family are you married into?"

I let out a big sigh. "Nasser Ziad's son!" I watched the smile slowly drain from Mohammed's face as he nodded gently, trying to conceal his shock.

"Telephone company Nasser Ziad?" he asked slowly.

As we were speaking, another man came into the room and asked if we needed his help; Karen looked at me seeking for my approval, but I told her I wanted the fewest people possible involved in my case. I recognised him as the man I'd spoken to the day before at the gates, and he went on to tell me that we needed to work together, because if I was successful in my application, he would be the one stamping my visa, so he joined us. Mohammed then went on to explain to both Karen and the other man the wealth and power of my in-laws.

Unlike Mohammed, Karen and her friend looked less fazed by

who my in-laws were, so we carried on trying to gather information to help our case. It was looking impossible to verify our identities, or find us another route out, but then I remembered someone who could, and would help.

"Uncle Jim, my foster dad!" I said excitedly. "I can give you his full name, and address, I can even get you his phone number! He can tell you everything you need to know, will that help?" Karen was over the moon to have someone in the UK who she could speak to, and took as much information as I could give her about Uncle Jim, which was a lot!

Yas and I had talked about him constantly throughout the years, and even though I myself hadn't written to him much because of my circumstances, Yas had been in regular contact with him, and he had never stopped offering his support to both of us.

It was around lunchtime by the time we finished and said our goodbyes to Karen, but not before she had arranged to pick me up later that afternoon, to take me to see the nursery for the job.

Later that afternoon when Karen arrived I decided to take Nasser with me to the nursery, and when we entered the nursery the first thing we saw was this huge garden that looked like a playground, swings, slides, everything!

Nasser immediately ran and started playing with the toys while I was greeted by a tall lady with blonde hair who was pregnant; she told me her name was Louise, and that she owned the nursery. It was also her home where she lived with her Yemeni husband; they already had a nine year old son, and were now expecting another baby.

Louise was surprised when Karen told her I had no experience in child care, but accepted that I needed a job, and agreed to put me on a trial basis. She asked me if I wanted to bring any of my own children to work with me, and was happy when I said I would like to bring Nasser because of his age, and the fact that I had no one to look after him at home. Although she was fine with me taking him, she was quick to tell me she wouldn't accept me showing him any special treatment over the other children, something I fully accepted.

She told me most of the children were fine and didn't misbehave, although she warned me she had a child called Andrew, who although from a German background spoke very good English; she told me he was a very challenging boy who was big for his age of four years.

She also asked me if I would be comfortable wearing westernised clothes, jeans and a top, she said she didn't mind me covering my hair but would rather I didn't wear a sharsharf inside the gates. I told her I had no problem with that, but I didn't have any clothes myself, so she took me into her bedroom and picked me out a few of her clothes for me to wear at work.

She asked me if I could start work the next morning and I accepted, then when she told me how much I was going to be paid each month, I wanted to scream with joy! 4000 rials! If I'd been able to call my family and tell them, I would have, if only just to rub salt into the wound; I didn't even think my Uncle Ahmed was earning that much a month and he was the most educated and highest paid of my uncles at the time!

When I got home I felt excited to tell my children, and proud when I saw the excitement in their eyes that their mother had accomplished something so big. Later that afternoon I took my children to show them where I was going to be working; although we didn't go inside, I wanted them to see it from outside. It was an easy place to find if they ever needed me in an emergency, all they needed to do was follow the main road.

On the way home I looked for a phone box, I wanted to let my sister know I was OK, and let her know about my new job, but when I dialled the number a man answered. The voice sounded like Abdul but in my panic I put the phone down, I couldn't take any chances. As I stood by the phone box I knew it was time to make another call, I'd been on the run for a few days now and there was someone who I really wanted to tell, someone I wanted to see.

As soon as he answered the phone, I recognized his voice. "Hello! Guess who this is?" I teased. I heard him gasp at the sound of my voice.

His giggle gave me butterflies in my stomach. "Oh I don't know, tell me a little bit about yourself and I will try and guess!" he joked.

"Well," I said happily, "I'm a girl on the run and I have a job in Sanaa!"

I could hear how excited Anwar was. "Don't joke with me! Are you joking with me?" I laughed at the desperation in his voice, it was sweet.

"I'm not lying, I promise. I wish I could see you later," I said sadly.

"You name the time and place, and I will be there," he responded without hesitation, but I told him we couldn't meet just yet, I had to make sure the children were settled first, but I promised I would call him in a few days. We chatted for a while, he told me he was doing well working at a school with young boys as a teacher, and after our chat I made my way back to the house. I had a sense of new found freedom, and everything around me looked, and smelt, different.

Once inside the gates I watched the children play as I took off my sharsharf, then while I was adjusting my head scarf I realized I didn't need to cover my hair inside the gates anymore. As I took off my scarf I ruffled my hair with my fingers to allow the fresh air to breeze through, and then I threw my scarf on the floor and went to play with the children.

They were surprised to see me with my hair uncovered; it was something they hadn't seen before. "Mum, what if someone sees you?" Tarek asked, concerned.

"No one can see us from outside the gates, but does it upset you?" I asked, unsure what his answer would be.

"No! I don't care, as long as you're happy," he smiled.

The night time came and the children fell asleep, their smiles were almost complete. I could see that the older two still had fears that their family, or mine, would turn up and take away our happiness. It was endearing yet upsetting to see how much they protected their younger siblings, but it was the way they had been brought up, loving each other and knowing when to shelter each other from harm's way.

I'd watched them play that afternoon, and how they would all automatically stop playing if a strange sound was heard outside the gates, whether it was a knock on a nearby gate, or a heavy truck pass by the nearby fields. Nasser would be the one they would run over to and pick up, and hush him to stay quiet, just in case the threat was a real. I'd spent the afternoon reassuring them that it was OK, nobody was coming to our new home, and that we were safe. As they slept I snuggled up beside them, and told myself the same, we were going to be OK!

The next morning I fed the children and gave the older two instructions for the day ahead. It wasn't a good feeling knowing I was going to be leaving them all alone, but they had been through much worse, and I knew I needed to provide for my children. With Nasser in my arms, I made my way to the nursery.

We got there before anyone else, and Louise took us inside to introduce us to her house staff, and familiarise ourselves with the house. She told me her husband had just left for work, but she hoped we could meet him another time. Her nanny was in the kitchen getting her son ready for school; her kitchen was beautiful, she had things in there I knew existed, but couldn't remember what they were called, or how they worked!

I remember looking around thinking she must be really rich because she could afford to have a washing machine and a real cooker! The fact that she had people working for her didn't make me think she was rich, many people could afford human labourers, it was the fact she possessed these materialistic items that are not easily accessible in Yemen which made her stand out! She also had a cleaner, and another nursery teacher called Jamela. Jamela was leaving the nursery in a few days, and I was her replacement!

Nasser was in awe of all the play areas, and his favourite was the soft play area; this was a completely padded out room with loads of soft cushions and toys, to ensure the children couldn't hurt themselves. It was called the blue room.

There was a class room with desks and chairs and full of paints, crayons, books etc. Also a room full of cots, mattresses, blankets and pillows for the children to take their naps! There was a room that was full of toys I'd never seen before; it had a rocking chair and rocking horse! Her bathroom had a bath, shower and toilet, something that confused Nasser!

Nasser was happy playing with the toys in the garden while I stood back and watched Jamela greet the children once they started to arrive. She opened the doors for them, and took them from their parents as they got dropped at the gate, but while I watched her greet the children it became obvious to me that she didn't have a natural connection with the children; she wasn't mean, but she wasn't warm.

After a few had been let in a little girl, no older than three years old, turned up at the gates; I couldn't take my eyes off her. She looked like a little doll that could break at any moment. She had the bluest eyes and beautiful blonde hair, and she was tiny. When Jamela took her from her mother she was crying, and after she closed the gates she immediately put her down, even though she was still crying over her mother!

I went to her and gently picked her up, mindful of the fact she didn't know me. "Hi, my name's Muna, what's yours?" I asked wiping away her tears, in between her sobs she told me her name was Carrie; she had a lovely English accent but I couldn't place it. After I quickly glanced over to make sure Nasser was still OK, I took Carrie into one of the rooms, chatting to her on the way, and reassuring her everything was going to be OK, while letting her know who I was and why I was there. I sat with Carrie in the rocking chair for all of a few minutes before she stopped crying and jumped off my lap, then ran back outside, ready to greet the rest of her friends who were still turning up.

I followed her outside and watched as the rest of the children came in. There was no mistaking Andrew when he turned up, he put a smile on my face as soon as he walked through the gates, and I knew from the start that I would develop a soft spot for him, no matter how naughty he was!

He was big for his age, he had blond, almost white hair, and he had a dummy firmly attached to his mouth, and with a squinty face he looked up and grunted at Jamela when she said hello. Then he stormed past her into the garden, where he stood firmly sucking on his dummy, as his eyes roamed around to see who was where, and playing with what. When he spotted me he approached Jamela and pointed at me. "Who's that?" he demanded to know in a squeaky voice that was muffled behind his dummy.

"That's Muna, she's going to be your new teacher because I'm leaving," Jamela responded half-heartedly, but Andrew looked happy with her answer. "Good, I'm glad you're leaving!" he yelled at her as he ran off to play on the swings.

I watched as Andrew approached Nasser, and I could see he was attempting to talk to him, but Nasser wasn't taking any notice, so I slowly walked over closer to where they were, aware that Nasser wasn't able to speak English, and wary of Louise's advice about Andrew being difficult to handle. As I was watching them and the other children play, Andrew came over to me.

"Who's that?" he asked, pointing over at Nasser.

"That's Nasser, he's a new child here," I answered.

"Why won't he speak to me?" Andrew asked, chewing on his dummy.

"Oh sweetheart, that's because he can't speak your language, but I can speak both his language and yours, do you want me to speak to him for you?"

Before Andrew could respond Louise came out from the house and blew a whistle to let the children know it was time to go inside, so I called Nasser over and told him what was happening, and to follow the children. On the way in Andrew attempted to sneak past Louise with his dummy in his mouth, but she stopped him, stretching her hand out in front of her, demanding his dummy. Although he grunted at her, Andrew reluctantly handed over his dummy and followed the other children inside. "We don't give them their dummies unless its nap time," Louise told me as we led the children into the play rooms.

As the morning went by I got to know the children, and although they came from all corners of the world, they all spoke English, some more than others. Carrie and Andrew were the two most difficult children in the nursery, and they took to me from day one. Whenever Carrie cried she would run to me for comfort; it would take her less than a few minutes to calm down and stop crying, and I really didn't see why Jamela was so intent on leaving her to cry for so long when all she needed was a little cuddle. She didn't cry because she wanted something, or wanted her own way; she was fragile, and would easily fall over and was always getting shouted at by the other children.

Andrew was a little terror, but I couldn't help but have a soft spot for him, he was forever getting told off for something, and whenever Jamela or Louise told him off he would come straight to me for confirmation that it was either right, or wrong for them to do so. Although he and Nasser couldn't communicate well with their language barrier, they played well most of the time, and Andrew would run back and forward asking me to tell him this, or tell him that.

By 1.30 pm all the parents had picked up their children, and I was happy the day was over; I'd been under the impression that I wouldn't be out of work until late afternoon, but Louise told me this was a normal working day at nursery.

After Jamela left, Louise asked me to join her in the kitchen for a drink and a chat; straight away I thought I'd done something wrong, and she was going to tell me off. I was over the moon when she started to praise me, telling me she thought I'd done extremely well that day. She told me Jamela was an experienced nursery teacher, but she felt that I had better interaction and intuition with the children than she did. Even though Andrew and Carrie were her most difficult children, she felt I'd handled them well, and was happy they felt they could come to me when they needed something, or felt they needed comfort.

I was skipping with joy that day when I left work; things were going well and I headed straight for the phone box to call my sister.

Amar answered the phone and I could hear voices in the background, so I was quick to tell him to let his mother know his Aunty Fothaliya was on the phone. This was Abdul's sister's name, so if anyone was at Yas's house looking for me, they wouldn't suspect anything. Yas quickly came to the phone and I let her know it was me; she reassured me nobody was at her home, just her children, so I went on to tell her all about what had been happening over the past few days.

She was so happy things were turning out well for me, but told me to be careful, she said Dad was in Sanaa looking for me, he had been to Nebat's house and Uncle Ahmed's. She said Nebat called her and was hysterical, thinking something bad had happened to us; she asked me if it was OK to let her know we were safe.

I knew in my heart we could trust Nebat not to tell anyone what we were doing, so I said yes, that she could let her know we were alright. She was our sister; I couldn't let her worry about us. She had so much to worry about already with her husband still ill from his accident; I knew she would protect our secret at all cost.

Yas also told me she was sending us some food with a friend, so we should expect a knock on the door that evening. I finished my call to Yas and I really wanted to call Anwar, but knew I couldn't; he was now working in a school for young boys, and he didn't finish work until later. Also, I knew I had to be very careful for my children; although I loved Anwar and wanted to be with him, we were not in a country that allowed you to be with a man just because you loved him! I knew my children also loved Anwar, and I knew Anwar also loved my children, more than their father loved them, but I didn't want any of my children to ever think I was disrespecting their father's honour.

I made my way home to my children, who were anxious as I knocked on the gate; we had made a secret knock to let them know it was me, and no one else, three knocks followed by another three. I was delighted to see they were all fine and nothing bad had happened whilst I was away at work. The older two were proud to let me know the details of the day's events, and how they had looked after their squabbling siblings. I told them I could never have done it without them, and I told the little ones how proud I was of them for keeping the noise down, even though Tarek and Izzy kept insisting they were not quiet at all, but noisy all day!

To show them how proud I was of them all, I'd stopped off at a little shop on the way home from work, and bought a few sweets. I knew we didn't have much money left, but I needed them to have a treat to see how well they had done, and how special they all are to me.

I told them I'd spoken to their aunty and that she was sending us some things later, so they shouldn't panic when they hear a knock on the gates. I left out the details that their grandfather was in Sanaa hunting us; I didn't want them to worry any more, they were just starting to settle down and it wasn't something they needed to know.

Later on that afternoon the jeep arrived with the food; the children helped me carry the boxes and sacks inside. Yas had sent us everything she could think of to keep us going for at least a month, until I got my wages. That evening the children played happily until they couldn't play anymore, before collapsing with exhaustion and falling sleep.

It was weeks before I heard back from Karen. She turned up at the nursery to let me know they had heard back from Uncle Jim, and that he had supplied them with all the information they had requested from him, so my British passport was approved.

The easiest bit was over, now came the part of getting my children out of Yemen.

They needed to find birth certificates so that they could get their passports, but most of all, they needed to find someone willing to sign those passports saying he was their father.

I struggled to find the words to tell Karen how much I needed her help, but I begged her to help us. She took my hands in hers. "I promise you I will do everything I can to make this happen!" she promised. "I need you to trust me, do you trust me?" she asked. I didn't hesitate in answering, I knew in my heart I could trust her from the first time I met her.

"Yes, I trust you!" I quickly told her. Karen quickly kissed me on both cheeks, and as she left she told me to wait until she contacted me, no matter how long that took! It sounded like we had a long wait, but at least I was working, and the children were happy.

Dad continued to look for us, and by now we had every uncle in Sanaa on the lookout, but I wasn't going to let that spoil my family's happiness or freedom!

On payday we all went to the nearby night market, I was covered with my veil, and the girls wore headscarves, we didn't stand out from any other family. The children had treats and from that first pay cheque we bought our very first TV. It was a tiny black and white portable but the children had never had their own TV, never mind in our own house, and for myself I bought a cassette/radio player.

On our way back from the market I stopped to call my sister; I called her every time I wanted to update her or let her know things were good, I knew she was always worrying about us and I wanted her to know that for once, we were doing OK!

After that call, with the children fussing over their treats, I decided to call Anwar; I'd called him a few times but hadn't made any arrangement's to meet up. While I whispered away to him, Tarek shouted over at me, "Can I talk to Anwar?"

"Oh hang on, we just got caught out, Tarek wants to speak to you!" I whispered down the phone.

Trying not to look worried, I casually handed Tarek the phone so he could chat to Anwar, but as soon as I did, all the other children jumped up wanting to talk to him, including Nasser, who usually never wanted to speak to anybody! The struggle ended with a compromise from Tarek, he told everyone he would speak to Anwar now, and they all get to speak to him later, because he wanted to invite Anwar over to our house the next afternoon.

With the children begging their very reluctant mother into saying OK and a very happy Anwar into agreeing, we devised a secret knock for him so we would know it was him!

I barely slept that night knowing that I was going to see Anwar again after all this time, and the next day work couldn't finish quickly enough. Time felt as though it was going so slowly, but finally, later that afternoon, Anwar came over to the house. The children were all waiting for his knock and as soon as he did they raced to the gate to welcome him in; I couldn't tell who was more excited to see him, the children or me.

I couldn't take my eyes off him as he spent the whole afternoon, and early evening, talking and playing with the children. Nasser, who would usually shy away from strangers, joined in with the fun and took an instant liking to Anwar. Once I tucked the children in for bed Izzy asked me a question. "Is Anwar going to stay?"

"No baby, he's going to stay for a bit so we can have a chat, but then he's going home," I told her as I went to get up. She made a sad face, hanging her bottom lip as low as she could.

"Why? Why can't he stay with us?" she sulked.

"Well…" I tried to think what to say, and a hundred answers went through my mind at that moment, but none that I wanted my daughter to hear, so not knowing what to say I gave her a kiss. "Because he's got his own house!"

Anwar and I made idle chit chat in the room next door until we were sure the children were fast asleep, and then we put a blanket on the floor and snuggled up in each other's arms, and in between our kisses and cuddles, we told each other everything we thought the other needed to know that night.

We both knew we had lots to catch up on, but we had lots of time to do that, we would see each other again soon. He told me he was extremely proud of everything I was doing, and would be behind every decision I made. He also made me promise never to let any man get in the way of mine or my children's happiness, and that included him.

Before we knew it the sun was rising and I was rushing him out the door in a silent hurry! I had to be in work in a few hours, and I'd had no sleep, so I told him I would call him very soon, I promised.

It was month two before Yas felt comfortable to come and visit and she just turned up one afternoon; even I was unaware she was coming. We were all in the garden playing, and the knock on the gate made Izzy quiver in fear as she ran towards me screaming.

"Please don't open the gate, it's Granddad; he's come to get us!"

She was petrified as I picked her up and walked her towards the gate. I could hear Yas calling out to Izzy, letting her know it was only her and her children, telling her children to call out and let my children know they were outside. Once Izzy heard her cousin's voices she calmed down and helped me open the gates, then enjoyed being fussed over as her aunty took her from me to apologise for upsetting her. Together they came up with a secret knock!

It was a great afternoon, and although Yas was a bit shocked to see half the roof missing in our new home, she was happy to see how happy we all were. It was difficult keeping Anwar a secret from my sister; I'd never asked my children to keep his visits a secret, I hadn't seen the need in that, we didn't see anyone other than my sister, and if they did mention him to her then I would deal with that if it happened. I knew in different circumstances she would have given her right arm to see me happy, with the man I loved, but my life was complicated enough! I didn't want her to know I'd made it much more complicated by falling in love!

Our children played and squabble as usual while we sat and chatted, and brought each other up to date on everything. She told me Dad was back in the village for now, but he would pass by her house on his trips to Sanaa, which was every week or few days to do his rounds to see if anyone had heard from me, or seen me.

She said he was still very angry, and according to him, he had many leads by now on our whereabouts. Yas felt this was just a tactic he would use to see if she would get worried and pass on information to us to see if we would hand ourselves over out of fear! She told me Nebat said he would tell her the same when he went to her house; he knew we were very close as sisters, he just didn't realise how close.

There had been no word from either Ziad or his family, no word where Ziad was, or that he had any interest in finding his children, or if he even knew we were missing. This was good for us; if he wasn't interested then we didn't have to worry about him looking for us, and we had no clue to what his father was up to, he wouldn't have taken my kidnapping his grandchildren lightly, even if he had disowned their father! This would have been looked upon as an act of defiance against the whole family name, his name!

Yas told us that even though Dad had put out word to all the family who worked in government to keep an eye out for us, she told us not to worry, because up until then neither Dad nor anyone else had knowledge of our whereabouts or intentions. She also said Nebat was going to pop around very soon for a visit so to expect her and to make sure I told the children so they didn't panic again when she knocked the gate.

This time when Yas left she didn't have to sneak me money, or wonder if we would be treated badly or abused as soon as she left the door. However we were now crippled by the knowledge that once our passports were available we were going to be separated once more, for what could be a lifetime. We were wary not to show our emotions as we said our goodbyes in front of our children. Me and my children stood by the gates and happily waved goodbye and shouted out that we loved them and would see each other soon.

Nebat came to visit a few weeks later; she only brought her oldest son Neshwan with her because she felt he was the only one she could trust at that time to keep a secret. Neshwan reminded me a lot of Tarek in his maturity and kindness towards his siblings.

He and Tarek stuck together like glue all afternoon, and it was so nice to finally see Tarek have some time to himself; whilst Izzy had my sister's daughter to play with, and the other children had cousins around their age, Tarek was a little older, and wasn't around children of his own age, especially because he wasn't in school anymore.

Nebat was so happy to see we were OK, and was hitting herself at realising how close we lived to her; we were only around 15 minutes' walk from her house! It was horrible to hear how ill Ahmed still was, and how Nebat was still struggling to cope with his care, Ahmed was still having angry outbursts since his accident, and even though she knew it wasn't his fault, she was struggling to cope with him.

Even though Nebat was strong he was physically much bigger and stronger than she was, and she said it took all her strength to settle him down when he became hostile. She admitted she was starting to understand him a bit more recently and found ways to calm him down through talking to him instead of shouting at him, but his recovery was extremely slow, and drained her own health. She was also struggling financially even though she had managed to find someone to work in Ahmed's workshop; luckily we had Yas, and just like she did for me, Yas helped Nebat and her family out with food and money whenever she could. It was lucky for us that Abdul was in charge of government food in the city where he worked, he would always help out families in need, and although we were not from his city at the time, we were very much in need!

I didn't go into a lot of detail with her about what I was doing, because some of the details I found difficult to understand myself, so it would have been impossible to try and get my sister to understand. While I'd had a few years of education back in England, Nebat had never picked up a pen and paper, she had never been inside a school, she had no clue what a birth certificate was, or why we needed them. Nebat's visits became regular, and of course she too had her own secret knock!

Yas visited as often as she could, which was around once every few weeks; sometimes she would drive to and from her house in Dhamar on the same day, therefore only staying for a few hours at a time, other times she would visit Abdul's parents' house and stay the night with them. They lived ten minutes' walk from my house, which meant we would get to see her more than once, which was good for a change.

Over the coming months things were good, the children were happy because they felt safe and loved, and I felt safe and loved. Anwar was coming around a few evenings a week, he wouldn't come until late afternoon because by then I'd be sure that neither Yas nor Nebat would turn up; women only went out to socialise early afternoon, or between certain times in the city.

The children would fight to get to the gate when they heard Anwar's knock and would hang on to his every word; they never stopped smiling when he was around, neither did I. We both made sure that he was always gone by sunrise and that my children always woke up with me asleep beside them.

We had previously spoken about plans for him to apply for a British visa on his passport; his was Sudanese and for some reason he was refused a visa from Yemen to Britain on his passport. He thought that he would have a better chance if he applied for a Yemeni passport, and then apply for a British visa, that way he could follow us once we had left for England.

We had also spoken of the possibility that things could turn out differently, and that we could be separated for life. We were both OK with that; although it was something neither of us wanted, we both understood enough to know it could happen. We spent almost every moment together awake, chatting, laughing, giggling, nodding off and then waking up, because we never wanted to waste a single second together.

Every time my pay cheque came in I made sure I took my children out to the night market and bought them something nice; it was a way of me showing them that things could be good, if you just put your mind to it and never give up. I was always cautious of our surroundings when we were out together in the night market; this wasn't like the small side street daily market where we would buy our groceries, this was a big market, brightly lit street stalls in the busy main streets.

They had lots of beautiful things in the market, a lot of which we couldn't afford! The gold stores sparkled with the most beautiful necklaces, bracelets, rings and earrings, and everything else women love to wear to show off their wealth, there was Yemeni clothes, even a few western clothes. I would buy them at least one piece of clothing each and I'd also bought myself a few treats; I had a few cassettes by now, Michael Jackson, Madonna and Lionel Richie. I loved listening to music, especially in the room that I'd spend time in during the day, it was also the room I'd spend my nights in with Anwar. That room had a little window in it that was slightly high up, and if I lay down and looked up through it I could see the sky, and I could also just about see the end branches of a large tree.

Some afternoons I would lie down with the cassette player on my belly and listen to English music whilst I looked up out the window at the sky and imagined I was back in England. I could hear the children playing outside and I'd imagine we were in a park back home, enjoying our freedom.

It was around this time that I started finding English stations on my radio, and English music! This was when I first heard Whitney Houston and her number one song 'All The Man I Need'. I remember listening to the words of that song, and immediately thinking how it reminded me of Anwar.

Time went by and before I knew it around six months had passed. Karen visited me a few times over that period and told me she couldn't get birth certificates for the children, but had decided to put the children on my British passport; however, they still needed to find the person who would be willing to sign it.

This was a huge risk for whoever signed it because just in case it got out that the Embassy had helped me, they would need to prove that someone had gone in and signed my passport saying he was my husband. Karen reassured me everything was going well, and asked me to have patience, she told me once again to wait for her to contact me, although anxious that Dad was still on our trail, and wary that time wasn't in our favour, I knew we had no option but to wait.

Yas had informed me that Dad's trips to Sanaa had increased and he was spending more and more time staying at Nebat's house; this meant that Nebat's visits were becoming fewer and fewer. Yas and her children weren't able to visit us as much as they used to either, as Abdul had been promoted yet again, and they had been moved to another city further away.

We were becoming more and more isolated, but I was thankful that at least I was working and providing for my children; but my luck was about to run a little low. One day at work Louise informed me that the nursery was closing. Something had happened and most of the children were leaving and going back to their home countries with their parents, therefore she could no longer afford to keep me working. I was devastated! I had saved a little money; I knew it wouldn't last us very long, I also knew the chance of me finding another well paid job, if any at all, was unlikely.

Karen tried her best to find me something else but failed, and before long, we found ourselves struggling once more. Anwar hadn't been able to visit for weeks by then, he had had to have another operation on his hip because the wound had become severely infected, he wasn't able to walk, and had been out of work because of this. Although I told Anwar I was out of work I didn't tell him how badly we were struggling; there was no point, he was also struggling so couldn't help us.

In the middle of all this Abdul's cousin came home from his army job to stay in his house next door to us; he was a very quiet and kind man. Whilst home he bought some rabbits, six in all, and built them a cage outside his front door, he got on well with the children and encouraged them to feed the rabbits grass from the nearby fields and play with them, and then asked them to look after them once he was called back to the army.

Anwar came to see us as soon as he left; he was walking on crutches, and he had some good news. "I've found you work!" he told me, all excited. It was in a small private hospital. It wasn't as well paid as my last job but it would get us by, it was as a receptionist. I had no clue what a receptionist was, or what I needed to do, but I knew I would do it!

This job was going to be much harder than the nursery; for a start I couldn't take Nasser with me, and I knew this would be difficult for the children. It was also longer hours. The next day Anwar met me to show me where to go and who to speak to; he had worked with this lady a few years earlier in a school, and felt she was trustworthy. She was an older lady from Somalia called Sahara, and we immediately became friends; she spoke really good English and put me to work straight away, doing her best to explain what I needed to do, or not do, as a receptionist.

The hospital was a private hospital for foreigners, and our job was filing papers and typing etc. I couldn't type at all, so my job was mainly filing and putting things in order. Although the change was a lot for the children to take in they didn't complain; Nasser was the biggest change to the routine, he was difficult for them to manage, but they handled him well. We struggled with food in our first month before my pay cheque came in and, not wanting to turn to anyone again for help, I turned to more drastic measures: the rabbits!

I knew the owner wouldn't be back for months, and I could tell him one just 'escaped' and he would be no wiser, and anyway, we were very hungry! One afternoon I told Tarek and Izzy that I needed their help so that I could kill one of the rabbits, and because I didn't want the younger ones to see me kill their 'pets', the plan was for Izzy to play with them inside, while Tarek helped me slaughter the rabbit around the back of the house. Things were going as planned; I'd been taught how to kill animals and had killed many animals before, in the Halal way. I thought a rabbit would be like a chicken, hold its arms and legs down, cut the throat, and drain the blood. Apparently not! As I cut its throat it let out a cry that sent shivers down my spine! Its cry was similar to the cry of a new born baby, and it made me let go of the rabbit, leaving it flapping about, all around the garden!

Tarek attempted to bring me back from my shock as I stood back covering my ears with my eyes closed, he grabbed my arm shoving me towards the dying rabbit. "Mum, it's just a rabbit, you need to finish what you were doing!" he urged, but it was too late, the sound of the rabbit's cry had brought the other children running out to see what was going on!

To try and spare them the scene of the rabbit in distress I hopped around after it, then listened to my children gasping in horror while I grabbed the rabbit and cut its head off; my hands were shaking as I held it upside down to drain the rest of the blood from its dripping neck, whilst I looked over at my children, who just stood there, their mouths wide open, staring up at me, waiting for an explanation!

I knew they were all hungry, they had spent the last few days eating stale bread and cups of tea, so with a very unsteady voice, and a fake smile, I shouted out, "Who wants rabbit soup?"

By the time my pay cheque came all six rabbits were gone; I hated killing them because of their cry, but it was something I needed to do to feed my children. We dug a hole next to the cage to pretend they had escaped, and when the owner came back and I told him his rabbits had escaped. He nodded and smiled, saying it was OK, and that he would buy the children some more before he left, I got the feeling he knew we had eaten them but didn't mind. I felt guilty not telling him the truth about his rabbits after he had been so kind to us, and decided I was going to tell him the truth the next time I saw him, but I never saw him again; he was called back to work without notice.

Chapter Twenty Three
A Promise to Myself

Anwar continued to come over to the house a few times a week, and whilst there he taught the children how to read and write. Tarek was his main pupil as he had been to school before and already knew a little, while the others mainly drew pictures and played. He was still waiting to hear if he was entitled to a Yemeni passport or not and we had been in hiding for nearly nine months when we got a visit from Karen. When I opened the gate she had the biggest smile on her face.

"We did it. We did it!"

She grabbed me and hugged me as I repeatedly asked her, "Did what? What? What?"

"We found someone!" she said happily, as she led me inside the house. Karen told me that they had found someone willing to pretend to be my husband, someone who had agreed to sign for all my children to leave Yemen on my passport.

I couldn't sit still with joy; I was asking question after question, why would he do this? What does he get in return? Who is he? Do I meet him? When can we go?

She revealed that she had misjudged my father in-law's position in Sanaa, or how powerful he was! She told me that this man was a sworn enemy of his, and though he never had any intention of letting him know he had done so, found it fitting that he could hurt him by helping us escape. There were strong bad feelings between both families, but this man wouldn't reveal what they were! She told me that this man wanted a British passport in return, and they had approved him one! She refused to tell me who he was, saying these were his terms, so I would not be meeting him.

Everything had been done and approved; now all that was needed was to buy our tickets, which they would do on the day we would travel. We were all set to go, except now they had the task of getting us through security at the airport. Karen told me that they had checked out the names of security officials, soldiers etc. who worked at the airport, and found that a high number of them were my family members. It was impossible for us to leave right now. I'd always known that I had family who worked at the airport, but I never thought they would be the reason our plans would come to a halt! With a little encouragement from Karen, and a heart full of determination, I told myself all would be OK! Karen promised me that if they couldn't find us a safe flight home soon, then they would find us another route out of Sanaa.

As soon as Karen left I headed for the phone box to call Yas. I told her the news and told her I needed to see her just in case they did find a way for us to leave. Karen had told me that if they found a window where they thought we could travel safely, they would just come for us without warning.

Yas arrived the next day, and however much she told me not to worry about her, that she would be fine. However much she promised that one day she would follow me, and we would be together again in England, I was worried! That's when I started to question if what I was doing was right. I'd never questioned my wanting to run away before, never questioned whether or not I should leave the Yemen. I knew we needed to get away from Ziad, I knew we needed to get away from my father, but now I was about to leave my sister behind. I started to question if I needed to leave Yemen at all? I'd proven to myself that I could find work and survive, I could feed my children. However I also knew I still couldn't keep them safe, we were constantly living in fear of being found and killed. I was torn. I was about to do the one thing I'd promised my sister I would never do, and that was leave her behind.

It felt as though even at times when saying goodbye was supposed to be based around times of hope, and happiness, it was once again filled with pain and sorrow!

It was early August and Yas had been visiting us every week, sometimes more, in case we were given the green light to fly home. Even though Dad was staying at Nebat's house more and more vigorously searching for us, Nebat would also manage to visit us, pretending to go to the market, or pretending to visit other women in the afternoons. My work at the hospital had come to an end - I wasn't given a good reason, just that I wasn't needed any more - but Yas made sure every time she came to visit she brought us food to keep us going, so we needed for nothing.

Rain season was in, and being in a house that was only half built was proving difficult. We survived a few nights of rain with the kitchen flooded and the roof leaking, but when the rain became too heavy we couldn't even shelter in a corner because the floors were flooded in every room.

Anwar came over one evening and told me he couldn't leave us in the house any more, he had spoken to his family about us, and they said for us to go and stay with them, he told me Thahaba wasn't there because she was in the village.

I was furious with him for letting his family know about us without asking me first, but he assured me he didn't tell them anything about our relationship, only that he was helping us escape Ziad. I was concerned that more and more people were learning of my whereabouts in Sanaa, I was also convinced his mother would suss me and Anwar out, and I refused to go, but when the rain got so bad that all our blankets and belongings were drenched, and the children were shivering with cold, I finally gave in.

Anwar's mother, who was called Zayneb, was kind and generous to the children, taking them into a room and making them beds to sleep for the night. This wasn't my first meeting with Zayneb, we had met when she first came to Yemen and I'd got on well with her then. Anwar's brother Jabil was also there, he always sat alone in his room; he was the total opposite of Anwar personality wise, he never spoke to anyone unless he really needed to. Salwa, his other sister, was working and was expected back later that evening. I felt guilty as I entered the kitchen and walked over to where Zayneb was in the kitchen, I was in her house under false pretences that I was merely a friend of her son, when in fact I was in love with him, and he with me.

I sat down next to her and offered to help with what she was doing, and without hesitation she took up my offer and we started chatting. We cooked food while Anwar sat with the children and it wasn't long before Salwa turned up; she was tall and beautiful and welcomed me into their home. She told me she had just come back from a trip abroad as an air stewardess, and although her family had heard all her stories before, I couldn't wait to put my children to bed so she could tell me all about them. Salwa told me all her stories, she hadn't long come back from the UK, and although she said she never stayed there because they flew straight back, she loved her job and the freedom it gave her!

The rain continued so we stayed at Anwar's house for a few more days. I called Yas and told her I was staying with a lady I'd met at the hospital where I last worked, just in case she came to visit. She didn't question me; all that mattered to her was that we were safe. I also called Karen and told her the truth, I told her about Anwar many months earlier. I asked for her help with his passport, but she told me she couldn't help because they had no control or say in Yemeni passports, and she didn't know anyone in the Yemeni Embassy that she trusted.

My time with Anwar and his family took me back to my time with Mana and his family; my time with Mana was very short, but peaceful. None of Anwar's family knew of our relationship, even though it was evident from the way we were together that we loved each other. Spending time with Anwar and his family made me wonder what we could have had if Anwar and I had been allowed to be together, but I knew this would never happen.

It was August 1992 when Karen turned up at the house. She told me that they thought we would have a chance of leaving very soon, as in the next week, or few days; she told me she felt this was very likely to happen, but she couldn't make an absolute promise. She told me to be prepared, to say my goodbyes, because the next time she saw us it would be to take us either to the airport or out of Sanaa.

I didn't tell the children what Karen told me, I didn't want them to get their hopes up just yet. They knew I'd been trying to get passports but I told them we had a long wait. I was worried about giving them the false hope that I'd had to bear so many times in my life. However, something inside me told me this time things were different, so I went straight to the phone box.

My first call was to Yas who made her way straight to Sanaa; she and Abdul decided to stay at his family home for a few days. She told me Karen had spoken to Abdul earlier that day and told him the same thing; they were already packing to leave when I called. Karen and Abdul had been talking between themselves for months by now to try and help each other with our situation.

My next call was to Anwar, we arranged for him to come over that night, and every night until we left.

Yas and Nebat visited every day, sometimes they would go back and forth more than once or twice a day, worried that I would be gone by morning. It was really difficult for them to do this by then because Dad had become increasingly obsessed about finding us and had been spending all his time between Abdul's house in the city where Yas and Abdul lived, and Nebat's house in Sanaa.

Every time I said goodbye to my sisters my heart would break; every day it got harder because I knew my departure got closer. On one day it became too much. Tarek caught me on my knees, crying. I'd collapsed after Yas left. He thought something bad had happened so I decided to tell him why I was so upset. I was happy we were finally leaving; I was upset that Aunty couldn't come with us. Tarek hugged me; I could see how upset he was because he was close to his aunty and cousins. Then he promised not to tell his siblings what Karen had said, but told me how excited he was that we were finally going to escape! Seeing the excitement in Tarek's face I decided to tell the others!

With some money that Yas had given us I took the children to the night market to buy our outfits for our travel back home. I didn't have a clue what the fashion was or what little children wore but I was determined that my children would have a new outfit to travel home in.

They needed hope just as much as I did, and buying them a new outfit for our travel home and storing it safe until that date, whenever in the future that may be, would give them hope. The boys chose matching outfits and so did the girls, very colourful, very Yemeni, but nice. As I looked around I couldn't see anything that stood out to me. I knew it was August and much colder than Yemen so I opted for an outfit that was a two piece, long black woolly trousers and a long sleeved black and white matching top. That was it; we were ready and waiting to go.

My nights with Anwar would feel like a dream that I didn't want to wake up from. We would stay awake until sunrise every night just talking and making plans for our future together. Until he could join me we would write to each other and phone each other. He made me promise that I would always allow the children to talk to him on the phone and write to him, and that I'd send him photos. I knew then that I would never love another man as much as I loved him.

It was August 28th, 1992. Anwar was back in work by then so he had arranged to come over later that evening, if we were still there! I heard a knock at the gates and went to open it, expecting to find him, but when I got to the gate and quietly asked who it was, my heart started beating when I heard Karen's voice.

"It's me, Karen, quickly open up!" I opened the gates to allow Karen and the car she had come in to drive into the garden.

"How long will it take you to get ready? You have a plane to catch!" she whispered as she stood in front of me, a huge smile on her face.

I stood there for a few seconds, my mouth wide open. At that moment I had an instant flashback of Yas's nickname for me, "Moo cow," saying that my eyes reminded her of a cow, because at that moment my eyes were open so wide!

Not believing our time had come to go home, I froze, but Karen snapped me out of my trance by ushering me towards the house.

"Well, come on! We haven't got long; you don't want to miss your flight do you?" She laughed. I ran towards the children's room shouting back at her.

"Five minutes! Give me five minutes!"

My hands were shaking, my legs felt like jelly, and the whole of my insides felt as though they were turning upside down as I quickly tried to wake the children, gently shaking them with the news that the time has finally come for us to go home to England.

The clothes we had bought from the market, along with a few other items, had been folded neatly in a bag and put to the side, waiting for this moment!

Karen told me we needed to be at the airport within the hour and didn't have much time, so I should just take the clothes with us and change everyone in the jeep on the way. Tarek and Izzy, as always, woke up straight away and took charge in helping me, while Sadig woke up and hung around for instructions on what to do next; he was always the quieter one of my children, very playful and very cheerful, but not very talkative!

Karen took Izzy and Sadig out to the car as I attempted to wake the other two; loving her sleep Dobia refused to wake up, shaking off any attempt to be woken from her sleep she pushed us away, and stuck her thumb in her mouth in her attempt to get back to her sleep. Nasser was in a deep sleep, and had to be flung around like a rag doll, and that's exactly what his brother Tarek did as he picked him up and flung him over his shoulder! I did the same with Dobia, whilst I grabbed my sharsharf and the bag of clothes. Karen came back in and took Nasser off Tarek.

"Where are your bags?" she asked, looking around, I held up the plastic bag in my hand.

"This is all we have, and this is all we need!" I told her as we walked to the jeep. Unlocking the gate, I turned to Karen.

"Oh no! Anwar, he's coming here tonight!" Even as I was saying the words I knew there was nothing I could do. I was leaving. Karen took Anwar's number from me and promised to call him as soon as she left the airport; she promised me she would keep on calling him until she spoke to him. On the way to the airport I put my sharsharf on and changed my children, while Karen talked us through things we needed to do at the airport.

She told me Abdul had been informed we were leaving tonight; he would be somewhere in the airport but we wouldn't see him, and if we did, we were not allowed to speak to him, or act as if we knew him. He was there purely to see how things went for us and to report back to Yas on whether or not we managed to escape! Karen told us once we were inside the airport we were totally alone, no matter what happened; if we got caught nobody would come to our rescue, or admit to having helped us in any way. This was to be the most terrifying time of my life.

Karen handed me my passport and I quickly flicked through the pages. My children's names on my British passport, in my hands! It felt heavy, as if it was made from gold! I held on to it as I hugged her goodbye, I didn't have the right words to make her understand how much she had done for us. Thank you just didn't seem enough, but it was all I had, and now it was her turn to ask me for something. She handed me her private address and number, and she made me promise that I would call her, and let her know we were OK once we had settled in back home.

She told me Uncle Jim had been kept informed throughout the time they had been trying to get us out, and that he would be waiting for us when we landed in the UK.

With all but Nasser now fully awake we headed into the airport; armed police and soldiers were a heavy presence at the airport, and I couldn't think back to when I'd ever felt so petrified. Tarek held on to Sadig's hand, leading him inside, and Izzy held on to her sisters. I could see Izzy was grasping tightly onto Dobia, and Dobia was twisting her hand to release her sister's grasp, so I had to tell her to ease up! Izzy said she was sorry, but she was worried her sister would run off because she never listened. To my relief, Nasser was still fast asleep over my shoulder.

As we approached the desk Karen had told us to go to, I handed Tarek the passport and tickets so that he could hand them to the man at the desk; it was wiser for me to show that I was allowing my oldest son to take charge when his father wasn't around, it showed respect for males, and I didn't want to bring any unwanted attention to us. The children had all been warned to stay silent and calm, and not to speak unless I nodded or gave them permission, it was only until we got on the aeroplane.

While the man behind the desk inspected our papers, I felt as though every person's eyes were on us, and my heart beat became so fast, and my breathing so shallow, I could feel my neck swelling up! His eyes darted from the passport to me, then to the children, then back, then forth, back and forth, and back and forth!

"No luggage?" he finally asked, handing the passport and

papers back to Tarek. Once again I froze not knowing what to say, I was travelling to England with five children, and a plastic bag!

"My uncle's bringing them in a few days, it's too much to carry," Tarek quickly said. "Where do we go now?" he asked the man, acting so grown up.

Happy that Tarek had got us out of that situation, we made our way over to an area where a group of people were sitting; most of them were foreigners but there were a few Arabic people. Karen had told me to listen out for a flight to Gatwick Airport, and to go to the gate as soon as I heard the callout for that flight.

While we sat and waited I looked around; my nerves were really bad as I watched the soldiers walking around the airport with their automatic guns by their sides. Every time my eyes accidently caught one of theirs my stomach would turn, I just kept imagining the worst, what if? I tried to keep my head down, but I was looking for Abdul or Karen. Karen was gone, if she was there I couldn't see her, but finally I saw Abdul!

For some unknown reason I had a glimmer of hope that my sister would be stood in the background next to Abdul to watch us escape. Even though I knew Abdul would never allow her to be there at the airport, it was a thought, almost a last wish that entered my head. Abdul thought that Yas was too weak to watch us leave, and maybe she was weak in her health, but to see us escape would have been something that would have brought her such joy, even if it was tainted with sorrow and sadness because of our separation.

Abdul was hiding right at the back behind a huge crowd and I quietly whispered to Tarek, telling him not to let the others know because they would become too obvious. Tarek slightly glanced at Abdul and gave a hint of a smile, then looked the other way and ignored him. The children all sat holding hands with their heads slightly down for what felt like hours, but were only a matter of minutes, and then I heard the call for Gatwick.

I quickly stood up and told the children to follow me and do as they were told, then once again handed Tarek the papers so that we could get through the gates onto the tarmac. The children's eyes lit up as soon as we got onto the tarmac and they saw the huge aeroplane in front of them, and as we followed the crowd across the tarmac Izzy and Dobia broke into a little skip and run, and immediately got shouted at by an armed soldier who was patrolling the tarmac.

Even though I was terrified I could sense the fear in Izzy as she grabbed her sister's hand and dragged her back to my side, holding on to the edge of my sharsharf.

"Sorry mummy!" she whispered. I could see her eyes were filling with tears because she thought she had done something wrong, so I grabbed her hand.

"There's nothing to be sorry about, in England you can skip anywhere you want to!" I whispered back as we walked up the steps to the aeroplane. I could see an armed soldier stood next to the aeroplane door, and I could hear the stewardesses welcoming the passengers and directing them to their seats, and when it was our turn my heart nearly jumped out of my chest: stood right in front of me was Salwa!

"Muna! What?" she said in shock.

"Salwa! Hi!" I got really close to her. "Please don't say anything, please!" I quickly begged. She immediately composed herself and told me not to worry.

"I have a letter for you from Anwar, he knew this day would come and made me carry it with me everywhere. I will bring it over to you later, I'm so happy for you!" she whispered, taking us to our seats, we had front seats with extra leg room and two seats behind, with Nasser on my lap.

Every moment that passed felt as though it was happening in slow motion, I watched everyone's movements as they entered the plane and took their seats. As I watched the armed soldier pace up and down the aeroplane doing his last inspection, and I watched the soldiers on the tarmac march from one side of the tarmac to the other, I could feel the sweat dripping from my body under my sharsharf.

After a while Salwa came over to us. "You need to put those belts around you," she said, showing the children how to put their belts on, and then she turned to me.

"Are you alright? What's happening?" she asked while she handed me an envelope. She could tell how nervous I was.

"I will be fine once we are in the air, and I will tell you all about it then!" I said, shoving the envelope down my top while looking around. Salwa told me not to worry as the doors started to close ready for take-off, and then she went off saying she would go and get some things to keep the children busy during the flight. I looked at the children and gave them a wink to let them know everything was OK, but Tarek saw through my fearful reassurances.

"Mum, stop worrying, we are safe now!" he pleaded.

"I know son, believe me I know. We are going home and we are going to be safe, but I will always worry, I'm your mother and that's what mums do!" I told him.

Tarek and Izzy sat behind me, while Sadig and Dobia sat beside me, and the plane prepared to take off. The engines started up and the aeroplane stared to speed down the runway, but the sounds of the engines were being drowned out by a voice in my own head.

"Please God! Please God! Please God!" I begged, worried that at any moment the soldiers would stop the plane and drag us out.

As we sped down the runway, and the plane lifted off into the air, I started to weep uncontrollably, trying to stay as silent as I possibly could, so not to bring attention to myself. When I finally stopped crying, and the plane was fully in flight, I ripped off my sharsharf. Then I made a promise to myself.

I would never allow what happened to me in my past affect the rest of my future, or those of my children!

Even though I knew we would always be hunted, I also knew we were going to be able to live the rest of our lives as free human beings. My children would never be forced into doing anything beyond their own wishes, and I would live my life the best I possibly could.

I also knew I needed to find out the truth about what really happened to my mother, and I would never stop fighting to be reunited with the ones I loved!